Miles

0   100   200   300   400   500

0      200      400      600      800

FINLAND

Helsinki

Tallinn

Riga

1941 RK OF
OSTLAND

Kaunas

Vilna

stenburg

Bug

Pripet

Warsaw
ENERAL
ublin
ERNMENT
racow
OF POLAND

IA

Košice

dapest

GARY

ROMANIA

Belgrade
SERBIA

Sofia

BULGARIA

Albania
Y

GREECE

Gorgopotamos

Athens

Peloponnese

Crete

Leningrad

Moscow

UNION    OF

S O V I E T

Kuybyshey

Volga

S O C I A L I S T

Stalingrad

Kharkov

Kiev

1941  RK OF
UKRAINE

R E P U B L I C S

Transnistria

Dniester

Bessarabia

Dnieper

Odessa

Crimea

Sevastopol

Ploeşti

Bucarest
Danube

B l a c k      S e a

Istanbul

Ankara

T U R K E Y

Izmir

SYRIA

LEBANON
Beirut

Damascus

N S H

# RESISTANCE

books by the same author include

*Men in Uniform* (Weidenfeld and Nicolson 1961)
*SOE in France* (HMSO 1966, 1968)
ed. *The Gladstone Diaries* (OUP 2 v 1968,
2 v with H. C. G. Matthew 1974)
ed. *War and Society* (Elek 1973)

# M. R. D. FOOT

# RESISTANCE

## AN ANALYSIS OF
## EUROPEAN RESISTANCE TO NAZISM
## 1940-1945

EYRE METHUEN · LONDON

*First published in 1976*
*by Eyre Methuen Ltd*
*11 New Fetter Lane, London* EC4P 4EE
*Reprinted with corrections 1977*
*Copyright © 1976 M. R. D. Foot*

*Printed in Great Britain*
*by Butler & Tanner Ltd, Frome and London*

ISBN 0 413 34710 9

# NI HAINE
# NI OUBLI

# CONTENTS

## MAPS[1]

[1] Grateful acknowledgement is due to H. C. Darby and H. Fullard, *New Cambridge Modern History* (Cambridge University Press 1970), xiv. 58–9; and to H-A. Jacobsen and H. Dollinger, *Der zweite Weltkrieg* (Desch, Munich 1962), i. 329.

# FOREWORD

Some thirty years ago, when Great Britain was still at grips with Hitler's Germany, and the dispersal and disintegration of the modern empire had hardly begun, it would have been unthinkable to publish a study that touched on such *arcana reservanda imperii* as the workings of MI5 and MI6. The past existence of these bodies is seldom officially acknowledged, even obliquely, down to the present day. But now that Britain is less often called great; now that no part of truncated Germany is called a Reich; now that the Indian and African empires have been handed back to their own inhabitants to govern; something can perhaps be said without offence about the struggles between the British and the German secret services during the war of 1939-45, and about the historical and social contexts of resistance in which these struggles were waged.[1]

This book has been prepared on its author's own initiative, without any sort of official encouragement, and without access to papers in government custody still officially regarded as secret. As Namier once said, 'A great many profound secrets are somewhere in print, but are most easily detected when one knows what to seek.'[2] It would be churlish to think of concealing what I freely and at once acknowledge: that the work I did fourteen years ago at government request, among the surviving papers of the Special Operations Executive, taught me a lot about what to seek. It did much, as well, to sustain and strengthen my interest in resistance; which dates back to the Ethiopian and Spanish struggles before the world war began, and was stimulated through some slight contacts with resisters during the years with which this book deals.

Yet the quasi-official history I wrote in the early 1960s[3] and this one are quite different. The first had for its main base a mass of original sources, from which much of the interest inherent in it derived; and covered, necessarily from a

---

[1] Contrast Goronwy Rees, *A Chapter of Accidents* (1972), 262.

[2] (Sir) L. B. Namier, *Diplomatic Prelude 1938-1939* (1948), v.

[3] *SOE in France* (HMSO 1966; second impression, revised, 1968; second edition, pigeonholed). Henceforward cited as: Foot.

restricted viewpoint, only part of the history of resistance in a single country. The present work treats a wider subject from a professionally less respectable base, that contains a much larger proportion of secondary sources. Necessarily, it is more superficial and less detailed; necessarily, it asks more questions than it is able to answer.

Resisters did not bother much about respectability, and even superficial knowledge can be better than none. It does seem worth while to gather up into the fabric of a single book several of the main threads of that brilliantly diverse skein, resistance; so that people treating of the history, politics, and society of the 1940s can (to vary the metaphor) prime their own canvases properly before they block in their designs. An outstanding, though not a senior, figure in the organizing of wartime resistance from London said recently, 'No one can write a book about resistance and get it straight; the reality was always more complex than what any author can express.'[1] This may be so; the historian's duty remains clear, to bring such order as he can perceive into the chaos of available fact.

An attempt is made below to analyse the whole field of wartime resistance to the nazis in Europe; to explain what kinds of thing resisters could and could not do; to assess, in outline, whether they achieved their aims; and to indicate points where more work needs to be done, preferably before all the eyewitnesses are dead. Resistance history is a flourishing academic sub-industry in most of continental Europe. The British, hardly occupied – the Channel Islands' case is marginal – like the Americans and Canadians who were never occupied, feel an understandable reticence about tackling a subject that is so loaded with emotional overtones for so many millions of people. Yet young historians in all three countries may now want to join their European contemporaries and colleagues in work on a war that is equally remote from all of them in time, if not in myth.

This book, with many aphorismic compressions, no doubt with many lacunae as well; with all its inadequacies; may yet help to get work in English moving. It is certainly in many respects incomplete; not least because it makes no attempt to rise to the romantic grandeur of the subject. History sometimes has to handle the themes of epic, but history is not poetry.

I am greatly indebted to the many friends and acquaintances whose conversation has helped me, over many years, to assemble material for this book; and also to the staffs of the invaluable London Library, Wiener Library, and British (Museum) Library. The last-named body has paid resistance history the compliment of treating it on a par with other specialized branches of research; and has thus made the book's hurried completion more easy.

To save the reader trouble and the printer temper, I have put all code names and pseudonyms into inverted commas – eg. 'Barbarossa', 'Overlord', 'Shelley'; save that I have not inflicted inverted commas on the pen-names by which Bernstein, Broz, Djugashvili, Nguyen Ai Quoc, and Ulyanov are known the world over.

To Her Majesty's Stationery Office I owe a particular debt; on John Morley's

[1] Conversation with Vera Atkins, 7 January 1975.

principle that, if you have to say a thing twice, you may as well say it in the same words, I have made several overlaps between my previous book on SOE and this one. The previous book is Crown copyright and the Controller, HMSO, has been so kind as to allow me to quote many extracts from it. I must also express my gratitude to all the other copyright owners quoted below, for their divers permissions.

A few phrases, sometimes whole sentences, are borrowed from articles of mine that have appeared elsewhere, or are now in the press: the Percival lecture for 1968, delivered at the invitation of the Manchester Literary and Philosophical Society, and printed as 'Reflections on SOE' in its *Memoirs and Proceedings*, cxi. 1 (1969); in Henri Michel's *Revue d'histoire de la deuxième guerre mondiale*[1] for April 1973; in an Open University history course on war and society; in Stephen Hawes and Ralph White's *Resistance in Europe 1939–1945* (Allen Lane 1975); in Casterman éditeurs, *Encyclopédie historique de la guerre de 1939 à 1945* (Brussels 1977);[2] and in two lectures given at King's College, London, in March 1973, to be published in G. W. Keeton and G. Schwarzenberger ed, *Year Book of World Affairs*, xxxi (Stevens 1977). Large parts of the sections on escape are based on a lecture delivered in the John Rylands Library, Manchester, in the same month. To all the authorities, editors, and publishers concerned I am duly and dutifully grateful. Unattributed translations are my own.

Mrs D. Phillips of Home Types Limited has wrestled impeccably with unfamiliar words in a strange handwriting, working against time, and deserves a special word of thanks. So does Mrs Walker who acted as cut-out between us.

Had I thought the book worthy of them, I would have dedicated it to those who died in furthering the causes of resistance. Instead, with the leave – for which I am most grateful – of the Mayor and of the Association des Déportés Internés Résistants et Patriotes of Tarbes in the Hautes-Pyrénées, this book's motto is taken from the war memorial there.

Anyone aware of errors or omissions, of which no doubt there are many, has only to notify them to the publishers; to whom I am greatly indebted, for long forbearance; as I am to Michael Sissons.

Much in resistance was out of the ordinary: most of its best hopes lay in being as different, as unusual as could be. Nevertheless the fact that it is usual for an author to say that his greatest debt is to his wife shall not keep me from saying the same.

Lastly, I must emphasize that responsibility for the contents is mine alone. The book, conceived long ago, was begun while I was a professor at Manchester. It could hardly be usefully continued in the rare interstices of work at a government discussion centre; which I left, in order to complete it. No university, no government department, no one but myself is answerable for what is in it.

4 July 1976                                               M.R.D.F.

[1] Henceforward: *RHDGM*.             [2] Henceforward: Casterman.

# NOTE TO
# SECOND IMPRESSION

I am particularly grateful to those who have already drawn my attention to deficiencies in this book, especially to Elisabeth Barker and Bickham Sweet-Escott; and am more indebted than ever to my publishers for their continued patience.

23 February 1977                                                      M.R.D.F.

# ABBREVIATIONS

| | |
|---|---|
| AA | anti-aircraft |
| AFHQ | Allied force headquarters [Mediterranean] |
| AI10 | cover name for SOE |
| AK | Armia Krajowa (Home Army) |
| AMF | Algerian-based country section of SOE working into France |
| AMGOT | Allied military government in occupied territory |
| | |
| BATS | Balkan air terminal service |
| BBC | British Broadcasting Corporation |
| BCRA(M) | Bureau central de renseignements et d'action (militaire) [Central office for intelligence and (military) operations] |
| *BFSP* | *British and foreign state papers* |
| BRAL | Bureau de recherches et d'action à Londres [Office for research and operations in London] |
| BSC | British security co-ordination |
| | |
| C | symbol of head of MI6 |
| CCO | Chief of Combined Operations |
| CFLN | Comité Français de Libération Nationale |
| CLN(AI) | Comitato de Liberazione Nationale (dell' Alta Italia) [national liberation committee of northern Italy] |
| CND | confrérie de Notre-Dame |
| CNR | Conseil National de la Résistance |
| COS | chiefs of staff |
| CPGB | Communist Party of Great Britain |
| CPSU(B) | Communist Party of the Soviet Union (bolsheviks) |
| CPY | Communist Party of Yugoslavia |
| | |
| D | decipher section of French SR |
| D | section of MI6, detached to form part of SOE |

| | |
|---|---|
| DF | west European escape section of SOE |
| DMI | director of military intelligence |
| DMR | délégué militaire régional |
| DNI | director of naval intelligence |
| | |
| EAM | ethnikon apeleftherotikon metopon [national liberation front] |
| ed | editor; edited by |
| EDES | ethnikos dimokraticos ellinikos syndesmos [national republican Greek league] |
| EKKA | ethniki kai koinoniki apeleftherosis [national and social liberation] |
| EKKI | Espolnityelnii komityet kommunisticheskogo internatsionala [executive committee of the communist international] |
| ELAS | ellenikos laikos apeleftherotikos stratos [Greek popular liberation army] |
| EMFFI | état-major des forces françaises de l'intérieur |
| *ERM* | *European resistance movements* [see p. 322] |
| EU/P | country section of SOE for Poles outside Poland |
| | |
| F | non-gaullist country section of SOE for France |
| FBI | Federal Bureau of Investigation |
| FFI | Forces françaises de l'Intérieur |
| FTP | Francs-tireurs et Partisans [sharpshooters and partisans] |
| | |
| GCCS | government code and cipher school |
| Gestapo | geheime Staatspolizei [secret state police] |
| GRU | Glavnoye Razvedyvatelnoye Upravlenie [chief intelligence directorate] |
| GSO | general staff officer |
| GS(R) | SOE Cairo |
| | |
| HQ | headquarters |
| | |
| IIIF | foreign section of the Abwehr |
| IO | intelligence officer |
| IS9 | intelligence school no. 9 [an MI9 cover name] |
| ISSU | inter-service signals unit [an SOE cover name] |
| IVF | foreign section of the SD |
| | |
| KKE | Kommunistikon Komma Ellados [Greek communist party] |
| KPD | Kommunistische Partei Deutschlands [German communist party] |
| | |
| LCS | London controlling section |
| LNC | Levitzia Nacional Clirimtare [national liberation movement] |
| LVF | Légion française des Vétérans et des volontaires de la révolution nationale |
| | |
| M | symbol of head of SOE's operations section |

| | |
|---|---|
| MI | military intelligence; specifically, |
| MI5 | security |
| MI6 | intelligence |
| MI9 | escape |
| MI14 | German army |
| MI19 | refugees |
| MIR | research |
| MMLA | missions militaires de liaison administrative |
| MO1(SP) | cover name for SOE |
| MO4 | SOE Cairo |
| MUR | mouvements unis de résistance |
| N | country section of SOE for the Netherlands |
| NAP | noyautage de l'administration publique |
| NID | naval intelligence division |
| NID(Q) | cover name for SOE |
| NKVD | Narodny Kommissariat Vnutrennich Dyel [people's commissariat for internal affairs] |
| NS | Nasjonal Samling [national unity] |
| NSB | Nationaal-Socialistische Beweging [national-socialist movement] |
| NSDAP | nazionalsozialistische deutsche Arbeiterpartei [national-socialist German workers' party] |
| OD | Ordedienst [service for order] |
| ON | Obrana Naroda [people's organization] |
| OSS | Office of Strategic Services |
| OT | Organisation Todt |
| OVRA | Organizzazione di Vigilanza e Repressione dell' Antifascismo [organization of vigilance for repressing antifascism] |
| PCF | Parti Communiste Français [French communist party] |
| PCI | Partito Communista Italiano [Italian communist party] |
| POUM | Partido Obrero de Unificación Marxista [workers' party of marxist unity] |
| PPA | Popski's Private Army |
| PWE | Political Warfare Executive |
| RCMP | Royal Canadian Mounted Police |
| RF | gaullist country section of SOE for France |
| RHDGM | *Revue d'historie de la deuxième guerre mondiale* |
| RSHA | Reichssicherheitshauptamt [imperial security headquarters] |
| RSS | radio security service |
| RUSIJ | *Royal United Services Institute Journal* |
| RVV | Raad van Verzet [resistance council] |
| SAS | Special Air Service |

| | |
|---|---|
| SBS | Special Boat Section |
| SD | Sicherheitsdienst [security service] |
| SIS | Secret Intelligence Service |
| SLU | Special liaison unit |
| SOE | Special Operations Executive |
| SR | Service renseignements [intelligence service] |
| SS | Schutzstaffel [protection squad] |
| T | country section of SOE for Belgium and Luxembourg |
| v | volume |
| V [Roman five] | security section of MI6 |
| V-mann | Vertrauensmann [trusty] |
| V1 | Vergeltungswaffe 1 [reprisal weapon one, pilotless aircraft] |
| V2 | Vergeltungswaffe 2 [reprisal weapon two, ballistic missile] |
| VNV | Vlaamsch Nationaal Verbond [Flemish national union] |
| W | inter-service committee handling most secret matters in London |
| X | country section of SOE for Germany |
| XX | double-cross committee |
| Y | wireless interception service |
| Z | symbol used by Sweet-Escott for C |

# CODENAMES

| | | |
|---|---|---|
| Anvil | renamed Dragoon | |
| Attila | German invasion of Vichy France | began 11 November 1942 |
| Barbarossa | German invasion of USSR | began 22 June 1941 |
| Bodyguard | renamed Fortitude | |
| Dragoon | Allied invasion of Vichy France | began 15 August 1944 |
| Enigma | commercial cipher machine, used with variants by Germans and Japanese | |
| Fortitude | cover for Overlord | |
| Husky | Allied invasion of Sicily | began 10 July 1943 |
| Jedburgh | Anglo-Franco-American teams stiffening maquis during Overlord | June–September 1944 |
| Magic | American interception of Japanese machine cipher traffic | |
| Neptune | assault on Normandy coast, opening phase of Overlord | 5/6 June 1944 |
| Overlord | Allied invasion of north-west Europe | began 5/6 June 1944 |
| Sussex | Anglo-Franco-American teams providing intelligence for Overlord | May–September 1944 |
| Torch | Anglo-American invasion of north-west Africa | began 8 November 1942 |
| Ultra | British interception of German machine cipher traffic | |

# 1  WHAT RESISTANCE WAS

The German Third Reich was to have lasted for a thousand years. The phrase *'das tausendjährige Reich'* resounded through the régime's propaganda, in broadcasts, in newspaper articles, in speeches on pompous occasions, with the deadly iteration of a yellowhammer, over and over and over again. It became for a while a tag as familiar as *'semper eadem'*, or *'la grande nation'*, or 'manifest destiny', or 'neo-colonialism'. The Reich took for its birthday 30 January 1933; when Adolf Hitler, leader of the national socialist German workers', or nazi, party, became Chancellor of the German republic. The infant grew fast. In the spring of 1935, when the party's internal faction fights had been stilled, Hitler re-created the large armoured army and the air force that Germany's victors had forbidden by the treaty of Versailles in 1919.[1] German tank crews and pilots had long been trained, by secret arrangement between the German and Russian governments, in the communist USSR; not till May 1935 was the German office in Moscow that supervised the details of this plan closed.[2] Next month the British, in a moment of aberration, made a treaty with the Germans which allowed the two powers equal numbers of submarines, another weapon forbidden to Germany at Versailles.[3] In March 1936, on Hitler's order, a thin screen of troops occupied the demilitarized zone on the left bank of the Rhine; beyond a little diplomatic finger-wagging, no one stirred. By the end of the year the new Luftwaffe was getting some practical training in Spain.[4] Hitler was less intimately involved than Mussolini in the Spanish right-wing revolt against the republican government,[5] but he approved its aims and methods and gave it ample air support in the consequent civil war.

Spain apart, 1937 was a year of preparation and training for the Reich. In 1938, uncomfortably soon from the German service staffs' point of view, a

[1] *BFSP* cxii. 86, 96.
[2] (Sir) J. W. Wheeler-Bennett, *The Nemesis of Power* (1953), 129.
[3] *BFSP* cxxxix. 182.
[4] Cp. Hugh Thomas, *The Spanish Civil War* (2 ed. 1965), 401–2.
[5] Cp. R. W. Seton-Watson, *Britain and the Dictators* (1938), 388.

serious career of conquest began. Austria was swallowed up in March, with no shot fired, except by suicides. Czechoslovakia was split by the Munich agreement of 29 September;[1] Germany took the fortified borderland, which had its first frontier change since the twelfth century. In the spring of 1939, the Reich gobbled up the rest of Bohemia and Moravia, and Slovakia became the first German satellite state.

In March, the Spanish republican government withdrew over the Pyrenees, to join in the limbo of exile such improbable companions as the Habsburg emperor and the Lion of Judah, emperor of Ethiopia; to be joined next month by King Zog whom Mussolini had started to evict from Albania on Good Friday. Franco ruled all Spain; at the time of writing he does so yet.[2] Spain has become a tourists' demi-paradise, where really hard-line resisters do not go.

But our main concern now is with Germany; with German nazism, rather than with Italian fascism that provided its model and became its servant, or with Spanish falangism whose devotees managed to maintain an equivocal attitude in the war that was about to break out. For in the late summer of 1939 the cup of Europe's misfortune began again to overflow: on 1 September Hitler's war began.

Why it began remains in dispute among historians.[3] But the final excuse for it has been quite clear for a generation: a clandestine operation mounted by a branch of the German secret police. A wireless station at Gleiwitz (now Gliwice), then comfortably on the German side of the frontier in Silesia, was attacked by a group of men in Polish uniforms, whose bodies were viewed by foreign journalists. They were in fact prisoners from German concentration camps, who had been deluded into thinking that by taking part in this attack as ordered they would save their lives.[4] Their attack was presented to the world as justifying the German onslaught on Poland; by an historic irony, the nazis started with a subterfuge a war in which subterfuges were to be used with deadly effect against them.

Within a week, Great Britain and France had declared war, on Poland's side;[5] though for the time they did little more. Within a month, all four of the British 'old dominions' had joined in as well. India and the British and French colonial empires were brought in without consultation. Within a year, the struggle had become a general European civil war, merging with the Greco-Italian war that began late in October 1940; in less than two years the German attack on the USSR spread it further; before the end of 1941 the Japanese attack on the USA

[1] *BFSP* cxlii. 438.

[2] He died, aged 82, on 20 November 1975, while this book was in the press.

[3] A. J. P. Taylor, *The Origins of the Second World War* (1961), one of the more wayward efforts of a brilliant historian, carries small conviction; though it has not yet been refuted in detail, see P. A. Reynolds, 'Hitler's War?' in *History*, xlvi. 212 (1961).

[4] Nuremberg trial, iii. 191–2, &c. See also the imaginative reconstruction in C. S. Forester, *The Nightmare* (1954), ch. i.

[5] See R. A. C. Parker, 'The British Government and the Coming of War with Germany, 1939', in M. R. D. Foot ed, *War and Society* (1973), 1.

made it world-wide, because Hitler for once kept a promise and declared war on the USA as well. Hence the popular title of 'the Second World War'.[1]

By the middle of 1942, the Germans had overrun the bulk of continental Europe, where only Sweden, Switzerland, Liechtenstein,[2] Monaco, southern France, Andorra, Spain and Portugal remained uninvaded. The USSR was unconquered, yet, but in dire peril. Leningrad and even Moscow were under siege;[3] the whole of the Ukraine, of White Russia, of the Don basin were in enemy hands; there were Germans on the right bank of the Volga and thrusting towards the Caucasus. Western north Africa preserved a precarious neutrality under the satellite régime of Vichy France. In eastern north Africa, Rommel was preparing a pounce on Alexandria. German submarines controlled much of the Atlantic and even of the Caribbean. Japanese submarines were raiding across the Indian ocean; the Japanese navy controlled the west Pacific, the army most of coastal China and of south-east Asia.

From this nearly catastrophic degree of defeat the united nations managed, in a little over three years, to recover. The naval battle of Midway in June, the officially still unrecognized first battle of El Alamein early in July, and the epic defence of Stalingrad in the late autumn of 1942 marked the turn of the tide. Italy crumpled comparatively fast, changing sides late in 1943; Germany surrendered in May 1945, a few days after Hitler's suicide; and the Japanese, beaten down by superior industrial power and awed by two atomic bombs, gave in on 2 September. The war had lasted six years and two days; the thousand-year Reich had lasted twelve years and three months.

The accepted historians' view, echoed by leader-writers, compilers of news bulletins, people in clubs, people in pubs, people in queues, is that the nazis were beaten by the Allied armed forces – army, navy, and air – which acted in rough concert with each other. The exact form taken by this accepted myth varies from place to place. In Russia the achievements of the Red Army are, perhaps unduly, stressed; to the neglect of everyone else. Given the existing political balance of forces in the USSR, this is a political and propaganda necessity. In the USA and in England the Red Army's achievements are, again perhaps unduly, understressed; for reasons of national pride – call it conceit – more is heard of the royal or US air forces and navies, and of the indomitable British infantryman or American GI. Most Americans, British, and Russians believe unthinkingly that without their own nation's share in it the war would have been lost. All may be right. And all agree that this great war was a military affair,

[1] I shall not use this title, which might be thought to apply with more historical justice to the great war of 1792–1815 (cp. Sir L. B. Namier, *England in the Age of the American Revolution* (1961), 339); but know my usage is idiosyncratic. In any case, a still greater historian than Namier, Sir George Clark, maintains there were world wars a century earlier still (his *History of England* (1971), 230–2, 276–7, 336–7, &c.).

[2] And Liechtenstein, it turned out in 1938, had been formally at war with Prussia since 1866.

[3] A former officer in a German tank unit told me that he was wounded while counting the turrets on the Kremlin through his field glasses.

decided by military methods – that is, by the armed forces of the combatant powers. Certainly devoted armies, navies, and air forces fought battles more tremendous than any history had so far recorded; in some unhappy countries there were rates of casualty even more dreadful than in the previous holocaust, which had been at its worst from 1914 to 1918.[1] Several decisive battles were fought, besides the three turning-points named just now; such as the battle of Britain, without which the war would have been a German walk-over, the battle of the Atlantic, the storming of Okinawa, the landings in Normandy, and the conclusive Russian advance on Berlin.

And yet – this was not a war of formal armed forces alone; still less a war confined to the armed forces of great powers. For the nations Germany overran managed to set up, or to keep in being, forces in exile; some of them, such as the Poles and the French, forces many ships, divisions, and air squadrons strong. And besides these forces in exile, fighting with exiles' desperation, occupied countries had a resource nearer home: their own peoples.

Common folk knew, when the Germans withdrew, that nazi military power had not been broken by the victorious armed forces of the Allies alone. Besides the sailors, the soldiers, the airmen, a fourth force had been at work: the resisters. No territory that the nazis occupied joyously accepted their embraces, and did their will with a whole heart. Even in their German homeland, and even in German-speaking occupied areas – Austria, Luxembourg, Alsace – resisters were to be found; in some of the remoter provinces the nazis conquered, such as Brittany or Bosnia, collaborators were rare outside the towns. In industrial areas, factory workers sometimes had social and political homogeneity enough to take a collective stand, through their trade unions or otherwise, against the occupier: as witness some great strikes in Holland, Denmark, France. The railwaymen of western Europe, as a body, acted more or less spontaneously in an anti-nazi sense, and provide a further series of strong examples of the influence a group of economically essential workers could exert. And in the countryside, where the tempo of life was slower, where custom and tradition counted for more, and ways of doing things had been settled for longer, it was comparatively easy for resistance to grow up inside the collective hostility with which each district, each village, regarded outsiders of all kinds. There were several good historic precedents for this: in the Irish countryside over a century before, for instance, 'It was next to impossible for outsiders to enter an organization whose members were all known to one another', and as late as the 1830s, the writ of the Dublin government did not always run far outside the Pale.[2] But the German general staff had no experience or understanding of this phenomenon, which lay outside

[1] This is remembered in England and France as 'the great war' or 'the 1914 war'; in America as 'the first world war'. For the Americans, it was the war of 1917–18; for the Russians, of 1914–20; for the Turks the war of 1911–22.

[2] Galen Broeker, *Rural Disorder and Police Reform in Ireland, 1812–36* (Routledge 1970), 18 and cp. ibid. 122–3, 133–4, &c. Michael Davitt's *Fall of Feudalism in Ireland* (1904) has some instances from half a century later still.

its sophisticated ken; except vague recollections of myths of the war of liberation against Napoleon in 1813.[1]

Though few people, as a rule, actually took part in overt acts of resistance, or even in clandestine ones, what brought resistance its eventual success was the eventual common agreement with its main aims of the mass of the populations in which it worked; as well as the arrival of the liberating armies. When people all over Europe rejoiced in being liberated, they were proud as well; for they knew that they had helped personally to drive the Germans out by making occupation unbearable for the occupier. This feeling of participation, even by those wholly non-combatant in spirit and in deed, was important for the future of this populous and troubled continent; for it gave people back the self-respect they had forfeited at the time of German conquest. An awareness that one has, once at least, taken part – if only as a silent witness – in something worth doing is a valuable companion afterwards; the more valuable, the more one's hopes at liberation are dimmed by later disappointments. The object of this book is to summarize the facts on which this awareness rested – so far as they are perceptible to a single, necessarily prejudiced, former minimal participant – and to examine how far it was justified.

Let us begin with the dictionary definition:

> In World War II; after F[rench] *Résistance*, an organized underground movement in a country occupied by enemy forces carried on with the assistance of armed fighters for the purpose of frustrating and damaging the occupying power.[2]

Armed fighters, as we shall see, are not an indispensable feature of resistance,[3] but before we part from the dictionary, we need to glance at the derivation of the word. *Résistance* comes from the Latin *resistere*, in which the *re* is an intensive prefix; which in turn is put on an intensive verb, *sistere*, the extra-strong form of *stare*, to stand. To resist therefore means to stand fast, doubly fast, to some position or principle; to what, remains for discussion below.[4] It is as well to bring in early this sense of cross-grained toughness, of obstinacy even: it was the leading characteristic of thousands of resisters, not all of them obscure.

More of resisters' leading characteristics in the next chapter; except for one almost as central as obstinacy, which was self-assurance. Not quite self-confidence, for anyone at all deep in this horribly perilous business was bound to have occasional qualms; but an inner certainty that, whether things went well or ill on any particular day, one was doing the right thing. Since the middle ages, levying

---

[1] Cp. (Sir) A. Conan Doyle, *The Exploits of Brigadier Gerard*, ch. vi (esp. pp. 218–19 in 1949 ed.).

[2] *Shorter Oxford English Dictionary*, ii. 2507 b (3 ed. 1969). The main *Dictionary's* postwar supplement (1972) does not yet run beyond the letter G.

[3] Eg. pp. 25, 114–15, 282 below.

[4] Especially in Chapter 4.

war had been the prerogative of sovereigns; save for chieftains on such out-boundaries of society as Appalachia or Afghanistan or Argyll or Annam. In the twentieth century, even these out-stations had learned the rule of law. Resisters were prepared to reassert the rule of law, against a régime that derided it; and to reassert it, if they had to, from an illegal stance.[1]

This was by no means the same as that respect for the letter of the law which earned for their chief opponent the nickname among academic Frenchmen of *Adolphe Légalité*. It was the capacity to move, with the rigid precision of a bolshevik, indeed of a piston-rod, in a predetermined direction; a direction laid down by the resister's conscience and upbringing. It would be a piece of grandiose priggery to claim that resisters loved their fellow men more dearly than other people did. What they did have – what their consciences gave them – was a strong sense that human dignity is something more than a phrase. They saw nazis treating men and women like cattle; and were quite sure this would not do.

Some maintain that the disintegration of ordered society which has set in during the 1960s and early 1970s is traceable back to resisters' independent-mindedness, to their readiness to usurp a sovereign's prerogative and start a private war. It would be interesting to see whether such a connexion could be traced; it is not a view that the present writer has seen evidence enough to support. On the contrary, the disintegration looks more like the work of the one of Hitler's enemies that was most expert in subversion, the USSR; but again, proof so far is lacking.

Popularly, 'resistance' is held, as it was often held at the time, to have been one; or at least one in each separate resisting country. Certainly, there were broad similarities between resisters' aims, all Europe over. They had many common enemies, from Hitler upwards, who wore crooked crosses. They had many common attitudes; some that were becoming old-fashioned even then, like patriotism;[2] some that good men have held and will hold for centuries, like self-respect and love of freedom and respect for other people's dignity. Yet seldom if ever were they able to act, even in a single country, as one. Everywhere, resistance had to be split into separate groups, chains, communities; for it could no more make itself effective as a single mass of unorganized and undirected citizens than a body of fifty thousand unitless, leaderless riflemen could make itself effective as an army corps. In resistance, as in industry, division of labour is necessary; and all the professionals in clandestine activity, even those whose ultimate aims included mass uprisings, always insisted on the need for *cloisonne-*

---

[1] This point was touched on, at a *colloque* in Paris on 28 October 1974, by Professor M. Blumenson.

[2] The Oxford Union's anti-patriotic motion, carried a few days after Hitler came to power, 'that this house would not fight for King and Country', rang round the world, and was almost as widely misunderstood as it was reported. The same body's motion 'that this house would go to war for Danzig', carried in a thinnish house in midsummer 1939 in the last debate of term – presided over by Hugh Fraser – went absolutely unnoticed by any newspaper, national or local. Before the vacation was over, those who voted for it combined with those who voted against, to do what it said.

*ment,* for the breaking down of resistance into small groups and cells, kept for security's sake wholly apart from each other. The most successful early groups were often the smallest; large groups were *ipso facto* suspect, till the final insurrection.

In practice, resistance was divided in every country into several sections, which differed partly in origin, partly in politics, and partly in function. Wholly spontaneous groups sprang into being in many countries, either during the paroxysms of occupation, or as soon as the first shock of defeat had worn off; but such groups were distinguished more for bravery than for prudence. They usually made a cult of openness and straight dealing, and their members were seldom wily enough to stay for long out of the clutches of the enemy secret police. Politically, communists tended to hold aloof from – and to be held aloof by – the rest. This was partly because their leaders had had training in clandestinity, often coupled with recent practical experience in Spain, and knew the importance of partitioning resisters off from each other; partly because, while memories were still keen of the Ribbentrop–Molotov pact that had given Hitler his green light to start the war,[1] the rest were not too ready to work with them. Extreme nationalists, at the other end of the political spectrum, also inclined to keep themselves to themselves. (Whether the political spectrum is linear or circular – with orange extreme right adjoining red extreme left – is not a question we need answer here.) And once the fact of resistance became thinkable for more than a handful of fanatic outcasts, survivors of prewar political parties' leading cadres began to look round for new opportunities.

For the military historian, it is more useful to analyse resistance by function than by party or by origin. What were people in it trying to do?

The fundamental problem was quite straightforward for everyone except the communists: it was, to get rid of the occupying power. This same problem had been confronted and surmounted within living memory, by the greatest resistance leader of the twentieth century: Michael Collins, who rose to be the military chief of the Irish Republican Army during the troubles of 1916–22 and died in the hour of victory. Collins, a clandestine genius, took everything on his own broad shoulders. But he was fighting in simpler times against a kinder enemy; nobody, not even Tito, was able to take on quite so large a burden in the war against nazism, and handle himself all the problems of strategy, intelligence, escape, subversion, and supply at once. Not many European resisters had heard of Collins; his enormous contribution to resistance was less direct, by force of example, than indirect through the impact he made on two young opponents who between them later founded SOE.[2] But we anticipate.

It is worth considering how the powers fighting Germany organized their own

[1] See L. B. Namier in *The Listener,* xxxix. 429–30, 11 March 1948, and xlii. 355–6, 1 September 1949.
[2] Cp. M. R. D. Foot, 'The IRA and the origins of SOE', in *War and Society,* 68–9.

ministries and secret services for dealing with resistance. The British, among several more or less separate and more or less highly secret organizations, had five distinct services:

MI5 the security service, working primarily at home
MI6 the secret intelligence service
MI9 the escape service
SOE the special operations executive, which handled sabotage and secret armies, and
PWE which handled propaganda

The first two of these dated from 1909; the other three were set up *ad hoc*, early in the war of 1939. The Americans, coming late to the 'great game',[1] had only two main services:

the long-standing FBI, to cover security on US territory, and the OSS, formed in mid-1942 to cover
intelligence
subversion
and research

The Russians dealt mainly through the NKVD, which was in general charge of state security in all its ramifications; a body much swollen in size and importance, if not in efficiency, at the end of the 1930s by the cares of the great purge which it was conducting for Stalin: the purge that arrested almost every senior officer in the USSR except his brother-in-law,[2] and so made the union's survival against a German *Blitzkrieg* nothing short of miraculous. There was also a much smaller, more efficient, and more secret body, the GRU, which dealt with military intelligence: a subject even less extricable from political intelligence in Russia than elsewhere.

Of the many governments-in-exile, a few are worth early notice. The free French had a single secret service, the BCRA, nominally under General de Gaulle's national committee; its head could deal direct with the general, and with several opposite numbers in the British and American secret services. The BCRA competed on the political front with the gaullist commissariat for the interior, which also sent agents into and conducted propaganda in France. Both leaned heavily on the BBC: as indeed did almost everybody else. The 'London' Poles also had two separate bodies seeking to direct clandestine activity in Poland: the quarrels between the free Polish ministries of defence and of the interior were legion. Other exiled governments, particularly the Belgians, had similar troubles.

But however intricate the wrangles between secret offices and staff officers in London, Moscow, Cairo, Washington, and later Algiers or Bari, the amount of direct and immediate influence that any member – however senior – of any

---

[1] See H. W. C. Davis, 'The Great Game in Asia', *Proceedings of the British Academy*, xii, 227 (1927): a reference owed to Professor Beloff.
[2] For some details, cp. R. Medvedev, *Let History Judge* (1972), 209–14.

secret service headquarters could exercise on what happened in the field was seldom if ever extensive. On the spot, resisters believed themselves to serve no masters but their country and their conscience. Few of them had heard, in any but the vaguest fashion, of the secret services that hoped to guide their activities; almost all would indignantly have repudiated any idea that they needed any sort of guidance, except on technical questions like how to use high explosive or how to receive an arms drop. Yet, necessarily, they had to operate in different – even if converging – groups and categories.

Historians are no more uniform in their treatment of resistance than the Allied secret services were at the time. Henri Bernard, who approaches the subject from the triple advantage of experience as an agent in the field, as responsible staff officer in London, and as professor of military history, propounds six groups;

information
sabotage
secret armies
secret newspapers, and other forms of psychological war
escape lines
help to Jews and others persecuted by the enemy.[1]

Henri Michel, somewhat more academic in his approach, but using a still deeper research base, proposes a different set, of ten:

passive resistance
go-slow
strikes
secret tracts and newspapers
escape lines
information
sabotage
assassination
maquis and guerilla
liberation movement[2]

In a later and much longer work, he puts forward a simplified alternative list, of another six:

passive and administrative resistance
sabotage
assassinations and plots
strikes
maquis and guerilla
national insurrection[3]

---

[1] H. Bernard, *La Résistance [belge] 1940–1945* (1968), 11–12.
[2] H. Michel, *Les Mouvements Clandestins en Europe* (1961), 11–16.
[3] H. Michel, tr. R. H. Barry, *The Shadow War* (1972), 195 ff.; henceforward Michel, *SW*.

In this he deliberately omits both intelligence and escape activities; to suit the more restricted subject-matter of his book.

With so many different systems to choose from, their analyst may set up his own. This book will divide resistance into three broad functional categories:

1 intelligence
2 escape
3 subversion

Of these, the last will be sub-divided into four:

a sabotage
b attacks on troops and individuals
c politics
d insurrection

The tasks that faced resisters of these several kinds were quite separate from each other. Different qualities of nerve and skill were needed to excel at each. A brilliant saboteur might be useless in an escape network, and worse than useless in an intelligence one; an exceptionally skilful forger of false papers might be no use at all in an ambush; the best and bravest of mountain guides might not know how to assemble a sten, or where to use a time pencil.

# 2 WHO RESISTED

Fashionable historians today like to lean on class interpretations of history; such interpretations do not fit the known facts of this particular case. Character, not class, made people into resisters, or collaborators, or would-be neutrals; character, not class, encouraged some of them to move from one of these roles to another, as the tides of war shifted.

It is often, though wrongly, believed that all hard-core resisters were communists. Most communists active in occupied countries after 22 June 1941 had good and some had excellent resistance records, but they by no means monopolized resistance, at any level; no more did their long-standing opponents the catholic country priests, many of whom also did remarkable things. Maybe good resisters, good communists, and good priests have points of character in common; forming categories that overlap, but are distinct.

Even among the communists, though most of them came from a proletarian background in western or a peasant background in eastern Europe, no rigid social rule laid down that they must come from one working class or the other. From Lenin's and Paul Levi's day, communism has exercised a strong appeal over some kinds of intellectual; people who come from bourgeois backgrounds and resent them, for a host of personal, social, economic, or moral reasons.

Self-evidently, the resisters who joined in the great resistance strikes were from the urban working class; the strikes were important, and exercised a perceptible effect on the nazi war economy. Yet few of them lasted long; the dice were loaded fiercely against them. Many, even most, working men could be persuaded to join in a particular strike on a particular day, for a special object: to protest at a cut in wages or rations, or to mark a singular nazi atrocity. Yet a great many ordinary workmen, however strongly they felt their solidarity with their working-class comrades, felt also their duties to their families; most of them were brave, but they were not all heroes. Which of them decided to undertake the long-term tasks of resistance, rather than the short-term task of a strike, depended on character, not on class origin.[1]

[1] That class origin has some influence on character is obvious; but this writer at least is not marxist enough to believe that the influence is often large, or at all decisive.

Character, again, laid down which peasants, or which professional men, joined resistance; character, and opportunity. Of peasant resistance more is said elsewhere.[1] Among the professions, those of scholar and doctor were of special use; scholars being good at assimilating, recording, condensing information, and doctors having more facilities than most for travel at odd hours. Streams of strangers, besides, could call at a town doctor's house without rousing suspicion: this made surgeries convenient rendezvous. Bookshops had similar advantages; as Tito, Rössler, and Brossolette had realized even before 1939. Teachers, engineers, lawyers, merchants, businessmen, civil servants, priests – especially priests – were often active as well.

Another profession of which the members were likely to be specially useful was of course that of fighting men: regular officers and NCOs of the forces the Germans scattered in 1939–41 had skills and capacities of enormous use to resistance, if only the regulars had characters flexible enough to let them contemplate joining in irregular warfare at all. Unluckily (in some ways) for resisters, most regulars trained in the 1920s and 1930s tended to be rigid, stolid, conformist types, long on obedience and short on initiative; so that they kept their professional skills to themselves. In France, the orders of the greatest living French soldier held them to collaboration with the invader. In Yugoslavia, they had their king's order to resist, and a royalist general to lead them; but as we shall see the course of south Slav politics made that general's leadership ineffectual. In Russia, there was a plethora of anti-Stalinist committees, but no single body with the weight of a collaborationist government; and the Germans muffed a chance to pose as liberators. Pursuing the insensate civil affairs policy that nazi racial philosophy laid down for them, they provided every incitement to the conquered population to resist. Any trained Red Army cadres who evaded their search policies (which were strict) knew their duty: to train and lead every fit man and woman in partisan units, which would get orders from the party high command.

In eastern Europe, in fact, nearness to the Soviet Union, the acceptance by the Russian general staff – well in advance of their opposite numbers in the Allied west – of the advantages of partisans as an auxiliary arm, and the comparative local strength of Russian-dominated communism as an inspiring creed, did make for some degree of social and political homogeneity among resisters. So, often enough, in the same territories – in the Balkans, in south-west Russia, in parts of Poland or Latvia or Slovakia – did dire necessity. Whole villages in remote areas might be forced to the choice: either resist, or be massacred, or starve. Sooner than be massacred, or starve in the ruins of their hovels, they took to the hills, or the marshes, or the forest, according to what countryside lay near them; and so escaped the comparatively road-bound Hun. They might come near enough to starving, even so, with very little to eat for months. Some Yugoslav partisan units, for example, survived a Bosnian winter on a diet of

[1] Ante, 4–5, and post, 19, 88, 182, 191–5, 225, &c.

which the main and recurrent item was stinging-nettles, boiled; varied by an occasional slice of mule, and enlivened by slivovits as well as spring water to drink. In these conditions, inconceivably tough to the housewife of Rochester or Solihull, whole villages could maintain some degree of peasant cohesion.

Farther west, resisters' diversity of social origin was marked. Some were aristocrats, such as the Graf von Stauffenberg who dared in the end a direct attempt on Hitler, or the Princesse de Caraman Chimay, or Noor Inayat Khan; some came from the landed gentry; many from workshop benches or railway yards. Railwaymen in fact, as a group, provide an exception to the rule set out at the start of this chapter: they are the solitary instance of a sub-class devoted *as such*, in many areas, to resistance; on grounds of class interest and class solidarity. Some of the most useful resisters came from a class that in those days was hardly perceived by social analysts, and still awaits full critical treatment: clerks.[1] Unobtrusive and apparently unimportant clerks, in such places as railway termini or large town halls, who had access to significant news or documents, could be invaluable; if they had the nerve and skill to abstract an extra copy of a list of impending train-loads, or specimens of a new type of ration card. A great many clerks had not got the enterprise or the inclination to do anything of the sort; conformist compatriots who helped the occupier were among the more exasperating burdens the occupied had to bear. But their more actively pro-Allied colleagues provided some intelligence triumphs.

In this corner of resistance, as in so many others, the Irish had shown the way: one of Michael Collins's best agents in 1919 was a quiet woman who had for years been one of the typists in Dublin Castle, and had risen by tact and seniority to type out all the really secret immediate material, such as the list of houses to be raided each night. When Jackie Fisher said 'Buggins's turn will be the ruin of the Empire yet', he spoke more truly than he knew.[2]

Resisters tend to be out of step with their time – usually in advance of it; to be thoughtful, earnest, naif, Pierre Bezukhovs, rather than Boris Drubetskoys who trim their sails to catch every puff of social wind that may lead to their personal advancement.[3] An example of this is to be found in the many significant roles that women have played in modern resistance, from the Countess Markiewicz who held St Stephen's Green (rather badly) in 1916 down to the Angela Davises and Bernadette Devlins of the present day. In the secret war against the nazis, women without number played an invaluable part, participating on terms of perfect equality with men. Again, they came from every social stratum. Two princesses were mentioned a moment ago, who worked in France and Belgium; the Polish Countess Skarbek, better known by her SOE name of Christine Granville, had had a colourful career arranging escape lines in east central Europe

[1] Humorists have long been at work in this field: Flaubert, in *Bouvard et Pécuchet*; Compton Mackenzie, in *The Red Tapeworm*; A. P. Herbert, C. N. Parkinson, and others have broken lances against the bureaucratic windmill. It grinds on unperturbed.

[2] *Memories* (1919), 39.

[3] Cp. Tolstoy, *War and Peace*, esp. book V ch. xix.

before ever SOE was formed,[1] and was one of fifty women agents sent to France under SOE's auspices; a few women parachuted into Belgium and Yugoslavia as well. Though much British newspaper attention has been lavished on this handful of brave women; though a great deal of what they did was valuable; still more valuable work was done by women who never left their homelands, unless they were caught and deported to Germany: by women who as organizers, couriers, safe-house-keepers, authors of pamphlets, mothers of families, cipher operators, nurses, drivers, or assassins showed that in this field at least the cry for women's liberation was just. Some of the most daring and most successful were prostitutes, who used their special opportunities to rifle their German customers' pockets and lower their morale.

Theirs was a way of life in which they were not much hampered by a brake on resistance activity that hindered a lot of people: a sense of respect for professional standards and for one's own standing in one's profession. The originality, unorthodoxy, and dash without which a successful resister was lost did not come easily to a great many professional men.

Originality necessarily came high on any list of characteristics desirable in resistance. One needed to be fond like Hopkins of 'All things counter, original, spare, strange',[2] and yet discreet enough not to let the strangeness show. One had to be ready to say, after Clemenceau, '*Moi, je suis contre*': but not to be so contrary that one said it too loud or too soon.

Among the other characteristics a resister needed, courage must come first: it was no task for cowards. Nor was the usual sort of courage of much use, that had inspired the common soldier at Borodino or at Waterloo, at Fontenoy or Inkerman or any of the thousand stricken fields of Europe's old wars. As was said elsewhere, 'Out here on the lonely margins of military life, heroes seem more heroic and blackguards more blackguardly than they do in the ordinary line of battle, where companionship keeps men steady and women are not expected to fight at all.'[3] A member of an intelligence circuit might easily never meet the person next to him – or her – along the information-passing chain; indeed it was safer for them both if they kept apart, since neither could in that case describe the other, if either were caught. Feelings of companionship and comradeship were intense enough; the more so, sometimes, for someone who remained a complete personal abstraction, about whom nothing disagreeable could be known.

Not only was an ordinarily brave man little more use than a coward: to succeed in resistance, you needed extra strong, steely, flexible nerves, no inhibitions at all, and uncanny quickness of wit. As witness – if we may jump a stride ahead to our narrative – 'Felix', a Jew of Alsatian-Polish origins who was assistant wireless operator to the young 'Alphonse', a British agent in southern France. He,

---

[1] See Bickham Sweet-Escott, *Baker Street Irregular* (Methuen 1965), 28; henceforward Sweet-Escott.
[2] G. M. Hopkins, 'Pied Beauty', 7.
[3] Foot, 142.

'Alphonse', and 'Emanuel' the wireless operator all got out of the same train at Toulouse; 'Felix', carrying the transmitter in its readily recognizable suitcase, went up to the barrier first. Two French policemen were conducting a cursory check on identity papers. Behind them, two uniformed SS men were sending everyone with a case or big package to the *consigne*, where more SS were making a methodical luggage search. 'Felix' took in the scene; ignored the French police; held his suitcase high; and called in authoritative German, 'Get me a car at once, I have a captured set.' He was driven away in a German-requisitioned car; had it pull up in a back street; killed the driver, and reported to 'Alphonse' with the set for orders.[1]

Close behind courage and swiftness came discretion. More groups of resisters must have been undone by careless talk than by anything else; particularly in those countries that had few or no secular memories of foreign tyranny – France, Denmark, Hungary, Russia. The Dutch, who had endured the Spaniards and the French; the Belgians, who had endured the Spaniards, the French, and the Dutch; the Greeks, who had fought off the Ottoman Turks; the south Slavs, who had fought both Ottoman and Habsburg; above all the Poles, who had endured Habsburg, Romanov, and Hohenzollern oppression all at once; knew something, from the nursery onwards, of the need to keep one's mouth shut. So did the lesser nationalities of the USSR. But the Great Russians, like the French and the Magyars, were more used to being a dominant than a dominated group; the Danes, like the French, had half-forgotten occupation; and the Norwegians had never known it.[2]

Though, for many of the people who joined it, resistance was an adventure – almost a game – people who went into it with too light a heart might soon be undeceived. For success, one had to be capable of silence: rather a rare gift. The main fault of resisters was that, being human, they *would talk*; and so drew towards themselves or their friends the attention of the large, and sometimes efficient, nazi police forces. To be inconspicuous, not to stand out in a crowd, never to attract a second glance, was the safest and most precious of a resister's gifts; still more, of a secret agent's. Some developed (and, to the confusion of inquirers, retain) the knack of always turning a probing question unexcitingly aside; a few bring up their children on Kipling's tag, 'Them that asks no questions isn't told a lie'.

To be observant, well beyond the common run, was a great help as well. Such gifts as being able to *see* fifteen objects at a glance, without having to count them; or to recall half a dozen different passers-by, in the order in which they passed; or never to forget an address; were as valuable as they are out of the ordinary. And someone who could promptly recognize familiar objects – cars,

[1] Conversation long afterwards (9 January 1970) with 'Alphonse', who did not date the incident; probably early 1943.

[2] Norway had at various times been governed from outside Norwegian soil, but without the apparatus of authority the Germans brought with them; the union with Sweden had been dissolved peaceably in 1905.

shops, individual clumps of trees, kinds of field gun, kinds of soldier – and store what he recognized in an exact brain, would have more time on hand to watch out for significant detail: such as markings on the truck that towed the gun, or a regimental number on the soldier's collar. People who had this gift developed unusually far, might do unusually well. It was one of the ways in which country-bred folk were likely to be better equipped for resistance life than towns-people.

What of the natural leaders of the countryside? The minor aristocracy and landed gentry of Europe have always thought it more important to be, than to do; apart from a little hunting and shooting, and a dance or two, there is nothing much to do with one's time except to be oneself, and to invite one's friends to dinner. So gentlemanly a way of life was useless in resistance: doing was essential, if one could command the capacity and the resource, as well as the tools and the occasion, to act. Capacity for many resistance tasks was inborn, some people having natural gifts of neat-fingeredness or retentive memories; but with practice most memories can be trained to be retentive, and a good instructor can teach all but the most ham-handed how to blow up a bridge or clear a bren gun stoppage. Some gift for acting a part convincingly was often needed. This came awkwardly to those who had been most carefully brought up always to tell the truth – that is, to just those groups who had on moral grounds the strongest objections to coming under nazi rule; even they overcame their distaste for living a lie, when they had to. The nicest and most straightforward of people had to learn to be devious, or go down. Many others found unsuspected abilities as actors inside themselves, and were delighted to exercise them.

Originality, unorthodoxy, dash, explain themselves: a similar quality, often much needed, was resourcefulness. Alert and inventive people make much better resisters than dullards; though there were some tasks for which a patient, angry dullard was better suited than someone more mercurial. The plain man's suspicion of mere cleverness played its part in this field as in others;[1] someone who was ostentatiously bright might well be cold-shouldered by resisters, and not only because brightness makes people ostentatious.

Anger was a useful quality in a resister, as long as it did not make him fool-hardy in his fury; it helped to give him driving force. So did something of the quality the psychologists call *Angst*: worry, concern, and a sensitive awareness of one's immediate surroundings. The best clandestines developed psychic antennae, a sort of sixth sense that warned them when they were in danger and had best move.[2] Yet moving too soon might stop anything from happening at all.[3] Sound judgement, and plain common sense, were indispensable; if they could be backed by an instinctive feel for what was going on, so much the better.

[1] About 1937, the writer recalls, he heard elderly relatives of his own dismissing the possibility that Churchill could ever return to high office, because he was 'too clever to be trustworthy'.

[2] Eg. George Millar, *Maquis* (1956 ed.), 44–6; Foot, 242.

[3] Ibid. 121; cp. p. 63 below.

Tenacity mattered also, above all when things started to go wrong. A man or a woman who could 'hold on when there is nothing in [them] Except the Will which says to them: "Hold on!" ' made a better person to go resisting with than one who quailed easily – or at all. When things went entirely wrong, and a whole group of resisters fell into the Gestapo's hands, anybody in that dismembered company was liable to quail in the end: only sublime sturdiness could keep a prisoner silent for ever. (Hence the working assumption, throughout resistance, that anything known to a prisoner would be known to the enemy as well within forty-eight hours of the arrest. This was often not the case, either because the prisoner's stout heart held, or because the enemy had not correctly identified him, or failed to interrogate him fully, or failed to distribute the interrogation report to those who needed it. But the assumption was a sensible one to make, on the staff college rule: Always plan for your worst case.)

Tenacity was important, though difficult, for a prisoner, who might have to hug to himself indefinitely the secret of an identity, an address, a coding system that the Germans would dearly have loved to know; it was also important, and often hardly less difficult, for a resister still at large. In the early days of occupation especially, when the trauma of defeat was still raw, and the prospect of victory – however sure – remote, it called for endurance well beyond the common run to hold one's purpose firm, and stick to one's resistant task. Besides, some forms of resistance were so difficult to get started at all, that only people of unusual perseverance were able to overcome the series of obstacles – not to say dangers – that lay in their path.

Patience was another quality, closely allied, that resisters needed; familiar enough as a virtue, but needed in unfamiliar strength. Simply to wait, for hours on end, in a hedge, for the noise of an approaching aircraft with a load of stores; to wait so, several nights running without result; and to be there again, waiting, at the next change of moon; these were the gifts of an ideal member of a reception committee. To wait, behind a boulder, on a Breton or Adriatic or Crimean beach, watching incessantly for a faint light signal from the sea that might never come; to sit, for days or weeks on end, within earshot of a telephone that might never ring; and to keep to oneself the fact that one was doing anything of the kind: these tasks were not entirely simple.

Someone endowed with all these various virtues, who did not mind turning a hand to vice as well if doing so would help the cause forward, might still never be able to strike a blow for resistance at all, if denied the opportunity. The ability to spot when and where a chance to resist was going to occur was one of the most valuable gifts a resistance leader could have: this in fact was one of the ways in which people established themselves as leaders. Leading from in front, they could take a force to the point of action, and act.

As Hemingway, who knew what he wrote about, once put it, 'When working with irregular troops you have no real discipline except that of example. As long as they believe in you they will fight if they are good elements. The minute they cease to believe in you, or in the mission to be accomplished, they disappear.'[1] One of the sure ways of encouraging irregulars to fight was by providing them with worthwhile targets; but none might offer. If none offered, there was nothing to do as a rule but stay quiet and hope. Those who went out to make trouble, usually got into it.

This brings us to the final, indispensable quality a resister needed: luck. Without one's fair share of luck, and a little more beside, one could get nowhere. With it, there were few heights one could not try to scale.

Published tales of resistance, true and false alike, teem with instances of luck; perhaps one more might be added, a true one, as an example to stand for the rest. There is no need to specify the country; it was one in which, at the time, resistance was becoming very active. A woman, trained by the British and her own countryfolk for an important clandestine mission, arrived at the large town containing the safe flat where she was to spend the night long after curfew, because minor but incessant interferences with the permanent way by resisters had delayed her train five or six hours. The German in charge of the station where she got out allowed, with uncommon courtesy, all the passengers a one-night pass to break curfew. She walked, dog tired, to the flat: where two Germans awaited her. They believed they recognized her, from descriptions; one of them observed they had a surer means of identifying her, and produced a pair of her own evening shoes. After so many hours' travel, her feet were swollen; her own shoes were clearly too small; and they let her go.[2]

Luck falls of course with the impartiality of God's rain; some people seem never to have it, others never to want it, but for most it comes and goes erratically. The extreme chanciness of resistance work provided much of its charm to the adventurous, and much of its horror to the timid. One simply could not tell from day to day whether the tenor of one's life would continue untroubled or not. Even for those who had decided that their character, their temperament, their career, or their family prevented them from running the risks – the appalling risks – that necessarily attended on resistance work, the call to take such work up might suddenly arrive. Like the old radical cry, 'John Ball has rungen your bell', the call might come at any moment to any household, to any random group in the street: then who would do what? Even if you habitually passed by on the other side, would you go on being such a Pharisee at the sight of one of your own countrymen being man-handled? Could you turn a terrified stranger away from your own door?

In a phrase of Mr Gladstone's, 'Principle can dwell in a man like fire in a flint'; given the necessary shock, a spark might be struck from anyone. There is a story, that deserves to be true, of a French resister who was recognized, in a Paris metro station during the rush hour, by some German policemen. They moved forward

[1] E. Hemingway. *By-Line*, 372 (Collins 1968).
[2] Conversation with her organizer, 1967.

to arrest him. He turned to the crowd round him with a cry: '*Résistance! Aidez-moi!*' They drew apart; he ran through; they re-closed behind him; and the Germans were baffled. Such a happening is credible enough in the closing stages of a resistance war, when almost everyone in an occupied area – the occupying troops included – is expecting their imminent retreat. Earlier on, it was far less likely: there was no consensus in any chance crowd about which side was going to win.

This did not prevent some groups of people, such as the inhabitants of a particular village, from reaching a collective opinion in advance of the rest of their fellow citizens, if circumstances were odd enough. Eric Newby, on the run in the Apennines above Parma as an escaped prisoner-of-war late in 1943, records an interesting example of peasant solidarity. A group of farmers, all drawn from two related families, sent for him. Their spokesman said: 'Many of the people in this village and in the farms round about have sons and relatives who are being hunted by the Germans. Three of them were taken the other day. Some of them have sons in Russia of whom, so far, there is no news and who may never return. They feel that you are in a similar condition to that of their sons who, they hope, are being given help wherever they are, and they think that it is their duty to help you through the coming winter, which otherwise you will not survive.' So they found him food and a hiding-place; even so, somebody's nerve was not strong enough, and later he was betrayed.[1]

Such concepts of conscience and duty were to be expected in communities brought up, over many centuries, to accept a Christian ethic; such betrayals, again, are commonly the fate of those who have adventures imposed on them in unquiet times. The example may help to illuminate a quality in resistance that has lasting fascination and wide appeal: choices of this sort might be forced on anybody, irrespective of race or class.

Few ordinary people ever know what political or military accident may bring them as neighbours: living in a large city, it is easy – even customary – to know little or nothing of the other people in one's street beyond their faces. This anonymity offers huge advantages to the clandestine; unfortunately for whom, it offers almost equal advantages to the secret police. The present writer lived unaware for a dozen years in the next house but one to Boris Pasternak's sister in peacetime Oxford. In wartime Paris, Henri Déricourt – *bon déricourtiste*, but otherwise of doubtful loyalty, alleged to have been at once an important agent in SOE and a leading agent for the *Sicherheitsdienst* – lived for some months in a flat absolutely next door to Sergeant Bleicher, the *Abwehr*'s best detective in Paris: each claimed to know the other only by sight: both may have been right.[2] In that same beautiful and desolate city, José Dupuis, who tripled courier work for Yeo Thomas with cipher work for an intelligence circuit and a cover job as a schoolmistress, decided, at the end of the summer term of 1944, to change her

[1] Eric Newby, *Love and War in the Apennines* (Hodder & Stoughton 1971), 162–3.
[2] Cp. Foot, ch. x; conversation with Bleicher, 1969.

cover job and her identity; got a new job as a clerk; and found an ideal flat, in a corner block, between two quiet neighbours. At the liberation she discovered both her neighbours to be fellow clandestines, working in different circuits.[1]

It will be clear already to readers that the author is a warm admirer of resisters, as a type of human being; in principle. He has met, and read of, too many to have a doubt that on the whole they are the salt of the earth. But it would be false to history to suggest that all of them were without blemish; or that there were not mean and ignoble motives for going into resistance, as well as those discussed so far.

Some were in it for the money.

The Gestapo offered substantial head-money – £5,000 or more – for information that led directly to the arrest of an agent of the Allied secret services; in some countries, resistance security was weak enough for a desperate man to entertain, as a business proposition, the idea of getting into an established circuit in order to betray its leader and claim the reward. In a few cases this could be, and even was, done.

Others may have been tempted by the prospect of hard cash – traditionally, golden sovereigns; but in modern times one often has to put up with paper[2] – provided for resistance purposes, but sequestered to private ones. Substantial sums were indeed parachuted into southern and north-western Europe by the American and British air forces, on behalf of various secret services; and a certain amount of this money, perhaps as much as a twentieth, may have stuck to fingers through which it passed. The head of one exiled secret service was arraigned, after his return to the country he had helped to liberate, on the charge of malversation of funds, and spent some months behind bars awaiting trial; he was released. Accounting systems at the dispatching end could be rudimentary,[3] but there is no known case of peculation at source in the secret service world. One agent, calling at his secret service's office in the capital of a newly freed country to return the balance of his operational funds, met another who said, 'Are you *mad*? I've bought a couple of nice hotels with mine';[4] but such cases could not be common – there was little enough money to go round.

Others were in it, in an era of famine, for a still more material benefit than cash; for food or tobacco. These were more readily to be got, of course, on the black market than by resistance raids. Black markets in all sorts of goods flourished in most of the occupied countries; come to that they were far from unknown on the Allied side either. Whenever there are shortages, shifty little men are to be found who purport to know the way round them; a full social history of the war would contain plenty of dingy tales, had not most black marketeers been

---

[1] Conversation with H. H. A. Thackthwaite, 1966.
[2] Cp. T. E. Lawrence, *Seven Pillars of Wisdom* (1935), 94, 321–2.
[3] Cp. Sweet-Escott, 23.
[4] Conversation with one of them, 1969.

good at covering their tracks. The sort of scale on which they could operate may be shown by a single statistic: illegal consumption of petrol in the United States during the war touched two and a half million gallons a day.[1] Several secret services dabbled in black markets of various kinds, notably the Gestapo. It suited the German aim of keeping people's morale in occupied territory low, and non-German administration there weak, to have parallel, illegal, and quasi-legal markets in operation for much-desired, and more or less essential goods: furs in Russia, wine in the south, food and tobacco everywhere. It also suited many Gestapo men to supplement their pay by crooked dealings among the people they supervised.[2]

Black markets in fact came, in some areas, to be so much run by the Gestapo that prudent local criminals avoided them, and tried to secure their goods through resistance groups instead: hence the impression that some gangs of outlaws have given, of having been nothing better than bandits.

In Joseph Kessel's phrase, then, they were not all angels; they were not all devils either. What, good and bad, weak and strong alike, were they trying to do?

---

[1] *Observer*, 24 August 1969, 21 ab.
[2] Eg. J. Delarue, *Trafics et crimes sous l'occupation*, part 1 (1968).

# 3 FORMS RESISTANCE TOOK

### Intelligence

One task for resisters stood out above all at the time, from the Allied staffs' point of view, and indeed from the point of view of every Allied commander, from a Zhukov or an Eisenhower down to a senior private leading a patrol. It was vital to know, from day to day, from minute even to minute, where the enemy was and what he was doing. In retrospect too we can see how important this task was, what indispensable aid it gave to any rapid Allied advance. Yet on the occupied spot, the indispensability of this task was seldom clear; and for the individual who prepared to turn spy in his own country, there was a stiff pair of hedges to be taken early in the course.

The first hedge was moral: how could one bring oneself to work against the constituted régime under which one lived? To break the ingrained habits of a lifetime, perhaps of many generations; to carry one's line of conduct and habits of thought back for years, perhaps hundreds of years, to the last time one's own country had been torn by a civil war; was a hard and desperate act, to which only desperate men and women were ready to resort.

Once this great choice had been taken, another presented itself at once; almost equally testing for a patriot, in an age and context in which love of country meant much. Most, almost all, of the data one could supply would be used initially for the benefit of some foreign country's armed forces. Bad as German occupation was, was it so bad that one wished to substitute for it occupation by Russians or British or Americans? Countries self-willed enough to develop strong resistance movements might well entertain doubts on this point; it had a notable impact in Poland, Yugoslavia, and France.[1]

For those who found it possible to get over these moral and political obstacles and to set out to become spies, there was a double task: to secure information, and to transmit it.

The information that was needed for use against the Germans was political,

---

[1] Cp. Alban Vistel, *La nuit sans ombre* (1970), 189, for secular French suspicions of the British intelligence service.

economic, and military. On the political side there was not much to report, even if anyone could be found to report it, because the nazis did not believe in elections, once they had come to power themselves. Normal open democratic political activity was at a standstill in occupied Europe: this was one of the main things the war was about. If it happened to be possible to get news of impending changes in what we may call for short the Quisling machine – which of the nazis' puppets was to be set up higher, and which put down – such news would be worth transmitting, if only for its use to the propaganda services of the nazis' enemies. But this did not amount to a great deal. Again, news of restrictions on movement was useful in a small way: knowledge about the hours of curfew, or the boundaries of coastal or fortified zones that were banned to strangers without permits (and where did one get, how could one forge the permits?), would be useful to someone planning a raid or a secret mission, or training aircrew in evasion.

Economic intelligence was another matter: less hard to come by, if one understood what it was and where to look for it; and of noticeable impact for the war effort, if it could be got into the right hands. Total wars may well be decided as much by the productive capacity as by the armed and unarmed forces of the combatants. One of the most economical uses of armed forces is to destroy the enemy's means of production; and to decide which target to attack, sound economic intelligence is indispensable.

Recognizing it for what it is, was not always straightforward. For example, the intelligence staffs of the British and American bomber commands sifted through a colossal body of data on the German aircraft industry, looking for weak points; and discovered that practically Germany's entire output of ball bearings was concentrated in a small area of Schweinfurt. Taking for granted that the factories there were working triple shifts, and gleaning from resistance sources some figures on the rate at which loaded trains left the factory area, they reckoned they had found what they were looking for. Hence, a great outpouring of effort, bomb load, and life. The impact of the bombing was simply to move the factories from single to double shift, to enable output to keep abreast of damage: nobody on the intelligence side having taken in the comparatively feeble degree to which manpower in Germany had been mobilized for war production.

A slighter, but quotable, example may be taken from another skip forward to our narrative. In the autumn of 1941, when the hunt for oil targets was up, SOE's country sections were busy devising targets for attack by saboteurs; a target section was formed in Baker Street, to oversee their work and to secure liaison with other interested bodies. A country section proudly submitted a long list of *raffineries* it had discovered from searching through the 1 : 80,000 French army map (an accurate document in its day, but diabolically hard to read). The authority in the target section *was* an authority; he had worked for many years in one of the largest industrial insurance firms in Paris. He pointed out that all the *raffineries* on this list refined sugar, not oil.[1]

[1] Conversation with him, 1968.

23

A great deal of his work was with the non- or rather less-secret side of the ministry of economic warfare, the body that provided official cover for SOE, and contained plenty of economists. Much could be gleaned, there and elsewhere, from newspapers, when available: shortages could be seen, even foreseen, and something could be done to assess the impact of various kinds of blockading policy. This is only another example of a point familiar to anyone who has ever had any serious intelligence or research work to do: on most subjects there is an enormous amount in print already. The difficulty is rather to know where to look for it, and to reduce it to a form that will be intelligible for the purpose at hand; whether that purpose is securing a doctorate or overthrowing a régime.

For example, a strategist planning an invasion – or indeed a tactician planning a raid – will do well to start by consulting works of geography from which he can garner the essential points about the ground he intends to send troops to fight over: types of soil, types of buildings, width and force of rivers, kinds of wood, kinds of weather. With any luck, harbour installations, bridges, power stations may have been built originally by firms from abroad who can supply the original plans, which offer a host of details about the vulnerability of the plant to those who know where to look. In the ideal case, the briefing officer can show the saboteur an air photograph or even a model of his target, and point out yard by yard how to approach it: cases in hard fact are seldom ideal.

There was one kind of ideal agent, for economic intelligence: the railway goods clerk, in a large junction, who compiled – perhaps as part of his paid day's work – statistics of what goods travelled in which directions. A few such existed;[1] worth their weight in platinum.

On the military side, what was most worth reporting?

Intentions, above all: as Sun Tzu remarked in the fourth century BC, in the chapter 'on the use of secret agents' in his *Art of War*, 'the reason why the enlightened prince and the wise general conquer the enemy whenever they move and their achievements surpass those of ordinary men is foreknowledge of his plans'.[2]

It hardly ever happened that a resister was able to get direct evidence of Axis intentions; though now and again this could be done. The *locus classicus* was the theft, by an alert French house decorator, of the plan for the Atlantic Wall; which was in London before a single block-house described in it was built.[3] 'Ultra' of course provided a mass of data about Hitler's plans, but only the initial stages of 'Ultra' can be credited to resistance; it too must be handled in detail later.[4]

What often indicated the enemy's intentions, and what was well within the range of a good intelligence network, was movement: the slightest indications

---

[1] I met one, now a distinguished international civil servant, in 1971.
[2] Ed. S. B. Griffith (Oxford 1963), 144.
[3] See p. 242 below.
[4] See pp. 308–10 below.

were worth having of arrivals and departures of units and headquarters, of ships, guns, tanks, vehicles, and aircraft. Obviously the more detailed reports of these movements were, the better. Any housewife who gave a moment's thought to it could count the funnels on a ship; or guess the calibre of a gun, if it went slowly down her village street; or see the colours of the shoulder-piping of the soldiers who came to her local café. If she could get close enough, she could count the number of engines on an aircraft, too; even though she could not tell a Ju 88 from a He 111. Obviously, she was not likely to lurk near a military airfield, taking notes; but why should she not push her baby's pram along the path that ran outside the perimeter wire?

Really observant agents, and those who had been trained in aircraft and tank recognition, could do a lot better than the chance housewife or the passing pigman. They would be on the lookout for indications of that great intelligence officers' shibboleth: order of battle. IOs in all armed forces were brought up to believe that one of their principal aims must be to establish the order of battle of the forces opposed to them; and the first object of most prisoner interrogations was to find out the prisoner's unit.

An enormous amount about German order of battle was found out from 'Ultra' sources, and discreetly leaked in due time via MI6 to the combatant arms. British divisional and brigade IOs had a yellow pocketbook entitled *Order of Battle of the German Army*, to which frequent amendments were issued by MI14, the apparent source: MI14 knew indeed a great deal about the peacetime *Wehrmacht*, and did what it could to allot each newly discovered division to one of the Reich's eighteen *Wehrkreise*. A clandestine agent in the field – a prostitute in an army brothel, for instance, going through a sleeping client's pockets – could learn easily enough where to hunt (paybook, envelopes of letters, shoulderstraps) for clues to the essential points: arm of service, number of regiment, date of enlistment.[1]

Earnest and attentive staff officers in London, Washington, and Moscow kept a regular eye on the number, quality, and location of the Axis armies' divisions; also on their internal organization. Reports from resistance could do a good deal to confirm and to clarify what was known or suspected already.[2]

Here it is necessary to reiterate what has been said above:[3] the task of the IO is quite as much editorial as original. A vast deal is in print on most subjects already; your really bright man is the man who knows where to look for it, and can assess with how much accuracy his predecessors have set it out. Donald McLachlan, an exceptionally bright star even in the constellation of NID, has explained this at length, in a passage that bears summary. Interceptions of

---

[1] On being taken prisoner, I was horrified – though I tried not to show it – when my cheque book was removed from my inner battledress blouse pocket; I should never have taken into the field a cheque stub made out to HQ SAS Troops. My interrogator, without examining the stubs, said 'You won't want this, will you?' and dropped it in the fire.

[2] Cp. p. 307 below.

[3] p. 23.

enemy signals are put first; we now know why. Next came captured documents; fixes of ships' positions (a naval speciality, beside our point); air photographs; and naval sightings. Only sixth came 'Information of all kinds from agents or friendly secret services: variously graded but all top secret.' Then he put what prisoners-of-war say; what can be gleaned from wireless traffic; and from the enemy's own propaganda; and from letter censorship. Next he places 'Topographical and technical information from open sources; friendly and neutral observers; what can be noticed of enemy tactics during battles; sightings, other than naval; relevant news from other services (sometimes to be placed at the top of the list); and lastly, communications through double agents.[1]

Again, a lot was known already about the weapons the Axis forces used; from their own publications, from captures on the fighting fronts, from neutral manufacturers (Oerlikon the Swiss gunmakers sold their excellent 20 mm cannon impartially to the air forces of both sides. Resistance's task here was to smuggle essential parts out for the RAF[2]). Yet in a technical age, technical matters became of overwhelming importance; every detail about the shape, size, colour, composition, location of almost any weapon was worth having. Here, what any housewife could spot was less important; what any metallurgist or engineer could detect mattered a lot more.

Construction details, fully within the engineer's province and not the sort of thing on which 'Ultra' was going to be any help, were an obvious intelligence target; which it was sometimes possible to hit. For example, hints from 'Ultra' and elsewhere drew attention to Peenemünde, the research station on the Baltic coast at which the Germans were experimenting with the V1 and V2. Reconnaissance photographs happened to catch activity in the open.[3] Efforts were made to insert an agent into the work force at the station; with interesting results.[4] And the Poles were told: hence their justly famous exploit, of racing the Germans to the wreck of one of the first V2s ever fired, which landed hopelessly off course in a bend of the river Bug. Poles managed to secure the engine and to send it out by air to London. Resistance also played its part in helping to dispose of the V3 and V4, in their colossal sites at Wissant and Mimoyecques; though sabotage exploits by actual agents inside these sites remain in the realm of fiction.[5]

Another important field in which news was welcome, if it could be obtained, was that of the enemy high command: the personality or at any rate the identity of formation and unit commanders always matters to their opponents. Here again resistance was only one among several sources; army lists, previous contacts, newspaper files might fill in a great deal of detail, but resistance would be likely to provide the best source for the one essential detail: the name of the

[1] D. H. McLachlan, *Room 39* (1968), 20-1.
[2] Cp. p. 216 below.
[3] Constance Babington Smith, *Evidence in Camera* (1961), ch. ix.
[4] See R. V. Jones, 'Scientific Intelligence', in *RUSIJ*, xcii. 362 (1947); and D. J. Dallin, *Soviet Espionage* (1955), 268.
[5] See p. 295 below.

man on the spot. The Y service would in fact be its only serious rival; apart from the accident of a posting order sent by 'Enigma' and successfully deciphered.

In fiction the task of the resistance heroine is to lure the enemy commander into bed; where she either emulates Judith's technique with Holofernes – messy[1] – or coaxes vital information from him about his plans, which she transmits through her true love next day – highly improbable.[2] History does not need to linger long on these romantic fantasies.

It needs to notice instead a last, and duller, intelligence requirement: news about the weather. For air force purposes, accurate weather forecasts were important. Customary weather maps, and tables of weather data, vanished from wartime newspapers; temperature, barometric pressure, extent of cloud cover became state secrets. Polish intelligence sources provided London, twice daily throughout the war, with weather data from Poland; which, married to those cabled from Stockholm and İstanbul, enabled bomber command's meteorologists to forecast the weather over Germany. *Per contra*, the Luftwaffe got reports twice daily from the German legation in Dublin and from Greenland.[3]

Observation, aided by a few common measuring tools such as barometers, rulers, field glasses, provided a great deal of this intelligence material. The next main source was subterfuge – eg. taking an extra copy of a document one was typing; which shaded fast into theft and burglary. An accomplished spy, or one exceptionally well placed on an enemy staff, could do a great deal with a camera, in the way of photographing supposedly secret documents; if he could get at them.

Fortunately for spies, people who have to handle highly secret material get used to doing so, and fall into routines. If you can get close enough to the material to study the routines, you may be able to lay hands on what you want. Safes are generally taken to be safe; and therefore left alone at night. Someone who had taken an impression of the key, or discovered the combination, might all the same be able to go through their contents, if clever enough to get into the same room.[4] Outside safes, filing cabinets – even if locked – presented no obstacle to a fully trained agent who had taken a lock-picking course, a matter of routine in any secret service's training section. Amateurs in the field might have more trouble; one could always, after due inquiry, take lessons from a locksmith.

Though the gaining of intelligence was the primary spy's task, it was quite as important to transmit it: untransmitted news might just as well, indeed better, not have been gathered. Transmission was the really dangerous stage, in a life no part of which was wholly safe.

The spy therefore, on top of living a double life, had to perform a task of

[1] Judith xiii. 6–10.

[2] Cp. Wayland Young, *The Profumo Affair* (1963), 85.

[3] J. Garliński, *Poland SOE and the Allies* (1969), 72, 78; Albert Speer, *Inside the Third Reich* (1971), 494; J. Piekalkiewicz, *Secret Agents, Spies and Saboteurs* (1974), 466–85.

[4] For a famous example, a joint MI6–SOE *coup* in Washington, see p. 154 below.

double complexity: having secured his material, he had to move it away towards its goal. Few of those engaged on this work in those years thought of themselves as being in any sense under the control of what is nowadays termed a spymaster; most in fact were. How they communicated will be discussed below.[1] Things had become a good deal more complicated in the twenty-five years since Blenkiron juggled with oranges in Constantinople.[2]

One other spy's task needs to be mentioned, a necessary preliminary to sending the material away: condensing it. This was straightforward enough, to those who had the art of précis; at which practice in any case makes perfect. If contact between spy and spymaster was reasonably swift, the spy would hear soon enough if over-compression had cut out some point of interest.

## Deception

Deception is a very ancient device in warfare; great commanders have used it repeatedly, from the legendary exploits of Ulysses to the actual triumphs of Giap. Here there really are security bars, which only the wilfully obtuse or the conscious fellow-traveller can resent; this is why it is the branch of the art of war most gingerly handled by the theorists. It gets less attention from them, proportionately to its weight in the scales of decision, than the other branches, on grounds both of security and of tact: everyone hates to look a fool, and people taken in by deceptions can look foolish indeed.

In the past two centuries or so the British have often shown themselves pastmasters of politico-military deceit. This mastery is probably a side effect of that gigantic confidence trick, the Raj: an Indian empire with a population numbered in hundreds of millions was controlled by an administrative class of less than 3,000 sahibs.[3] The sahibs behaved as if it never crossed their minds that anyone would fail to do what they said; and apart from the mutiny of 1857-8, the system worked. Comparable imperturbability, steered still closer to the brink of death, was shown by the crews of Q-ships in the anti-submarine campaigns of 1915-18.[4] A single staff officer with iron nerves and a worn haversack-strap, by pretending to be flustered, planted bogus papers on the Turks and thus enabled Allenby to capture Gaza in 1917.[5]

Could such *coups* be repeated in a resistance context?

The more expensive, and extensive, wars become, the more valuable successful deceptions are. Hence, even more were attempted in the wars of 1939-45 than before. The Germans brought off a particularly useful one in the winter and spring of 1939-40: they spread all over western Europe, as much by innuendo as

[1] At pp. 98-127.
[2] John Buchan, *Greenmantle* (1916), 169-70.
[3] See Judith M. Brown in Foot ed, *War and Society*, 89 (1973).
[4] See Gordon Campbell, VC, *My Mystery Ships* (1928), 279-80. The *coup* was not usefully repeatable: see A. J. Marder, *From the Dardanelles to Oran* (1974), 49.
[5] See Wavell, *Allenby* (1940), i. 201-2, 210.

by direct statement, the idea that they had a large and highly organized 'fifth column' of clandestine supporters all over the lands they were going to conquer. Though in fact this fifth column had hardly any real existence, the belief that it was there had a powerful influence, stimulating panic among millions of civilians, and so creating in rear areas a state of confusion ideal for an opposing *Blitzkrieg* attack.[1] The *coup* was presumably originated by Goebbels, on a suggestion of Hitler's own: it is one of the many subjects we shall meet with still worth further study.

Strategic deceptions, like this one, were – had to be – handled only at the politico-military summit: with nothing, or hardly anything, put on paper. Directing heads of state, one or two essential ministers, chiefs of staff, and the necessary minimum of staff officers and executants would be the only people involved. One individual would be in charge of the whole project, and would be wholly absorbed by it. Only the intricacies of camouflage detail could be left to subordinates; even those would need occasional checking from the top. Some of the staff officers would know little, and some of the executants nothing, of what they were really doing. Deadly, permanent secrecy was the condition of success.

Imperatives of security therefore made it impossible for resisters to play much active part in deceptions, and difficult for them to play any part at all.

Passively, they were sometimes able to help. For instance, when Eisenhower and Alexander were clearing North Africa of Axis troops in the late spring of 1943, it became important to confuse the Germans about where the next blow in the Mediterranean would be struck. An elaborate deception scheme, of which the centrepiece was the washing up of a body carrying really secret letters on the coast of Spain, succeeded: the Germans anticipated landings in Sardinia and in southern Greece, and neglected to protect Sicily properly. Among other misguided troop movements, they sent the 1st Panzer Division from France to the Peloponnese: where it provided targets at least, as well as trouble, for Greek resistance.[2]

Later, in the autumn of the same year, it remained important to keep the Axis powers confused about Allied landing intentions. By this time the system of sending messages to parties of organized resisters through the BBC, to trigger off extra alertness or even sabotage activity, had reached such a degree of sophistication that the German security forces wasted much time in trying to decode the messages; and had captured some as well.[3] A lot of warning messages were sent to SOE's circuits in south-west France in early October; they were never followed by action messages, there was no real operation impending on the Biscay coast which action could have aided,[4] and the warnings can be presumed to be part of some deception so grand that no other detail of it has become known.

MI5 meanwhile was busy with a deception so vast that it puts even the

---

[1] See L. de Jong, *The German Fifth Column in the Second World War*, tr. (1956).
[2] Ewen Montagu, *The Man Who Never Was* (Penguin 1956), esp. 109–10.
[3] Eg. Foot, 304, 388.     [4] Personal knowledge.

*Abwehr's* achievement in the Netherlands[1] into the shade: a great professional stroke, and one with important implications for resisters all Europe over. One of its branches, Bɪa, played back to Germany most of the clandestine transmitters the Germans dispatched to this country; in so deft a fashion that the German secret services never discovered – till it was too late, and Germany had lost the war for certain – that every one of the agents they believed to be operating for them in Great Britain was in fact working under British control.[2]

The operation called 'Fortitude' which the British and Americans mounted, to confuse and deceive the Germans about when and where their main assault on north-west Europe was taking place, was one of their most striking and least expensive victories. It was mounted partly with the help of the double-crossing agents; partly through camouflage; and partly through bogus wireless traffic, which simulated non-existent armies in Scotland and East Anglia. It mattered for resisters in several ways. Above all, it mattered because it hastened the end of the war. Less agreeably, for those on the spot, it sharpened German police awareness in the areas it threatened – Norway, Denmark, Belgium, France north of the river Somme – and made it even more dangerous to be an active resister in those areas than it had been already. In a small way, resisters in intelligence networks were able to help the work of 'Fortitude' along, by routine reports of German troop movements and other precautionary measures; these reports helped the deception staffs – which had by now necessarily grown – to assess how far they were succeeding.

Reports from resisters, as well as those from other channels, were of course useful to deception planners in general, quite apart from 'Fortitude', for the same purpose of judging whether they were hitting the targets at which they aimed. A section of SOE, left behind in it when PWE split off, indulged in the spreading of 'sibs' – plausible anecdotes likely to lower enemy morale, or such catches for children to sing as:

Pas de feu, vive Pucheu!

Pas de pain, vive Pétain!

Sibs were devised by an inter-service committee and spread by those who could; as often as not, they were first tried out in club and canteen bars in London, before being exported. Resisters, quite unconscious of what was going on, could usefully report back results.[3]

Another way in which resisters could take part in deception lay in booby-trapping areas through which enemy troops were about to pass; as part of one of resistance's main tasks, attacks on troops.[4] SOE had an extensive camouflage

---

[1] Cp. pp. 264–6 below.

[2] (Sir) J. C. Masterman, *The Double-Cross System in the War of 1939 to 1945* (Yale 1972), is a mildly bowdlerized version of his official report, as head of the section, written in 1945 before he went back to academic life. Less official details in Sefton Delmer, *The Counterfeit Spy* (1973), which follows the fortunes of one of the agents.

[3] Eg. Delmer, *Counterfeit Spy*, 244–8.

[4] See pp. 49–57 below.

section, which amused itself devising explosive cowpats and similar toys; these could be parachuted in to agents who needed to use them. Appropriately enough, the camouflage section was housed in one of the South Kensington museums that had provided entertainment for generations of schoolboys.[1] As a matter of fact, a more efficient tyre-burster than a pile of plastic dung was a scaled-down version of the renaissance caltrop, a formidable obstacle to cavalry; scaled-down caltrops could also be supplied by SOE.

But we are getting away from deception. Not much is yet known about it, even after Masterman's book; there is a great deal more waiting to be discovered.

To sum up, resistance provided some of the stage settings and a few walk-on parts; but the stars, and the directors, for the dramas of deception belonged elsewhere.

## Escape

The craft of escaping has an ancient and honourable history; it is no doubt older even than the craft of war. To authenticate it as a subject for scholarly attention, the case of an eminent escaper and still more eminent scholar may be cited: Hugo Grotius. During the troubles of the early seventeenth century he was imprisoned in the castle of Loevestein; whence his friends carried him away, on 22 March 1621, in a large case believed by his guards to contain books he had finished reading.[2] Airey Neave's *Saturday at MI9*[3] provides a recent instance of an informative and thoroughly scholarly treatment of a sizeable slice of our present subject; by someone who himself escaped from Saxony to England, and then held a responsible post in the British escape organization.

The subject of escape from the nazis is not yet quite ripe for full historical analysis; so far as it is treatable from the records at all. Not all the surviving archive material is yet available for research; and parts of this subject are still wrapped in some degree of security cover. In the British archives, the public record office so far contains one, only one, highly suggestive summary.[4] The summary consists of a nominal roll of people in the armed forces of the British crown who escaped from, or evaded, German capture in the near east in 1941-4. There were, in all, 2,807 of them – counting the wife of a British private who escaped from Crete with him in a caïque in November 1941. The first 534 names on the roll are missing; leaving a quotable first entry, about a yeomanry trooper, H. L. Addicott. He had been captured in Greece, when attached to 50 Commando, on 23 March 1941, and arrived in Turkey that October. 'Method:

[1] L. Bell, *Sabotage!* (1957), frontispiece.
[2] The case was on show in the Rijksmuseum at Amsterdam in September 1972.
[3] Hodder & Stoughton, 1969; henceforward, Neave. Cp. also his superior, J. M. Langley, *Fight Another Day* (Collins 1974).
[4] I am much indebted to Group Captain E. B. Haslam, head of the air historical branch of the Ministry of Defence, for drawing my attention to PRO AIR 20/2330 and for other useful advice.

Swam.'[1] This in fact can only be an interim report, about the problems of escape in Hitler's war; preparing the way for a full analysis someone can make later.

Five simple analytic points need to be made early; in a field not wholly familiar, even the obvious is worth stating.

1    The first may seem merely verbal; but verbal distinctions do sometimes matter, and this one is important. An evader is not the same as an escaper. An escaper is someone who has been in enemy hands, and gets away. An evader is someone who, for one reason or another, finds himself on enemy territory but not under enemy control, and gets away without having been in enemy hands at all.

It often happened to people in the army, in parachute or commando units; or to members of secret services; or to aircrew whose aircraft had been shot down; that they found themselves in enemy territory, with no set task left to perform, but with their exact whereabouts – or, better still from the evaders' point of view, the fact of their existence – unknown to the enemy. Of course, if there had been an air raid or an important demolition, there would be a local state of alert, and many authorities would be on the lookout for uniformed strangers; but this was not always so. An aircraft's crew, for instance, might have to bale out hundreds of miles from their target, because anti-aircraft fire had damaged their aircraft to an extent that only became uncontrollable after a time. Now aircrew, commandos, parachutists, anyone else who might find themselves in an evader's predicament, had had it firmly instilled into them that it was their duty to evade, rather than to surrender. They had all been trained, with much trouble and expense; their capacities were still needed in the war; and their task was to get away. Many evaders were tempted, when they saw some worthwhile sabotage target they thought they could encompass, to attack it; most of them resisted the temptation. Common prudence suggested they had difficulties enough already; their units, and their families, called them back – on two different wavelengths, but loud and clear on each.

2    Secondly – again, an obvious but an important point – escape (or evasion) for civilians was not the same as it was for members of armed forces. In the context of getting away from the nazis, entirely different risks were run by each. The risks run depended partly on whom and where one was getting away from, partly on where one was going. It was dinned into uniformed potential escapers, during their escape training before ever they went into enemy territory, that their uniform should provide them with some degree of protection, under the Geneva convention; and that even if they got out of uniform, usually a sensible step if they contemplated a long journey across occupied Europe, they should in the event of recapture announce their true rank, name, and number, and claim the convention's safeguards. It sometimes happened that aircrew got lynched by people they had set out to attack; it only too often happened that commandos and parachutists who fell into German hands were executed under Hitler's

[1] Loc. cit., f. 1.

notorious order of 14 October 1942;[1] and there were a few equally notorious instances of recaptured escapers who were shot.[2] But as a rule aircrew, and recaptured escapers from prisoner-of-war camps, had nothing worse awaiting them than prison. Prison, also, might be the worst fate awaiting captured secret service agents, if the service running them had remembered to give them officer status, and they claimed it. Even the SS were oddly reluctant, off the battlefield, to execute an officer – such was the strength of the *Offizierkorps* tradition.[3]

This was not the case with civilians who helped them. If detected, they could expect no mercy, and received little. They would be tried by a military court; acquittals were unknown. The sentence was invariably deportation to Germany, or death at once; a great many of those deported did not come back. It posed an extra problem for an escaper or evader, if he had to have help to get away: was this the sort of danger he could reasonably ask someone else's family to run?

Destination – where one was going – threw up some odd results, even in this odd world; one or two cases may be cited. Perhaps the oddest was Gustav Herling's.[4] He was a student when the Germans overran Poland in 1939; evaded capture; and went home. Hearing by bush telegraph that Polish forces were continuing the struggle abroad, he decided to join them. After the fourth partition of Poland, he tried to cross into Lithuania, but was caught by Soviet frontier guards. He was mistaken for a cousin of Göring's, and sent to Leningrad; where he was put in the Peresylka prison. By a clerical error he was put in a cell with some seventy people; including many Red Army officers, much his seniors, who were doing time during the great purge. They interrogated him exhaustively about the conduct of the German and Russian invasions of Poland; once he had established his private identity, no one else interrogated him at all, nor was he tried. He was sent to a labour camp in the far north, of which his book gives a piercingly moving account; by the spring of 1942 he was near death from starvation. Suddenly he heard his name on the camp loud-speaker; hobbled to the office; and was given a free ticket to the Persian border. The wheel of fortune had turned a full half-circle, and his captors by now looked with favour on anti-German Poles; he could go.

A great many civilians, a few of them of world eminence such as Einstein and Freud, and most of them like these two Jewish, got away from Germany before ever the war began. A total of 280,000 Jews are recorded as having left the continent, some to England, some to South America, some to the United States; some to Japan.[5] What did it feel like to be a rich German Jew who had bought his way out of Germany and gone to Japan, when Japan and Germany joined in the war on the same side? – a macabre example of the importance of thinking where one is going. A sizeable proportion of the German Jewish intelligentsia

[1] Nuremberg document 498-PS, USA-501.
[2] Cp. Neave, *Saturday at MI9*, 24.
[3] Ibid. 33–4.
[4] See G. Herling, *A World Apart* (1951).
[5] *New Cambridge Modern History*, xiv, map 60 (1970).

seems to have escaped; some like Gustav Stolper to New York, many to Oxford, where G. D. H. Cole and others did a great deal of unobtrusive but effective work to fit them into the university.

Escape was by no means simple for these people; as Jews, they were naturally on the frontier police black list; even non-Jews did not find it easy to leave the nazi paradise. The nazis, being what they were, enjoyed devising traps for those rash enough to want to flee. The simplest way out was bribery: find the official in charge of the case, find out how much he hints at, double it, and hope. A few escaped by bluff. The least bright stayed, and went in the end to the extermination camps, whence none was meant to return.[1]

Walter Gropius's case deserves mention also. As leader of the *Bauhaus* group, he had already exercised a cardinal influence on the growth of modern architecture; but he and the new régime did not see eye to eye, on matters either of style or of conduct. In 1934 he was invited by some Italians interested in *Bauhaus* ideas to visit Rome; and did so, accompanied by his attractive, much younger, and visibly nordic wife. She smiled at everybody, and allowed herself to be taken in to dinner on the arm of Mussolini's party secretary. Her husband called at the German embassy to inquire whether their Lufthansa return tickets from Munich might be varied to allow a return via Zürich, where he wanted to call on a friend. 'But of course, Herr Doktor – did we not see the Frau Doktor with Signor Starace last night? No sort of difficulty.' So they flew to Zürich; and did not go on to Munich. They went to London instead.

Gropius kept in touch with the south German press. Reading in it that a former assistant of his was in trouble with the nazis on charges he knew not to be true, with great daring he went back; gave evidence, successfully, on his friend's behalf; and was arrested as he left the court. Fortunately for him, he was so eminent that the nazis did not dare to hold him, and he was released; spending the war in America, and dying quite recently at a great age. His widow is still alive to tell the story.[2]

There are a great many other tales to be told about civilian escapes; but not here.

3   Thirdly, there is a distinction to be made, among those escaping or evading, between those who travel by themselves, and those who are moved along some kind of escape line. If the phrase is not too brash, we may call them 'loners' and 'liners'.

Some 'loners' brought off remarkable escapes. The Polish Count Dżiefgowski, parachuted (at the fourth attempt) into south-west France to make some inquiries for SOE in the autumn of 1941, made his own way from Perpignan to Gibraltar six months later.[3] A very few, very tough, very brave men could attempt this kind of thing; but most people needed help. Compare for example

---

[1] See H. Krausnick *et al.*, *Anatomy of the SS State* (1968), esp. 464–504.
[2] *Times* obituary, 7 July 1969, 10f, information from J. C. Pritchard, 1975.
[3] If we may believe the citation for his military cross; Foot, 101, 176–7.

the pair of airmen, still in RAF battledress, who blundered accidentally into a café in Toulouse much used by the Gestapo, which was also the heart of a particularly securely organized clandestine circuit; sought help; got it; and reported their find as a 'safe' address when they got home.[1]

There was an English infantry private who got left behind at Dunkirk, who walked from Dunkirk to the foothills of the Jura; taking four months to do it. His French was limited to *oui* and *non*; he had no money. He moved by night; slept rough in the day; and lived on what he could steal in the fields and woods. He steered by maps lifted from telephone-boxes; but as each of these showed only a single *département*, and some (unobserved by him) had east and some had no th at the top, his course was erratic. He avoided all officials, French or German, and all controls. In the end he bumped into an English boy of eighteen who happened to have Swiss papers and bilingual French; who took charge of him, took him down to Marseilles, and saw him onto an escape line. Both survive.[2]

'Saw him onto an escape line' – was it as simple as seeing someone onto a train? Not by any means; but if one had any kind of flair for the clandestine life, one could probably ferret out some way of getting in touch with a line. A line that was well organized would certainly have strict rules encouraging its passengers to think of themselves as parcels being moved along it,[3] and they would need to behave in quite a different way from the 'loners'. They would be given clothes and papers to cover false identities (of all this more shortly), and would probably do much of their travelling by train.

4　Among escape lines, there was an important distinction: between those running eastward into the Soviet zone, and those that ran elsewhere. The others ran southward from Poland into Hungary, and then in Hannay's footsteps down the Danube into Turkey; northward or eastward from Denmark or Norway into Sweden; from Greece into Turkey or Egypt; and along all sorts of routes through the Netherlands, Belgium, and France, either into Iberia or into Switzerland.

Of the eastbound lines, very little is known. They must have existed; it would have been absurd for an organization of the size and nature of the Comintern to fail to maintain them. It is known that there was a clandestine system for slipping western European communists, on their way to join the international brigades in Spain in 1936–7, through from Paris to Barcelona without trouble from the French police. It was run by a Croat called Josip Broz, later world-famous as Marshal Tito. Twenty-four south Slavs he sent down his line became generals in the Yugoslav army.[4] Another obvious case: Maurice Thorez, secretary of the French communist party when Daladier's government used its special powers against it in the autumn of 1939, disappeared; and turned up months later in

---

[1] Ibid. 98.

[2] Cp. ibid. 218; and conversation with one of them, after they had again met and reminisced, late 1966.

[3] Cp. ibid. 97.

[4] Hugh Thomas, *Spanish Civil War*, 381, 778.

Moscow, helped onto an 'underground railway' by a soviet diplomatic contact in Brussels.

Soviet security is even denser than security in the western world, because the soviet authorities have a close control over press and wireless. Beyond a few bald facts, such as the two just cited, virtually nothing is known about the existence of these lines; even less, about how they worked. It may simply be that communist security is excellent, so that nothing at all leaks out. During the war, it was not always absolutely perfect; as many books about the 'Red Orchestra', the espionage network betrayed through a sub-sub-agent's indiscretion, show.[1] And it may also be that the communists could do very little during the war in the way of moving people about; particularly in the early days of mistrust.[2]

5 Fifthly, it is worth noting that a prisoner-of-war was not the same as a captured clandestine agent or resister; though a good captured agent might succeed in pretending to be a prisoner-of-war. Yeo-Thomas, for instance, who performed the almost unexampled feat of escaping from Buchenwald, was soon thereafter recaptured; he managed to pass himself off as an escaped French air force officer, was put in an Oflag, and soon escaped again with new-made friends, with whom he found his way into Allied hands.[3] But ordinary prisoners-of-war, from the ordinary armed forces, separated into officers' and other ranks' camps, were in a wholly different category from captured clandestine agents known to be such. For these the Germans had special arrangements, special measures of security and supervision even within the concentration camps to which they were sent; from which no prisoner was meant to emerge alive.

About escapes from ordinary service prisoner-of-war camps there is a massive literature, which there is no need even to summarize here; of the many books Eric Williams's *The Wooden Horse* (1949) is the best known, and one of the best.

What is a prisoner-of-war, or an imprisoned resister, trying to do when he plans an escape? When all else fails, he can make more work and more worry for the enemy, and thus by however slight an amount divert resources from a more important battlefield. If one can do nothing else, one can at least pin people around one's camp, trying to keep one in it, when they might be more use to the enemy war effort doing something else.[4] Of course, much stronger personal motives apply as well. Prison is prison; dullness, monotony, discomfort, lack of freedom are not easily borne, quite apart from the feeling one is playing little or no useful part in a war worth fighting.

Moreover, once one does escape, one has a moment of sublime elation. To quote a prisoner from a much earlier war, Captain O'Brien remarked of his first

[1] Heinz Höhne, *Codeword: Direktor* (1971), is the latest in English. Cp. also 'Alexander Foote' [no relation], *Handbook for Spies* (1949), and P. Accoce and P. Quet, *The Lucy Ring* (1967), for a sub-network on which more remains to be told.

[2] Cp. pp. 83–4 below.     [3] Cp. Bruce Marshall, *The White Rabbit* (1954), 257–63.

[4] I am proud to record that the small prisoner-of-war camp I was in maintained so high a rate of escape that there were always more guards than prisoners. The reader will allow a few more autobiographical fragments in a moment.

escape on 30 August 1807, near Nancy, 'The happiness we even at this moment felt, was inexpressible; we considered ourselves literally as regenerated creatures.'[1] The feeling one has on actually getting beyond the wire is comparable to the feeling one has when one's parachute has opened properly after all; or to that ecstatic feeling lovers have sometimes at their closest moments. As a human experience, it has superlative quality.

And to achieve it, the thing most necessary was nerve. It was important to have maps, it was frequently indispensable to have money, food, and clothes, it was useful to have a compass; but without nerve, none of these things could help much. Just before an escape, one experienced what the Gladstones used to call in their family language 'bathing-feel' – what one felt as a small boy, just before committing oneself to the bathing-woman and entering the sea;[2] one's state of nervous tension was high. It was kept high not only by the apprehension of danger and the sense of adventure, but by the knowledge that at least one was going to make trouble for the Germans, even if one did not get clean away oneself.

It is no secret that tools were provided to help people who might fall into enemy hands to get away.[3] Aircrew, commandos, and so on carried flat plastic boxes, about $20 \times 10 \times 2$ cm, containing a water bottle, water-purifying tablets, a razor, soap, a fishing line with hooks, three days' worth of highly compressed food, and half a dozen tablets of benzedrine. No one (so far as I know) became a benzedrine addict after using this stimulant to help him on an Alpine or Pyrenean crossing. Silk maps, of a scale of about $1 : 4,000,000$ with enlargements of frontier areas, were available too; you can still pick them up in the Portobello Road.[4] There were all sorts of compasses – collar studs, fly-buttons, and so on; Pierre Lorain has published a detailed diagram of the type I have carried for thirty years.[5] The escape boxes also contained a file, easily enough overlooked as a fragment of scrap – one survived a search of my clothes while I was not wearing them – and usable, by a patient man not liable to cramp in his fingers, to cut through bars. Bars put up by amateurs quite often turn out, on close inspection, to depend on one or two quite slender strips of metal, which an escape kit file can readily cut.[6] Once through the bars, wire remains as an obstacle; but temporary prisoner-of-war-camp wire and the impenetrable entanglements of the old front line of 1914–18, that only armour could cross unscathed, were two quite different kinds of barrier. A barbed-wire fence four or five feet thick, or twelve or fourteen feet high, is no obstacle to determined men in a hurry, unless an expert has put it up.[7]

An old soldiers' maxim states that obstacles are useless, if they are not covered by fire. If you choose your night for escaping carefully enough, the sentries may

---

[1] *The Escapes of Captain D. H. O'Brien, R.N.* (1932), 51.
[2] Cp. Lord Lyttelton, *Glynnese Glossary* (1851), 38.
[3] See Clayton Hutton, *Official Secret* (1960), rather an angry book.
[4] *Vidi.*
[5] *Les armes clandestins* (1972), 96; henceforward: Lorain.
[6] Personal knowledge.  [7] Personal knowledge.

be deep enough in a doze to render wire obstacles slight. The snoozing sentry, not provided for in anyone's tactical handbook, was a fact of war.[1]

Tools, whether more or less elaborate, were not indispensable for escapes; simple methods remained the best. Here is an example, of which I was an eye-witness, from a small camp at St Nazaire in September 1944. Among the FFI prisoners in it was a lad, just turned seventeen, who looked younger; he set off with a *Landwehr* lance-corporal in his forties on a water fatigue. The older man carried a rifle, slung; the lad, a bucket in each hand. They walked away through the ruins, that resembled the desolate next world in Cocteau's *Orphée*. About a furlong from the camp, the lad put down his buckets – and ran off. 'Ach so!' cried the lance-corporal, 'Achtung! Achtung! Zurück, zurück!' The boy, who spoke no German, ran on. The lance-corporal remembered his rifle, unslung it, found a cartridge, loaded, and fired. By that time, the boy was a hundred yards away, and zig-zagging; the lance-corporal fired again, and again missed. The shots ought to have raised a general alarm; but the camp was full of rats, which the Germans had been shooting for food. The other Germans thought, Lucky Jozef; rat for supper.

Nearly ten minutes passed before Jozef got back into camp, bearing two empty buckets, to explain that his prisoner had got away. The hue and cry was not well organized; and the escaper vanished. He bolted into the first surviving house he found that looked safe to him; dyed his hair; borrowed a pair of shorts; and was evacuated a fortnight later, as a child under twelve, under the nose of the man who had interrogated him when captured. It was an enterprising and sensible escape.

Once one had got outside a camp, the main question to settle was – where to go? You could try Spain; a long way away, and full of typhus-ridden transit camps where wandering strangers might spend months before some service attaché traced and rescued them. Switzerland was closer to camps in Germany or Poland; but, once in Switzerland, it was hard to get farther. One man – one – got away from Brittany in his own private light aeroplane, having saved up the petrol for the journey to Cornwall;[2] one other, from Denmark to Sweden. A few escaped by sea across the Channel, hundreds across the Baltic. There was a quite active sea line across the central Aegean, running in caïques via Skiathos, Skopelos, and Skyros to Chios and İzmir.[3] A resourceful New Zealand sergeant managed to hire a boat at Marathon to take himself and five companions away in October 1941.[4]

Sea escapes could sometimes be horribly crowded. HMS *Thrasher*, not an enormous submarine, collected 67 escapers in one load from Crete that July; HMS *Torbay* collected 125 a few weeks later.[5] In September 1942, a French acquaintance spent a week travelling between the Riviera and Gibraltar in a

[1] Personal knowledge.   [2] Michel, *SW*, 75.
[3] C. M. Woodhouse, *Apple of Discord* (1948), 41–2; PRO AIR 20/2330, passim.
[4] Ibid.   [5] Ibid.

twenty-ton felucca with 90 companions. The inconceivable discomfort was worth it, for the sake of not being in nazi hands.[1]

SOE ran the Gibraltar felucca line, in 1941–2;[2] and ran also, in 1943–4, a small efficient escape line for secret agents between the north coast of Brittany and Helford in Cornwall.[3] This was the line that used a beach only forty feet from an occupied pillbox, where the sergeant in charge wanted no trouble and took care not to look.[4] Another, lonelier beach was at the back of the ridge of land on which the yachting port of St Cast lies, not far west of Dinard. The same cove had been used, a century and a half before, by British parties communicating clandestinely with revolutionary France.[5] By a splendid instance of nature imitating art, the path up the ridge from the cove is thick with a plant rather rare on that coast – the scarlet pimpernel.[6]

Let us turn back from sea to land travel. A prime difficulty for the land escaper who had no time to hide all day and creep about the countryside in the dark was, what would the locals make of him? In German-speaking territories, he could take the population's hostility for granted, if any hint of what he was slipped out; though by the middle of the war so many millions had been deported to labour in Germany that strange physiognomies and strange accents were more commonplace than security-minded planners of escape lines always realized. Bluff might carry a confident man through.

In Italy one needed more than bluff. Let an eyewitness testify:

> It was very difficult to get out of a prison camp in Italy. Italian soldiers might be figures of fun to us, but some of them were extraordinarily observant and very suspicious and far better at guarding prisoners than the Germans were. It was also very difficult to travel in Italy if you did get out. The Italians are fascinated by minutiae of dress and the behaviour of their fellow men, perhaps to a greater degree than almost any other race in Europe, and the ingenious subterfuges and disguises which escaping prisoners of war habitually resorted to and which were often enough to take in the Germans: the documents, train tickets, and ration cards, lovingly fabricated by the camp's staff of expert forgers; the suits made from dyed blankets; the desert boots cut down to look like shoes and the carefully bleached army shirts were hardly ever sufficiently genuine-looking to fool even the most myopic Italian ticket collector and get the owner past the barrier, let alone survive the scrutiny of the occupants of a compartment on an Italian train. The kind of going over to which an escaping Anglo-Saxon was subjected by other travellers was usually enough to finish him off unless he was a professional actor or spoke fluent Italian. And in Italy,

---

[1] Conversation with Henri Frenay, 1967.
[2] Foot, 67–8.    [3] Ibid. 69–71.
[4] Ibid. 62, and conversation with beach lieutenant, August 1967.
[5] *Ex inf.* M. G. Hutt, confirmed by him in conversation with E. P. Deman who did the work for SOE.
[6] *Vidi.*

before the Armistice, there were no members of the Resistance or railway employees of the Left, as there were in France, to help escaping prisoners out of the country along an organised route.[1]

There were only too many fascist narks about instead.

In an occupied country, there was much more hope of help from ordinary people; and even the local police might be persuaded to look the other way.[2] The extent to which one could rely on help varied of course with time and place; the later in the war, the stronger the chances that the Germans would lose and the more likely people would be to help an anti-German stranger.

The usual advice to escapers or evaders was to keep as clear as possible of built-up areas, and to look out for a church, preferably an isolated one; then to throw oneself on the mercy of the priest. There is no known instance of anyone who did this and had cause to regret it; for country priests, unlike many of their superiors, were solid in their opposition to nazism.

Failing a priest, the next best hope was a railwayman; not a station-master, who might well have been picked by the occupying régime, but a porter, whom one might hope to intercept on his way home as he came off shift. Railway escapes were many and various.[3] Failing a priest or a porter, one could try a schoolteacher; but this was more risky. Teachers were not stupid, but might well be opinionated; or, even worse, sympathetic to the régime.

Thoroughly resourceful people could manage on their own. The prize for toughness and enterprise must surely go to an SOE agent, Harry Peulevé. He got away from his first mission by escaping over the Pyrenees on crutches, and then breaking out of the Spanish internment camp at Jaraba. He went back to France; was arrested; and was wounded in an attempt to escape from Fresnes. He was sent to Buchenwald; whence, like Yeo-Thomas, he got away. He stole some clothes, and had picked his way quite close to the battle front when he bumped into two Belgian SS. They asked for his papers; he had none. They proposed to shoot him. He reminded them – this was April 1945 – that they would shortly be in Allied hands. Then, they said, let us change clothes; all three started to undress. Peulevé picked up one of their pistols, and took them both prisoner.

This was a sublime piece of nerve; alas, it did not hold out when the dullness of peace closed round its owner, and he died before his time.[4]

A conceivable alternative to the lone escape was the mass escape; a desperate device, seldom tried at all and hardly ever successful. For many, perhaps for most ordinary prisoners a prisoner-of-war camp with all its indignities and discomforts is preferable to a battlefield. Officer types can try to leaven this mass of ignoble content; but, prisoners themselves, can no longer be sure they will be

---

[1] Eric Newby, *Love and War in the Apennines*, 30.
[2] Eg. George Millar, *Maquis*, 51–4.
[3] See , eg., B. H. Cowburn, *No Cloak, No Dagger* (1960), 107, 115.
[4] See Foot, 199, 281, 398, 426–7; and *Times* obituary, 25 March 1963, 12e.

followed if they lead the way. There was one successful mass escape from Auschwitz, in which over a hundred Polish prisoners managed to disappear into the surrounding Polish countryside, and another from Sobibór. Some 200 hopeless Russians once, unarmed, stormed the gate at Mauthausen. About thirty got out; *one* got away. At Sobibór prisoners did still better; at a ghastly price.[1]

Once out of a camp, an escaper could not normally make touch with an escape line automatically; but the lines were there, and contact with them was (as we have seen already) not impossible. To work in a line one needed a combination of characteristics that was not quite usual: courage, discretion, and quickness of wit. Sure friends, a sound memory, and plenty of money were needed as well; so were some tools of the trade. One of these tools, plenty of forged papers, forms a problem so complex that it must be handled elsewhere.[2] Wireless contact with abroad, also dealt with below,[3] was not absolutely indispensable, and brought its own dangers of detection by the enemy with it; but it was desirable from the line's point of view, and highly desirable for the secret service to which the line was working.

The friends were needed to provide the safe houses, in which escapers could be kept hidden while the next stage of their journey was prepared. Loneliness in the country, or thick curtains and two exits in town, were important features of safe houses; and travellers on the lines had to be disciplined enough not to want to slip out of them for a walk or a drink, lest they imperilled everybody. Their owners were usually elderly maiden ladies, or couples without children: children, like Italians, ask too many questions.

Quite as important as forged papers, safe houses, or clothes was a system of cut-outs, 'the nearest thing to a safe device in underground warfare',[4] a means by which agents could get in touch with others while providing the minimum target for the hostile police. One of SOE's escape lines for agents, to give a specific example, ran via a Paris bookseller, who could be asked by telephone, 'Have you any of Hugo's *Les Misérables* in stock?', and would reply, 'No, mademoiselle, none I'm afraid,' or 'Two volumes have just come in,' according to whether the safe flat in the Avenue Victor Hugo was empty or full. Through further intermediaries, a senior agent of the line would approach the flat if it was full; first telephoning, to make sure the coast was clear; and then set about the detailed business of interviewing the travellers and deciding how, and how fast, to move them on.

An adequate cut-out system ensured that, if the Germans did break into a line, it did not rip and rot entirely; a cut-out ought to be able to give away only, at worst, the people on either side of him or her in the system. If everybody was alert enough, if one of them was caught, all hid, changing addresses and identities

[1] See p. 294 below.
[2] At pp. 95–8 below.  [3] At pp. 102–7.
[4] Foot, 94; pp. 94–101 for details of some particular secure escape lines' methods.

at once. Senior escape line agents made a practice of making such changes anyhow, every few months; hence their own high rate of survival.

It must have been hard to remember, from month to month, who one was.

## Subversion

Subversion, the overthrowing of the occupier's direct régime or of such satellite authorities as did the occupier's will, was a game that anyone could play who felt inclined: as the case of the old lady in the Paris metro, whose umbrella somehow kept getting entangled in German field boots, makes clear.[1] It was played best by those who knew what they were playing it for: hence the advantages long enjoyed by professional revolutionary communists, which rather outweighed those enjoyed by agents of SOE or OSS. The communists' training is almost as protracted as the jesuits', and like the jesuits, they keep their eyes fixed on their final goal; far apart though their final goals are. Less well trained clandestines were more liable to lose sight of their goal in the turmoil of subversive work, and to pursue whatever was most easy to do, and obviously exasperating to the enemy, without making sure where that most easy course would lead them.

Timing is all-important in subversion, as in any other kind of war; and those working under external orders to suit a long-drawn-out strategy had to remember to fit their activity to it, sometimes needing tactical dexterity to hold back hotheads on the spot. Perfectibilitarians tried to get and to keep everything just so; but subversion is often imprecise and messy. It is one of the fields where 'resistance thrives on a mixture of muddle and luck'.[2]

In every case, it was a critical business to time the final push from inside a régime, that would topple it, to coincide with the final push from outside, by one of the great Allied armies, that would have the same effect. The NKVD emerged in power in most of the European countries the Red Army conquered – in all of them, in fact, except Austria, Czechoslovakia, Finland, and Yugoslavia; and in Czechoslovakia there were less than three years to wait. Germany split, the Red-Army-conquered part (West Berlin always excepted) going into the communist zone; from Austria, as from Finland, Iran, and Manchuria, the Red Army did in the end withdraw. SOE was not a body designed to retain political power; those who had worked with it were prominent in the postwar politics of most of the countries freed by the western Allies.

These political results will need further treatment below;[3] it may yet be useful for the reader to hold this rough outline in his head as we take a closer look at subversion. It will be handled here under four headings, sabotage, attacks, propaganda, and insurrection; but the division into these four headings, though convenient, is not cast-iron. There were not always hard-and-fast lines dividing

---

[1] Philippe de Vomécourt, *Who Lived to See the Day* (1961), 26.
[2] Foot at King's College, London, 7 March 1973.
[3] At pp. 316–17.

one category from another; nor was it (or is it) always easy to say when for instance attacks on troops had become so incessant, so nation-wide that they had reached the scale of insurrection.

The point resisters often sought to take was surprise, that oldest and best trick of war: to promote sudden catastrophe, all the more catastrophic for being sudden. But how to set about it?

### Sabotage

Sabotage, as its name suggests, can be a pretty rough business. It is named after the actions of dissident French workers in the early machine age, who tossed a *sabot* into a moving machine to wreck it: still an effective device when *sabots* came back into use with the leather shortage of the early 1940s. Throwing a spanner, or a brick, into the works of any delicate machine was just as harmful, and easy to do – it only called for nerve; nor was it always simple to trace the act back to the person who had done it.

Given a little imagination and a stout hammer, a saboteur had a great many openings available, if he had the run of a factory or even of a storeroom: with a hammer, one could wreck in half an hour the output of an optical glassworks for half a year. A glassworks making rangefinder eyepieces would, it is true, probably be guarded with some care, like any other armament factory; a glassworks making chemical retorts might not be so well watched, and might offer a resister a target worth the trouble. For by damaging the enemy's chemical industry, one would be doing something to impair the enemy war effort; even if somewhat indirectly.

Being untraceable – *insaississable*, a staff catch-phrase in the early days of French resistance – was an important quality for an act of sabotage; often a help to the saboteur, always a perplexity to the police.

Some methods available on the railways fell in this category, for operations as elaborate as those on main line railway networks were bound to offer chances to those with the spirit to take them. Abrasive grease, which wears out the parts it appears to lubricate – a speciality of SOE's – provides an obvious example: mild discretion on the operator's part was all that was needed to protect him while he wreaked plentiful damage.[1] But abrasive grease could only be got by saboteurs in touch with one of SOE's circuits, which could have supplies sent in. A more widely available means of making trouble lay in a system the Germans had devised for their own protection.

Goods moving by rail under *Wehrmacht* orders, or to any German or German-controlled address, travelled in sealed trucks; so that a glance at the seals would show German police whether the truck's contents had been interfered with. Each truck bore, low on its side, a small wire grille behind which a label was stuck, indicating the destination in a railway code. Wherever goods trains were made up or shunted, railway men sorted the trucks out according to what the

[1] Cp. Foot, 269.

labels said; and fresh sets of labels were issued at main interchange stations. All the saboteur needed to do was to mix the labels up a trifle; putting the top one at the bottom of the pile would do. One or two trivial, untraceable, apparently clerical errors of this kind caused disproportionate delay, dislocation, and annoyance; truckloads of acid for U-boat batteries reached steelworks in Bohemia, truckloads of women's underclothes reached fighter airfields, trucks for Mulhouse went to Nantes, trucks for Colmar went to Copenhagen; and nobody could be shot for what seemed to be nobody's fault.[1]

Similar apparently accidental inattention by a clerk could wreak no end of havoc in a card index. A persistently incompetent clerk would be likely to get the sack; so if one went in for sabotage of this kind, it was important at least to appear willing and efficient to one's immediate boss. While doing so, there would be plenty of scope for mislaying essential papers, mistyping important ones, adding a thousand and one minor miseries to one's boss's life.

A frequent refinement on this technique was to adopt the methods in the previous great war of that sublime resister in fiction, Šveik.[2] He was as affable and courteous and willing-to-oblige as could be; he was also hopelessly incompetent. His Czech compatriots were past-masters at following his example; millions of others followed it as well, not always in conscious imitation, but because it seemed a good idea.

And one could always do a job competently, but maddeningly slowly; explaining to any German who protested that, as the job was being done for the Germans, it was not one that could be skimped. When the Canadians re-entered Dieppe on 1 September 1944, an anxious transport staff officer went to the railway workshops, to see what locomotives he might have available to move stores landed through the port. Parts of a dozen were scattered everywhere, in huge confusion; and a blackboard indicated when they would be ready for use – in six weeks', eight weeks', twenty-eight weeks' time. His heart sank; were things, he asked the foreman, really as bad as that? 'O that was for the Germans,' said the foreman, wiping the board clean; 'for the Allies, we shall have ten ready in forty-eight hours.'

This is a particular instance of the railway go-slow in France, part of the general railway go-slow in western Europe that has been noticed already.[3] This finally reached a stage at which a rueful and authoritative German technical survey was drawn up for the general who had commanded the railways of occupied France and Belgium, when the Allies had overrun his area that autumn:

> it was not so much the actual damage inflicted by the allied air forces, or even the incessant minor demolitions of the saboteurs, that made the railways unworkable; it was the permanent attitude of non-co-operation

---

[1] Cp. de Vomécourt, *Who Lived to See the Day*, 33–5.
[2] Jaroslavl Hašek, tr. Sir C. Parrott, *The Good Soldier Šveik* (1973).
[3] p. 13 above.

and go slow of the railway staff, even when they were not on strike, that made it impracticable to clear up enough of the mess for trains to run.[1]

As bodies as disparate in their outlook as the BBC and Radio Moscow were both encouraging the captive labour force not to over-exert itself in the German interest, the wide appeal of go-slow as a doctrine of resistance will be apparent. From east and west alike, workers were also encouraged to engage in direct sabotage; using such tools as they could find.

Much more serious, professional sabotage could be undertaken by those specially trained and equipped for the task.

SOE had an experimental section, Station XII near Welwyn in Hertfordshire, that took over the work of Jefferis' technical sub-section of MIR and of the technicians in Section D who had been working on time fuses.[2] Their end products included, beside twelve million pencil time fuses, a midget submarine (called the Welman) and a nasty piece of tubing, a foot long and not much over an inch wide, with a detachable four-inch butt. It was a single-shot 7·65 mm silent pistol, called the welrod; an ideal weapon for the clandestine agent, both because it was silent and because it could so easily be hidden in a trouser-leg.[3]

Plastic explosive was from a saboteur's point of view their most important discovery (it was already available in June 1940, before SOE itself had formally been set up). It looks much like butter, which it resembles in consistency, save that it is still more malleable. SOE's director of scientific research said that it

> consists of cyclonite mixed with a plasticising medium; it is considered to be one of the safest explosives and will not detonate if struck by a rifle bullet or when subject to the ordinary shocks of transit; it requires a detonator well embedded in the mass of the explosive. It is particularly useful to us as in addition to its insensitivity, it is plastic and can be moulded into shape like dough.[4]

Various people discovered that, like many other explosives, it will burn peaceably; and two people ate some, by mistake, without disaster.[5]

It was packed in quarter- or half-pound sticks, or five pound bricks, or quarter- or half-kilogram blocks, or (being so mouldable) made up to any shape that pleased the operator using it. SOE devised a kilogram box of it with six strong magnets attached, called a limpet mine; this was about the size of a British steel helmet and could sink a ship. Indeed in the hands of frogmen, commandos, and saboteurs, it quite often did. Above water, plastic could be stuck on a vertical piece of metal simply by smearing it with Vaseline; or of course with a piece of adhesive tape or even gummed paper. There was also a rubber tube filled with plastic, about twenty inches long with its fuse, which could be hidden under a pilot's seat or near an aircraft's rudder hinge; the fuse

---

[1] Foot, 411.　　[2] Cp. ibid. 3.
[3] Cp. drawing in Lorain, 146.
[4] 30 March 1942, from Foot, 56.　　　　[5] Ibid.

was actuated by a fall in air pressure, and could be set to cause an explosion at 5,000 or at 10,000 feet.[1] This illustrates a weakness in SOE's trap-design department; it was rather too diabolically ingenious to be much use 'in the field', as Luftwaffe aircraft were seldom if ever accessible, between servicing and take-off, to the passing saboteur.

A pocket incendiary bomb intended to burn furiously for fifty seconds after a set delay – varying from 30 seconds to 24 hours – was a much more useful device, and SOE provided several other thermite incendiaries as well. Little plastic tyre-bursters, disguised as cowpats or plain, exploded on being driven over; they had pressure fuses. The camouflage department was particularly proud of its dead rat, plastic-stuffed, with a fuse that was armed by the action of a stoker shovelling it into a ship's boiler: which was then to blow up. The gammon grenade, containing a kilogram of plastic and fused to burst on impact, was a more directly combative weapon.[2] Brigitte Bardot's explosive cigar provides comment enough on the booby-trap designers.[3]

If plastic was unavailable, saboteurs would use anything else they could get; such as miners' dynamite, or gelignite, or – SOE's favoured alternative – Nobel 808 with its strong smell of bitter almonds. (The best quality plastic was odourless; less perfect kinds had a perceptible almondy smell, much slighter than 808's.) Routine instruction, at the NKVD's courses in Siberia or at SOE's in Inverness-shire or Ontario, passed on to tens of thousands of willing amateurs behind the German lines, taught people how to lay and tamp explosive. Plastic is so powerful that it does not need to be tamped, unless some particular direction for its shock is sought. Primers, about the size and shape of a tapering cork for a medicine bottle, were in plentiful supply from secret sources. A saboteur, having placed and shaped his plastic charge, and linked it up if necessary with neighbour charges by cordtex safety fuse,[4] had only to select – by its colour code – a time pencil with a suitable delay; press it into the primer; remember to activate it (surprisingly easy to forget); camouflage what he had done, if tactical necessity demanded it; and scarper. Delays, much as with the pocket incendiary, varied; between half an hour and a week.[5] Inevitably, there were occasional errors, such as two-hour fuses going off after half an hour; seldom fatal to the saboteurs.

Details of these techniques were taught at SOE's Station XVII, near Hertford, by a remarkable man, George Rheam, the founder of modern industrial sabotage. He taught his many willing pupils how to work economically: how to spot in a factory which were the essential tools, the tools of which the breakdown would bring a whole production line to a standstill. Then he taught them how to look at a tool or a machine. Has it a cast-iron base? Hit it with a hammer – cast-iron

[1] Drawings in Lorain, 151, 155.
[2] Details and drawings ibid. 150–5.
[3] *Babette Goes to War* (1959), ad fin.
[4] See the illustration of 'Acolyte' (misnamed in the first edition) tackling some railway points in Foot, after 196.
[5] Numerous details and diagrams in Lorain, 150–5.

fractures easily. Has it some irreplaceable small part? Bend, break, or abstract it. Can it be set to produce a disaster to itself, or to the adjoining machine, when next started up? Then set it accordingly. And take care that the machine you wreck cannot be repaired at once by cannibalizing its neighbour or its spare.

If for instance you attack railway engines – an excellent and fairly freely available target – go for their cylinders, which are readily exposed to the saboteur, and expensive to the replacing manufacturer; and take care that you blow up the right-hand cylinder of every engine in the shed, not the left cylinder on some and the right cylinder on others. Why blow up more than a cylinder? The engine cannot work without it; and though wrecking engines is fun,[1] it will make trouble for your own side later, after the enemy has gone and you want your railways back.

A layman might think a less dangerous form of railway sabotage than a visit to the engine-shed, which would be likely to have some sort of night watchman at least near it, would be to remove a rail in a quiet part of the countryside instead. Life was not quite so simple. Removing a rail is a much more lengthy and noisy job than the layman would imagine; and in any case needs a railwayman's special spanner as well as great physical strength. And, the rail once removed, how pleased will the layman feel if the next train along the line is full of children being evacuated or of wounded prisoners-of-war? Track in any case would probably be patrolled if of serious importance to the enemy. This helped to disperse his or his satellites' effort; and presented no severe obstacle to the alert saboteur.

A surer and swifter way of destroying track lay in the explosive mine. A couple of kilograms of plastic explosive, six feet farther apart than the wheelbase of the engine they were to derail, could be fused by a fog-signal type pressure fuse[2] and the necessary length of cordtex. This was an advance on Lawrence's 'tulip' mining of the Hejaz railway;[3] and if like Lawrence's larger mines the prospective wreck was covered by a firing party, and care was taken – with the help of good local railway intelligence – only to attack troop trains, tactically interesting results might follow.[4] But we are moving over to our next section, while a little more needs to be said about sabotage.

Road transport was just as open to attack as rail. Showers of miniature caltrops, four-pointed metal spikes devised in renaissance times to stop cavalry, formed efficient tyre-bursters, and could make trouble for a motorized column: SOE supplied them. Road mines could be prepared, and fired at a critical moment; bridge mines were more common. Only a few pounds of plastic were needed to cut most country bridges, and on grand occasions teams of saboteurs could

[1] See last illustration but one in Foot.
[2] Diagram in Lorain, 153.
[3] T. E. Lawrence, *Seven Pillars of Wisdom*, 594–6.
[4] There is a well-known, somewhat romanticized example in René Clément's film *La Bataille du Rail*, which was made in the early autumn of 1944, just after the Germans left France.

tackle full-size viaducts and destroy them too. Again, these obstacles were all much more efficient German-killers if they could be kept covered by fire; though this goes against the saboteur's traditional instinct, which is to throw his *sabot* and run away.

Parked lorries or cars were fair game for him (or her: women, given the opportunity, were quite as good at sabotage as men). As with locomotives, if one had a dozen or so similar vehicles to treat at once, one did one's best to treat them all at the same spot. A small bomb that broke the front axle was well thought of; so was a thermite afterthought, to burn up the wreck. Apt pupils of Rheam's, or indeed of his unidentified soviet opposite number, were good at devising consecutive traps, such as laying a bomb, in putting out the fire caused by which people would set off a second bomb. Recent events in Ulster show that such techniques have not yet been forgotten.

If no other recourse was open, it was always worth while slashing an enemy vehicle's tyres.[1] Only the most niminipiministic of soldiers would mind driving on his wheel-rims on a battlefield; but only the toughest of staff officers would envisage long journeys on rims behind the lines. Rubber, even synthetic rubber, was short for the Germans, and every slashed tyre would make it shorter.

Petrol was an obvious and important saboteur's target. The pocket incendiary was useful here, particularly if the tap of a petrol storage tank was left unlocked. Plastic explosive used against petrol or oil in such a way that it came in contact with either before it went off, needed a watertight covering, since both petrol and oil destroyed it.

Telephones, again, provided a target that was both accessible and important. Any fool can blow down, or cut down, a telegraph pole: only a crass fool would forget to cut any wires that survived intact. But, as any fool signalman knows, a cut wire is soon enough traced and repaired. Much more sophisticated forms of sabotage were workable on the telegraph–telephone front by skilled operators. Such people would know how to enter and how to destroy junction boxes, even exchanges; or, subtler, how to jumble the cables in a junction box, so as to provoke a long run of wrong numbers and exasperation; or, subtler still, how to listen in to enemy conversations and thus secure invaluable intelligence.[2] On a few occasions, whole telephone networks were available for resistance.[3]

An advantage that regularly followed sabotage of long-distance telephone lines was that it provoked an increase in enemy wireless traffic; all of which was intercepted, and much of it unravelled, by the Y service and similar organizations. This in turn meant that the Allied high command was more thoroughly informed than ever about the enemy's strength and intentions.

Such points were set out in a brief and pungent pamphlet called 'How to use

[1] Lorain, 157, illustrates a commando fighting knife, which could do this well, and mentions SOE's 'saboteur's knife', an ordinary pocket knife in appearance, with a long blade for slicing explosive and a specially strengthened short blade for bursting tyres.
[2] Cp. p. 243 below.
[3] Eg. p. 269 below.

high explosive', clearly written and amply illustrated. Hundreds of thousands of copies, in most European languages, were distributed by parachute on SOE's behalf during the war.[1] Gubbins,[2] who had written it in the spring of 1939, never needed to revise it; and had much to do with putting it into practice.

### Attacks on troops

A really desperate citizen of an occupied country could always fall back on the slogan Churchill had ready for the English, and mercifully never had to issue, in the late summer of 1940: 'You can always take one with you.' Someone past caring about his own life could do a lot of harm to a bunch of enemy troops with a stolen grenade. With any luck, he could dispose of two or three with that readily available weapon, a sharp kitchen knife.

One instance of this doctrine's use is too vivid to leave unquoted. At the very bottom of the nazi pyramid, in Mauthausen concentration camp, prisoners worked all day in a deep quarry; except for an hour's interval at midday, when they drank soup and listened to the camp orchestra. It was accepted that those who could bear it no longer could go up to the top of the quarry and jump off. A few SS rather liked loitering at the top, to look and listen. Two French Jewish prisoners, brothers, decided to jump. They spent the midday interval shaking hands with all their friends; and when the whistle blew, walked up to the top of the quarry. Two of the usual jeering SS were there. They shook hands with them too, held on tight, and jumped; each took one with him.[3]

There was no need to sacrifice oneself as well as one's enemy, except when pressed to the very last resort. There were other simple kinds of Hun-trap, some almost as readily available as the kitchen knife. A stout wire, for instance, fastened between two trees on opposite sides of a lane at the height of the average motor-cyclist's Adam's apple, could easily slice the head off a German dispatch-rider; thus incidentally providing his dispatches, pistol, boots, paybook, and tyres for resistance as well. But some care needed to be taken. It was as well to have a hidden sentry, to warn off a friendly cyclist in time; and as we have seen a well-known military adage lays down that obstacles are useless, unless they are covered by fire. Who was going to fire at the motor-cyclist, and with what, if he was bent so low over his handlebars that the wire only bruised his back, and he set out pistol in hand to see who had tried to trap him? Arms, weapon pits from which to use them, and a means of rapid retreat were all needed if a trap of this kind was to be a tactical success.

Why a means of retreat? Because frightful reprisals were likely to be exacted, if not on the perpetrators, then on the witnesses of what the Germans held to be a terrorist outrage. They were not particular whom they shot, so long as they shot somebody.

[1] The French version may be read in Marc Leproux, *Nous, les Terroristes* (Monte Carlo 1947), i. 278–88.
[2] See p. 139 below.    [3] Eyewitness account, 1971.

The atrocities of Lidice and Oradour-sur-Glane have become world-famous; mainly because they were atrocities of reprisal. The statistically even more ghastly atrocity of Kharkov, which is much less well known in the west – about a hundred thousand people massacred in an afternoon[1] – was another kind of atrocity: racial hatred plus maladministration, rather than racial hatred *in terrorem*. In the war of 1870–1, the Prussians had found a few summary executions an excellent way of securing their lines of communication against francs-tireurs; the habit stayed with them.

There was some tendency in Europe to think that the unoccupied Allies were inclined to order – or to suggest – resistance activity for irrelevant or even frivolous reasons, without regard to the reprisal casualties that were sure to follow; relics of the idea held by some dogged supporters of Vichy, that England would always fight to the last Frenchman. There was nothing in this: on the contrary, the British and American high command was painfully sensitive about reprisals, and very senior officers – Marshall, Brooke, Mountbatten, if the scheme passed Donovan or Gubbins – were known to forbid proposed irregular operations on the ground that the danger to the civilian population in the raided area would be too great. And of course the staffs of governments-in-exile in London or Cairo or Algiers or Bari could be extremely sensitive about dangers proposed to be inflicted on their own fellow citizens. Churchill's favourite quotation from Lactantius, that the blood of the martyrs is the seed of the church, was sometimes on impetuous young staff officers' lips; their elders generally put them down.

It is easy to suppose a short answer to the nazi problem: the assassination of Hitler. But 'the utter futility of assassination as a political weapon'[2] is one of the few clearly legible lessons of modern history. The knifing of Lord Frederick Cavendish in the Phoenix Park put back the cause of Irish freedom forty years. The shooting of the Habsburg archduke, Franz Ferdinand, at Sarajevo brought down the Habsburg empire, and three others with it, delivering to the spiral of history a downward twist from which it has yet to recover. Nicholas II's disappearance at Ekaterinburg brought great discredit to its perpetrators, as most discovered killings of prisoners do. (His death was ordered by the politburo of the CPSU, including Lenin. Recent rumours that he and his family were spirited away, at the request of his cousin the king of England, to a peaceable old age on some remote estate on British soil show how far are the limits of human gullibility. No evidence for this, worth the snap of a real historian's fingers, has yet appeared.) Matteotti's murder was never forgiven Mussolini.

Yet – the thought cannot help darting – how much agony might the world have been spared, if an assassin had disposed of Hitler in time? Mason-Macfarlane, the British military attaché in Berlin, proposed the step in 1938. 'I could

---

[1] Conversation with a survivor, 1953.
[2] Tom Corfe, *The Phoenix Park Murders* (1968), 266.

pick the bastard off from here as easy as winking,' he told a friend as they watched a reviewing stand going up near his drawing-room window, 'and what's more I'm thinking of doing it'; the British government turned it down.[1]

SOE's headquarters in Cairo did once brief a man for the job; a Macedonian terrorist who used the name of Vilmar, and was certainly a crack shot. Unfortunately for the plan, he was also a heavy drinker. He was equipped with cover as a Bulgarian businessman, a pistol, and some money; and got, via Lisbon, as far as Vienna, where he secured an invitation to a diplomatic reception at which Hitler was to be present. London had not been informed; Vilmar was out on his own. He was so much on his own that he went to a nightclub, got very drunk, and boasted of what he was going to do. Someone sent for the police; he finished the night in jail, and was shortly deported to Bulgaria, where he vanished.[2]

Hitler himself was well aware of the likelihood that someone would want to get rid of him, and devoted time and thought to frustrating any would-be assassin: he made it a rule never to follow a routine, frequently changed his plans, and was used to setting off on long journeys at a few minutes' notice.[3] His long-continued interest in, even preoccupation with, this subject shows that he had some fellow-feelings for resisters, and for sly sudden underhand action. This after all was where his movement had sprung from: he had struggled too long for power on the streets of south German towns ever to be able to forget how he had done so. Unfortunately for the course of resistance, of this aspect of it he was the master. None of the few direct attempts on his life that got past the starting-gate succeeded, till he killed himself.

Technically, the feat would not have been impossible in the years just before the war, as Mason-Macfarlane saw. Geoffrey Household, in one of the best thrillers ever written, advocated a big-game hunter's rifle wielded from an upper story as the right weapon for picking off a head of state; perhaps his advice was taken by Lee Oswald in the fatal November of 1963.[4] At closer range, Hitler took unusually stout precautions against personal attack, as Stalin did. A couple of secret police gunmen, drawn in random rotation from a team, were habitually on guard in the immediate neighbourhood of each; either in the same room or vehicle, or watching through a spy hole what purported to be private conversations. Hitler hardly ever saw strangers; though when he did, they were not searched before they entered his presence. So someone of iron nerve, very fast

[1] Ewan Butler, *Mason-Mac* (1972), 75–6.

[2] Julian Amery, *Approach March* (1973), 240–1. The XX committee was more cautious than SOE Cairo: see Masterman, *Double-Cross System*, 132, 122–3.

[3] P. Hoffmann, *Widerstand Staatsstreich Attentat* (Munich 1969), 639 ff.

[4] Geoffrey Household, *Rogue Male* (1939), ad fin. That Oswald, like his victim, read Ian Fleming on his last night on earth is known; had he read Household too, or did he reach the same conclusion independently? His victim indicated the morning before he was shot, that he knew of the method and accepted it as one of the risks of his trade (Arthur M. Schlesinger, jr, *A Thousand Days* [Deutsch 1965], 867).

on the draw, might then have done for him. (Mussolini was far more accessible, but any stranger on his way into the duce's study was frisked.)[1]

During the war, the guard on Hitler was intensified, to a point at which the passing assassin had no chance against him at all.[2] He came to spend a great deal of his time in the Wolfschanze at Rastenburg, remote from the actual life of his troops, his citizenry, or the countries his armies occupied. Nothing was ordinary about his life any more, and he was inaccessible to resisters: unless some were to be found within his own entourage. In the end, as is well known, the heroic attempt of 20 July 1944 miscarried.[3] Even had it, or any earlier effort, succeeded, things might have got worse, not better. The nazi movement was not entirely Hitler's own creation: the response it called out from the German people showed as much. Once he was dead, his régime did not survive him ten days; that was because he had already held on to the bitter end. The German people, armed by Speer, terrified by Himmler, sustained by Goebbels, held on with him. Before the end became so bitter, the movement had a life of its own; it is not quite stone dead yet, either inside Germany or elsewhere. Even if Hitler had been an available resister's target, to replace him by Himmler or Göring might have produced a change for the worse.

It is doubtful whether the one killing of a leading nazi that resistance did bring off, the death of Reinhard Heydrich, did much real good. Nobody would call Kaltenbrunner, his successor, much of an improvement on him; can anybody but their families be sorry both are dead? In the short run, Heydrich's death brought massacres to Lidice and Ležáky, some two thousand more deaths, and a massive check to the cause of resistance in Czechoslovakia. In the middle run, Beneš came back; for three years. What followed? A régime as conservative as Francis Joseph's, disguised in revolutionary scarves.

To mount serious attacks on enemy forces, resisters needed several things besides that courage which runs as a continuing theme through all that they attempted. To start with, any attack needs a leader. There is a popular fallacy, encouraged by shelves of fiction, that successful resistance leaders must have a dash of the blackguard in them; or at least should be ready and willing to make love in the intervals between operations. Ernest Hemingway's Robert Jordan has a good deal to answer for on this score.[4]

Of the amorous side of resistance – and there certainly was one – this is not the place to speak. In hard fact, the popular fallacy is as unsound as any other fallacy; but that quality of enterprise which distinguishes an adventurous lover does have similarities with the dash and enterprise that are needed to lead irregular troops, often on forlorn hopes.

[1] Conversation with Vernon Bartlett, who had interviewed both him and Hitler, 4 December 1936.

[2] Hoffmann, 655–69.

[3] Ibid. 473–6; and see p. 303 below.

[4] E. Hemingway, *For Whom the Bell Tolls* (1940).

Some sort of tactical training, and a little battle experience as well, were a great help; though neither was quite indispensable. Tactical training was, naturally enough, common in countries which held to the usual civilized doctrine that every man owes his society the duty to be trained in arms to defend it: that is, wherever the Germans went except the Channel Islands.[1] Battle experience was not unknown; much of it, in 1940, had been in how to run away, but this was an indispensable art for resisters. Their strength came from vanishing, not from holding ground. Heroic last-man-last-round stands of the Glières or Vercors type are magnificent, but they are not irregular war.

One of the arrangements for which SOE, OSS, and the NKVD all went in, in rather different ways, was the parachuting in to bodies of resisters – French or Belgian maquisards, Norwegian skiers, Polish, Slovak, Ukrainian, Russian, or Yugoslav partisans – of well-trained young officers who could instruct them in sabotage methods and elementary tactics. Former soldiers would know how to shoot, and how to throw a grenade, and would have mastered simple tactical points such as covering fire, or moving round a flank; but might not know the difference between plastic and margarine, let alone which colour of time pencil delay fuse did what. The young needed to learn everything. There were a great many active young in resistance; the revolting student of today, who believes he is the first to start on a journey to a new heaven and a new earth, is only following where his parents trod, as like as not, before him.

The best form of training is example. Casualties among these young officers were therefore on the high side; it was their job to take plenty of risks. Further example, and still tougher stiffening, could be provided for resistance by small bodies of uniformed troops, sent in by air or sea to fight alongside resisters.

Several units in the British army were designed for this purpose, besides Orde Wingate's long-range penetration groups, the Chindits, who cannot concern us here – they fought in Burma. The Special Air Service Regiment, formed in north Africa in 1941, had grown to brigade strength by 1944. It was a truly international brigade – mainly British and French, but including also Belgians, Yugoslavs, a few Poles, Spaniards, even (under cover names) Germans. 'Almost the whole brigade strength of some 2,200 men was committed to battle in the three months that followed D-day' in Normandy, 6 June 1944.[2] A summary of its work prepared for supreme headquarters by an officer in SOE – a rival organization; therefore, a reporter not predisposed in the brigade's favour – said of its troops that 'they supplied the trained military direction which the FFI inevitably lacked, and in the areas where they operated, formed the hard core of French resistance in the field'.[3]

OSS trained and dispatched similar bodies, called Operational Groups –

---

[1] Why the United Kingdom has abandoned, for most of its history since 1815, the practice of conscription is a curious problem in military politics, which this – again – is not the place to answer.

[2] Foot, 402, and map 4.    [3] Ibid. 402, 7 September 1944.

usually about thirty strong, and usually (unlike many SAS) fluent in the language of the country in which they were to work. Their enthusiasm, fighting skills, and gallantry were marked, and they too were well equipped to serve as a hard core for fighting resistance: in the closing stages of a campaign of liberation. At earlier stages, an offshoot from SAS, the Special Boat Section, had kept the pot of anti-German activity boiling busily in the Aegean; and fought its way up the Adriatic on the right flank of the British Eighth Army in 1944–5. Yet SBS's activities were tied in, as were SAS's, to the needs of the Allied high command; they were less of a help to resistance, more of a rival to the commandos.[1] The same might be said of Popski's Private Army; and the Long Range Desert Group hardly operated in Europe, though it provided the SAS brigade with its two best intelligence officers.

One might well ask why, if the SAS brigade was so useful, it was not used elsewhere as well; why several brigades were not formed to work systematically in (say) Italy, Yugoslavia, Norway, as well as north-west Europe. The ostensible reason was shortage of suitable men. SAS, though then the newest, was also one of the most accomplished regiments in the British army; everyone in it was a volunteer; and the rest of the army's fighting units felt they had had cream enough skimmed off them already. This genuine objection apart, the fact remains that most British high commanders were suspicious of 'private armies', as they called bodies such as SAS or SOE, as of other military novelties; soldiering tends to be an intensely conservative profession, so there was unlikely to be any initiative for forming more SAS brigades at a level likely to produce results; and sure to be some powerful obstruction.

Moreover, political difficulties might attend the use of SAS. Only the Norwegian, of the governments in exile, was likely to raise no troubles at all. The Italian set-up was already intricate enough; and the Yugoslav, about as smooth as an angry porcupine's back. Both the royal Yugoslav and the soviet governments would have been furious, although for opposite reasons, if there had been SAS missions with Tito's partisans.

Though it was the Red Army that had revived the ancient sport of parachuting, the course the war on the eastern front took swallowed up almost all its parachute units as ground infantry; and though SOE had a communist equivalent, SAS had not. The kind of individualist enterprise that SAS favoured was not popular in the USSR, where the party high command liked to keep a firm hold on events. The body that operated extensively on the eastern front in uniform across the fixed fighting lines was of nazi, not communist, inspiration: the *Lehrregiment Brandenburg*, later expanded to a division. The uniforms it used were usually Russian; and when not beyond the Red Army's lines, its units were often employed in chasing partisans.

The arrival, or the impending arrival, or even the hope of the arrival of an SAS or OSS party in an area where armed resisters hoped to be active could have

[1] For examples of lack of liaison between commandos and resistance, see ibid. 182–8.

one effect, unfortunate for the resistance cause, to counterbalance the benefits of training, leadership, contact with the free world, and supplies. It might lead people to cherish unjustified hopes of setting up, on their own territory, some sort of national redoubt: an area where the national flag could be flown, and the national anthem played, and the old laws and customs followed, without fear of reprisal.

A number of famous disasters derived from this conception. When Bourgoin took his SAS unit – the *2e Régiment de Chasseurs Parachutistes* – into Brittany in June 1944, the local peasant women put on national costume to flock to the landing-ground, where their men tore open containers in the hope of a decent pair of trousers or of boots, quite as much as of a rifle or a sten; '*c'était une kermesse*', was the colonel's disgusted comment.[1] As soon as the Germans leant on him, he spirited his troops and their supporters away: so that only a few participants and experts remember Saint Marcel, while millions mourn the dead of the Vercors, and the Warsaw rising has become a name of horror.

SAS and suchlike bodies depended for their success on constant, reliable, reiterated supply from the air. There were two alternative sources of supply, besides the air, for resistance forces; both largely illusory. A communist slogan laid down, 'Any household has a knife; if you have a knife, you can get a pistol; if you have a pistol, you can get a rifle; if you have a rifle, you can get a machine-gun. Get on with it comrades: get armed!' This was fine; if every communist was brave, and every enemy soldier dumb. No one has yet produced a useful proof that this slogan brought in a lot of arms.

The other possible, but not as it turned out productive, source of arms lay in the depots of the recently defeated local army: Danish, Dutch, Czech, or whatever it might be. The armistice terms would certainly lay down restrictions on these depots, and on the carrying of arms by those who remained in the losing side's uniform: if anybody did. In some conquered areas, such as Alsace, the men of military age became liable to conscription into the German armed forces,[2] and the previously existing forces were simply dissolved.[3] The armed forces of Vichy France were reduced to 100,000 men in 1940, because victorious France had imposed that limitation on Germany's army in 1919.[4] The vichyste army retained quite sizeable depots, and a few of its officers engaged in secret stocking of arms against the day when France could fight Germany again; with disappointing results in 1942, and slight ones in 1944.

Even if one managed to secure some arms, by a private *coup de main* against either the enemy or a depot, one would run into an immediate difficulty: ammu-

---

[1] R. Leroux, 'Le Combat de Saint–Marcel', in *RHDGM*, July 1964, 15.

[2] By a ludicrous irony of history, most of the individuals who were caught and tried years later for the Oradour massacre were Alsatians who had been put into the Waffen-SS; whose citizenship had now changed back from German to French. Hence a series of exceptionally complicated legal tangles: see J. Kruuse, *Madness at Oradour* (1969), 146–7.

[3] Eg. *BFSP* cxliv. 403, the Franco-German armistice of 22 June 1940.

[4] *BFSP* cxii. 82; H. Michel, *Vichy année 40* (1966), 72.

nition supply. The best of Lüger pistols, picked from a dead German officer's holster, might have rounds enough in its magazine to serve for a single hold-up; but what then, unless the hold-up by some unlikely chance was of a lorry bearing a case of Lüger pistol ammunition ? Untrained or half-trained troops are notoriously much less economical with bullets than are seasoned soldiers, and keeping them supplied with bullets enough to keep up their own morale was a real problem.

The answer, inevitably, for those who could manage it, lay in supply by parachute. Supply by sea, the only feasible alternative, was used to some effect by SOE in Norway, by the Red Navy in the Black Sea, and by SBS, SOE and commandos in the Aegean and Adriatic. Efforts to use it from SOE's base near Algiers into south-western Europe, or from Helford into Brittany, were most of them vain till the late summer of 1944 – that is, till the closing stages of the war in France.[1]

Of the details of parachute landings, more in a later section.[2] Once the arms had been landed, they posed yet another problem for the resister: where were they to be hidden ? Only the crazily bellicose were going to carry them straight into action, unless they were dropped onto the edge of a battle in progress; they would have to be stored. Where and how to store them was a lasting perplexity.

Obviously enough, arms drops were made in the country, rather than in towns: such crises as Warsaw or Arnhem apart. Countrymen are good at hiding things from townsmen; and their natural gifts of this kind were sharpened during the war by contacts with policemen and black marketeers. Every conceivable sort of hiding-place was used; arms were buried, hung in trees, put behind piles of logs or backs of ovens or rows of empty casks, put into false cask or wardrobe bottoms, into milk churns, into bracken, into ponds, into plough, into dung. Obviously again, this did not do them any good. They were dispatched well covered in grease, but the grease would not last for ever; after a year or so, the stoutest buried weapon might start to deteriorate, and buried explosive – other than plastic – might have become highly dangerous.

Moreover, weapons have an awkward, in the context of searches a fatal, characteristic. A few secret agents' toys apart, they are impossible to disguise,[3] and once found, they cannot be explained away. One of the principal aims of the German security forces in occupied Europe was to discover these dumps of clandestine arms, and 'Where have you hidden your weapons ?' must have been one of the commonest questions put to captured resisters. Cunning agents would have an outlying small dump of arms, that could comparatively lightly be betrayed, not far from a main one; cunning policemen would dig up, or at least dig across, the whole of a farm, having once found something there, to discover whether there was more.

---

[1] See Foot, 471–2.　　　　　　　　　　　　　[2] At pp. 119–26 below.
[3] See Lorain, 156, for a single-shot pistol that just might be overlooked as a fountain pen.

What sorts of arms were dropped will be discussed below.[1] One point needs to be made about them straight away. Almost every resister inclined to believe that the fate of the war centred round what happened in his own district; and wherever there was a prospect that a large partisan force could be set up, people started asking for heavy weapons. Often they complained that they only got sub-machine-guns, instead.

If this problem is looked at from the angle of the supply staff, instead of the receiving partisan, the predominance of sub-machine-guns is more easy to explain. The high command believed that, in Gubbins's phrase, 'Guerilla actions will usually take place at point blank range as the result of an ambush or raid. . . . Undoubtedly, therefore, the most effective weapon for the guerilla is the sub-machine gun'.[2] Heavier arms would therefore only be an encumbrance; besides, there were never quite enough of them on the main fighting fronts. Moreover sub-machine-guns were cheap, and ammunition for them plentiful.

Bodies of resisters who clamoured for artillery were victims of the fallacy of the national redoubt, discussed just now; and of the old-fashioned idea that a soldier should stand and fight. The irregular soldier is usually much more use to his cause if he runs away, and fights in some other time and place of his own choosing.

Just as guerilla bands in the country were likely to do best when they had a core of fully experienced fighting men to lead them – for instance the French SAS in Brittany, or the best of Ponomarenko's or Tito's partisans in the Pripet marshes or in Bosnia – so, in large industrial cities, one might expect there to have been the most successful uprisings where the trained revolutionaries of the communist party were most numerous. In practice there were few memorable urban risings. Of the three that are remembered in the west, Warsaw was a tragedy from which the communists ostentatiously held aloof, Prague came right at the end of the war, and Paris as we shall see was really almost as much farce as triumph. The other spontaneous popular uprising in a great city, at Naples in September 1943, was a four days' massacre: no one except the Germans having done the indispensable preparation.[3]

### Political subversion

Just as fingers were made before forks, there was news to be had before there were newspapers. Occupied countries often had to turn back to primitive means of circulating news, by word of mouth between neighbours; without the years of experience, that make the bush telegraph so fascinatingly fast, to guide them.

Disseminating news was the first object of the political subverter. The further aim was to convince opinion, overwhelmed by the fact of nazi conquest, that this conquest was not irreversible; not a sort of political death; only a setback, however severe; something that could and should be overturned.

[1] At pp. 125–31.  [2] Foot, 4; from a 1939 pamphlet.
[3] A few details below, pp. 298–300, 209, 253, 226.

No one really knew then, or indeed knows now, what public opinion is. Dr Gallup's and other investigations into how to measure it – begun, at manufacturers' request, in the American advertising industry, to counter the sales resistance built up in the great depression of 1929–33 – were still in their early stages, and did not receive even the flattery of imitation by the occupiers. Clearly enough no one was going to conduct an opinion poll in Pontarlier, or the Piraeus, to find out what people thought about the Germans as occupiers, or whether or how people would like to see them shown the door. We were, and are, equally ignorant about why people change their minds in matters of politics.

Nevertheless a great many people devoted their war effort to the business of propaganda, on the Axis side, or counter-propaganda, on that of the Allies. A fierce psychological war had been waged under Goebbels' direction, ever since the seizure of power in 1933; a war aimed at riveting on the world the convictions that the aryan race was undoubtedly the master race in all creation, and Adolf Hitler the most marvellous man ever born. Against Goebbels' genius – crooked, but genius all the same – even the rugged straightforwardness of a Reith or a Murrow could hardly hope to prevail.

Reith's unshakeable uprightness left a mark on the BBC that came to mean much, as the war went on. The tradition of honesty was implanted so firmly in Broadcasting House that such major disasters as the evacuations from Dunkirk, or Narvik, or Nauplia could not shake it; BBC news bulletins reported the facts, as facts, as soon as they were known. There was only one equivalent in this war to the celebrated censorship *gaffe* of 1914, when the loss of HMS *Audacious* – a new and powerful battleship that went down off the Irish coast in sight of the crowded rail of a transatlantic liner in September 1914 – was left four years unreported. The loss of the *Lancastria*, with some 5,000 souls on board – four-fifths of whom were drowned – off St Nazaire on 17 June 1940, though the second greatest single disaster ever known at sea, remained known only to a restricted circle till the war's end; simply because everyone concerned in London at the time was too busy to release the news for publication.[1]

This anxiety always strictly to tell the truth, however unpalatable the truth might be to a patriotic ear, turned out before long to have been a devastatingly effective stroke in psychological warfare. As the BBC always stated the facts, so far as they were known in London, and German- and Italian-controlled broadcasts continued their prewar habits of boasting, exaggeration, and propaganda, those who were able to listen to both sides were quickly able to conclude which was the more reliable.

From the comparative accuracy of their news bulletins, available in over fifty languages by the middle of the war, BBC broadcasts thus got a long start in

[1] (Sir) W. S. Churchill, *The World Crisis* (1939 ed.), i. 355–7; *Second World War*, ii. 172. Resistance gained a great leader from this disaster. Maurice Southgate was one of the few people who managed to swim ashore; felt his life had been given back to him; and devoted it to France.

holding the attention of continental listeners; this in turn provided advantages for the British propaganda services. About these we know something already from Asa Briggs's incomparable history of the BBC, from Sefton Delmer, a leading participant, and from other sources;[1] and we have the tone of the early ministry of information picked out by the insolently accurate ear of the war's greatest novelist.[2] No official history of PWE has been published; here is a gap crying out to be filled.

An even greater gap arises from our ignorance, by and large, of communist propaganda strategy during the war. Radio Moscow had a Johnsonian determination not to let the capitalist dogs get the better of any propaganda bones that were to be gnawed, and never ceased to glorify – whenever it had a chance to do so – the achievements of the soviet forces, the correctness of the current communist party line, and the sublime sagacity of Stalin. Indeed on the first and third of these points British broadcasts (after 22 June 1941) were quite often, and American broadcasts occasionally, almost as warm as Russian.

These great broadcasting corporations, the soviet one under direct state control, the British one responsive to government advice, the American ones more independent, all cooperated (after 7 December 1941) in one joint effort: to convince, as best they could, the occupied populations of the worthlessness of the nazi cause. That the nazis were certain to lose, none of these bodies' broadcasters allowed himself by the slightest inflexion of the voice to doubt; thus hurling back in Goebbels' teeth that arrogant tone which had helped to rouse most of the rest of the world against nazism.

Alongside them there operated in much more clandestine conditions a whole series of 'black' stations, run by PWE, OSS, the NKVD; aimed at disrupting German armed forces' morale, above all, and thus important to resisters, but not really à propos, or needing more than mention, here.

What does need more than a passing mention in this chapter of general survey is a function of broadcasts, news broadcasts in particular, that was of cardinal impact to resistance. The reader will think at once of the streams of personal messages that signalled impending operations; but these are handled elsewhere.[3] Less immediately urgent, but quite as significant, was the role of broadcasting in providing for a news-starved public much of the main content of the clandestine press.

Historians are in a difficulty here. They like solid evidence; contemporary written testimony is best. (Being wary of forgeries is second nature to historians; forgery is not our present purpose, but in this context needs not to be forgotten. The thorough researcher will find in the Bibliothèque Nationale in Paris two versions of the clandestine *Humanité zone nord*, one more accurate and one more

---

[1] A. Briggs, *The War of Words* (1970), S. Delmer, *Black Boomerang* (1952), Duff Cooper, *Old Men Forget* (1953), Andrew Boyle, '*Poor Dear Brendan*' (1974), ch. ix, &c.

[2] Evelyn Waugh, *Put Out More Flags* (1942).

[3] See below, pp. 108–9.

'correct' than the other.) Of a parachute drop onto grass, Sherlock Holmes himself could hardly find solid evidence a week later, in western European weather. There might be a contemporary jotting, on the back of an IO's envelope; converted once a month into an entry in an RAF squadron's operational record book; and likely to be no more informative than 'Fireman: 12 containers, 2 packages. France.' The wireless operator who arranged it would be crazy to keep his copy of the relevant message, whether in code or in clear; he should at any rate have burned it as soon as sent. Home station's records are said now to have been destroyed.

But of a clandestine newspaper, run off in several hundred, or several thousand copies, a few copies might easily survive; and indeed millions do. Over a thousand separate clandestine newspapers appeared in France alone; one, *Défense de la France*, printing as many as 450,000 copies a time in January 1944. The Belgians, who had run an active clandestine press in 1914–18, were not far behind the French. The Dutch were if anything ahead of them, one paper dating back to 15 May 1940.[1] In eastern Europe, with lower literacy rates, presses were still active; the Poles used them a lot, and J. B. Priestley wrote the commentary for a film showing one at work *al fresco* for a soviet partisan band.

Work for these newspapers was just as intricate and just as dangerous as any other kind of work in resistance. You were just as sure to be sent to a concentration camp – at best: you might get more summary treatment – if you were caught carrying a haversack-full of roneoed leaflets, as if the haversack was full of Mills grenades. Danger never deterred anybody who had the soul of a resister; and the type of work was one that appealed particularly to intellectuals. Some of the greatest literary names of the 1940s wrote for the underground press: Geyl, Malraux, Sartre, de Beauvoir, Camus, Aragon, Croce, are names enough.

As has been hinted already, it is far from easy to explain what influence the underground press in fact exerted. One day, some revisionist sceptic may seek to prove it had none: a difficult, but not an inconceivable task. Certainly the present writer does not believe this press was negligible, or useless; he seeks only to bring out the danger of laying too much emphasis on it. This temptation to over-emphasize will be particularly strong for those brought up at the knee of some great intellectual figure of the war, or of one of his (or her) pupils. Intellectuals always enjoy most writing about, or against, each other. But they need to realize that resistance, outside the teaching profession,[2] was not a business in which intellectual qualities were of leading importance; and must not let any abundance of surviving material overbalance their judgements about what work had most effect at the time.

The effect towards which all subversive work moved was a simple, profound one. It was to create a degree of popular enthusiasm for anti-nazism, and of popular certainty that the nazis were going quite shortly to lose the war, so

[1] L. de Jong, *Het Koninkrijk der Nederlanden*, iv. 688 (1972).
[2] Cp. p. 282 below.

strong that a resister would have nine chances in ten of getting shelter when he asked for it, at random, on the run. Once a fugitive feels he can knock on any door, call at any farm; say, 'They're after me – they'll be round that corner any minute – hide me'; and get hidden, at once, no questions asked, in loft or barn or cellar; subversion's work is nearly done. That particular fugitive may or may not be found; but the country is ripe for the closing stage: insurrection.

### Insurrection

This corner of resistance history is nowadays fashionable enough, in English-speaking countries; had indeed received a lot of attention, though in contemporary rather than wartime contexts. The rules for a successful rising have not altered at all, except in technical detail, since Malaparte and Lenin laid them down; indeed, most of them are to be found in Thucydides and Aristotle.[1] And forcible seizures of power are becoming so common in modern times that, if we may believe a thorough recent study, there have been over four hundred of them in the present century.[2]

The sort of uprising that we need to consider at this point is a good deal more widespread, in its popular base and in its political impact, than a palace revolution, such as Simović's coup in Belgrade on 27 March 1941 that ousted the regent of Yugoslavia in favour of the young king Peter.[3] Subversive propagandists sought not merely to change the titular head of state, but to generate a sustained overwhelming popular conviction, affecting whole provinces at a time: the conviction that the rule of the nazi occupier was no longer bearable at all, and that the moment for a complete overthrow of the local pro-nazi régime had now arrived. Ideally, people would no longer take their lawsuits to the courts of the collaborationist régime, but to resistance courts (as the Irish peasantry got used to doing in 1920). Ideally, people would not merely not cheer at a formal German parade in a city; not even absent themselves; but turn up and jeer.

The ideal world and the real are usually quite far apart. As we shall see, a few approximations of one to the other could be made, where resistance was strongest: in Poland, Yugoslavia, Norway, France.[4] The Poles of course had had, from mid-September 1939 onward, something approaching the unanimity of hatred for the occupier that the previous paragraph sketched out; but, having just undergone a total military collapse, had not the minimum of power needed to enforce their will on the two states that had occupied them. And, being human, the bulk of their town population had the normal urban dweller's instinct to do as he or she is bid, by whoever is in the street or the town hall directing what goes on

---

[1] 'C. Malaparte', *Technique du coup d'état* (1931), V. I. Lenin, *State and Revolution* (1916), Thucydides, *Peloponnesian War*, book iii, Aristotle, *Politics*, book v.

[2] P. Calvert, *A Study of Revolution* (1970), appx. Incessant confusions over namesakes beset resistance and its history. Peter Calvert, a don at Southampton, is no more identical with Michael Calvert the Chindit leader and authority on guerilla than the present writer is identical with the current (July 1976) leader of the house of commons.

[3] Cp. p. 188 below.     [4] See pp. 292–4, 195–7, 281–2, 239–41

Duly constituted authorities, or authorities that appear at least to be duly constituted, have a flying start in getting peoples' civil obedience.[1]

As the war went on, a number of Poles decided to throw in their lot with the communist cause; as did a substantial number of people in other occupied countries. This put them into the company of dedicated revolutionaries, whose business it was supposed to be to precipitate and to direct insurrections. How successful the communists were in this task is a matter for sharp disputes between their friends and their enemies; and, again, will need our attention later.[2] In many places there is a myth, and in some places it may be that it was the fact, that the advance of the Red Army was accompanied by a popular uprising that was in favour of the resultant communist régime. Elsewhere, no; with two singular and important exceptions.

One was Yugoslavia, of which only the north-eastern quarter was crossed by the Russian advance. In the rest of the country, Tito had by 1944 managed to secure a large degree of support, and a still larger degree of acquiescence, for the national revolution that he had launched in the summer of 1941, and carried round the mountains with him since. This peripatetic nation-in-arms will call for closer scrutiny; as will the egregious case of the Albanian risings.[3]

Tito and Hoxha were both big enough men to soar above the obstacle that seems to have hampered so many other communist leaders as the struggle for power reached a critical stage: security. With security in principle the following section will deal; but we need to glance at it at once, as it affected insurrection.

Everybody who had to deal with the communists in clandestinity found their dealings maddeningly slow. Everything to do with them had to pass (unless one was an agent actually parachuted to an important leader; and even then, there might be inexplicable hold-ups) through cut-outs, whole zarebas of them, and committees; which took weeks for certain, and might take months. Communications probably did not allow for all major decisions to be referred to Moscow; but the party system, particularly just after the great purge, was not one that offered much encouragement to individual initiative. 'Opportunist' had been one of Lenin's favourite terms of invective, for hurling at such past opponents as Kautsky; and the leading comrades, deeply read in Lenin, were so frightened of being labelled 'opportunist' that they may have missed a number of opportunities.

Sixteen years after the war, there were some sharp exchanges between Washington and Moscow; one of which is so *à propos* that it needs to be cited here, out of its chronological context. J. F. Kennedy addresses Nikita Krushchov, the day after the disaster at the Bay of Pigs:

> I believe, Mr Chairman, that you should recognise that free peoples in all
> parts of the world do not accept the claim of historical inevitability for
> communist revolution. What your Government believes is its own business;
> what it does in the world is the world's business. The great revolution in the

[1] Cp. p. 22 above.      [2] Cp. p. 316 below.      [3] Cp. pp. 195–7, 184–5.

history of man, past and future, is the revolution of those determined to be free.[1]

This was the revolution that counted, that made its durable mark on history; it was for this that most resisters strove.

## Security

As the nazis had come to power with the help of dirty tricks, they knew a lot about how such dirty tricks departments of their enemies as the NKVD or SOE or OSS might work. As a matter of drill, they kept a sharp lookout for signs of clandestine trouble; relying on their own past experience to know what to seek. Anyone in the SD who was over twenty-five in 1940 was likely to have worked as a subversive himself,[2] in the years before the nazi seizure of power. This would give him an advantage in combating resistance, since it gave him some insight into resisters' probable lines of thought and action.

Any competent resistance leader expected enemy attempts to break into his group; in fact, if they did not take place, he could regard it as a reflexion of his own lack of impact on the war. Good commanders of clandestine networks (usually known as circuits) were constantly watching out for trouble, and kept a firm rein on recruiting. There was only one certain way of keeping double agents – those who worked with both sides, leaving their real loyalty with the wrong one – out of a circuit. That was, only to admit to it people who could be vouched for, from many years' personal knowledge, by those who were in it already. Admittedly, this was a counsel of perfection. Those who could stick to it, remained perfectly safe; they were liable also to be perfectly ineffectual. 'Caution axiomatic', in an excellent phrase of one of SOE's men in Stamboul, 'but over-caution results in nothing done.'[3]

SOE had a drill, to which dutiful agents conformed when time and circumstance allowed. No one was supposed to be recruited into an SOE circuit until his full name, current address, occupation, and date and place of birth had been reported to, and approved by, the country section headquarters concerned. The country section could search in SOE's chaotic files, and have inquiries made in the supposedly enormous dossiers of MI5. Only after receiving clearance from Baker Street was the circuit supposed to go ahead and approach the person in view. This again was a counsel of perfection. Once business in the field began to be brisk, there was no time for such niceties; leaving aside the rumour that MI5's main filing system underwent a disaster in the autumn of 1940.

(Should any readers remember my earlier book clearly, they are asked to

[1] Schlesinger, *A Thousand Days*, 250–1.
[2] There were women in the SD, but outside fiction their work was clerical and domestic; so there is no need to insert the 'or herself' so often needed when we discuss resistance. Women in resistance proved (if a proof were needed) the case for 'women's liberation', slogan of the sixties.
[3] March 1945, cited from Foot, 121.

forgive some repetition in the next few pages; for some of the points made in its chapter on security[1] remain valid.)

Resisters, whether local or infiltrated from abroad, needed to keep themselves safe from several overlapping police jurisdictions; some German, some indigenous. With all the current difficulties of a world teetering on the brink of slump, and a Britain rocked by intermittent Irish bombs and racked by wage-hunting trade unionists, we do still live in a comparatively free society. Though a distant police car's hooter sounds as these words are again penned, we are removed by some distance in time and space from the immediate urgencies of war, hunger, occupation, and repression. It is easy to forget how difficult life was to resisters at all levels. Hunger and bombing or shellfire presented, in some areas and at some times, severe strains; occasionally, all together. And on top of that, every step in everybody's everyday existence might be reported, considered, commented on by one secret police force or another. Some of these police forces were of exceptional savagery.

The nazis secured their hold on power in Germany by a carefully thought-out series of manœuvres based on three premises: that maximum power is the most desirable of objects, that Adolf Hitler's orders for securing it are always to be obeyed, and that absolutely no regard is to be paid to any other code or precept. Hitler had done the thinking out, and had his gangs trained already to obey him. On this foundation of limitless bad faith the 'new order' arose. The German security services' performance was erratic, and did not always bear out the sedulously fostered myths that they knew everything and would stick at nothing. Once in their hands, many millions of people died in agony, and no one could feel safe; least of all an agent of a hostile power. Yet their senior staffs were obsessed by service intrigues, and their junior staffs were often as incompetent as they were cruel. Several SOE agents who were over-enthusiastic, or under-trained, or both, for their work in France [or elsewhere] were able to elude arrest and returned to recount their adventures: more thanks to the Germans' inefficiency than to their own discretion. The nature of the nazi state machine ensured that many German counter-espionage agents were more interested in promoting the status of their own organization as compared with its rivals at home than in actually coping with the activities of allied agents in the field.[2]

More of the Germans' various services later;[3] but theirs was only one arm of the police cross that resisters had to carry. As well as the *Abwehr* and the *Sicherheitsdienst*, the resister – outside the enlarged Reich – had also to fend off his own local, municipal police; who might, if he too was a local, know him all too well. Different manners, different kinds of bluff were needed to get past the two sorts of control, if one was stopped at a chance barrier by either.[4] In some

---

[1] Foot, 115–25.    [2] Ibid. 115–16.    [3] At pp. 148–9 below.
[4] Examples of how to deal with both at once on p. 15 above: if your nerves were strong. Will the reader forgive another personal anecdote? Once, about midnight of a very dark

countries, and on some points, the local police were less easily satisfied than the Germans. The fifteen separate police organizations of Vichy France were, particularly in 1941, painstakingly bureaucratic. Right down to the liberation in 1944 the French *milice*, a paramilitary body of 'some 45,000 toughs and fascist fanatics ready to shoot it out with the *maquis*',[1] was busy in arms against resisters, in the name of 'public order'. Over 8,000 Jews were deported from Vichy France to German concentration camps, by the French police, in the early autumn of 1942,[2] and Vichy and Gestapo authorities cooperated in tracking down clandestine wireless sets.

Much of this pro-German zeal was encouraged by collaborationist ministers of the interior, and enforced on police bodies from the top; not all of it. We must not let the resistance myth captivate us so much that we forget all about the collaborators; that would be as foolish as being captivated by the collaborationist myth, which holds that resisters were really only a sort of bandit. It was not only in France that there were collaborationist policemen. Some 12,000 Dutchmen, for instance, took up police and security work under the nazis – this excludes the 17,000 in the Waffen-SS. Even in Norway there were over 500 volunteers for an SS guard battalion raised for security duties inside Norway, and Norwegians could be found to help the SD unravel resistance networks.[3] The Italian police, and ticket inspectorate, we have seen at work already.[4]

Nevertheless, a lot of village policemen and junior town gendarmes and even some of the more enterprising and less regulation-bound members of detective departments, were prepared to help resisters; at least, to start with, they were prepared to look the other way, instead of stepping forward and questioning someone whom they had reason to suspect of being on a resistance mission. Gradually, as more and more people came to detest the occupiers, more and more policemen came to keep in step with the bulk of their own countrymen; till, as the Allied armies approached, the police were sometimes found leading an official change of sides.

Rome provides the leading case: when Mussolini, after over twenty years in office, fell, he was quietly taken away in an ambulance by a captain in the military police, who acted on orders from his commanding general.[5] The Athenian case is odder: Colonel Evert, the police chief there, 'succeeded in winning and retaining the confidence both of the German authorities and of the British organisers of resistance'.[6] On a much lower, but still to a resister a cheering, level,

---

night, I and a fellow escaper stumbled on a Waffen-SS sentry, who gave us a rather sloppy challenge. My companion said instantly, in perfectly fluent German (which was not his native tongue), 'You bloody well stand to attention when you speak to an officer!' '*Zu Befehl!*' ('Sir!') said the sentry, clicking his heels smartly; and we passed by.

[1] Robert O. Paxton, *Vichy France* (Barrie & Jenkins, 1972), 298.

[2] Ibid. 296.     [3] D. Littlejohn, *The Patriotic Traitors* (1972), 128, 45.

[4] Above, pp. 39–40.

[5] (Sir) F. W. Deakin, *The Brutal Friendship* (Pelican 1966), i. 514–17.

[6] C. M. Woodhouse in *European Resistance Movements 1939–1945* (Maxwell 1960), i. 380: henceforward *ERM*.

two French police inspectors engaged so whole heartedly in the work of circuits of SOE's F section that they came out, when their own stations got too hot to hold them, over the Pyrenees; and later went back to lead circuits of their own.[1]

In general, though, resisters could not rely on police friendship, and had to look out for police hostility. For the NKVD's agents, this was straightforward; they were brought up to believe that all police forces are the tools of the governing class; that their own police force was, therefore, immaculate because it was chosen by the vanguard of the revolutionary proletariat, the CPSU(B); and that all capitalist and fascist police forces were necessarily nefarious (though nor incorruptible). For an American or British agent, or for a Dutch or Danish citizen brought up to an entirely different and much more friendly view of the police, a correctly suspicious attitude was sometimes hard to take.

One police force everyone could agree in dreading – even its own nationals dreaded it: the Gestapo. Just after the great purge, the *Yezhovshchina*, the NKVD did not come at all far behind it in its capacity to inspire alarm: among those who knew. Outside the soviet union, so far few did.

What should a resister do, to keep himself secure among these uniformed and plain-clothed enemies? Keep alert; keep (so far as his duty allowed him) to the rules, with his papers in perfect order; remember who he is, and above all, keep his mouth shut. Routine police methods are the same the world over. What the police look out for is anything out of the ordinary. Your most successful resister (again, contrast the spy of fiction) is therefore likely to be someone so ordinary-looking that he will never attract a gendarme's second glance.

Conscientious and well-trained resisters used to practise, constantly running over the answers in their minds, what they would say if asked at a snap control the usual routine questions: who are you? where are you (a nasty one, sometimes, for a parachutist just off the dropping zone)? where have you come from? how? where are you going? why? where do you live? how much money have you got on you? If asked all eight questions in a row, the resister would suspect something was up; normally police only ask two or three of them, more or less at random, to satisfy themselves that they are not dealing with a suspicious character. If a resister found he had suddenly had to transport himself, at short or no notice, into some quite different social milieu and some quite new personality, he (or she) would do well to practise this exercise often; otherwise a stumble in conversation at a road block might lead to a fall into bad hands. The great gift on these occasions is the gift of saying very little, very dully: been at my cousin's, came by train, walking home, &c; presenting no jagged or unexpected edge to be seized on and taken up, and never volunteering anything at all.

Some of the best and dourest of resisters were consequently rather indifferent company; some were not. On the continent, at the time, every resister

had to combine discretion and daring in a formula he had to work out for himself, in the light of his training and personality, and of the actual

[1] Foot, 120.

circumstances facing him in the field. 'Security is really only a question of care and common sense', said one of the [SOE] section histories, 'and if agents are well-trained security will become second-nature to them. The danger lies, not in themselves, but in the people they have to contact in the field.' . . . Here lay the key to security: picking colleagues trustworthy enough not to gossip. Anyone who has had secrets to handle knows how strong the temptation is to impart them to somebody; sophisticated but undisciplined people who had to know [resistance] secrets . . . were often careless in their choice of people to confide in, and so word got round too fast and too far. The only guard against this was constant caution: never make a rash approach, never enrol chatterers, never tell anybody anything bearing on secret work unless the telling will directly help the work forward. The extent to which [a resister] could follow these precepts varied with his role; people . . . conducting sabotage or guerilla had to take more risks, and expose themselves more often, than escape line staffs or traditional clandestine intelligence agents. . . . How each [resister] worked out his private formula for security was, of course, an individual matter; it would depend on the nature and completeness of his cover, and on his orders [if he accepted any], which depended in turn on the tactical and strategic objects of his mission; naturally it would depend also on his character. Happy-go-lucky people did not bother very much about all this; a few of them survived. Others, more suspicious-minded, thought of little else; most of these extra-cautious ones lived to tell, and a few of the most energetic of them could put beside a record of complete discretion a distinguished subversive record. Yet not even the most meticulous and devoted . . . could always save themselves from howlers.[1]

From these they could only be rescued by luck; always important in war, and in secret war all-important.[2] 'Good luck in fact might supplement good security. What was always dangerous and often fatal was to rely on good luck to outweigh bad security';[3] gamblers could carry their gambling instincts too far. 'A perfectionist kept even his private address and his usual cover identity to himself, so that if a [colleague] was caught no harm to himself and little to the circuit was likely to follow; not many [resisters] were so careful.'[4]

Security may roughly be equated with what, in some armed forces, is called counter-intelligence: by no means exactly the same thing as counter-espionage, to which we need to turn next. Let us quote an expert:

Counter-espionage, usually called simply by its initials CE, is a widely misunderstood branch of secret operations. Its purpose is not to apprehend enemy agents; that is an aim of the security forces. It is the word 'counter' which causes the trouble, since it is generally interpreted to mean 'against';

[1] Ibid. 121–2.    [2] Examples ibid. 122–3.
[3] Ibid. 123.    [4] Ibid. 123.

a defensive operation against the enemy's intelligence operations. Quite to the contrary, CE is an offensive operation, a means of obtaining intelligence about the opposition by using – or, more usually, attempting to use – the opposition's operations ... The ultimate goal of all CE operations is to penetrate the opposition's own secret operations apparatus; to become, obviously without the opposition's knowledge, an integral and functioning part of their calculations ... so far as intelligence is concerned, you know what he knows. You have thereby annulled, in one stroke, the value to him of his secret intelligence about you ... you are in a position to control his actions.[1]

Part of the historic importance of resistance, unknown to resisters at the time and not likely to have been much appreciated by them if it had been known, lay in this: that it provided several secret services with a field in which their counter-espionage departments could exercise.

Of all the fields we touch on that are still in part covered by security blankets, this remains the most sensitive; there is little that is known, and still less that can be said. Of the supreme work of counter-intelligence, a successful deception scheme, something has been said already.[2] Numerous efforts were made by all concerned to penetrate each other's services; only once with outstanding effect.

There are rumours that the head of the *Abwehr*, Admiral Canaris, was in fact a British agent; there is no solid evidence whatever to support the rumours, and only the most tenuous of indications that the head of MI6, as one gentleman to another, did not feel too savagely towards his enemy opposite number.[3] There seems in fact to have been an informal understanding between most of the warring secret services that they would leave each other's head offices alone; broken twice, by Beria of the NKVD who had his men planted in MI6 and SOE – his nominal allies – and by Moravec, the head of Czech intelligence, who organized the killing of Reinhard Heydrich, the nazi ruler of Bohemia.

More opportunities lost, it may be. There are odd tales of the penetrability of SOE's main offices in Baker Street, during air raid alerts. And the sister of a great French resister – she was not in active resistance at the time – had the SD's Paris headquarters in the Avenue Foch to herself for half an hour when she called one lunch-time in December 1943 to make a routine inquiry about her missing brother.[4]

The SD infiltrated double agents successfully into a number of British circuits in France, and the *Abwehr* brought off a classic of counter-espionage in Holland; MI6 appears to have had a man on von Choltitz's staff in Paris; MI5's effort with 'Fortitude' outclassed all the rest, and had a considerable influence on the course of the war.[5] Beria's men remained quietly embedded, to

1 'C. Felix', *The Spy and His Masters* (Secker & Warburg 1963), 129–30.
2 At pp. 28–31 above.
3 Ian Colvin, *Canaris* (1958), 42.
4 Conversation with Mlle Laure Moulin, 1967.
5 See pp. 249–50, 264–6, 253 and 29–30.

exercise their influence on the peace. Newspaper sensations need not blind readers to the truth about 'spies': the really important ones are the ones who are never unmasked.

A closing point: in spite, again, of rumours to the contrary – often started by the SD, to soften up prisoners under interrogation – there was no German agent working into France from SOE headquarters.[1]

[1] Proof in Foot, 125.

# 4 POLITICS AND WAR

By convention, in ordinary English usage, wars are held to be two-sided. Propaganda, usually aimed at the lowest common multiple of a people, takes for granted that 'our side' is locked in a single struggle with 'the enemy'; and Hitler and Hitlerism appeared so singularly nasty in wartime that they were very widely regarded as the one foe. In their own gloomiest moments in the cold early months of 1945, ardent nazis could even take morose pleasure in their *Weltfeindlichkeit*, in the way every un-nazi man's and woman's hand seemed to be against them.

Yet the nazis' opponents were far from seeing eye to eye on political, any more than on military affairs.

An old-fashioned marxist's class interpretation of the war would show the working class, acting through communist parties the world over and particularly through the CPSU(B), on one side; and rival combinations of aggressive capitalist states, the Axis powers and their western enemies, on two others. As a matter of expediency, the working class could work with the western powers against the Axis; but, once the Axis was beaten locally, must be ready to exert itself against the next class enemy.[1]

This was precisely what happened in Greece in December 1944. In September of the same year, it was widely expected to happen in France and Belgium; though, for reasons that have never satisfactorily been cleared up, it did not. The local communist parties in western Europe, though much more numerous and even more sophisticated than their Greek opposite numbers, made no effective move towards seizing power in either of these two western countries; though they remained ready to seize such propaganda advantages as they could from maintaining, in the teeth of the evidence, that they alone had provided the real core of resistance. Perhaps they had no orders to move; perhaps they judged the Americans were too strong for them. Certainly, though they had some power bases athwart the western allies' lines of communication, they did not command the degree of popular support that enabled Makhno's anarchists in

[1] Casterman [see p. 321], s.v. Guerres multilaterales, tr.

the Ukraine to scupper Denikin in 1919 and almost to scupper Trotsky in 1920.[1]

The Allied troops that entered Paris, Lille, Brussels, Liège, and other large towns in north-east France and Belgium in August–September 1944 received a welcome so rapturous that it imposed a perceptible delay on their eastward advance. This was a spontaneous bubbling-up of joy that the Germans had gone; it was also a reminder of the personal and political bases on which war rests. That it could happen at all was a justification of the policies towards resistance that both the British and the Americans had for some time pursued.

SOE's role in all this, which was considerable, expressed in microcosm the role of the United Kingdom and, later in the war, of the United States. If we may attempt a metaphor from hydraulics, SOE's task might be seen as keeping the mechanism of the canal gates of freedom oiled and in decent working order, till the water levels of fluctuating opinion could move up and down again when the immediate necessities of war were over. Yet in hydraulics water can only flow down, or be pumped up; and a merely two-directional metaphor does not meet the complexity of some of the wars of 1939–45. Several of those were triangular – in Poland, 1939–44, and in Greece, 1941–5, for instance; one or two, particularly in Yugoslavia from 1941 to 1946, had so many potentially or actually hostile factions they could better be called polygonal.

In such a pass, any act of resistance had political overtones; indeed the best judge of SOE's work laid down that SOE could do nothing that was not political.[2] What politics did it pursue?

Its agents often claimed that they were unpolitical. So in one important sense they were, if they were British subjects operating abroad; for they would be certain to go away after the war's end, if they survived it, and were therefore bound to be innocent of any desire to feather their own local political nest through any line of policy they pursued in the field. The same could by no means always be said of those with whom they were working; thousands of them beneficiaries of SOE and some few of them directly in its pay. Much the same applied to agents of OSS; in each service, personal political sympathies (unless one was a communist; and of those there were few indeed[3]) counted for nothing at all. One was under orders, and carried out – within wide bounds of local initiative – the policy of one's government.

What, in turn, was that?

Where Europe was concerned, it could be summed up in two adjectives: anti-nazi, and constitutionalist. The military advantages of seeing that there was armed resistance to the nazis, that intelligence was secured from their domain, and that fugitives could escape across it are obvious enough; some dividend at

---

[1] See David Footman, 'Nestor Makhno', in *St Antony's Papers*, no. 6 (Oxford 1959), 105–6, 118–20.
[2] Foreign Office file, seen 1960.    [3] But see p. 198 below.

least could be expected, and Chapter 7 will discuss how large the dividend was. The constitutionalist side deserves a closer look here.

The Americans have been stout constitutionalists since 1787, or at any rate since the end of the war between the states in 1865. Enormous importance had been attached to the United States constitution in every American school attended by their wartime leaders; American troops abroad never lost an opportunity of preaching its virtues to benighted Europeans. They regarded constitutional government, summed up in Lincoln's Gettysburg phrase as government of the people by the people for the people, as the only proper political end, and its restoration to those parts of occupied Europe that had known it before as one of their main aims in the war.

The British, though taunted often enough by foreigners for having no constitution, are in fact much hedged in by precedent and formality. Our constitutional arrangements are, it is true, unusually flexible; consider the case of the Emergency Powers (Defence) Act, 1940, which gave the crown more or less unlimited authority over the persons and property of its subjects, and passed through every stage from introduction to royal assent on the single day of 22 May 1940.[1] Yet even in so dire a crisis, the forms were gone through; and the political world at Westminster was determined only to act so hurriedly when the crisis really was dire. Churchill was for many purposes a dictator; one of his close colleagues indeed is said to have described his system as 'dictatorship by monologue – none of us could get a word in edgeways'.[2] In his own phrase, 'All I wanted was compliance with my wishes after reasonable discussion.'[3] But he, like everyone round him, was aware that he was a dictator of the old Roman, not the new fascist, type; that he would be accountable at the war's end for what he had done. As he put it proudly, 'all the responsibility was laid upon the five War Cabinet Ministers. They were the only ones who had the right to have their heads cut off on Tower Hill if we did not win.'[4] As a strong romantic, as well as a strong realist, he would have been appalled even to contemplate acting unconstitutionally, on any matter of significance; and as his father's son, and with his own past career lodged in his mind, he was always a devoted house of commons man. This inbred parliamentarianism goverened all his relations with secret services, as well as the other forces of the crown. The heads of British secret services felt responsible – through intervening ministers – to him; and he helped to shape their policies.

His control over the war was so complete that for once the historian can legitimately put what was done, and left undone, in these directly personal terms;[5] he was, while the war lasted, more of a president than a prime minister.

[1] *Parliamentary Papers 1939–40*, i. 569; 361 H.C. Deb. 5s, 151–85; 116 H.L. Deb. 5s, 381–8.
[2] Conversation with T. E. Utley, 1945; who had it direct from source.
[3] W. S. Churchill, *The Second World War*, iv. 78 (1951).
[4] Ibid. ii. 12 (1949).
[5] Cp. A. J. P. Taylor, *English History 1914–1945* (Pelican 1970), 581–95.

The American president, Roosevelt, had *ex officio* the power of commander-in-chief of all the armed forces of the USA, and had the FBI, and later OSS also, under his own direct control. He and Churchill, acquaintances of long standing, cooperated fairly closely; neither controlling the other. As American strength developed with the passage of time, Roosevelt took over from Churchill as the more dominant personality of the two; till in the last few months of his life his health began to fail. Of their joint political views, the Atlantic Charter of 12 August 1941 – before the Americans were in the war – remains the best short statement.

It includes the phrases, crucial for their political views, that 'they respect the right of all peoples to choose the form of government under which they will live; and they wish to see sovereign rights and self-government restored to those who have been forcibly deprived of them'.[1] This was really the political nub of the war, as it has been of the cold war; though often obscured and overlaid by irrelevances brought into the argument by nastier-minded politicians anxious to obfuscate the issue. Neither Roosevelt nor Churchill thought recent conquest a sound foundation for a state; both meant what they said, when they said they wanted to return to the peoples of Europe the right of choice. The central political task performed by SOE and OSS was to prepare such a reorganization of occupied Europe as would lead to the widest possible free elections when the Germans had been driven out.

One one subject of leading political import Roosevelt and Churchill did not always see eye to eye: relations with the USSR. The British were inclined – the most cautious of them would say, over-inclined – to trust their soviet allies, during the phase of nazi–soviet hostility; the Americans inclined to trust them even more. There are even indications that at times Roosevelt ganged up with Stalin against Churchill; relying on those passionate anti-imperialist feelings that were held almost universally by his electorate, nearly all of whom looked on Great Britain as – what indeed she then was – the world's leading imperialist power, and remembered their own colonialist revolt of 1775–83, their war of independence.[2]

Yet both in Washington and in London, experts on soviet relations feared a revival of the Hitler–Stalin/Ribbentrop–Molotov pact of August 1939; while the Russians, suffering still from the birth trauma of their second 1917 revolution, still feared a notional alliance of world capitalism against them. That is, the only real identity of aim lay, if it lay anywhere, in the desire to secure the military defeat of nazi Germany. The Russians – as almost everybody called them at the time; sovietologists will wince, but let us here follow common usage – the Russians adopted a uniformly surly attitude towards the Americans and British alike, where policy towards resistance was concerned as well as in other affairs.

[1] *BFSP* cxliv. 683–4.
[2] H. Feis, *Churchill Roosevelt Stalin* (Princeton 1957), 214–15, 516–17.

The NKVD occasionally demanded facilities for putting its own agents into areas it could only conveniently reach through British or American bases, and took for granted that if the carrying aircraft went unserviceable at the last moment or the proposed dropping zone was obscured by fog, there was a capitalist plot to prevent it from carrying out its revolutionary task. No return facilities were ever offered.

It is important, though difficult, to remember that though the NKVD's manners often seemed frightful, to western staff officers brought up in utterly different modes of social thought, its leading men were neither ragamuffins nor careerists, but dedicated communists. They held to their creed, nauseating though it seemed to many of their opposite numbers, with the strength of a persecuted minority that has faith in its eventual success. Indeed, devout atheists though they had to be, it is not absurd to compare the strength of their feeling with that of religious fanatics. Communist readers, or readers much thrown into contact with communists, will recognize as one of the leading traits of this political species, *certainty*: dogmatic insistence that whatever the party currently says, is right. Communist resistance policy was comparatively simple: it was to spread this certainty over as wide an area as could be; to the greater eventual glory of a world communist revolution they were brought up to believe was inevitable. This feeling that you and history are on the same side, if you can communicate it to other people, makes (as we shall see in a moment) a powerful political magnet. But history books, unless written by reliable members of the communist party, are not popular reading among communists; they too often indicate that the party made mistakes, an inadmissible point.

It is also important, though difficult, to remember that in 1942-3-4 'our gallant soviet ally' became a catch-phrase in British and American journalism almost as prevalent as the thousand-year Reich in Goebbels' Germany. The Russians were undergoing a tremendous battering from the *Wehrmacht*, and incurring – and inflicting – casualties by the million, while a few British divisions were scurrying to and fro across the western desert and a few Americans were being killed in the Pacific. The free world depended for its survival on the Russian wing of the bound world; people with the upbringing of the American or British governing classes of those years felt that this dependence created obligations. Hence what later demagogues, in the then unforeseen 'cold war' of 1947 onwards,[1] decried as 'softness to Russia'; a mood that culminated in the tragedy of 1945-6 when over a million soviet citizens were forcibly returned to the USSR; where, more forcibly still, they were all sent to camps in Siberia.[2]

For the governing class of the soviet union is unhampered by bourgeois prejudices about good manners or gratitude. The governing party is still the CPSU; though it has undergone various changes of leadership, and has dropped

[1] 1962 is often given as a closing date for the cold war; which, however much politicians prattle of détente, has no more closed than the earth has stopped rotating.
[2] See Nicholas Bethell, *The Last Secret* (1974).

from its title the concluding (B) for Bolshevik – majority: acquired originally at a meeting in a chapel off the Tottenham Court Road in 1903. Politics in Russia remain completely dominated by this party, and various practices abhorred in the west, such as delation of parents by children or prolonged detention without trial, are common form.

The iniquities – if they are iniquities: *chaque nation à son goût* – of the soviet system were perfectly well known to the American and British governments during the war; though anyone who tried to draw attention to them in the years of Russia's severest struggle was regarded at best as a crank. Pity was the principal emotion felt by western troops stationed at such places as Murmansk. Great Britain and the USA were not fighting against the single-party system as such: they had too many single-party friends of their own, such as Salazar or Batista. They were fighting – they had been forced to fight – against the nazis' special application of it, that proposed to spread the rule of a single party far beyond the bounds of a single nation's historic reach. The nazis had picked up a German nationalist slogan, *Weltmacht oder Niedergang*, world power or downfall; half of it – fortunately for the rest of us, the second half of it – they carried through.

Practical writing on politics is as full as a net is full of holes with unexpressed assumptions about how people act; no doubt the pages above are no exception. Now and again, stress needs to be laid on a point that has seemed so obvious that no one has bothered to write it down; such a point arises here.

Most people prefer to be on the winning side.

Many changes of minds by voters during election campaigns are made so that the changers may align themselves with the apparent favourites; shifts of opinion in wartime are often made for similar reasons. Revolutions and *coups d'état* are usually made by handfuls of discontented men and women who see a chance to grab power, have the nerve to seize it, and have the stronger nerve to hold on. The success of counter-revolutions against them depends partly on luck, partly on technique; but more than either, on which side looks to the populace at large as if it is going to win. Harold Wilson's well-known remark that 'a week is a long time in politics' applies with particular force in revolutionary crises: think of Robespierre on 2 Thermidor, l'an II, safely in power, or of Lenin in mid-October 1917, on the run. Sudden men, people of quick decision who can spot an opening and pounce on it, are the men who make *coups*; they then need to convince everybody that they have won. Once the idea starts to spread, 'nothing succeeds like success'. (Nothing fails like failure, either; but as Lady Macbeth said, 'Screw your courage to the sticking place, And we'll not fail.' Politicians may think better of her than plain men do.)

Crises in resistance, as the last section showed, were sometimes revolutionary in form. In many cases there was, during this war, an extra political complication superimposed on all the normal difficulties of a wartime insurrection: a government in exile, or even – as in the Polish case – two rival governments in exile, wanting to have a deciding voice in what went on. Generalization here would be pointless; each separate case will need to be glanced at in Chapter 6.

Each government in exile believed itself legitimate; and each had some connexion with the party system in the country it believed itself in some sense to represent. To party we can now turn.

## Nationalism

In occupied countries that the Germans regarded as racially akin to themselves there was a temptation for nationalist parties to throw in their lot with the occupier. This was just what the Norwegian *Nasjonal Samling*, Møller's Danish and van Rappard's Dutch nazi parties, Mussert's larger *Nationaal-Socialistische Beweging* in the Netherlands, de Clercq's *Vlaamsch Nationaal Verbond* and lesser fascist groupings in Belgium, did. Yet none of them commanded a large following, and they were as a rule treated by the nazis, as by the bulk of their fellow countrymen, with barely concealed contempt.

In two provinces of conquered successor states, the German occupation provided facilities for a nationalist movement to assert itself much more fully than before; hence a brief period of quasi-independence for Slovakia, and much more hair-raising results in Croatia where the *Ustashe* ran out of hand.[1]

Italian fascists at first inclined to patronize the nazis, as promising political younger brothers. They found themselves successively outclassed, impoverished, and – their Duce apart – ignored.

In eastern Europe, the nazis muffed a magnificent chance to pose as liberators of the oppressed nationalities of the eastern Baltic, the Ukraine, and the Caucasus. The necessities of their racial myth led them to treat all the conquered populations alike as sub-humans, a sort of superior cattle. This produced ludicrous results: millions of deserters who volunteered to join the Germans against their hated communist masters were treated with local enthusiasm, by fellow front-line soldiers who could appreciate their fighting qualities, but then with official disdain. Some were put into local security units to fight the communist-dominated partisans, which they did willingly enough. Others joined Vlasov's army, put on *Wehrmacht* uniform, and became occupying troops in quiet or supposedly quiet corners of Europe, where in 1944 a high proportion of them deserted again, to the forces of the western Allies; only, in the long run, to be sent back to the USSR from whence they came.

Nationalist resistance, both to the German and to the soviet authorities simultaneously, was too complicated an affair to be set up in a hurry. No effort to encourage it could be contemplated by the British or American secret services; and, for lack both of outside assistance and of local opportunity, practically nothing came of it.

[1] Details in sections on Czechoslovakia, pp. 202–9, and Yugoslavia, pp. 186–9, below.

In the Balkans and in occupied Latin Europe – France, francophone Belgium, later Italy; and Romania, straddling both categories – there was more opportunity than in ex-soviet territory for nationalism to assert itself as a leading element in resistance; just indeed as it asserted itself, given time and chance, in those areas of vaguely aryan ethnic origin with which this section began.[1] The Dutch for instance, conscious like the Swedes and the Spanish of having once been a great power, had strong historic reasons for wishing to be left alone. So had the French.[2] The Belgians had had the Germans before, well within living memory. Many Italians still treasured memories of the national resurgence against Habsburg and Bourbon tyranny, in which their grandfathers had fought in 1859–61; though it was sensible, when governed through the OVRA, to keep such memories to oneself. The Greeks, from whose language the words politics and democracy come, remembered having got rid with British help of the Turks; similar memories were fresh all over the Balkans.

As one who was once described as a foreigner by a fellow Englishman, and indeed a fellow householder in the same borough, who lived on the other side of the city centre, the present writer can appreciate that people's views of who their countrymen are can be narrow. But enough has perhaps been said to show that national feeling could provide – in fact was likely to provide – a strong political motive for resisters. This was not a matter in which party links were of great importance; outside those fringe parties, glanced at already, whose members looked on nazism with favour.

A separate point about national feeling needs notice.

This great war, like others, acted as an accelerator: that is, it pushed on more rapidly historical processes that had already begun. In Africa and Asia, of which the affairs do not directly concern us here, there was a marked acceleration of the shift against colonialism – or against non-marxist colonialism at least. Burmese, Koreans, Ghanaians, Nigerians, Malays, and many other renascent nationalities began to feel separate and to desire independence of any outside political control. On the other hand, within Europe some thoughtful people began to reconsider the wisdom of the policies of entire national independence that most European states had pursued since 1848.

The governments in exile in London of Belgium, Luxembourg, and the Netherlands agreed in principle, during the war, on the Benelux customs union; of which some of the key principles were hammered out in the maquis of the Ardennes.[3] From this grew eventually the European Economic Community; with all that implies for the future of the continent and the world.

A powerful personality at work behind the scenes, who strove towards the

---

[1] (Sir) Julian Huxley and A. C. Haddon, *We Europeans* (1935), is a particularly lucid and compelling exposure of the nazi racial myth.
[2] The French case was for several reasons peculiarly complicated: see pp. 235–9 below.
[3] *BFSP* clii. 166; and conversation with Baron Snoy et d'Oppuers, 1973.

ideal of some sort of democratic organization in Europe that would transcend national boundaries, was Gladwyn Jebb. He had been seconded from the diplomatic service to SOE, ostensibly 'to keep an eye on the wild Dalton', the first minister in charge of it;[1] but that was only cover. His was one of the main directing characters in the earliest and in some ways the most formative months of SOE's development, when that body was working out the main guidelines along which it hoped resistance would develop in turn. He always had in the back of his mind an idea of a great European politico-economic body, including Great Britain, France, and a Germany purged of nazism as three of its main working parts, that would bring all the benefits of Hitler's 'new order' without any of the dictatorial disadvantages.[2] So did George Taylor, the widely travelled and knowledgeable business man who was in effect Jebb's chief of staff, and worked with him closely.

Part of resistance's importance lay in this: that it unsettled people's thinking from the set ruts of ordinary long-established life, and made them more ready to entertain new ideas; of which, the idea of membership in some sort of supranational organization was not the least important.

## Conservatism

Let us next consider the non-fascist parties of the right: the supporters of established order, rights of landlords, rights of property, a settled system of society in which everybody knows his place, and nothing changes fast or often.

There was a lot in nazism to offend people of this kind, for nazism's adherents constantly proclaimed it to be a revolutionary doctrine; and wherever they went – except in Denmark in the early stages of occupation – they seemed positively to delight in turning everything topsy-turvy. As most parents know, there is a very tough conservative vein in most children, and a firm dislike of anything new or original is carried through from childhood by a sizeable proportion of adult mankind. Such people were liable to be outraged by the manners of nazi overlords, and by the matter of some of their decrees; sometimes they were so outraged that they would overcome their own distrust of novelty enough to contemplate resistance, or even to engage in it. This was more likely to happen in the country, or in small towns, than in large ones; and more likely to happen in areas with a turbulent recent past – Galicia, Macedonia, Montenegro, for instance – than in ones that had not often lately been fought over, such as Norway or the Bordelais (two areas by the by in which resistance was exceptionally active; but for different reasons).

There was not much in the way of political organization for this staid, conventionalist, right-wing feeling that could easily connect with resistance. Indeed all over Europe parties of the right, if not helping to run dictatorships, were in

[1] Foot, 17.
[2] Conversations with him, 1967 and 1973; and see his *The European Idea* (1966, 1967).

the early 1940s distinctly under a cloud; except in Great Britain. Even there, some members of the one party that unashamedly called itself conservative quite often preferred to cloak their political views in the label of unionist – a label that dated back to the political earthquake of the mid-1880s, when their liberal opponents had sought to grant to Ireland part of the independent status the Irish seized for themselves in 1920–22. Other conservatives preferred the label national, which dated from the more recent panic election of 1931. Whatever their name – let us call them tories for short, as their opponents did and do – the parliamentary members of this party had secured in the general election of 1935 a majority of all the votes cast in the country: the latest occasion[1] on which this has happened. The eccentricities of the British electoral system brought with this majority of votes a majority of some 240 seats in the house of commons, the controlling house of parliament; larger, again, than any party has enjoyed since.

This parliament perpetuated itself, beyond its statutory five-year term, in yearly bounds, for almost five years more; as everyone thought a general election impracticable during a war against a European neighbour. At the end of the war in Europe, the general election of July 1945 gave the tories' main opponents, the labour party, much the largest majority they have ever had – over 200 seats; and replaced the great war leader Churchill by the meticulous Attlee. This result gives a fair indication of how far British opinion had shifted against conservatism, as a suitable line of policy for a peacetime government, during the previous ten years.

Continental conservative parties were less openly named. For instance, the extreme right of the French third republic's chamber of deputies was occupied by a party that called itself the democratic republican union; it foundered in 1940. In the Netherlands, the extreme non-nazi right was guarded by a party popularly known as the liberals, formally entitled the people's party for freedom and democracy.

In the 1930s, social democrats had run Scandinavia quietly; popular front governments had, with a good deal of disturbance, failed to run Spain or France; in the Spanish case precipitating a civil war, and in the French, a mild rightward reversion. In several countries, parliamentary government was no more than a pretence: Poland, Turkey, Portugal, Romania, Spain, Greece were all under virtual or proclaimed dictatorships by 1939, as well as the directly fascist dictatorships of Italy and Germany. None of these governments of the right had been able or willing to prevent the war.

During the war, as we shall shortly see, there were strong leftward swings in most resisting countries and movements; but there were countercurrents as well. A not very large, but quite influential body of people inclined to say 'I told you so'; and to maintain that what Kipling called the Gods of the Copybook Headings[2] had been quite right. Part of Churchill's greatness lay in the fact that he never, never once during the war, said 'I told you so'; lesser men were less

---

[1] Writing in July 1976.    [2] *Rudyard Kipling's Verse*, definitive edition (1940), 793.

bound in honour and politics to silence. Simple concepts of duty to one's country, traditions of upright behaviour, respect for decency, came to mean more under nazi occupation than under whatever régime had preceded it, even if that régime had been mean or feeble or obscurantist: as in some countries it had.

The concept of Christian duty had its part to play as well. This is not the place to do more than glance at the thorny, often debated problem of the church's role in the struggle against Hitler and Hitlerism; but one or two things do need to be said.

The Roman catholic church was one of the few bodies of such world stature that it could deal with nazi Germany from an equal, or even a superior stand. Though the Vatican's ambassadors were always too tactful to rub in the fact that their organization had nineteen hundred years' start over Hitler's, they could never forget that brute figure, which few nazis could bear to remember. Time runs slowly for an institution so old, and so august; this in fact was among the catholics' handicaps in dealing with an immediate crisis, such as war and resistance often presented.

By the late 1930s, the outspoken menace of communism to all Christian thoughts and attitudes was clear, and the troubles in Spain helped to enlist the church's interest and activity in the anti-communist camp. But the cardinal secretary of state, Pacelli, who became pope as Pius XII in March 1939, knew Germany well – he had worked there for twelve years – and disliked nazism much. He had much to do with the anti-nazi papal encyclical, *Mit brennender Sorge* – 'with burning sorrow' – issued in 1937; but he would not go so far as to encourage Germans in civil or military disobedience to their state machine, when that state was fighting for its life. No doubt he might have done more to save Jews in Germany; no doubt, again, at the risk of frightful reprisals against some German catholics, a risk he did not choose to run. In Italy, he does seem to have exercised direct influence towards the protection of Italian Jewry.

Italian political interests predominated with him, no doubt, in the last year of the war, when communist influence in Lombardy grew great; but again, the intricate relations between the PCI and the Vatican deserve a separate monograph, rather than analysis here. Only one other comment needs to be made now on Pius XII: it is, that his twelve years as a nuncio in Munich and Berlin may have made too much of a diplomat of him to fit him altogether to stand up to the barbarities of a Himmler.

Within Italy, his views on church and political affairs normally carried decisive weight. Outside it, they were propagated through a church establishment of very long standing; most of the senior members of which were devoted to whatever political order was established round them. There were a few highly distinguished exceptions; but the catholic prelacy, on the whole, was cool towards resistance.

As we have seen already, the opposite was true of the country priests;[1] though

1 See p. 40 above.

the abbé who sat in the porch of a church in Picardy with a loaded sten gun hidden in the folds of his soutane, while one of SOE's wireless operators worked his set in the vestry, went rather farther than most of his colleagues.[1]

## Liberalism and rationalism

The word 'liberal', in an international context, is a source of ambiguities and confusions, for it means quite different things in different countries. For a Dutchman, as we saw just now, it carries overtones of order, regularity, keeping things as they have always been. For an Englishman on the contrary, if we may accept John Stuart Mill's definition, 'A Liberal is he who looks forward for his principles of government; a Tory looks backward.'[2] For us the word carries overtones of freedom, political and commercial: free speech, free choice, free access, free trade; shading off sometimes into a confusion between liberty and license. For a Spaniard, from whose language the word in its political application comes, it carries overtones of anti-clericalism as well as constitutionalism; as it does for a Belgian. For a Frenchman, similar but even stronger overtones are almost revolutionary in their intensity.

There is nothing anti-clerical at all about an English liberal; Gladstone, the greatest leader of its liberal party that the Westminster parliament has ever seen, was also an exceptionally devout high anglican, who only went into politics because his father would not let him be a priest. Equally there is nothing anti-clerical about an English freemason. Freemasonry in Britain seems to have become an intensely respectable, moneyed, conformist movement, with strong links with the city, and royal dukes among its most eminent members. Continental freemasronry has been, like continental liberalism, at times passionately anti-clerical, and has had close links with revolutionary secret societies, in Italy especially.

What part, if any, freemasonry played in resistance remains unknown, to this writer at least; and would be worth research, if one could get at the evidence. There certainly were some masons, or former masons (once a mason, surely always a mason), in quite senior positions in the resistance struggle; but their craft security remains excellent, impenetrable to the unqualified historian. It is much to be hoped that someone better placed will one day square the record up.

In nazi Germany masonic lodges were specifically forbidden, outlawed under the single-party laws of the spring of 1933. In Vichy France also they were declared illegal, like all other secret societies, by a law of 13 August 1940, passed to curry favour with the Germans. Over a thousand schoolmasters were dismissed in consequence.[3]

Schoolmasters provide in many countries the channel through which rational and liberal ideas – using 'liberal' now in its old, broad, general, apolitical sense –

[1] SOE file.
[2] *Morning Star*, 6 July 1865, *selon* OED.
[3] R. O. Paxton, *Vichy France*, 172–3, 156.

get spread through a nation.[1] A really good teacher, at any level, shakes a pupil's mind as a really good housewife shakes a rug; knocks all the cant out of it; and encourages the pupil to think for him- or herself.

Occupation could sometimes prove as good as the best of teachers, for shaking up people's ideas. One of the main services the nazis provided, wholly unintentionally, for Europe was that they forced millions of people to try to think through again the foundations on which their society rested. Everybody had to wonder, during the dislocations of war, whether granny's ideas about the limited number of tasks women ought to perform were right. Many individual couples, separated by force of military circumstance – when the man was crippled, or reported missing believed killed, or simply disappeared – had to make agonizing choices about whether to be faithful to each other: it was 'the time of the great separation when there were no more families and no more homes, when men and women worked for the most part a long way away from each other and only occasionally met to kiss goodbye. Living away from people that you like is not very satisfactory. . . It gives men a measure, nevertheless, of the things that they want in the world.'[2]

On a more mundane, economic, plane, factory managers and factory workers had to revise many of their long-held views about what sort of work could be handled by what sort of labour. Prewar rules against dilution of skilled workers by unskilled, or of men by women, rapidly went by the board; and the advantages of free trade were seldom so clearly seen as when all trade was controlled.

Over-control brought thoughts of freedom, and its advantages; just as over-exposure to propaganda made people more suspicious of fraud. There was an enormous fund of political and moral goodwill – will towards good, that is; but it was unharnessed, and probably unharnessable, to any immediate military or political end or to any organized party.

## Socialism

The second, socialist international never really recovered from the catastrophe of 1914. The socialist parties of industrial Europe had agreed at their Amsterdam congress in 1908 that any threat of a general war was to be met by a general strike. When it came to the crunch, the accident of a mad assassin's bullet silenced the great voice of Jean Jaurès, and the working classes of Europe marched away joyfully to massacre each other. Every socialist party found a chauvinist reason for evading its Amsterdam pledge. A few of the bravest and most devoted –

[1] There is some evidence to suggest that, as part of a long-term process of softening up, communist agents have been infiltrated – most of them, without declaring their real sympathies – into the British educational system, where they are some of them now in positions of authority. Has it ever occurred to the politburo that sent them that this weapon may be a boomerang?

[2] John Mulgan – himself a New Zealander – *Report on Experience* (Oxford University Press 1947), 142.

a Karl Liebknecht, a Herbert Morrison – went to prison; the rest, if of military age, went to fight, or if too old manned the recruiting platforms. This gave a superb propaganda advantage to the third, communist international, which till Stalin told it to change its mind in 1935 devoted quite as much effort to denouncing social-democrats (as social-chauvinists, social-fascists, &c) as to denouncing capitalists.

Socialist remedies for the world depression that began in 1929 were hardly applied, except in the USA where everyone took care not to call them socialist. Through the 1930s the position of many social-democratic parties seemed to worsen, outside Scandinavia and New Zealand where they began to build successful welfare states. The Austrian socialists, for example, were crushed into silence by the successive repressions of Dollfuss in 1934 and Seyss-Inquart in 1938. The comintern's *volte face* in 1935 produced popular front governments, extending far enough 'left' to include both socialists and communists, in 1936 in Spain and in France. Spain promptly dissolved into civil war, and France though outwardly more secure was deeply divided within, by mistrust between citizens and classes.

The catastrophe of occupation drove most European socialist parties into temporary silence. The French party, the largest and strongest of them, which by calling itself the *Section Française de l'Internationale Ouvrière* reminded all its members that its aims were not merely national, split: an anti-fascist grouping behind its last prime minister Léon Blum, and an anti-war grouping behind Paul Faure the party chairman. Faure's followers, and the Danish socialists, were prepared to accept occupation as a fact of political life, and to work inside it. For other socialist parties, the socialist element in German national socialism was less evident than the national, and they were opposed in principle; likely indeed to resist in the end, if they found a chance.

Outside the formal, official ranks of active politicians and card-carrying party members, there was a lot of lively interest in socialism as a doctrine, particularly among intelligent young people. The dry, elegant persuasiveness of such writers as G. D. H. Cole, Stafford Cripps, Bernard Shaw, R. H. Tawney, Barbara Wootton, did not have any precise continental equivalent; but similar influences were being quietly exerted all over the industrial world, where the voice of reasoned debate could pierce the carapace of totalitarian systems, and wherever discussion was still free. The concept that profit-making, as well as profiteering, was not merely unnecessary but undesirable, even immoral, began to take hold. People who thought this, and people who admired Jaurès, were not likely to make placid subjects for Hitler.

## Communism

'It took a strong man', John Mulgan wrote, 'to enjoy the smile on Stalin's face, pictured shaking hands with Ribbentrop, and featured in every paper in the world.'[1] It would be absurd to shirk the pact concluded between Germany and the USSR on the night of 23/24 August 1939, signed in Stalin's presence by Ribbentrop and Molotov.[2] The pact set the communist parties of Europe formally on the nazis' side; the comintern, whose agents had up to the previous week been attacking the nazis, performed another somersault and acted in their previous enemies' support. It would be equally absurd to forget that within two years, on 22 June 1941, the comintern performed a back-somersault. For on that day 'Barbarossa', the German attack on the USSR, began; and Europe's communists were formally released from a stance few of them had found agreeable.[3]

Understandably, devout communists do not enjoy being reminded about the pact; and a lot of communist historians have been at pains to show how their comrades were active in resistance before 'Barbarossa' began. This, even their dourest opponents would be foolish not to concede; of course there were communists who could see beyond the end of their noses, and appreciate the dangers to world communism inherent in the nazi régime. Even the dourest communist might, if he conceded anything – which is impossible – admit that there were awkward passages meanwhile.

There was for instance the appalling incident on the bridge at Brest-Litovsk, on the demarcation line between German- and Russian-occupied Poland, when the Gestapo and the NKVD exchanged parties of refugees – people fleeing from one terror, who had taken refuge in the country of the other: not an exchange liable to encourage anyone who heard of it to change sides.[4] There were comparatively minor oddities as well, such as the agreement between the French communist party and the nazi propaganda services in Paris that L'Humanité should reappear on the news-stands; an arrangement frustrated by the Paris police, who remained resolutely anti-communist.[5]

None of these incidents, however macabre, can obscure the grand fact: the communists alone had foreseen the possibility of resistance war, and once engaged in it, did marvels. In some areas and at some times they exercised indeed a predominant influence on resistance. They were usually important; they were hardly ever all-important. Much propaganda effort has gone in the past thirty years into attempts to pooh-pooh non-communist resisters; which would be ludicrous. It would be quite as ludicrous to maintain that the communist impact on resistance was only slight.

[1] Report on Experience, 31
[2] Text, including secret clauses, in Nazi–Soviet Relations (Washington 1948), 76–8. And cp. p. 7 above.
[3] An anecdote from student politics may be allowed a footnote. It is said that the secretary of the Oxford University communist party happened to hear the BBC's eight o'clock news bulletin that Sunday morning; rang up party headquarters in King Street, Covent Garden, to inquire whether the party line had changed; and was asked to hold on, as the central committee was about to decide.
[4] Robert Conquest, The Great Terror (1971 ed.), 578–9.
[5] Histoire du Parti Communiste Français (1962), ii. 24–8.

Many leading communists had had prewar experience of clandestine life; many had fought in Spain; all were used to the basic practices of clandestinity, were ready to live under false names, were adept at using cover stories, had thought about where to find arms, knew some of the elementary rules about disguise, pursuit, and safety; were hardened liars, when party duty demanded it; and knew how to keep quiet. Their followers and hangers-on were many of them less fully trained, but were ready and willing to learn.

All or almost all were in those four years of Russo-German war – June 1941 to May 1945 – entirely devoted to Stalin, who at the time stood head and shoulders above every other living communist, and was treated as a co-equal with three of the movement's four principal characters: Marx, Engels, and Lenin. Trotsky was by this time in his Mexican grave, the object then as now of unlimited anathemas from stalinists;[1] and Stalin's intellectual inferiority to the other four only became clear after his own death in 1953. It was masked meanwhile behind the prestige of his office (this in a movement that formally disowns prestige) and by the brute fact that he had the power.

The theoretical training in marxism–leninism through which all dutiful comrades put themselves, if they missed the compulsory classes in it that were and are set features of life in the soviet armed forces, did provide useful backing for work in resistance, for marxists have long recognized clandestine war as an important channel through which the class struggle can be waged. Mao Tse-tung's elaborations on guerilla theory, which were being put into practice in China at the time, were unavailable in Europe during the war, and would in any case have been unwelcome in the stalinocentric system of the comintern; Mao and Stalin had not seen eye to eye since 1927.[2] Tito, who was putting them into practice simultaneously, seems to have arrived at similar conclusions by the light of his own experience.

At all events, 'Barbarossa' released onto the scene of resistance a large number of efficient underground leaders, some of whom brought off remarkable triumphs, which Chapter 6 will notice. Till 'Barbarossa', as Henri Bernard put it, 'the USSR had pretended not to be interested in resistance';[3] thenceforward every resistance movement that was not itself manifestly anti-communist had Moscow's moral support at least, and within the rapidly lost lands of the western USSR the partisan movement was taken in hand promptly.

There were three main difficulties, from the non-communist resister's point of view, about dealing with the communists in resistance. The first arose from the course of battle between the nazi and soviet armies: the Russians soon found themselves in a desperate, backs-to-the-wall military crisis, and subordinated everything else to the cause of national survival. This was understandable enough;

[1] At training schools for the NKVD's secret agents in the late 1940s, each morning began with a hate session directed against Trotsky, exactly like the hate sessions in Orwell's *1984*. (Conversation with a participant, 1952.)

[2] See B. I. Schwarz, *Chinese Communism and the Rise of Mao* (1952).

[3] *La Résistance 1940–1945*, 22, tr.

was what any other nation would do in a similar fix. But it did make them exceptionally unforthcoming, surly, and difficult to deal with.

Secondly, the state of development of their air force was not such as to enable them to engage in much long-range air supply. They hardly ever (so far as is known) tried to drop men or supplies more than a couple of hundred kilometres away from their own front line; their missions sent by air to Yugoslavia, for example, travelled from Allied bases in Italy and in Allied aircraft, borrowed by Russian pilots for the occasion.[1]

And thirdly – a legacy, this, from the wars of intervention of 1918–20 – they were intensely suspicious of the British and Americans; much more their co-belligerents than their allies; and were inclined to spot a capitalist plot in every parachuted haversack. A depressing side effect of this suspicion afflicted people in the field who had to have dealings with communists, even on quite trivial points. Communist security was so dense that communications were painfully slow; it usually took a month to get an answer to the simplest question. This was not because everything, no matter how trivial, was submitted to Moscow: Moscow was too busy, and communications were too sparse. It was because everything, trivial or tremendous, had to go before a committee; even Tito, whose nickname – it means 'Do this!' – indicates a readiness to take command, was much bound in by committees, dominant though his personal influence on them might be. Assembling a committee with full regard for the rules of clandestine security might take a week; passing the answer back might take longer, even if the committee made up its mind at once, which, in this atmosphere of perpetual suspicion, it would be unlikely to do.

Forcible communist commanders sometimes found themselves members of Jackie Fisher's ideal committee – no more than three members, and two of them unavoidably absent; but one had to be very sure of oneself to undertake the responsibility of a decision, for which one might well have to answer later with one's head if one decided wrong.

Looking back on this period in the growth and decline of world communism, it is easy through the binoculars of hindsight to see that it came straight after the *Yezhovshchina*, what Robert Conquest has named the Great Terror, and to suppose that much communist caution was induced by plain fright. Such a supposition would be quite wrong: whatever the communist wartime resistance leaders were, they were not cowards. In a desperately dangerous way of life, they were on the contrary among the bravest of the brave. The truth is that surprisingly little was known about the *Yezhovshchina* till long after it was over, outside the ranks of its victims. They it is true were numbered in millions; but they were all dead or in Siberia – the SOE proverb, 'Three can keep a secret if two of them are dead', is painfully in point. Beria covered Yezhov's tracks thoroughly; not foreseeing how exactly he was to follow them himself.

Similarly, the comintern's foreign supporters pursued steadily what they

[1] Cp. Kenneth Macksey, *The Partisans of Europe in World War II* (1975), 74–5.

believed to be the comintern's objectives; not knowing that, after the war, many of the leading survivors would be summoned to Siberia in their turn. They all kept their eyes steadily fixed on the importance of spreading communist power as widely as possible; in an era when there was only one communist power centre, the Kremlin.

Only the innocent will believe that during the hiatus between the dissolution of the comintern – an uncharacteristically graceful gesture by Stalin in 1943 – and the setting up of the cominform in 1947 there was no central direction of world communist effort.

### Terror and counter-terror

So far we have been considering communism rather as it appeared from the comparative immunity of south-eastern England in the 1930s and early 1940s;[1] in a minute we must look at the dark side of the moon. Terror did play a part in securing support for some resistance movements, especially those with communist backing in Greece, Poland, and elsewhere in eastern Europe; it was not unknown in the west, either. Indeed as a matter of propaganda routine, the occupying authorities habitually referred to 'terrorist attacks' when resistance against them became noticeably active. Those who disliked resisters, or some particular group of them, were ready enough to accuse them all of banditry, and to say outright, 'That's quite simple, if he is a terrorist we shoot him straight away';[2] though they did not always have the power to do so.

By and large, terror was more the nazis' weapon than it was the weapon of their enemies: their régime was founded on it, at home in Germany quite as much as abroad. It took and can take several forms, worth distinguishing from each other.

Mass terror we can put first. Under it the population of a whole province, a whole state, half a continent even, become convinced that they had all better do what the régime says, or else Worse will befall. Exactly what form Worse will take, is usually left half-expressed in rumour, rather than made explicit; but no one is left in doubt that it will be remarkably unpleasant. Such a system can work passably well if it is really thoroughly organized; the nazis with their watchmen scattered through the great towns buttoned up the German proletariat thoroughly. Every apartment building had its *Blockwart*, who made it his job to know and report who was doing what with whom, throughout the building in his care; who was well, who was ill, who was sleeping around, who failed to turn out for demonstrations.[3] A kind of approval for conformity can be generated quite fast, at the price of a few nonconformists who are beaten up in public and

[1] Cp. Mulgan, *Report on Experience*, 26–31.

[2] A phrase (tr.) used about the author, in his hearing, by a German intelligence officer, unaware that he spoke German; or, fortunately, that by the IO's definition he *was* a terrorist; in August 1944.

[3] Conversation with D. H. McLachlan, 1936.

hustled away to prison by party gangs. The system works better in towns than in the country; even in the country, a well-staged incident or two at a crowded market would have its effect.

Mass terror needs another support, besides the *Blockwart*: delation. Now free men regard delation as a vice, and rather a low one at that; but in a closed society it is often regarded as a civic virtue, and even taught as one in schools and youth movements. Children are expected to eavesdrop their parents' conversations, and to report to teacher anything that suggests their parents are not wholehearted in support of the party in power. Neighbours are expected to be unneighbourly enough to report unusual comings and goings next door, or across the street, or politically unsuitable conversation overheard through the party wall from the adjoining flat. In a country where delation has become an accepted social custom, the police's difficulty will lie rather in sifting denunciations than in seeking them out.[1] As one of Evelyn Waugh's characters puts it, 'Nowadays it is not what you do that counts, but who informs against you.'[2]

What happened to someone who was delated? He would probably be pulled in for questioning; and might well then become subject to another weapon in terror's arsenal, blackmail. Unless you cooperate with us, the police would put it, and inform us fully about everybody you know who feels as you do, we shall tell your wife about that incident with a blonde typist after last year's Christmas office party; or whatever other shabby little secret happened to be on file. (Most people over thirty have at least one shabby little secret; which may be less secret than they think.)

Blackmail, people in free countries generally agree, is the crime of crimes; which would the reader regard more kindly, the murderer of a blackmailer, or the blackmailer of a murderer? Your ordinary, decent man may, just may, have the strength to resist it, as he can resist propaganda. If he resists it, force follows.

> Men who are strong and unscrupulous have learned a new and formidable technique of government. Propaganda and newspapers are small things. The common sense of ordinary, decent men will break them down. I would back the shrewd sagacity of a Greek mountain peasant to smell out most falsehoods. But behind this lies the second element of hard, physical power which can break an individual because it is organized and has discipline and knows no moral limits and has only one objective, to take power and keep it.[3]

Most ordinary people will break after a very little force is applied to them: a few jumps on their bare toes, or a knee in the groin will do. The Gestapo often went much farther. There was a nasty man in the SD in Brittany called Bonner – I name him: Interpol looked long for him – who began by stripping his prisoners

---

[1] For some recent developments, see Dev Murarka in *New Statesman*, 3 January 1975, 10–11.

[2] *Scott-King's Modern Europe* (1947), 64–5.

[3] Mulgan, *Report on Experience*, 124; based on what he met in Greece in 1944.

naked, tying their wrists to their ankles behind their backs with barbed wire, and leaving them untended for a night and a day on a concrete floor; then he appeared, twitching a riding-crop, and started to ask questions. His colleagues elsewhere did not disdain the mediaeval thumbscrew, or the modern dentist's drill, or pliers for pulling out nails; was it one of them who invented the electric shock to the genitals, that has become a commonplace of over-sophisticated conduct since?

The general assumption, throughout resistance, was that no one is invulnerable to torture; therefore, if the nazis were known to have caught someone, all the secrets the prisoner had known were at risk. One was expected to do one's best to say nothing for two days; thus giving one's companions some chance to move, to hide, to change the colour of their hair and the nature of their cover story. The best guard against saying too much, surprisingly simple and surprisingly effective, was supposed to be counting to oneself under one's breath.[1] A few extremely brave people, though put under the sharpest duress, never spoke at all: Jean Moulin the most famous of them.[2] A compatriot of his deserves mention in the next breath, Raymond Basset ('Mary'). He was arrested in 1941 near the demarcation line in France, close to his own home in Burgundy; on evidence that he had been smuggling people across it. He was strapped into a dentist's chair, and had a perfectly sound tooth wrenched out of his jaw.

This completely prostrated him; 'had they started to question me at that instant,' he said many years later, 'there was nothing I would not have told them.' But they got excited; and pulled out all the rest of his teeth. By the time they had done with his mouth, he was so angry that he refused to talk at all; promptly escaped; and moved on to a much more vigorous and distinguished career in resistance.[3]

Torture, in fact, one could over-use; force short of torture, equally, could be carried too far, to the point where it created total revulsion against its users. But what political weight does revulsion carry, without power? We must quote John Mulgan again, generalizing from the troubles he watched in Greece:

> Ordinary society, and least of all a revolutionary army, have nothing that corresponds to a secret police, and no way of fighting it. Two men in every village who are prepared to kill can hold the village. One political adviser beside every officer keeps the army in order. If the men that belong to this small internal organization, this army within the army, are ruthless enough, and if their discipline is good enough, they can always win.[4]

The extremest case of the use of force, irrespective of what people would make of it abroad – if they ever heard what was going on – is to be found in what Max Beloff has described as the characteristic political institution of the

---

[1] Denis Rake, *Rake's Progress* (1968), 132.
[2] See Henri Michel, *Jean Moulin l'unificateur* (1964), ad fin.
[3] Conversation with him, 1969, and see Foot, 248–50.
[4] Mulgan, *Report on Experience*, 122.

twentieth century: the concentration camp. 'The best justification for the war and all its losses is that it destroyed the régime which let these camps exist' in Germany.[1]

On their horrors, proverbial already as about the most frightful things human beings have ever done to each other, there is no need to expatiate here. And even inside these infernos, resisters subjected to their discipline were not completely cowed. In Theresienstadt, towards the end, large crowds used to collect in the hour before lights out in one of the huts; where Rabbi Leo Baeck talked, never raising his own quiet voice; just talked, gently, for forty or fifty minutes on end, about Herodotus or Thucydides, about Aristotle or Plato, or recited (in his own German translation) choruses from Euripides or Aeschylus. He took care never to touch on current politics or nazi philosophy; he stayed firmly in the ancient world. He had managed to lose his identity; his captors by now thought he was somebody else. But to open his mouth at all was an act of resistance.[2] Again, there arrived in Buchenwald early in 1944 an English prisoner, Christopher Burney, who had just spent eighteen months in solitary confinement near Paris, because he would not reveal what work he had been parachuted into France to do for SOE. Instead of succumbing to Buchenwald's régime, he started on collecting friends who would one day help him to seize control of the camp; and survived.[3] And a Pole, Witold Pilecki, actually let himself be arrested in order that he might be sent to Auschwitz; where he set up a viable resistance circuit before he escaped to report what he had done.[4]

These are examples of how terror, like any other weapon, is liable to slip in the user's hand, and wound himself instead of his enemy. Resistance did in fact make use of terror, and counter-terror, as deliberate tools for breaking nazi morale and thus breaking the nazis' hold on occupied Europe.

For the soviet government, this was simply to carry on with an existing tradition. The CPSU descended, politically speaking, from those bands of late-nineteenth-century terrorists whose most distinguished victim had been Tsar Alexander II; Lenin's own elder brother had been executed for taking part in a plot against his successor. During the civil wars of 1918–20, Dzerzhinsky's secret police had played a part hardly, if at all, less important than Trotsky's Red Army in asserting the party's hold on power. During the fourth and least publicized Russian revolution, the imposition of collective farming on the peasantry – who had supported the Bolsheviks in the civil wars because that seemed the best way to get the land for themselves – the main work was done by the secret police: at a cost in lives still not accurately counted, but amounting to one million at least. Routine comintern underground organization in Germany in the 1920s and 1930s included terror squads besides the usual intelligence and security squads.[5]

---

[1] Foot, xxii.     [2] A. H. Friedlander, *Leo Baeck* (1973), 3–4.
[3] Christopher Burney, *The Dungeon Democracy* (1945), a most remarkable book.
[4] J. Garliński, *Fighting Auschwitz* (1975).     [5] D. J. Dallin, *Soviet Espionage*, 179–86.

Yezhov's great purge, with its millions of arrests, was hardly over when the Germans attacked Poland.

So terror was a probable accompaniment of partisan operations on the eastern front; it would not occur to Beria, the partisans' ultimate controller below Stalin, that there was any other sure way of getting people to do what he wanted. Terror was used in two directions: to terrorize what was left of the civilian population into supporting the partisan bands, with shelter, food, information, and (when questioned by the Germans) silence; and to terrorize the Germans' rear area troops into withdrawal directly, by making their existence as short and uncomfortable as possible at every opportunity of attacking them.

In the west and south of Europe also,

> There is no doubt that the French communist party, acting through its militant wing the FTP [and comparable parties and armies in several other countries], did a great deal of work towards sapping [German morale], through the assassination of individual German uniformed officers and men. Useful as this policy of terrorism was in making the Germans jumpy, it undoubtedly – indeed deliberately – attracted severe reprisals, usually wreaked on the neighbourhood where the killing had taken place and not on the men who had done the job. This did not worry the communists, who believed that they were thus 'precipitating a revolutionary situation', a jargon term carrying conviction to them alone. Many of SOE's sabotage coups were unnerving to German morale in a more sophisticated way, less prodigal of lives.[1]

Among SOE's *coups*, if the break in tone at this point is not too sharp, the reader should refer to Harry Rée's strictly practical, almost light-hearted account of how he was able to use a sort of laudable blackmail for resistance purposes: persuading a manufacturer to let him arrange for the discreet sabotage of an arms factory, lest it be attacked – with inevitably heavy damage and casualties – by the RAF.[2] This was a brilliant joint invention by Rée and Rheam; an excellent example of that principle of economy of effort, preached so insistently in every staff college and practised rather more rarely by great commanders; but discovered too late in the war for the widespread use it deserved. Other forms of terror were used instead: 'the air staffs were set on sending great coveys of Halifaxes and Lancasters nightly along that road to Calvary from which so many never returned',[3] and catastrophic damage to German housing resulted. Whether that catastrophe was either desirable or necessary – but these are questions to be taken up another time.[4]

A final example, a mild one even – if the phrase is not a contradiction in terms – of the use of terror in resistance comes from Amsterdam. A large Dutch clandestine newspaper there shared its presses with a legitimate journal called *Volk*, which

---

[1] Foot, 439.
[2] Rée in Hawes and White, *Resistance in Europe*, 43–5; and cp. Foot, 287–8, 506.
[3] Ibid. 438.                    [4] See pp. 313–4 below.

was frankly nazi. Surely, a courier bringing copy for the underground paper inquired, it was very dangerous printing there? Several nazis must know what was going on? 'Yes,' a secret compositor replied, 'we have five of them; and we have made it perfectly clear to them that if any of them talk, all five will have a nasty professional accident. You can lose an arm, or worse, in a moment in a busy press; and there is plenty of molten lead.' The underground paper printed up to 80,000 copies; no one talked.[1]

The trouble about terror is, it becomes habit-forming; like alcohol. People enjoy the effect, and need stronger and stronger doses. It is not, therefore, a method of political action likely to promote long-term social peace.

## Anarchism

Ever since Marx's quarrels with Bakunin in the 1860s and 1870s, marxists have been aware that there is a rival view of how life should be organized, which lies close to their own in the political spectrum, and appeals to much the same sort of people as those who lean towards their own creed: anarchism. Next to social democrats – that is, non-revolutionary socialists – anarchists have at times been the communists' worst enemies; on one or two occasions they have been (if we may borrow a phrase from American gangster-hunting) the bolsheviks' Public Enemy Number One. Such an occasion was the winter of 1920–21, when Trotsky broke Makhno's movement in the Ukraine; after which he could boast that 'At last the Soviet government, with an iron broom, has rid Russia of anarchism.'[2] Stalin was not above taking a leaf or two out of Trotsky's book when the chance offered. In 1936 the iron broom was taken out of the cupboard, dusted, and sent to Spain.

Spain was the one country where anarchism had any substantial popular following, after the black flag had been hauled down in the Ukraine and Mussolini's police, the OVRA, had made sure it was no longer raised in Italy. When Franco's rebellion against the popular front republican government began in July 1936, the anarchists did all they could to oppose it; in Catalonia and Andalusia especially, anarchist groups – necessarily informal – took over the running of many factories and villages, in the republican interest and in the interest of that wholly unbridled, free society in which every anarchist believes.

In the course of the next three years, they were crushed: ground to powder between the upper millstone of Franco's eventually victorious armies, and the lower millstone of Stalin's secret police. The war, that credulous leftists (such as the present writer in his teens) regarded as a struggle between rebellious evil and democratic good, was beneath that propaganda surface a still harder affair. The USSR, popularly believed to be the Spanish republic's principal external prop, was through its agents busy eating away two of the main internal props on

[1] Conversation with (Rector) H. Brugmans, the inquirer, 1974; and private information.
[2] James Joll, *The Anarchists* (1964), 191.

which the republic's strength rested: the largely trotskyist POUM, and the anarchists.[1] By the time the civil war was over, anarchism was for the time being unavailable as an effective anti-fascist force.

## The anti-politicals

One more sizeable body of resisters to nazism remains for mention: those who hated politics of all kinds. They took to resistance because they were sick and tired of politics and parties as institutions and of politicians of all kinds as men. So far as they could see, political events since about the turn of the century had been almost without exception at variance, often ruinously at variance, with every standard of decent upright and straightforward conduct that good men are brought up to follow.

Any sincere Christian, and any sincere rationalist, who considers the evidence for this must agree that there is a good deal in it. The strictly nationalist attitude taken, in both the latest world wars, by almost every religious body except the Society of Friends speaks eloquently to the point. These anti-politicals were not looking for any total and immediate reform of whatever system they lived under, but for its total and immediate abolition. They were not anarchists – not, at any rate, consciously so. Most of them were conventional men and women, yet pursuing a far from conventional, revolutionary aim.

They felt that mood of despair for the republic that in less cramped conditions would lead people to emigrate.[2] Unluckily, emigrating from a fascist dictatorship, always difficult, is in wartime next to impossible; so they stayed to fight.

What against, is clear enough; but what for? Unluckily, again, no one has yet come up with anything better than politics – with all the built-in faults of politics – as a way of running societies or states. Many of the leading people among these anti-politicals came from the old landed gentry; were descendants, that is, of the local ruling class of pre-industrial Europe. Not all of them had yet – have yet – been driven from their lands into rentiers' flats or poverty or exile. They were brought up to feel that, in any emergency, their place was at the head of their local people. A great many countrymen were ready to follow wherever they led: keepers, grooms, gardeners, butlers, families with strong traditions of service to the leading local family. Some atavistic feelings of needing-to-lead and needing-to-follow may have helped to form them into fighting groups and to maintain some cohesion among them.

Separate bodies of anti-politicals were sometimes to be found among the intelligentsia.[3]

In the end, they never had to prove what sort of *ancien* or *nouveau régime* they

---

[1] Hugh Thomas, *The Spanish Civil War*, 578–81, 626.
[2] Compare the mood that led over seven million British voters not to vote for either of the main political parties in February 1974.
[3] Example on p. 317.

wanted to establish or re-establish: the politicians were uniformly too nimble for them. All of them, without exception, either died – sometimes in tragic, even appalling ways; or took to politics themselves; or, when the war was done, gave the struggle up and went back to dig their gardens.

# 5 TECHNICALITIES

We cannot understand anything about resistance activity unless we know something about the methods of work and living that conditioned it, and about the composition of the secret service staffs who hoped (sometimes rather against hope) that they were directing it.

Anyone who thinks this chapter will tell him how to run a contemporary terrorist or resistance body, should think again. The nazi threat was an altogether peculiar one, and called out a series of unique ripostes, on a continental scale. Most of the methods used against it are now obsolescent or obsolete; many of the things a modern freedom-fighter/terrorist can do were not to be done in the 1940s, and some things could be done then that it would be a nonsense to attempt today. The pages that follow are meant to bring the subsequent narrative into sharper technical focus, and to remind later readers of how different things were then.

## Forged papers

This was one of the points at which you could tell the men from the boys: resisters who meant to do any serious clandestine work in any but the wildest areas, and in any but the dying stages of the occupying régime, had to have access to the products of a first-class forger. Here was yet another point where resistance work went against what any nice girl had learned in the nursery, or any nice boy at school; and here was the point at which contact with a professional secret service was all but indispensable. A few exceptionally gifted Poles, Belgians, Czechs might try to improvise; hundreds of prisoners-of-war tried to improvise as well, but their amateur efforts were seldom successful. The professional could do much better.

SOE included 'people who could produce, between a Friday and a Monday morning, a virtually indistinguishable copy of a document part printed and part written, first manufacturing and water-marking the paper to do it on and cutting the type to do it with'. Those same people 'got so good at forging French ration cards that a revised version was once put into circulation by the Vichy authorities and by SOE on the same day'.[1] By 1943 indeed the body boasted 'that there was nothing it could not counterfeit'.[2] And SOE was (rightly or wrongly) despised by MI6 as a comparatively amateur body, not up to MI6's exacting standards. Much economy of effort could have been secured, had MI6 been ready to co-operate with SOE, instead of compelling the newcomer to duplicate several of 6's servicing facilities; the tale of their long and bitter rivalry is not one over which we can linger. Certainly SOE made some early floaters. Two of its agents, professing not to know each other, happened to be dining at the same French hotel – at separate tables – in 1942, during a routine police check of identity cards; they were unable to explain why their cards, issued in different *départements*, were made out in the same handwriting.[3]

The difficulty lay in one of the minor, but unavoidable characteristics of the nazi régime – the wallet-full of papers one had to carry if one left one's own village, and might be asked by any police authority to produce for inspection. Inspection might be, often was, cursory; equally, it might be thorough. Police authorities were legion; Vichy France for instance had fifteen distinct ones. Every grown citizen had to carry, firstly, an identity card, stating name, parentage, date and place of birth, and marital state, in most countries incorporating a photograph, and in a few a thumbprint; secondly, if at work, a work permit, stating trade qualifications and place of employment; thirdly, a ration card; fourthly, a tobacco card (whether one smoked or not); fifthly, if near the coast or a frontier, a permit to be in the coastal or frontier zone; sixthly, if a man, de-mobilization papers, showing when and where and from what unit and on what conditions he had been discharged from armed service; seventhly, most men needed also to carry, after midsummer 1942, a medical certificate – signed by an identifiable doctor – to explain why the state of their health exempted them from immediate deportation for forced labour in Germany.

In Germany, German citizens had for a time to carry the birth certificates of all four of their grandparents, to demonstrate how purely aryan their descent was;[4] this was a refinement with which travelling escaped prisoners, or visiting resisters, hardly needed to bother, as their cover would usually in any case be that of a foreigner.

Moreover, if travelling – improbably enough – at the wheel of a car or lorry, one needed a driving licence, and an insurance certificate for the vehicle; and if travelling by train, one often had to have a seat reservation as well as a ticket for a particular journey.[5]

---

[1] Foot, 41, 94, citing the relevant SOE section history.
[2] David E. Walker, *The Modern Smuggler* (1960), 176.    [3] Foot, 197.
[4] *Ex inf.* an evader, three of whose grandparents were Jews, who was asked on a routine train control in south Germany in 1939 for the birth certificate of his mother's mother. She was indisputably aryan, so he passed through.
[5] Travel was more awkward still at the time in the Soviet Union: cp. A. Solzhenitsyn, *One Day in the Life of Ivan Denisovich* (Penguin 1973), 75.

We do not need to go through every item on this list in detail: the first, the identity card, raises problems enough. To start with, you need the correct official form: impossible for an amateur to forge, but conceivably available from a friend in a local government office. And you need the correct authenticating stamps and signatures; here an amateur who knows what to do with a recently hard-boiled egg (and can find the egg) has got a chance.[1] A more tricky problem is: whose identity will you take? At a severe identity control, not only is everyone's face compared with some care with her or his photograph (nostrils? ear lobes? eyebrows?), but some attempt may be made to verify anyone's date and place of birth. Hence the large proportion of people in resistance whose papers showed them to have been born in a place of which all the records had been destroyed; such as St Pierre in Martinique, which in 1902 suffered Pompeii's fate.

Records could of course be destroyed on purpose, by resisters, as well as by natural catastrophe. The Dutch are proud of the achievement of a resistance group which, with strong popular approval and support, burned all the registration cards for the province of Amsterdam, thus intending to stymie nazi attempts either to identify Jews, or to extract young Dutchmen to work in Germany; alas, the destruction was incomplete.

Another Dutch example may illustrate how thoroughly a resister, in this case someone working in a large escape line, could equip himself with papers for supply to those moving along it. According to Giskes, the senior *Abwehr* officer who unravelled SOE's work in Holland, he met in Brussels in the spring of 1944 a Dutchman named Christiaan Lindemans, known in the underground as 'King Kong'. Lindemans claimed to have been working in escape lines for four years, and offered Giskes cooperation in return for his own younger brother's release from chance arrest. Giskes accepted. Lindemans poured onto the table beside them 'A heap of papers, forms, documents, parcels, personal identity papers, a number of German official rubber stamps, facsimile signatures . . . the travel documents for the OT and Wehrmacht had Field Post numbers and signatures inserted, and lacked simply the name of the user.'[2] Lindemans in fact had got himself thoroughly organized, in a way that it would be absurd to call amateur: as the professional admiration of Giskes shows. The case was of course a special one – all cases are special; Lindemans might be called the Dutch Déricourt, and we do not need to judge him here. He was introduced at this point simply to show how far one man could get in the forged-paper business.

Large resistance circuits either made contact with some professional secret service whose forgers' work they could use, or founded a team of forgers of their own. It was not a trade one could pick up as fast as, say, ironing; those who had already spent half a lifetime at it far excelled the work of newcomers.

---

[1] Cp. J. M. Langley, *Fight Another Day*, 82–3.

[2] H. J. Giskes, *London Calling North Pole* (tr. anon.; Kimber 1953), 144. Photographs of both in Anne Laurens, *L'Affaire King Kong* (1969), 32–3. Neave does not mention this story.

This was where the Russians had an enormous advantage over all other powers. The USSR had been in the business of forgery ever since the foundation of the comintern in 1919, so the communists had twenty years' start on almost everybody else. Providing forged identity cards was child's play to an organization that was used to providing forged passports – and good forged passports too, from respectable bourgeois powers, not banana republics – for important agents at a few hours' notice. When the comintern set up an organization in a foreign country, it included a forgery section automatically, just as it included sections for intelligence, sabotage, security, propaganda, and terror. One of the forgery section's first tasks was to supply itself with ample quantities of the usual forms – driving licence, employment card, identity card, &c – in common use in the country concerned, and with any stamps or other special addenda required; if need be, the sabotage section could steal some. By 1941, skilled forgers in all the countries the Germans occupied were already available, equipped, alert, ready to work in the communist interest.

The successes gained by communists in resistance work, many of them started from this simple point. They were much less hemmed in by nazi restrictions and controls on movement than were the local amateurs, or even envoys from rival secret services whose forgery departments were less accomplished than the comintern's. Indeed it may be that much of the communists' high reputation for skill and achievement in resistance derives from this simple, technical point.

They had taken the trouble to think ahead; they believed Camberley's advice, always plan for your worst case; and they reaped a reward.

## Communications

Everyone is now familiar with the marxist tenet that the ownership of the means of production determines the shape of society. As this century's reshapings of society have developed, a fresh focus has emerged. Ownership of the means of communication often matters still more. Certainly in the early 1940s it determined success or failure in the clandestine war; as in many other aspects of life. Here is a point at which directing brains can affect society, channel the shapes and the aims of other people's thoughts, to an unusual degree.

As 'one of the most iniquitous of the Gestapo's Paris staff', a Frenchman, put it, 'my object was always to break up the liaisons, even more than arresting the chaps; what could they do without communications?'[1] Indeed the best informed of spies could do nothing with their material, however extensive, however urgent it was, unless they could communicate; a secret army *in posse* could not be got onto the essential battlefield unless it could be mobilized; escape lines that ran without sure communications, soon ran into danger. The logistic problem of

[1] Foot, 60, quoting 'Masuy' from 'Rémy', *Une affaire de trahison* (Monte Carlo 1947), 45, tr. For photographs of 'Masuy', see Gustave Bertrand – his involuntary guest – *Enigma* (1973), plates 49–50.

arming secret forces was largely one of communications: how were the arms to be sent and received? Quite apart from the question we looked at earlier, how were they to be stored?[1] An immense effort of detail, by a few devoted people, was needed to organize any delivery of arms: a point overlooked often enough by people who write of parachute drops as if they simply happened, like showers of rain.

The whole nazi system hinged on control: controlling what people thought, what they did, where they went. Resisters were out to break that control; particularly, control on freedom of movement. In this battle for freedom, free communication was of prime importance.

### Messenger

Messengers, the oldest form of communication between people out of sight and sound of each other, have been useful from palaeolithic times to the present, and without them day-to-day work against nazism would have been impossible for many resisters. Lateral communication between resistance networks was severely frowned on by all the professionals; the communists even maintained that 'There should be no horizontal communications of any kind.'[2] But not all resisters were professionals. Transmitting messages by word of mouth is notoriously fallible;[3] so prudent people put them into writing, unless they were extremely simple – as simple as 'be there at midnight tonight'. If written, they were dangerous to carry, because they could not be explained away; unless they were camouflaged.

The nearest to a safe way of carrying a dangerous message was to have it written (or write it) on cigarette paper; wrap the paper round a needle; and insert it into a cigarette. A perfectibilitarian smoked a few puffs of the cigarette, stubbed it out, and carried the stub in his hand, ready to drop in the gutter in case of alarm.[4]

A message could be camouflaged by writing it in secret ink; or by encoding it; or both. Most trained agents knew about secret inks; so did most good security officers. At a careful control, a policeman would sit at a table with a couple of pots of secret-ink-developer and a brush, and would brush saltire-wise across any piece of suspicious paper: woe betide the carrier if the secret ink showed up, as it probably would, because she was carrying something she could hardly explain away (she, or he; most secret messengers were women). Such crosses on wartime letters that travelled between different countries will one day puzzle archivists; they were part of the everyday security routines of war. Failing a bottle of developer, a magnifying glass would probably reveal the supposedly invisible penstrokes. Secret inks, in fact, can hardly have been worth the trouble expended on them.[5]

---

[1] p. 56 above.  [2] Spring 1941; quoted in Foot, 111.
[3] See Marc Bloch, *Apologie pour l'histoire* (1948), 19.
[4] Foot, 112–13.  [5] Some formulae in Lorain, 70.

An alternative to secret ink lay in writing an apparently innocent letter, with the message concealed in it. This called for care and prearrangement, but could work; prearrange, for example, that from the third sentence of a letter, the second letter of every third word is to be extracted, and quite a lot can be conveyed; if the writer has the time, the ingenuity, and the imagination needed for the task of composition.[1]

Private codes were another matter. A simple arrangement by which, when one said sheep, one meant tanks might be quite effective; one might run out of suitable domestic animals quite soon, and an excuse to cover (say) kinds of bird might take quite some inventing. A good private code was virtually unbreakable, but good ones were rare.

Ciphers – more elaborate codes – were another matter still: again, something that if discovered could not be explained away; but at least a ciphered message was likely, even if intercepted, to impose some delay on the enemy's understanding of what was happening. A shortish message, only four or five lines long, in even a simple code such as Playfair might be unbreakable, or at least unbreakable quickly, if it was the sole example the other side was able to see. More of ciphers in a minute, in a context where larger fragments were liable to be read by the wrong side.[2]

How was the messenger to know whom to meet? Once again, the advantage of operating among old friends, and excluding every kind of stranger, was clear; old friends would know each other. 'Within circuits, it was seldom necessary to make arrangements that were at all elaborate for contact between members who did not know each other. "Look out for a dark man with curly hair and tell him you come from Pierre" was the sort of plain instruction that would usually do; agents had little but common sense to guard them against German penetration in this perfectly simple way.'[3] Only too often, newcomers to resistance circuits stood out like sore thumbs from the ordinary people round them; never having been trained, either as actors or as agents, they were visibly apprehensive, fidgeted incessantly, or stood far too long and far too conspicuously immobile.[4] They had not taken in the supremely valuable lesson for an agent, that he must absorb himself totally in his cover personality, must *be* it, so that he sinks unobtrusively into the background of day-to-day life and never catches anybody's eye unless he wants to.

SOE's agents were trained in various simple spies' tricks for recognizing each other. There were a whole series of drills about passwords and catchwords, for which people could learn to look out. They do not seem to have been much more elaborate than what Kipling told us Kim learned, at the knee of Lurgan Sahib and Mahbub Ali; writing ten years before the modern official secrets act could have silenced him. Each of SOE's large circuits, in France at least, had a circuit password, a ritual exchange of anodyne phrases – 'I come from – er – Celestín'.

---

[1] Elaborate example ibid. 70–2.  
[2] See pp. 108–12 below.  
[3] Foot, 113.  
[4] Cp. ibid. 254.

'Oh yes, the – er – wine merchant'[1] – by which people could establish their bona fides.

In this as in any other walk of life, people could find themselves, under sudden pressures from stronger-willed colleagues or acquaintances, succumbing to courses of action against their better judgement. And it was not a task either for elderly or for stupid people; one needed to have all one's wits awake.

There is a pathetic story of a very senior French officer, quite new to clandestine life, who had to pass through Paris – staying overnight at a safe house – on his way to a new secret command. He remembered the address of the safe house; rang the bell; but found himself, when a delightful girl answered the door, quite unable to remember the password. She could not let him in without it; after a few minutes' embarrassed and inconsequential talk, he raised his hat and walked away to an hotel. There he absent-mindedly registered in his own real name; and was arrested early next day. He was taken to Germany, and did not return.

One obvious means of correspondence has been left unmentioned: the various services provided by the post office. There were some exceptionally efficient resistance networks which operated inside the post office machine; following unaware in the footsteps of Michael Collins, who founded his extraordinary intelligence career on what he had observed as a boy clerk in the General Post Office in central London.[2] For the most interesting of them, the French source called K, no milder adjective than brilliant is adequate;[3] there were others as well.

Yet for the bulk of resisters, post, telegraph and telephone were alike taboo; as government organs, they were far too liable to nazi interception. Escape lines had to make it a rule that 'Members were warned never to call on any safe house, without first checking the security of the house by telephone'; a simple inversion covered this inquiry, 'if the coast was clear, the safe-house-keeper said it would not be convenient to be called on, and the phrase "By all means do come," meant "The Germans are here" '.[4] Otherwise, people used the telephone as little as they could, and always in code; telegrams not at all; and post, never unless they had to. Wartime posts were notoriously slow, and certain to be censored; just as all telephone calls were liable to be intercepted.

One English agent, escaping to Switzerland after a particularly harrowing spell in occupied territory, sent – without telling anybody that he was going to do so – a postcard to his own wife at his own English home; it was unsigned, and simply read 'Skiing here marvellous'. She knew the handwriting; the Germans did not.[5]

---

[1] Ibid., 503 tr.; and the example ibid. 306–7, a ludicrous amateurs' muddle.
[2] Foot, *War and Society*, 62.
[3] p. 243 below.
[4] Foot, 97.
[5] Private information.

## Wireless[1]

Two kinds of object dominated the relations between resisters in occupied countries, and their friends outside: parachutes, with which we deal later in this chapter,[2] and clandestine wireless transmitters. 'Without these links,' as Gubbins of SOE said of wirelesses, 'we would have been groping in the dark.'[3] Nowadays they are always called radios, and the word 'radio' was replacing the word 'wireless' in English, imported from American, even during the war; wireless operators were quite often called radio operators, *radios* for short in French. The older term will be used here; both because it was the formally correct one, and to help to mark the difference between those times and these.

The exact methods used for the purpose of clandestine transmissions fall into rather an odd category of secret. It is one of those subjects that is hardly ever discussed in public; but is yet one on which a country's enemies are likely to be almost as fully informed as its own practitioners. Nothing at all, so far as I know, has ever been published about the technical side of the NKVD's wireless equipment; one of the many silences in 'Alexander Foote's' book covers such points as wavelengths used and transmitter design. SIS's and MI9's and even OSS's sets are equally supposed to be unknown. But much the same guiding principles of physics and geography must have affected them, as affected SOE; and about SOE's sets it happens that we know quite a lot – including the fact that the earliest ones it used were provided by SIS. SIS is unlikely to have given SOE anything better than it had for its own operators, but there is no reason to believe that it tried to fob SOE off with grossly inferior sets.

What were these physical limiting conditions?

Long- and medium-wave broadcasting then required far more cumbrously large aerials than any clandestine agent could hope to carry about with him, or safely deploy. Very short and ultra-short-wave broadcasts cannot be received over great distances. But one group of wavelengths (frequencies) can: short waves, oscillating at a rate of 1·5 to 30 megacycles a second. These waves bounce back off the ionosphere, bounce again off the earth, bounce off the ionosphere again, and so continue round the planet; so that a short-wave transmitter using only ten watts of power – and a bright reading-light uses 100 – could transmit without trouble from Buenos Aires to London, or Sydney to Singapore. This phenomenon, known as skip, was what made the clandestine wireless war possible.

There were some geographical limits, besides those imposed by skip, on how and where people could conveniently operate. Mountains might interfere with transmission; some types of soil were more favourable as transmitting bases than others. The immediate neighbourhood of a power station, or an ordinary commercial transmitter, or a *Wehrmacht* wireless station, were also to be avoided.

[1] This section relies heavily on Pierre Lorain, *Armement Clandestin*, 12–49, 90–5 and 161–72, to which the reader is strongly recommended for illustrations and technical details.

[2] At pp. 119–26.

[3] Quoted from Foot, 102.

Some types of building were less absorbent of wireless waves than others. What to seek, and what to avoid, were dinned into operators during training. By 1944, they had every detail of their equipment worked out for them, and were under stringent orders not, on any account, to be bullied by their companions into moving out of their designated work area; because if they did, their sets might not be able to reach the home station that listened out for them.

SOE had four of these home stations – at Grendon Underwood, and at Poundon, both on the Oxfordshire–Buckinghamshire border; at Bicester, from April to November 1944 only; and at Dunbar.[1] They were staffed for the most part by girls in their late teens; intelligent young women, good both at cipher work and at operating wirelesses and teleprinters.

Very short range, very high frequency radio-telephony was developed in the 1930s, and was incessantly used during the air fighting of 1940; ground to air, air to ground, and air to air. No one who heard them or took part in them will every quite forget the rhythm, tension, drama of these exchanges; but for secret war they were ill fitted. They were far too public, too easy to overhear; and their range was so short that they might well endanger the aircraft that went to collect the message, as well as the agent who sent it. Joseph Kessel nevertheless relates[2] that he was a pilot in one of the special duty flights, which carried on voiced conversations with agents who could get within fifty miles or so of Dover. This was a good but dangerous method of getting information quickly, during the drive to find out about 'ski-sites' – sites for launching V1 pilotless rockets – in the winter of 1943–4. One of its dangers was discovered, to his considerable astonishment, by an agent who had been briefed that he would be working on a wavelength quite unknown to the Germans, and therefore impossible to inter-cept. He was arrested at the end of his first conversation, on the outskirts of Calais; where he had been using the precise frequency of the local tank regiment.[3]

Interception was, technically, only too easy; by a process, cumbrously enough named radiogoniometry, that any intelligent signals unit could work. Early in the war, the Germans worked the process clumsily, but by the spring of 1943 they had main intercepting stations in Augsburg, Berlin, Brest, Nuremberg, and no doubt elsewhere, in which a twenty-four-hour scan of the whole short-wave band was maintained. Once a transmission was spotted, a few seconds only were needed for cross-bearings to be taken; a telephone call thereupon sent Gestapo wireless vans to the three corners of a triangle that might have fifteen-kilometre sides. If the transmission was still going on when they got there, they could narrow the triangle to something under two kilometres at once; and within half an hour from starting, should be at the building concerned.[4]

There were several counters to this. One was to change the frequency of the transmission at brief intervals. The operator could do this easily enough, pulling out a plug in his set that contained his crystal – a piece of laminated quartz, about

[1] Lorain, 9, 70.    [2] *Images Reportages Aventures* (1969), 131–4.
[3] Private information.    [4] Details in Lorain, 13–14, 24–9.

the size of a thumb-nail, cut to very precise dimensions, which determined the frequency he sent on – and putting in another plug, bearing another crystal. A good operator, working from a good site with a set in perfect condition, could effect this change in a matter of moments; the girl at home station receiving him, if forewarned, simply picked up the earphones of another receiver, already tuned to the new frequency. The Germans met this counter, quite effectively, by instituting a continuous sweep by cathode ray tube over the whole short-wave band, so that they could pick up any new transmission at once and carry on with their interception.

Another counter, which puzzled the Germans for a little while, was to drop any attempt at exchange of messages between agent and home station. The agent simply broadcast his message into the blue, and waited only a few seconds for home station to reply, in a single code letter, which indicated whether he had been heard well or badly. If badly, there was a set time for him to repeat; later, and probably on another frequency. By 1944 all clandestine traffic on SOE's sets passed from occupied Europe by day, and to it by night; home station broadcasting with transmitters so powerful, at 250 watts, that they were likely to crash through any jamming; a 15-kilowatt transmitter was in reserve for severe cases.[1] This called for exceptionally strict discipline on the clandestine operator's part; he had to live by the clock, and so regulate his life that he could be at his set for a few essential minutes several times each day and night.[2]

The Germans got the hang of this system also before long. This threw clandestines back onto their most important safeguard: short messages, or at least short transmission times. The high-speed transmitter, familiar to readers of the modern spy trial, was devised by a Dane working with SOE in Denmark, a real expert; but was unavailable outside Denmark, and in any case was not invented in time to play any large part in the operations we have to consider.[3]

Nor was the miniature transmitter, that finally resolved one of the great troubles that beset early wireless operators, how to transport their sets without trouble. It is worth setting out a few details of these sets in tabular form.[4] (See facing page.)

Of these the B2 was from SOE's point of view much the commonest. A sharp-eyed passer-by at Marylebone station was able to pick out dozens of SOE's wireless operators in training, because they all took identical suitcases home with them on weekend leave from the training school at Thame Park.[5]

---

[1] Lorain, 168, with wiring diagram of one of SOE's base stations.

[2] Specimen timetables in T. Revesz-Long, *Combat des Ondes* (Lyon 1975), 43–4.

[3] See p. 276 below.

[4] There is a photograph of a B2 in J. D. Drummond, *But for These men* (1962), at 112. For comparison, see the German sets dropped into England shown in E. H. Cookridge, *Secrets of the British Secret Service* (1947), at 89, 120, and the larger one used from Prague to Moscow in J. Doležal and J. Křen, *La Tchécoslovaquie en Lutte* (Prague 1961), pl. 8.

[5] Conversation with her, 1961. This story was directly denied by an early Thame Park pupil, to whom it was repeated in 1975; he had not been allowed to take his set out of the grounds, except on exercises. No doubt the rules were changed.

**Table 1** SOME CLANDESTINE WIRELESS SETS 1938–45[1]

| Name | Date | Maker | Size mm | Total weight kg | Power watts | Valves send and receive | Frequency mc/s | Notes |
|---|---|---|---|---|---|---|---|---|
| Mark XV | 1938? | SIS | 132 × 72 × ? | 20 | 15–20 | 2+3 | 3·5–13 | In three packages. One set in Paris army museum |
| Paraset | 1939? | SIS | 220 × 140 × 111 | 18 | 4–5 | 1+2 | 3·3–7·6 | Silent key |
| AP4 | 1941? | Poles in exile | 280 × 210 × 95 | 4 | 8 | 2+3 | 2–8 | |
| BP3 | 1943 | Poles in exile | 280 × 210 × 95 | 10 | 30 | 2+4 | 2–8 | |
| A Mark II | Oct. 1942 | SOE | 225 × 300 × 80 | 9 | 5 | 1+3 | 3–9 | One set in Paris museum of liberation |
| B2 | 1943 | SOE | 241 × 272 × 123 | 14–18 | 20 | 2+4 | 3–15·5 | In a single suitcase. One in Imperial War Museum |
| A Mark IV | 1944? | SOE | 235 × 290 × 80 | 4 | 5 | 2+4 | 3–9 | |
| 51/1 | 1945 | SOE? | 146 × 120 × 38 | ·565 | 3–4 | 3+2 | 3–10·5 | Pocket size |

A thoroughly competent operator, wireless mechanic enough to maintain his own sets, clandestine enough not to draw unavoidable attention to himself, genial enough to have several friends ready to hide transmitters[2] for him, should have been safe enough, and several – Floiras, Chapman, Yvonne Cormeau, to take three examples from a single section, one of SOE's six that worked into France – were able to transmit without difficulty for many months on end. Madame Cormeau indeed broke rule one in the operators' training book with impunity, and worked from the same spot for over six months. The Germans knew there was a secret transmitter somewhere in the Pyrenean foothills where she lived, and heard from a source they trusted that it was worked by a British officer; so never visited her village, because it did not have the piped water supply on which they assumed a British officer would insist. She did not even need a

[1] Condensed from Lorain, 32–49.
[2] Strictly, these sets should be called transceivers: all those shown in table 1 could both transmit and receive.

protection squad, for she could overlook from her working table several kilometres of the only approach road.[1] Protection squads were normal in more
crowded places. They watched out for Gestapo vehicles, and for fat men who
seemed to keep their eyes on their wrist-watches; these men might be watching
a wrist indicator, powered by a detector hidden under their coats, which would
tell them whether they were approaching or receding from the transmitter they
sought.[2] A sensible operator practised hiding his (or her) set and vanishing
quickly; not always easy, if a sensible policeman had cordoned off the area
before closing in for the kill.

Unhappily for some agents, quick-witted members of the German secret
service soon learned to be as sharp-eyed as the girl who lived in Marylebone,
and transporting sets – B2s especially – became more dangerous than ever.
There is a tale worth repeating of the operator who reached a big terminus by
train, carrying only his B2 in its little case; saw a boy of about twelve struggling
with a big one; and said genially (in the local language) 'Let's change loads,
shall we?' He took care to go through in front of the boy; there was no trouble.
Round the first corner, they changed cases back. The boy said, 'It's as well they
didn't stop you; mine's full of revolvers.'[3] Moral, don't employ children.[4]

The camouflage section of SOE made some attempt to disguise its sets as
ordinary household receivers, but the attempt would not deceive for more than
a few seconds an enemy expert who unscrewed the back and looked inside. The
day of the transistorized set, which offers camouflage much wider opportunities,
was yet to come.

One other point about these sets was operationally important: who was working them. SOE's operators at least were told when under training that every
morse key signaller's touch is slightly different, and that home station would
be sure to notice if the 'fist' or 'handwriting' of the operator they knew had
changed. Indeed, in 1943–4–5 operators had their style recorded on tape before
they left England, so that a detailed check could be made later.[5] The difficulty
that SOE was not quite able to master was that operators' styles, like hand-
writings, can be imitated by an accomplished forger; of whom the Germans had
many. Several of SOE's sets in Holland and France were taken over by the
Germans, with some fatal results.[6]

There was a quite independent method, in use at the same time, for telling
who was working the set: known as the security check. This consisted initially
of a deliberate mistake introduced by the operator at a fixed point early or late
in the message; soon supplemented by a second deliberate mistake, to be introduced at a slightly different point; and known as the bluff and the true check
respectively. A message which arrived with the bluff check present, and the true
check absent, ought to have indicated to London that the operator had been

---

[1] Private information.      [2] Lorain, 25–7.
[3] Private information: se non è vero, è ben trovato.
[4] Cp. Foot, 97, 410.      [5] Details in Lorain, 162–5.      [6] pp. 264–7, 249–50 below.

captured, and had given away his bluff check under pressure. London would then verify, for example, by asking 'Do you need cigarettes?', to which the prearranged reply would be 'My aunt's eyes are brown', but to which the Germans would be more likely to respond 'Cigarettes welcome': thus giving the game away, and opening a wide field for deception.

There were troubles about security checks, as about recognizing operators' styles. The Germans discovered, from some unfortunate indiscretions by junior SOE staff,[1] that there were two checks, and were sometimes by severe pressure able to extract both from captured operators; thus making their own deception work more easy. On a few occasions they were able to simulate captured operators only too well.

One resource remained, if London retained suspicions: a staff officer could fly over the occupied area where the resistance circuit was supposed to be operating, and have a few words with its organizer by radio-telephony, if the circuit had an S-phone.

The S-phone, an invention of which SOE's research and signals sections were proud, was an ultra-high-frequency device of which the prime purpose was navigational. An aircraft (or a ship) carried one, fairly hefty, half of it; the other half could easily be carried by a single man on a set of webbing braces. Its only dangerous feature was that it could not possibly be explained away as anything else if it was discovered at a chance control.

It could be intercepted – up to 1,500 metres from the point of use, only – on the ground; otherwise it was virtually invulnerable. An aircraft could talk to it from 30 or 40 miles away, at a height of 10,000 feet, as easily as two people can talk by telephone in a single city.[2] With the help of a direction indicator in the aircraft, the pilot could fly straight towards the speaker; this was an enormous help in locating dropping zones in difficult country, and provided the equipment's *raison d'être*. The security advantage it also provided was a bonus.

The same researchers in SOE, cooperating with other scientists, devised another navigational device, a form of mobile radar in two halves called Eureka and Rebecca. Rebecca, again the heftier half, was airborne; even Eureka weighed almost a hundredweight, but was just portable and parachutable. Eureka was a radar beacon, to be set up in a dropping zone, coded to reply only to a particular signal from Rebecca; which could activate it from some 70 miles away. Both were equipped with devices which would blow them up if anyone tried to examine them.[3] Their combined margin of error was within 200 yards; they were therefore of enormous potential value to resistance.

They were used extensively by British and American airborne troops in the great airborne landings of 1944-5; with marked success. Their clandestine career, for which they had been designed, was a good deal less distinguished: in the

[1] Foot, 329-30.
[2] Sketch and diagrams in Lorain, 91-3, 173-4.
[3] Details ibid. 94-5.

words of the relevant SOE section history, 'a large proportion of the Eurekas despatched were never heard of again'.[1] The RAF, justly obsessed with difficulties about finding their way to particular fields by moonlight, besought SOE to arrange a Eureka grid, which would much have simplified their problem.

Earnest requests and peremptory orders to the field were alike disregarded: agents simply did not understand the importance of these intricate boxes of valves, and regarded them as tiresomely bulky liabilities, impossible to explain away to a snap control. Equally they did not appreciate the tactical advantages that would have followed the establishment of a Eureka grid, in the shape of far more reliable and more extensive supplies for themselves.[2] The few who did set up their Eurekas were delighted with the results; old mine shafts, deep river beds, old quarries hold the rest.

*Codes and ciphers.* Codes have been touched on already in this chapter,[3] but a little more needs to be said about them. A good code, like a good cipher, is unbreakable within the time for which it is needed; which may be a matter of minutes or of years. Simple battle codes, such as fighter aircraft or tank crew used, had no role to play in the underground war; simple coding systems such as Playfair[4] were taught to well-trained agents, and might be a great help – for a little time. As readers of Conan Doyle and Dorothy Sayers know, intelligent people can break some simple codes quickly.

But others are impermeable to anything but luck: witness 'the most conspicuous thing SOE ever did: the nightly broadcasting on the BBC's foreign programme, through some of the most powerful transmitters in the world, of scores of sentences which sounded either like family greetings or like Carrollian nonsense.'[5] This system, originated by SOE in the autumn of 1941, was of great value to resistance in several fields; MI6, MI9, and OSS were not slow to borrow it. Once there was prompt and full contact between London and occupied territory – not merely that mysterious state of Being in Touch with London, on which Henri Michel so rightly insists,[6] but constant and frequent touch by wireless – it was possible for the BBC to broadcast prearranged messages which would convey important, immediate, operational news to a small group of listeners, or even to an individual; but would be meaningless to everyone else who heard them outside England. 'Benedictine is a sweet liqueur', 'I see green eyes everywhere', 'Is Napoleon's hat still at Perros-Guirec?' – to take three French examples – were impenetrable to the Germans. They indicated respectively to the tank turret manufacturer at Montbéliard that Harry Rée was an effective agent; to a group of 'Xavier's' saboteurs in the Ain that they were about to get a

---

[1] Foot, 86.    [2] Ibid.
[3] pp. 99–100 above.
[4] Lorain, 57–8, expounding Playfair, remarks that if everyone had his rights it would be called Wheatstone; after the practical inventor of the telegraph and the concertina, who was himself no mean cryptologist.
[5] Foot, 110.    [6] Michel, *SW*, 254.

drop of arms; and to every armed Breton resister who was in touch with SAS that he was to parade with his weapon, in his village square, at five minutes to midnight that night. A few survivors of the 'Var' escape line will recognize the message about Napoleon's hat also; they had employed it earlier. It was one of the side advantages of this system that messages could be used several times over.

The system was of enormous use for mobilizing parachute reception committees – or for telling them that they need not break curfew after all, as the drop proposed for that night had had to be deferred; and it provided, as the Benedictine instance just given shows, a way in which agents could establish their bona fides. It had one frightful countervailing disadvantage: the Germans might in particular circumstances come to know in advance of the meaning attached to a particular message. Sometimes a captured agent might break down, and betray what a message meant; there are even tales, of doubtful reliability, of agents being captured with some hundreds of messages on them in writing.[1] Undoubtedly on one important occasion the Germans did hear in advance about a message that mattered: they had prior knowledge that gave them a few hours' warning of the Normandy invasion, 'Neptune'.

They had been warned so often before that they did not take as much notice as they might have done; the invasion achieved tactical surprise.[2] The fable of the boy who cried wolf is in point.

People who want to recapture the sound and spirit of blocks of these messages are referred to the opening of Cocteau's film *Orphée*, which catches their tone exactly. What particular messages meant to particular resisters, in terms of fright, relief, elation, or anxiety, can hardly be communicated any more.

The Germans expended a great deal of effort in attempts foredoomed to failure, to unravel what these messages meant; which could have been more usefully devoted to decipher.

Before we come to decipher, another use of code needs a word. Most agents working with resisters, and many resistance leaders working with secret services outside their own territory, had a personal code, which they had to memorize; they could use it to pass messages back to the secret headquarters to which they worked. Most SOE agents in western Europe had to memorize as well an address in Portugal, and a formula by which they could encode a postcard which, when interpreted, meant 'I am in hiding at the address on this card, and waiting for instructions from an escape line about how to get away.' But a personal code was more elaborate: a Playfair key word at its simplest, perhaps a string of numbers to guide in transposition, perhaps a transposition key as long as a couplet or a quatrain of some easily memorizable poem.

In a safely conducted circuit, this personal code would only be used, for additional security beyond the wireless operator's cipher, in a message that was going to be put into cipher anyhow. In less rigidly professional, more daring, and

[1] Eg. Foot, 304.　　　　[2] Ibid. 388.

more active bodies, a risk was taken: people were spared the trouble of constructing an 'innocent' letter as a veil for their code message, in what was oddly known as a barn code,[1] and were allowed to write straightforward reports in which the place and personal names, and any other obviously 'sensitive' points – and only those – were encoded.

This was far from safe. Those who arranged it might have remembered the agents' golden rule, *dubito ergo sum*, I doubt therefore I survive: no one could be sure what would happen to reports of this kind on their journey. Even if the agent who wrote them intended to put them himself into the hands of a pilot who flew over to collect them,[2] he might be arrested on the way there, or the pilot be shot down on the way back. If the reports went through the hands of intermediaries, that multiplied the chances of interception. Indeed, a sizeable group of SOE's agents who congregated (against orders) in Paris in the summer of 1943 were undone, largely by this very means: they wrote copious reports, lightly coded, which they transmitted through a man who showed them all to the SD, who in turn kept photocopies of them.[3] Many of these reports included encoded place names, which could easily be guessed from the context; with that much help, extracting the code for anything more supposedly secret took even an inexpert reader only a few minutes.[4] This was one of the not very numerous aspects of SOE's work which could correctly be derided as unprofessional by SIS or the NKVD.

Decipher proper was very much a matter for experts; as was the preparing of indecipherable messages.

This whole subject, which has fascinated one type of very clever mind since ancient times, has been exhaustively handled by David Kahn in a masterpiece of readable erudition.[5] The nearest to a blemish in his massive accumulation of detail is that he indicates that the British, after the admiralty's Room 40 had performed such prodigies in 1916–17, had rather tended to rest on their oars, and had fallen somewhat behind their competitors: an impression brusquely enough removed by some still more recent work. British security was too dense for him to be able to pierce it a decade ago; things have eased up since.

Lorain, expounding the relevant corners of Kahn from extra light thrown into them by well-informed friends, points out that all systems of enciphering, however simple or however elaborate, boil down to one of two methods: transposition or substitution.[6] The first is simply a matter of rearranging the letters in the original text, anagrammatically: something your skilled crossword puzzler can do, on a good day, practically at sight. Unhappily for resisters, competent anagrammatists are spread more or less evenly over Europe; so transposition ciphers were no use.

---

[1] p. 100 above.  [2] This could be done easily enough: see pp. 126–7 below.
[3] Cp. Foot, ch. x.  [4] *Feci.*
[5] *The Codebreakers* (1966).  [6] Lorain, 52–75.

The security of a substitution cipher varies with the length of the key that is used. Ideally, the key will be so long that, sooner or later, every letter in the original will have substituted for it every other letter in the alphabet, in some more or less random rotation; this merely – the reader will forgive the term of art – in monogrammatic (that is, single-letter) substitution. Bigrammatic substitution, dealing with the letters of the original text in pairs instead of singly, adds to the density of the mixture; so of course – forgive again – does superencipherment, the putting of the ciphered message through the mill of a second substitution-cipher before it is transmitted.

The arrival of the computer, as a readily available business tool, has made superencipherment child's play. The modern substitution key can contain hundreds of thousands of letters, and for all the plain man knows can be enciphered and re-enciphered hundreds of thousands of times, by machines that cannot make mistakes (if the people who set them to run make none: a big if). But this brings us back to the practical difficulties of the resister in the years before the computerized flood. Most resisters were, in Malory's phrase, good men of their hands, rather than Great Brains; remembering anything exactly was difficult enough, and remembering long intricate strings of unassociated letters or figures was plumb impossible. They had never heard of Vignère or Kasiski, polyalphabetism was to them a meaningless noise.

There was one important invariable, which reduced the value of substitution keys, however long; the number of letters in the alphabet. This varies from 23 in Greek, through our more familiar 26, to 32 in Russian; even with the ten digits added, this only made for 42 possible variants for which any single cipher-letter could stand. Figures were more usually spelt out, in messages, than sent as figures; thus giving an extra handle for the decipherer to grasp. With any luck for him, a key short enough for an agent to remember would repeat itself during a message of any length; and he could start by treating repeating passages to see if they would yield up words for numbers, a useful limiting of the field of search.

The patience of a computer was far from exhausted after 42 shots at a cipher target. Can teams of 42 decipherers have been quite unknown, at some German main cryptologists' headquarters; working with teutonic thoroughness through every alternative? But the subject is highly technical, only of real interest to technicians; and there is little more than can usefully be said here.

The Germans and the Japanese had both gone in for machine ciphers – adding extra bits to the commercial machine called 'Enigma' – and worked them secure in the belief that they were wholly indecipherable: an expensive mistake.[1] Resistance, and the Allied secret and diplomatic services, made do for the first half of the war with ciphers that they hoped, but did not know, were safe. In the second half, from 1943 onward, the British at least adopted a system, invented independently in Germany and the USA some twenty years before, which the

[1] See pp. 243, 292, 306 below.

Germans would have been well advised to use themselves, because it was at that time – and may indeed remain – undecipherable.

This system is called one-time pad (OTP).[1] Under it, two copies and only two copies are made of a pad of pages of random letters, arranged in columns. The encipherer has one, the cipher operator to whom the message goes has the only other. An agreed signal at the start of the message indicates which page is being used, and at what point on it work begins. A random substitution key of adequate length, never repeating, is thus provided. When the en- or de-ciphering has been completed and checked by the cipher operator at work in enemy territory, the page is torn off the pad and destroyed.[2]

Only two difficulties attended this system. One was that an OTP, like a transmitter, could not be disguised as anything else; it was simply an essential weapon in the clandestine war, and possessing one was another of the risks resisters had to run. This risk, everyone agreed, was worth it. To make the pad more easy to hide, it was usually printed on silk; so that, with any luck, it might get overlooked in the search of a suitcase full of clothing. This brought on the second catch: the silk burned rather slowly.

Till the invention, late in the world war, of the high-speed transmitter, it remained essential for operators to spend the minimum of time on the air, and a final word may be devoted to a coding device, used by SOE and SAS at least, which helped to shorten transmission times. This code was also printed on silk; it looked at a glance like a slightly grubby white silk handkerchief. Four-letter phrases, alternating vowels and consonants, through the alphabet from ABAB to ZUZU, were printed in columns, with the prearranged meaning attached to each; so that AKAK FOUR DODO LONA might signify 'parachute at next opportunity four container-loads bren gun ammunition in magazines'. These codes would obviously enough be surenciphered, not sent in clear.

One unhappy combination of weak staff work and signals inattention sent a message of this sort, from the combined headquarters of French resistance in London to a maquis in Savoy, in clear in July 1944: announcing a parachute drop that night. The floater is recorded; the result is not.

### Land lines

Most of the intricacies of land lines have already been discussed.[3] A few more need mention; headed by an important point of principle, which is often overlooked by people who live in open societies.

Nazism, like other dictatorships – whether of right or left – was a closed society, and in it the police had a position of special authority. Everybody in a nazi-conquered country came automatically under police control; whether direct

---

[1] Cp. Kahn, op. cit., 398–402.

[2] Examples in M-M. Fourcade, *L'Arche de Noé* (1968), before 513, as used by MI6; and in Revesz-Long, *Combat des Ondes*, 47, as used by SOE.

[3] In sections on escape, pp. 31–42; on security, pp. 64–7; on forged papers, pp. 95–8, and on messengers, pp. 99–101.

Gestapo control, or control by other German or by local police forces acting under the ultimate authority of Himmler, who in turn was Hitler's loyal subordinate. Anybody making any journey, however long or short – whether travelling a thousand miles, across several frontiers, on business, or walking a dozen yards to the corner shop to try to buy a box of matches – had to be ready to explain to the police where he was going, and why his journey was both innocent and necessary.

This was the point at which resisters' capacity to act a part was critical; it was also the point at which they most needed to be inconspicuous. Shabbily dressed men who looked like solicitors' clerks in towns, or obvious peasants in the countryside, were the ideal physical types. The problem for an escape line courier of shepherding the Texan crew of a shot-down B-24, the shortest of them 1·90 m tall, all blond, none speaking a word of the local language, across an area inhabited by dark-haired people averaging 1·65 m in height, was to put it mildly stiff: one deaf and dumb Dutch cousin might be conceivable, seven would strain anyone's credulity. Dozens of shot-down Texans are alive still to bear witness that some girls' nerves were up to solving even problems as stiff as this.

A condition for success was that passengers on escape lines surrendered all initiative to their guides, who alone could know and judge the dangers that surrounded them in any perilous spot. People who prided themselves on their tactical acumen had to swallow their pride and do what they were told; even if told to do it by a teen-age civilian.

One pretty girl is reputed to have used a simple, effective device when conveying passengers – one at a time – by train. They travelled first-class. When the routine police control of the moving train approached her carriage, she retired to the lavatory with her companion; hid him behind the door; stripped to her underclothes; and had no trouble with embarrassed policemen. This would not work against every police force, and placed extra strains on some escapers; and the same girl could not use the trick often on the same train.

Resisters not working or travelling on escape lines far outnumbered the rest; they too might always run into difficulty when moving about, peaceably or on active operations. People who lived in large towns soon got used to the Germans' techniques for snap street controls. Several vehicles would suddenly stop at a selected point; rough wooden barriers would be put up; and all passers-by in sight would have to pass through the barriers, showing their papers. Correct papers and a correct bearing were all that one needed as a rule. The staff manning the barriers was likely to include at least one quite senior policeman in plain clothes, who would stand aside from the routine work, scrutinize some faces very carefully, and pull in an occasional walker for further questioning: what was your mother's maiden name? how many sisters has she? their names? where is your father buried? what was your last platoon sergeant called? why have you not drawn your tobacco ration this week? where did you buy those shoes? Anyone who stumbled in his answers might be taken away and questioned thoroughly.

Whether this was an efficient way for policemen to spend their time is a cost-accountant's question, rather than an historian's. Certainly the existence of the system helped to keep resisters on their toes; it was presumably also of some use to the Germans, if only as an extra filter for catching people to be deported to Germany as forced labourers.

Similar systems could be applied in the country. Usually there would be a sudden check at a cross-roads. Sometimes an empty barn would be taken over at random, tables set up in it, and the passengers in every passing vehicle be made to explain who they were, and why they were going where. One English SOE agent has never been able to forget being pulled in to a control of this last kind; being kept waiting his turn for ten minutes; surviving five minutes' perfunctory questions with no trouble at all; being told he could go; and then, peremptorily, as he walked out, being called back. He at once remembered warnings he had received under training, about alternating soft and hard methods of cross-questioning. 'Where's your identity card?' He produced it again; a London forgery, but a good one. His furious interrogator strode over to the next table, held it under the nose of the military police corporal there, said *'That's* what an identity card is, you bloody fool', and handed it back to its terrified owner with a bow. The owner kept his fright out of his face, tottered safely back to his car, and drove away.[1]

Snap controls might crop up anywhere; they were a standing hazard in and near large towns, and some particular Paris metro stations were notoriously likely places for them. Deep in the country, they were much less likely, except in the 25-kilometre-deep forbidden zone round every frontier.

For frontier crossings, wise resisters put themselves in the hands of professionals: the smugglers, whose business it had always been to know how to evade the frontier guards. Good smugglers, paid in advance in full, never gave any trouble. Unhappily for many people trying to flee from nazism, some obvious staging points for refugees – Budapest late in 1939, Marseilles late in 1940, Perpignan late in 1942, for example – tended to silt up with crooks: people who offered themselves as *passeurs*, drew their fees, and scarpered with the cash. Sound and well-informed resisters kept well clear of these sharks, and some enterprising resisters set up highly efficient frontier-crossing systems of their own.

These always depended on minute knowledge of the ground – not merely mile by mile, wood by wood; but tree by tree, bush by bush, strand by strand of the frontier wire; and footfall by footfall of the patrols as well. 'Christine Granville' set up a line running on skis through the Carpathians in the winter of 1939–40 so audacious and so successful that even her fellow Poles could hardly credit that

---

[1] Conversation with him, 1967.

she was managing it without some degree of German complicity.[1] Several of SOE's agents in France and Italy had their private ports of entry into Switzerland. One brave Frenchwoman travelled fortnightly first-class by train between Paris and Geneva for the first six months of 1944 – her cover was that she was a bright young thing, comforting the bedside of a sick Swiss aunt – bringing back with her fortnightly in the false bottom of her suitcase the money the gaullist resisters in Paris needed for the next two weeks.[2] After Normandy D-day, she reckoned she was too well known, dyed her hair, and made her last journey on foot over the Col des Montets; she was then relieved, hardly before time.

The false bottoms of suitcases represent one of the oldest tricks in the modern smuggler's book; still, in the 1940s, worth attempting. A false bottom to a milk-churn was ideal, for minor smuggling on such comparatively open frontiers as the demarcation line in France or the Belgian–Luxembourg border: what village policeman is going to search fifty milk-churns, driven by a man he knows, carefully? Larger parcels than these were movable, but with some trouble; usually under an armed guard that would be prepared to shoot it out if a patrol unexpectedly came by (and what is the good of a frontier patrol if it is expected?). SOE handled a good deal of business with Oerlikon and other firms across the Swiss border; this enabled it to pay back part of the large debt it owed the RAF.[3] There are no known incidents of consignments that went astray.

### Sea lines

At sea, as on land or in the air,

> weather was a far more severe brake on clandestine working into [Europe] than were German activities of any kind, outside the heavily defended areas. Weather's effect varied of course with the element involved: cloud or rain might make air operations impossible and sea ones difficult on a night when it made a land frontier crossing easy. Above all, there was the moon. The whole of SOE's early life was geared to its phases. Clandestine aircraft could not land without it; clandestine boating parties could not land with it. Techniques grew more sophisticated with time; but it was always desirable, and in the early days it was essential, for parachute operations to take place while a moon, more than half full, was well up in the sky. As a senior officer put it much later, in SOE 'for at least two years the moon was as much of a goddess as she ever was in a near eastern religion'.[4]

Several extensive and deeply indented tracts of the European coastline were difficult to guard and impossible to patrol continuously, and in those early days of radar could be quite easily approached or left by undetected small boats. In all these areas there were fishing industries of long standing, whose sailors knew

[1] See *Christine*, her life by Madeleine Masson (1975 Hamish Hamilton).
[2] Conversation with her – Madame G. D. A. Gadoffre – 1968.
[3] See Geoffrey Parker, *Black Scalpel* (1968), 70–6.
[4] Foot, 61; quoting Robin Brook – formerly a colonel, then a merchant banker – to foreign office, 1964.

the coastal waters, the shoals, dangers, and landfalls, as well as they knew the shapes of their own bedrooms ashore. Maps of the Aegean, the Adriatic, Brittany, Frisia, Norway make these opportunities clear at a glance.

They were at once perceived by the Germans, who instituted a mass of controls at fishing ports: licences, passes, fuel controls, curfew hours, guard boats, every restriction they thought necessary to ensure that fisher-folk did not slip away. But fisher-folk who work in small boats are an independent-minded lot, much more wary of sea and weather than of man; it was far from easy to control them. Few were quite as independent-minded as the whole male population of the Ile de Sein, off the coast of Finisterre, who all took ship for England in late June 1940, and put a pretty set of administrative and security problems when they arrived two days later. For all the Germans' efforts, the possibility of a sea escape, even from a port as busy as Concarneau or Stavanger, was always open; and away from busy ports there was little real control the Germans could exercise, except over fuel for boats' engines and by offshore patrols. One could always attempt to eke out the fuel ration by sailing; Hitler no more controlled the winds than Canute had controlled the tides over 900 years before. But a sailing ship once spotted by an engined patrol craft was helpless, unless heavily armed, or unbelievably lucky with fog.

Private sailing for pleasure, still then mainly a rich man's pastime, was closed down wherever the Germans came; they were taking no chances on having the subjects of their new order in Europe sail away from their paradise.

And they used air patrols as well as sea patrols. To the incompetence of one of these Churchill owed his life; the attention of those who doubt that grave events can hinge on slight ones is drawn to the incident.[1] Air cover and air attack raised serious difficulties for small boats doing resistance work on the Dalmatian coast and among the islands of the Aegean in 1943-4. Hiding stationary craft was a straightforward problem of camouflage; but a craft moving over water by day cannot be hidden, because it leaves a perceptible wake. The craft available did not always have the speed to be able to confine their work to night-time, and could seldom carry serious anti-aircraft guns.

What craft were in fact available?

SOE and SIS had at one time two rival private navies, based a few miles from each other in Cornwall, each seeking to work into the same parts of France. Eventually, in June 1943, the two little flotillas were amalgamated at Helford, five miles south-west of Falmouth; as it turned out, to their joint delight, and to the vast benefit of the rest of their work.[2] They ran French-style fishing boats, motor torpedo boats, and a couple of motor gunboats, with which they did a lot of ferrying work; bringing escaped aircrew and agents over to England, and less often infiltrating agents into France.[3]

[1] See H. van Thal ed, *The Prime Ministers*, ii. 308 (1975).
[2] Foot, 66.
[3] Numerous details of SOE's part in this ibid. 61–73.

Across the southern North Sea, a very little of the same sort could be done by motor torpedo boats operating from Harwich; but only a very little. The Belgian and Dutch coasts were all but impenetrable, as they were so full of infantry, and of anti-aircraft troops who sought to make their skies impenetrable as well. What little could be done inevitably had a tang of comic opera to it.[1] The west Danish coast, also smooth and open, offered slightly more chances; and slipping across the Sound to Sweden was almost straightforward.

Norway was quite another matter. Thousands of Norwegian fishermen were at sea when Norway fell, and sailed their boats into British or American harbours. Thousands more escaped, many of them by sea; so there was no problem in providing boats which – once they had reached the Norwegian coast – could pass as local, nor in finding the crews to man them and risk the dangers of air or sea interception on the way. Nothing else was available to help, apart from an occasional motor torpedo boat, till in the late summer of 1943 Admiral Nimitz's generosity provided three new powerful submarine-chasers, 110 feet long and bristling with light AA artillery. This enabled SOE to extend much farther a range of operations that had already become known all over Norway as 'the Shetland bus'.[2]

Mention of submarine chasers will remind the reader of submarines: ideal craft for clandestine operations in some ways, for they leave no wake when submerged with periscope down, and can arrive and depart unobtrusively. They have compensating disadvantages: none then afloat[3] was designed to carry passengers, who could get horribly in the way and were bound to be uncomfortable; and they could only make room for extra warlike stores in any quantity by reducing their efficacy for their own work, as the arm that was striving to be dominant in naval war. SOE's and SIS's agents were occasionally carried by submarine – there is one recorded operation on the Biscay coast in the spring of 1941, and there were several to the south of France and to Albania; of one of the French operations, as a passenger saw it, Emmanuel d'Astier has left a poetic account.[4] Notoriously, an American general visited Algeria secretly a few days before Eisenhower's armies landed there, travelling both ways by submarine.

What submarine, or indeed surface, operations were carried out in the Black Sea we have no means yet of knowing: nothing has come out about them at all. There is every probability that occasional landings were made behind the Germans' sea flank; no details seem to be known.

In the Mediterranean, calmer, warmer, and much less disturbed by tides than the Atlantic or the North Sea, there was plenty of scope for small-boat operations. We have noticed already MI9's fleet of caïques that plied across the Aegean.[5] SOE's formidable pair of feluccas, with a crew described by Sikorski

[1] Cp. p. 262 below.
[2] See David Howarth's book of that title (1951); and some details on p. 280 below.
[3] Unless the Russians had some that have remained on the secret list.
[4] *Seven Times Seven Days* (tr. Humphrey Hare, 1958), 63–70.
[5] p. 38 above.

as 'too rough even for the Polish navy',[1] must one day provide the subject for a superb adventure story; they worked north-eastward from Gibraltar in 1941–2. There is a book already about *Fidelity*, but most of the data for it have vanished, as she has, for ever.[2] This odd craft, a small marseillais trawler by origin, worked for MI9 with a mixed crew – mixed in every sense – that once included Albert Guérisse, who through being unable to rejoin her was launched on the most celebrated clandestine career of the war. *Fidelity* was lost not long afterwards. SOE, for which she had done a little work on the side,[3] continued small-boat operations onto the French and Italian rivieras from its new base, called 'Massingham', opened west of Algiers in the winter of 1942–3. Various small-boat squadrons of the Royal and United States navies were operating in the Adriatic and the Aegean in 1943–5; so was the Special Boat Section, which cooperated extensively with Greek, Yugoslav, and Italian resistance and was a law unto itself.[4] SOE had its own Levant Fishing Patrol as well.[5]

All sea resistance operations had points in common. Dark nights were on the whole preferred to moonlit ones – for SOE's escape operations, at least, this was an inflexible rule. Great emphasis was laid on silence: silent engines, greased rowlocks, muffled oars. Some elementary knowledge of small-boat work was a great advantage: the woman agent newly recruited in France, who fell out of a dinghy into the sea, dropping her suitcase, and stood on the beach in a dripping fur coat lamenting her lost underwear aloud, was not popular.[6] A safe house close to the beach was a great advantage, but not an indispensable one: young, tough resisters could get on by themselves, with luck.

### Air

In the previous great war, both sides had made extensive use of aircraft for landing, collecting, and occasionally parachuting spies; with the low landing speeds and wing loadings of 1914–18, almost any large flat field could accommodate an aeroplane, and pilots were used to landing and taking off again more or less impromptu. Tactical and technical conditions had become wholly different by 1939.

British experience, developed from what the Arab revolt had undergone at the hands of Turkish air in 1918, had been devoted to the mild disciplining of Iraqi and Afghan tribesmen; comparable, if barely comparable, to forces of resistance *en maquis* in the early 1940s. The German air force's doctrines of army–air cooperation had gone into much sharper detail about how bodies of troops in open country could be harassed from the air; and the Luftwaffe put them into practice with conspicuous success in Poland in 1939 and in Norway and France in 1940, before embarking on the Balkan and eastern campaigns

---

[1] Foot, 67.   [2] M. Savill, *HMS Fidelity* (1975).
[3] Peter Kemp, *No Colours or Crest* (1960 ed.), 30–3.
[4] See John Lodwick, *The Filibusters* (1946). He joined SBS after an unsuccessful mission into France for SOE.   [5] Sweet-Escott, 196, 222–5.
[6] Foot, 191.

of 1941. No one from 1940 onwards could engage in war, and neglect the air, without peril.

A further run of technical developments, in the use of parachutes, affected resistance directly.

*Dropping men.* Parachuting has now become a familiar spectacle, even in some countries a sport. Yet for every parachutist, the moment when the parachute opens always lifts the heart. This has been so from the times of the earliest Greek and Chinese trials; and remains so although parachute accidents – which are usually fatal – have become *faits divers* rather than splash headlines in the newspapers.

The Russian army manœuvres in 1930 showed the impact that a band of trained parachutists could have in dislocating an opponent's command structure; a subaltern and half-a-dozen men put a corps headquarters out of action. Gubbins, later head of SOE, saw a film of this; Wavell, the best brain in the British army, saw a more extensive exercise in the Russians' 1936 manœuvres;[1] both were duly impressed. The Germans, who also had had eyewitnesses present, made copious notes, and in April and May 1940 used parachuted troops with shattering effect in Norway and the low countries. During that summer they dropped a few spies into Britain; and in May 1941, at the price of a naval defeat, they captured Crete by airborne force alone. When all the bills were in, the price for Crete turned out to include also the exhaustion of their airborne corps, thenceforward usually sent into the line on foot instead of being wafted behind it on aircraft.

Though the Russians had embarked on the business of military parachuting first, their armed forces were not in any state in the aftermath of the great purge for any kind of novelty or experiment. That they organized some parachuting of agents and weapons to partisan bands, and conducted some pick-up operations as well, is known;[2] but details are not. It is only clear that at this stage they made no startling innovations.

For the British, in the early years of the war – 1939–40–41 – where clandestine warfare was concerned the whole business was still in the experimental stage; new kinds of parachute and parachute harness were being tried out as late as July 1942. Exiles from the continent were at first wholly dependent on the British; and sometimes gloomy enough about what was offered them. The head of de Gaulle's secret services for example was treated to a demonstration near Manchester, in the spring of 1941: 'we were taken out to the airfield "to give us confidence". We watched sandbags being parachuted; a good half of the parachutes did not open, and the bags thudded onto the ground with a dull, flat noise that brought us no confidence at all. We looked at each other, rather pale – still, after all, some parachutes had managed to open; so we might be

[1] (Sir) Bernard Fergusson (now Lord Ballantrae), *Wavell* (1961), 31–2.
[2] Conversation with E. Boltin, 1962; Macksey, *Partisans*, 72–4, &c.

lucky.'[1] The Americans, at this stage, were following some distance behind the British.

The principal trouble was lack of aircraft; which derived in turn from British grand strategy. Bomber command of the RAF alone had suitable aircraft in any quantity; and bomber command, in the grip of the theories of Douhet and Trenchard, was not going to part with precious aircraft and still more precious aircrew beyond necessity. As Portal, the chief of the air staff, put it to a leading figure in SOE, 'your work is a gamble which may give us a valuable dividend or may produce nothing. It is anybody's guess. My bombing offensive is not a gamble. Its dividend is certain; it is a gilt-edged investment. I cannot divert aircraft from a certainty to a gamble which may be a gold-mine or may be completely worthless.'[2]

The total number of English-based aircraft available for full-time (or almost full-time) work with resistance was only five till August 1941, was still under thirty by the end of 1942, and never reached sixty; while bomber command frequently marshalled a thousand bombers on fine nights in 1944–5. In the earliest thousand-bomber raids, the special duty squadrons assigned to resistance work were also conscribed to take part.

There were two of these squadrons, formed on Newmarket racecourse, of all splendidly English places: 138 in August 1941 and 161 six months later. From March 1942 they were based on a carefully camouflaged airfield at Tempsford near Cambridge.[3] This was sequestered to their secret purposes, as was a corner of the busy fighter base at Tangmere, by Selsey Bill. Some extra help was to be got from transport command, particularly from 295 squadron's Whitleys at Hurn in 1941–2;[4] but in no great quantity. Nor were the secret services able to claim it as of right, as they could from Tempsford. Two USAAF bomber squadrons, the 36th and the 406th, flying Liberators and Dakotas, were available from English bases for clandestine work from January 1944, and two more squadrons, the 788th and 850th, joined them in May.[5] An exceptional daylight effort by the ordinary USAAF bomber force is noted in the French section of the following chapter.[6]

In the Mediterranean, another RAF bomber squadron, 624, bore the main brunt of clandestine work in 1941–3, operating successively from Cairo, Derna, Protville, and Bari. 334 wing RAF was formed in November 1943 to coordinate air operations in support of resistance. It commanded, as well as 624 squadron and a Polish bomber flight, several American squadrons: the 122nd (renumbered

---

[1] 'Passy', *Souvenirs*, i. 139 (Monte Carlo 1947), tr.

[2] Foot, 13; cp. ibid. 74–5.

[3] Equipment details in Foot, 76. Jerrard Tickell, *Moon Squadron* (1956), gives a romanticized account of Tempsford that nevertheless catches part of its mood.

[4] Conversations with Wing Commanders Briggs, 1974, and Ensor, 1975.

[5] They were renumbered as the 856th, 857th, 858th, and 859th from August. W. F. Craven and J. L. Cate ed, *The Army Air Forces in World War II*, iii. 498 (Chicago 1951).

[6] p. 249 below.

885th in June) from April 1944, a Liberator unit at Blida, and the 7th and 51st with Dakotas from February. From April 1944 these last were replaced by the 60th troop carrier group, comprising four squadrons, who operated vigorously into Yugoslavia and Albania from the same base at Brindisi.[1]

The Lancaster, that incomparable bomber, was never available for drops to resistance at all. When Harris, the bomber commander-in-chief, had to release some squadrons to help drop stores in the winter of 1943-4, he sent his least effective large aircraft, Stirlings. Till late in 1942, 138 squadron was still using the ponderous Whitley, which, though rough to fly, had at least a long working radius of 850 miles; and 161 squadron was still flying Wellingtons, aircraft of beautiful design and larger carrying capacity, but shorter range, till May 1944. Both types of aircraft were twin-engined; both, particularly the Whitley, were by 1943 obsolescent. By that year the Tempsford squadrons had got some four-engined Halifaxes, good and sturdy machines, though hardly longer in reach than a Whitley: in 1944 they proved just, and only just, able to reach Warsaw from Bari. Liberators could range about two hundred miles farther.

A moment with a map and a ruler will show that, unless they could land in soviet territory to refuel, none of these aircraft working from British or American-held bases could operate over eastern Poland, Finland, or the western USSR at all; except for Liberators, which in fact were hardly ever used on secret missions north of the Carpathians. Superfortresses and Catalinas were never available for clandestine drops. Soviet policy, practically without exception, was to exclude all aircraft on duty for other secret services from soviet territory: this policy carried particular weight for Poland.

Modifying a bomber to drop men was quite simple. A round hole about a metre wide was cut in the fuselage floor, aft of the bomb bay, and fitted with a removable cover. Near it, inside the fuselage, a rail was fitted to which parachutes' static lines could be clipped. A signal light, worked by the pilot, shone red when the dropping zone was near, and green when the first man was to jump. All – all! – that the parachutist had to do was to jump through the hole in the floor; his (or her) own weight broke the static line, after the line had twitched the parachute out of its package. The rest was supposed to follow automatically; and usually did. It brought a moment of wild elation; followed, a very few seconds later, by the bump of landing.[2] Those who want to know what landing felt like can try jumping from a fourteen-foot wall; it would be as well to learn first the trick of how to roll when landing.

Dakotas were more easy to jump from than other aircraft, since they had a door through which one leaped; a less unnatural action than shuffling on hands and bottom up to the hole, swinging one's legs into it while gripping its edge, and then springing to attention when the dispatcher cried Go. Albemarles,

---

[1] Craven and Cate, *Army Air Forces*, iii. 505–10.
[2] Personal knowledge.

available for SAS though not for SOE, had an oblong hole so long that five men could stand astride it at once, and all jump together by springing to attention at the word of command. The hardest jump of all was the first training jump, from a basket beneath a moored balloon: from that still and cold-blooded act several brave people withdrew. On the other hand, it was a mistake to be too hot-blooded. An unlucky young British sergeant was so excited at being allowed to join a mission to a savoyard maquis, and everyone else in the aircraft was so elated as well, that neither he nor his dispatcher remembered to hook up his static line, and he plummeted straight to his death.[1]

Drops were ideally made from about 600 feet. This gave the parachute plenty of time to open, and did not expose the parachutist to more than about ten seconds of dangling from it while deciding whether simply to let the ground come up to meet one (which it did inexorably fast), or to attempt a simple turn, by hauling on one's lift-webs, to enable one to meet it at a kinder angle. People dropped from too low were usually hurt; people dropped from too high might drift, if there was any wind, and make trouble for the reception committee.

Reception committees were not compulsory; versatile people could be dropped blind, to establish their own whereabouts as best they could. It was more usual to use a party to break curfew and meet the new arrivals. Here we need to turn again to the French book.

The task of these committees bristled with difficulties before hand, and might develop even more after the drop. They had to light and to guard the dropping zone, to guide any agents who were parachuted, and to dispose of parachutes and stores without trace. Guarding and lighting were comparatively simple. Three men held torches or bicycle lamps out in a row, along the direction of the wind, in the middle of a flat space of open ground about half a mile across. The commander of the party stood with a fourth torch so that the lit torches looked from the air like a reversed capital L. When a distant rumble in the sky announced that an aircraft was near, all the torches were pointed towards it; the leader's torch flashing a previously agreed morse letter. Provided the aircraft did see the lights and the letter was correct, it released its load above them and was gone as soon as it could, so as to attract as little local attention as possible. It might carry an extra package of leaflets to be distributed over some nearby town to provide some cover for the low flight.[2]

Needless to say, a heavy bomber in the act of dropping [men or] supplies, flying just above stalling speed with its flaps down, with almost all the crew's attention concentrated on the ground, was from a night fighter's point of view a sitting duck; particularly if the dropping zone was shut in between lines of hills, thus further reducing the pilot's chances of successful evasive action. Curiously enough there seems to have been no occasion

[1] Foot, 79, and Lorain, 179.
[2] Foot, 83.

. . . when a clandestine dropping aircraft was thus caught in the act from the air; and dropping zones were always well out of the way of flak.[1]
The aircraft casualty rate in special duty dropping operations was by bomber command's standards light: usually varying between 1·5 and 3 per cent.[2]
Nevertheless this special work called for special aptitude from the aircrew who did it: for concentration, endurance, and patience above all. And as the air minister put it at the end of the war, 'In difficult country the navigation risks were almost as formidable as the risks from the enemy.'[3] Their history remarks that

> the difficulties of navigation were especially acute for the S[pecial] D[uties] crew, the success of whose work necessitated pin-point accuracy on a small often ill-defined target after hours of flying across enemy country. The navigation, both on the journey and on the approach to the target, must obviously be of a very high order. Reception Committees were instructed to choose sites for their dropping grounds which could easily be seen from the air; but for many reasons this was often not possible for them, and the aircraft, after having found its target area, might have to search for some time before discovering lights half hidden by a wood, or obscured in a valley . . . the navigator nearly always had to rely on map-reading and D[ead] R[eckoning] and in order to enable him to do this, the pilot would take his aircraft across enemy-occupied Europe at a low altitude.[4]

[Navigation apart], the most probable source of trouble was the interception of members of the committee on their way to or from the reception; hence the care taken by some agents to forge themselves a gamekeeper's or doctor's travel permit, which allowed them to move about after curfew.[5] What with navigation difficulties in the air, and police difficulties on the ground, and the unpredictable weather that might cloud a dropping zone over in a few minutes, it is not surprising that some two-fifths of the sorties flown . . . by special duties dropping aircraft were abortive. The proportion of successes for night operations rose as the war went on, from about 45 per cent at first, to 65 per cent, or two successes to one failure, in the first nine months of 1944. The daylight dropping operations [in France] of the USAAF after D-day, flown in large formations, had the high proportion of 562 attempted and 556 successful sorties; three aircraft were lost and three had to turn back.[6] About a tenth of the night failures were due, on the pilot's own admission, to inaccurate navigating; they could not find their dropping zones. Under 5 per cent were due to

[1] Ibid. 85.
[2] Contrast Sir C. Webster and A. N. Frankland, *Strategic Air Offensive*, ii. 155–6 (1961).
[3] 400 H.C. Deb. 5s, 1860, 6 March 1945.
[4] Foot, 85.
[5] A gamekeeper's permit is illustrated in M. J. Buckmaster, *Specially Employed* (1953) at 144.
[6] Craven and Cate, *Army Air Forces*, iii, 503–5.

mechanical defects in the aircraft, for Tempsford's [and Brindisi's] maintenance was good. Between a quarter and a third of the failures were due to bad weather, according to the time of year; so bad that either the aircraft had to turn back before it had reached the target area, or when it got there the dropping zone was obscured. The rest – half or two-thirds – were due to failure by the reception committee to put in an appearance at the same time as the aircraft; normally, as the airmen fully understood, for reasons outside the committee's control.

Even if aircraft and committee did both reach the ground, there might be troubles in the actual drop. Only the most practised pilots could gauge the height of their run-in exactly. If they dropped from too low, containers might be stove in on impact and agents might well be injured; and if the drop was made from even a trifle high, and there was any wind at all, stores and agents would probably be scattered. Wise reception organizers did their best to place one man at least as a long-stop well up wind of the dropping zone, to mark down where each parachute fell; with drops by moonlight, this was not difficult. A perfectionist would have two separate long-stops with luminous prismatic compasses, to take cross-bearings; but reception committees were seldom run by perfectionists. It was often a shock for newly landed agents, who had practised reception drill during their training in rigorous conditions of silence and security, to find themselves in a patch of countryside covered by men smoking, shouting, laughing and shining torches instead of creeping decorously from dark hedgerow to hedgerow; a few drew their pistols quickly, and were only with difficulty prevented from shooting the friends they mistook for enemies.[1]

To sum up, parachuting people in lonely country could be perfectly secure, if only a small party – not more than half-a-dozen – landed, and no crowd turned out to meet them; provided everybody did his work punctually and accurately, provided the weather was all right, and provided no German patrol happened to pass by. As Michel has remarked, the continent is large;[2] not even the Gestapo could be everywhere at once.

*Dropping stores.* Dropping stores was even more simple than dropping people; and a wide variety of stores were dropped, including small arms for over a million men, and explosives for tens of thousands of demolitions.

The largest object parachuted was a jeep. That took six parachutes, as well as careful packing. Ideally, it was possible to drive it straight off the dropping zone, once the parachutes and a few rough timber supports had been cleared away; SAS, to whom alone jeeps were dropped, found that they lost about a quarter of them, one way and another, as a result of parachuting and landing accidents. And once dropped, they needed of course continual re-supply; lucky

---

[1] A vivid example of the sort of confusion that could result is in Millar, *Maquis* (1956), 28–38. These two paragraphs are from Foot, 86–7.      [2] Michel, *SW*, 270.

indeed was the SAS party that could keep its jeeps either in petrol, or in ammunition, from resources found on the spot. Each jeep carried three RAF surplus Vickers machine guns, on simple swivel mounts; this made them formidable, for sudden attacks in the dark on such targets as lorry convoys. But they needed handling by the trained men who drove them, and cannot be counted as normal resistance weapons.

Nor can the other heavy object dropped, a six-pounder (57 mm) anti-tank gun with which Fraser's SAS squadron in the Morvan was able suddenly to confound a German armoured car.[1] This again was not something any passer-by would know how to handle; and its ammunition supply was necessarily limited.

Much more usual loads were small arms, ammunition, explosives – plastic's stability helped here – clothing and especially boots. SOE did a great deal of experimental work on methods of packing. Kapok proved a suitable material for packing wireless sets, or suitcases (of continental type, naturally) for agents' clothes. Arms usually went in cylindrical metal containers, called either C type – nearly six feet long, with three inner canisters if required – or H type, five separate cylinders bolted together by a pair of long rods. 'The H type was the invention of an ingenious Pole who thought it inconvenient and dangerous to cart an object the size of a man, weighing over a tenth of a ton, round enemy territory.'[2] Kapok or wooden packing material could be burned; containers, being metal, could not. They could not be explained away, either, and mine detectors could help to find them: these were extra burdens laid by parachute drops on resisters on the ground.[3] All agreed these were burdens worth bearing, because of what the containers held: weapons that were a people's tools for helping to make itself free.

The difficulty of disposal was a real one, and cannot be shrugged off as unimportant. A point to remember when choosing a dropping zone was transport away from it; another was the nearness of some good hiding place. These were points necessarily much in the minds of people at the receiving end; who were troubled also by a tiresome procedural detail. They habitually opened containers, the moment they got them, to verify what was inside. But only the craftsmen who packed containers before they were dropped ever seemed to be able to repack everything into them, once they had been opened.

Occasionally there were absurdities. What bloody-minded quartermaster's incompetence can have been behind the parachuting of an aircraft-load of boots to rag-shod Yugoslav partisans, all of them boots for the left foot?[4] Or what passion for keeping up one's statistics led another quartermaster to send a maquis in trouble a package of lampshades?[5] One staff officer who handled a

---

[1] Foot, 404.            [2] Ibid. 80.

[3] Cp. p. 56 above for storage problems. An SOE staff officer, working in Paris in September 1944 in an hotel formerly used by the Gestapo, noticed that the wastepaper baskets were the end-pieces of C type containers. (Conversation with him, 1975.)

[4] (Sir) F. W. D. Deakin, *The Embattled Mountain* (1971), 81.

[5] Foot, 81.

lot of this work remembered most clearly in retrospect the wide variety of objects agents asked for: hair oil, cocaine, skis, sealing wax, boot wax, contraceptives, hatpins, starch, nibs, used motor-bicycle tyres, delousing powder, handcuffs, a gaff, a myriad of other things; all supplied as soon as weather allowed.

All these things were light, portable, parachutable; heavier ones could be carried in and air landed, even in those early days of air freight.

*Pick-ups.* At a time when travelling by air has become about as exciting as travelling by bus was fifty years ago; when on fine summer Saturdays thousands of people amuse themselves in light aircraft; when the police and customs forces of western Europe have almost given up the attempt to maintain strict frontier controls; it is not perfectly easy to recall the tension, drama, and difficulty that could attend on light aircraft flights between Axis-occupied and Allied territory during the war. Those who took it least tensely had least trouble. It was in fact perfectly simple to fly into Europe, land, take off again a few minutes later, and fly out: given luck, as always, and given drill.

The drill is explained in detail, and with unruffled clarity, by Hugh Verity who performed the operation twenty-nine times successfully in 1943; in a paper too long to set out here, but still available in print.[1] He gives a great many particulars about how to prepare and conduct a clandestine landing – known for short as a pick-up; especially about the problems of navigating over blacked-out countryside in search of a particular field. The technique at the ground end for receiving, clearing, and dispatching an aircraft has been in print since 1947.[2] It is clearly shown in that splendid historian's companion, Lorain; together with diagrams of two of the aircraft used into France, the Westland Lysander and the Lockheed Hudson.[3]

Of the Lysander it has been said, as Voltaire said of God, that had it not existed it would have had to be invented. It was a small slow high-wing monoplane, weighing less than five tons unladen, with a radius of 450 miles. Besides the pilot, it could carry two passengers easily, three at a pinch, or four in a crisis; and it could land and take off over five or six hundred yards of firm flat grass or clover. The Hudson, an American twin-engined light bomber with a crew of four, was large enough to hold a 'Rebecca' aerial (the Lysander was not), and could comfortably carry a dozen passengers and a ton of arms or documents; it was a little less manœuvrable than the Lysander, as it needed a good kilometre of flat meadow as a landing ground.

So did the third aircraft used, the Douglas C-47 Dakota; which made a few trips into France and a great many into Yugoslavia. One Dakota damaged its tail when landing in the Ain; was hidden all next day, camouflaged by bushes; received a new tail unit next night from another aircraft in the same squadron, and flew out with it.

[1] Appx. D in Foot, 478 ff.
[2] R. Leproux, *Nous, les terroristes*, i. 268–72.                    [3] Lorain, 86–9.

About 700 people were moved in and out of France by pick-up during the war, on SOE's account alone.[1] How many were moved for SIS and MI9 we do not yet know; certainly Lysander operations, with suitcases full of intelligence data, were important for the work of SIS.[2] In Yugoslavia there were many more pick-up operations, a lot of them by day; for by the summer of 1944 Tito's partisans controlled so sizeable an amount of Yugoslav territory that USAAF Dakotas – sometimes with Russian pilots – could operate in daylight. A body with the ludicrous acronym of BATS – the Balkan Air Terminal Service – ran at one time or another no fewer than thirty-six airstrips for the 60th troop carrier group.[3] Over 5,000 tons of warlike stores were moved in this way into Yugoslavia; and over 4,000 of Tito's wounded were flown out to hospitals in Italy. This relieved the partisan army of a crippling tactical burden, and thus much enhanced its striking power.

The French at least sometimes treated this work light-heartedly; and the British found it necessary to give the following firm instruction to agents in charge of it:

> You are in charge of a military operation. Whatever the rank or importance of your passengers they must be under your orders.
>
> There must be no family parties on the field. If the pilot sees a crowd he may not land. Ensure that at the moment of landing you and your passengers and NOBODY ELSE are on the left of Light A. and your Assistant on the left of Light B. Anybody anywhere else, especially anybody approaching the aircraft from the right, is liable to be shot by the pilot.[4]

### Weapons

Administration – 'the real crux of generalship, to my mind,' said Wavell[5] – varied so enormously from one place and one time to another that this book cannot attempt to treat it generally, and will only refer to it in passing as a rule; weapons, which varied much less, are worth a word.

On the purely technical front, Lorain can confidently be recommended: he contains precise drawings of five types of revolver, ten types of sub-machine-gun, five rifles, the bren, the bazooka, and various other close combat arms such as the silent carbine, the piat, and the Mills grenade: everything in fact that he could hear and write about, that was sent into France by air during the war.[6] All the arms he describes were British or American in origin; all were widely dispersed over Europe, not confined to French resistance. A few more outline points need to be made to supplement him.

All over Europe, elementary weapons were to be found on the spot. Any farm

---

[1] Details in Foot, 89–90.

[2] Eg. M. M. Fourcade, *Noah's Ark*, passim.

[3] Craven and Cate, *Army Air Forces*, iii. 508–10. Has no member of BATS written his war memoirs?  [4] Foot, 92; from an SOE file.

[5] *Soldiers and Soldiering* (1953), 14.  [6] His pp. 108–57.

has a pitchfork, with which one strong man – or woman – can quickly kill another; any household as we have seen has a kitchen knife. Most farms and most country houses in those days had a shotgun and a handful of cartridges: lethal enough at close quarters. The tale bears repeating of the Germans' arrival at a country house in the Balkans, which belonged to a former colonel in the service of the Habsburgs; an old military family, with a score of sporting rifles, all duly registered with the police. A German sergeant, who had seen the police register, came up to the house to take over the guns. Inexplicably, the gun room was found to be locked. After some delay, he got in, and collected all the guns, but none of their bolts: which the youngest son of the house, aged fourteen, had just removed and thrown into the lake.[1]

This was no more than a well-judged pinprick; even sporting rifles, with which you can kill a man as easily as a deer, might raise problems of ammunition supply, and they were only useful in the hands of marksmen, properly trained to wield them. Resistance offered no opportunities to train marksmen; in fact few of its fighting units lived in country so remote that their members could have any target practice with live ammunition at all. Where every single cartridge had to be flown in by air, economy with ammunition hardly needed preaching: most young resisters who used firearms at all, used them for the first time in action.

Home-made or impromptu weapons, in short, might be available to suit some local crisis; but were not there on a scale to encourage more than local and temporary war, extending over a few fields and copses at most.

On the other hand, in every occupied country, there were the German, and often till September 1943 the Italian, and occasionally other lesser, armed forces: engaged on the wrong side. Were they a fruitful source of arms?

In communist theory, certainly they were. As the left slogan ran, If you have a knife you can get a pistol, and so on;[2] in practice it was not so easy, till everybody's nerves were on edge as the moment of a national uprising approached. Those who secured most weapons by these means were probably communists: who, true to the party's traditions of secretiveness, have said little or nothing about what they secured.

From outside their closed nets, one conspicuous example can be seen of the importance of captured arms: in Greece and Yugoslavia in September 1943, when on the Italians' surrender much of their equipment and stored ammunition fell into partisan hands. Otherwise, on the southern and western fronts at least there do not seem to have been important captures of enemy weapons to aid resistance, unless in the very last closing stages of a disorderly withdrawal: Romania, perhaps, or Gascony, in August 1944. As a normal piece of drill, the German armed forces kept proper guards over their own stores, as efficient armed forces feel they should; a point to which we will need to revert. A large army moving

[1] Information from the middle brother, thirty-three years later.
[2] See p. 55 above.

across open country is always bound to shed a certain amount of fighting equipment, and a good scavenging resister is always likely to pick it up; but as a serious, long-term, large-scale method for arming resistance, raiding enemy dumps does not seem to have been much more useful than old men girding on their old swords.

There was no substitute in fact, on the arms front, for help from an outside power: the special case of the partisans in Yugoslavia apart.[1] In 1870-1 and in 1914-15 there had been no outside power available and willing to arm resisters in occupied territory: hence the comparative ineffectiveness of the original francs-tireurs in eastern France, of the Libyan Senussi, of the brilliant Wassmuss in Persia. As the war of 1914-18 developed, the need for subversive intervention became clear. The German general staff, by authorizing Lenin's return to Russia, cleared a major enemy from their path; and could have rescued themselves from the perils of a war on two fronts, had the administrative flywheel not developed such powerful inertia. They still had a million men idling in Russia in March-April 1918, when they just failed to break through in Flanders. The British, operating simultaneously through MO4 in Cairo, provided the Arab revolt with gold, mortars, machine guns, armoured cars, air support, and the genius of T. E. Lawrence; thus helping to topple Turkey from the war, an early-falling domino that helped bring down the rest. And the bolsheviks, having seized power by a neatly judged *coup*, needed no encouragement to provide arms, for sure hands, where power might result. The NKVD, SOE, and OSS all did serious work in arming resisters.

SOE at least stuck to a principle Gubbins had laid down in MIR before the war began, in a booklet – never sold in a bookshop, but distributed by parachute, in thousands of copies, in several languages, during the war – on 'The Art of Guerilla Warfare'. We have already met his view, based on direct experience in Ireland during the Troubles and much reflexion since, that undoubtedly 'the most effective weapon for the guerilla is the sub-machine gun'.[2] The TSMG, as the British army called it – the Chicago gangsters' tommy-gun – had with its ·45-inch bullet tremendous stopping power; but it was heavy to hold, kicked like a young mule, and was hard to hide. Amery and Smiley, officers on an important Balkan mission, each had Marlin sub-machine-guns, accurate up to a furlong and devastating in an ambush;[3] but these weapons were not always available.[4]

SOE, followed by OSS, settled instead for the sten: a weapon simple enough for a child of ten to assemble, and as every Cypriot housewife knows inconspicuous enough to be tucked, in three parts, into the bottom of a shopping-bag. For ambush purposes it was nearly ideal. It would take most 9 mm cartridges, a common calibre on the continent; it was fairly robust; above all, in an age

[1] Palestine is also an exception, on the edge of our subject: see pp. 162-3 below.
[2] p. 57 above.
[3] Julian Amery, *Sons of the Eagle* (1948), 91.
[4] Illustrations and description of the Marlin by Pierre Lorain in *Gazette des Armes*, no. 33 (December 1975), 14-19.

already cost-conscious, it was cheap – it cost about thirty shillings, mass produced. Enormous quantities of it were distributed, after tests had shown its
virtues; to the list of which we should add that it made a loud noise, encouraging
to the user.

There were some snags. It jammed easily. At point-blank range it was,
as intended, pretty lethal. But its barrel was short, to help make it light and easy
to hide; and a consequence of this was that at longer ranges than ten feet or so it
was unreliable. (A fellow soldier of the author's, about to be shot with a party
of captured SAS, noticed that the economical firing-party were only armed with
stens, captured from SOE; so ran away into the surrounding forest, and survived
the fusillade.)[1] And a side effect of corner-cutting, cost-cutting mass production
was that stens were too often sent out into the field defective. The most usual
fault was to leave a bur of steel in the barrel; if this was not noticed and removed,
the gun burst at the first round fired. The trigger mechanism, though simple, was
light; and a gun very likely to go off if dropped was not the perfect weapon to
provide for amateurs laying their first ambush.

Still, there the sten was; and for all its faults it provided a source of joy and
pride to hundreds of thousands of resisters, hitherto short of both, when they
got into their hands this tool for killing Germans. That a bad workman blames his
tools is a widespread proverb; not many of the juniors in resistance blamed the
sten.

Some more senior people did. The history of most strong armed resistance
movements is studded in its closing stages with unanswered appeals for heavy
weapons: unanswered and in the view of the British high command at least
unanswerable for the simple reason that the weapons were not there to spare. The
main armies needed every gun barrel, every mortar bomb they could get. The
clamour for mortars, heavy machine guns, light artillery, went up regularly
from those who were set on creating a national redoubt: from those in fact who
were still trying in 1944 to fight the war of 1940 or more probably of 1916,
without having taken in the proper function of guerilla. When counter-attacked,
a good guerilla vanishes; he does not stand and fight. He should be as impossible
to pin down, or to pick up, as a blob of mercury.

So there were sound tactical as well as logistic reasons to be urged against
providing heavy weapons for resisters; quite apart from the political ones, that
in highly politicized countries such as France or Yugoslavia were believed to
carry weight. Not many staff officers in SOE or OSS, not all staff officers even in
the NKVD, were aware of the political implications of what they did: they were
too busy with their day-to-day tasks of managing signals and supplies, pacifying
superiors, conciliating colleagues, doing all they possibly could for their agents
in the real dangers of work in the field. A few sharp directing brains, and a few
powerful personalities in key positions, were sometimes able to exercise notable
political influence through supplying or withholding weapons. There is probably,

[1] Foot, 405, based on conversation with him, 1944.

for example, something to be made of Roosevelt's strong if uninformed enthusiasm for resistance, as a force to counteract the official inertia of the American armament supply staffs.

By 1944 the minor war industry of parachute container packing had worked out its own drills, details, and loading tables; and a coded request from the field for a particular standard load would provide – weather and luck permitting – rifles, stens, light machine guns, or bazookas, with appropriate ammunition, in predetermined quantities.[1] The bazooka was almost as efficient as a six-pounder anti-tank gun, and a great deal more easy to carry and to hide: a pair of men could fire it easily and conceal it in moments.[2]

Mention needs to be made also of a few more specialist weapons. SOE invented an abrasive grease, which looked like ordinary grease, but wore out the parts it was supposed to lubricate. This made an admirable device for untraceable sabotage to railway engines. SOE, or rather one of its immediate predecessors, had also as we have seen invented plastic explosive; and produced over twelve million pencil time fuses. These fuses were all colour coded: only those who knew the colour code could make intelligent use of the fuses, and without careful fusing plastic in turn might be unusable. This provides yet another instance of the value of links with an outside power.

There is a famous example of an ill-fused bomb, which was planted by a German staff officer in Hitler's aircraft, but never exploded.[3] This may have been the result of mishandling; or of deterioration, wear and tear of the material over time; or of over-ingenuity by the original designers. The professional booby-trap-devisers in SOE knew quite a lot about the less reputable side of human nature, and took a slant delight in devising means by which the evil-schoolboy element in young nazis might be turned to nazi destruction: hence such saboteurs' luxuries as the explosive cowpat. These were toys. But stens, brens, rifles were serious tools of war.

### Money

One other administrative point is too important to be left out: money. Glancing references have been made to it already.[4] Young and innocent readers may ask, why was it needed at all? Was not work in resistance honour enough? To this the answer is, yes, but: it was an honour, and a high honour, but not one that everybody could afford unpaid.

Several people with large private fortunes expended them, usually without avail, in various resistance interests. Either from delicacy, or from lack of contact, or from backing the wrong horse in their home politics, or worse from falling into German hands, few if any of them were in the end able to submit accounts and get reimbursed by a régime they had saved.[5] The normal clandestine agent

---

[1] Details and examples in Foot, 475–7, and in Leproux, *Nous, les terroristes*, i. 275–7.
[2] Eg. Millar, *Maquis*, 182–3.        [3] Hoffmann, *Widerstand*, 332–4.
[4] Eg. pp. 20, 66.                         [5] Conversations with two of them, 1969.

setting off on a mission was supplied automatically, by the service that sent him, with currency suitable to support his cover; and the normal clandestine organizer required a regular source of hard cash, in quantities suitable to support the members of his network who – because their time was taken up with secret toil – could not work for their living.

If this was not done, it would get noticed; and thus break the resisters' golden rule, never do anything that attracts notice if you can avoid it. Police forces – not only the German ones – in occupied Europe were, or might be, inquisitive about everything, and occasions for them to be inquisitive had to be kept as few as could be. Indeed the danger that money supply brought with it, was that the enemy police knew it to be necessary, just as the secret services which provided the money did; and it provided one of the points to look for, when seeking how to break into a resistance network.

Parachuting the money was simple enough. Notes of small denominations were needed – big ones were far too easy to trace; but the quantities were never too exorbitantly large to fit into a suitcase. There was even a special technique for delivering a single package or container-load, by light dive bomber, by daylight.

Securing the money might be more awkward. SOE at least was forbidden, by the treasury, to forge it.[1] There is an interesting book, or at least an interesting learned article, waiting to be written – or is it only waiting to be published ? – on foreign currency movements during the war. Wing Commander Venner, the financial genius of SOE, knew all about it; but is dead.[2]

## Directing staffs

Few resisters were prepared to admit, unless they were communists, that they were working for – or under the direction of – any country but their own; if they were communists, in those comparatively undivided days they felt as a rule that their country was 'really' the USSR, for the victory of which they strove. Tito in Europe, and Mao in Asia, showed that national feeling could be even stronger than political, and broke away from soviet tutelage: providing extreme examples of the point at issue, which can be simply put. Leaders of resistance movements each believed that he ran his own show; but readily admitted that for some purposes – ammunition and explosive supply, almost always; arms supply, in most cases; strategic direction in some – he had to depend on some principal power fighting the Axis. All important resistance movements had links of liaison, at least, with one or more of the main anti-nazi secret services; and through them with the relevant general staff and war leadership. Hence, there could be some coordination between resistance effort and general strategy; even where the leadership and the inspiration were both entirely local.

[1] Contrast p. 165 below.
[2] See the éloge in Sweet-Escott, 42, 254.

What were these special services with which resisters dealt? Almost all of them were, or became, large offices, with all the defects of large-office intrigue; complicated by the extra zest which the extra security precautions carried. London had three small, extra secret, inter-service committees which remained small and extra secret, and thus retained power – they were called LCS, W and XX – and one secret service which was both small and efficient, MI9. Otherwise, there as elsewhere staffs swelled and efficiency tended to dwindle.[1]

On the whole, of the staffs of secret services the least said, the soonest mended; though a few comments in detail will be essential later. Through these refracting media, resisters made contact with the intelligence and operational staffs of armed forces; most of whom were reasonably bright. It was Aldous Huxley who originally remarked on *Britannica*'s distinction, in separate articles, between Intelligence, human; Intelligence, animal; and Intelligence, military.[2] The idea that there was something inhuman about military intelligence was sometimes fostered in wartime by the gaps fighting troops could perceive between the facts of life on the battlefield and the pictures painted by staff intelligence summaries. In fact a good intelligence or planning officer, who had managed to retain some flexibility of intellect and some imaginative grasp while working in a large headquarters (in itself no easy task), might be able to see into the mind of the original agent who had provided a report, or perceive how a given body of resisters could work to assist a particular operation.

### British

According to myth, there is but one British secret service, its ramifications as boundless as its power. Myth and fact are here quite far apart.

From 1909 there were two permanent secret services; the secret intelligence service (SIS or MI6), established as an unavowable outcrop from the foreign office, and the security service (MI5). Both have, obviously enough, worked in steady cooperation with the service departments, particularly with their chiefs of intelligence. MI6 had, again obviously enough, links with the foreign office, and MI5 with the police and the aliens branch of the home office. Formally, MI6 came under the foreign and MI5 under the home secretary, though the head of each service had the right of direct access to the prime minister.

During the war of 1914–18, the cipher section of the naval intelligence department grew so much that it was virtually a third secret service; and in the war of 1939–45 several fresh ones were created. The full list would include MI5, MI6, MI9, RSS, GCCS, SOE and PWE; on the edge of it would hover such empyrean authorities as HDE and the W committee, and such bodies as Colonel Turner's department of the air ministry and the LCS.

Of MI5 there is little that needs to be said, beyond a reference to its work for

---

[1] Cp. A. Zweig, *The Case of Sergeant Grischa* (tr. E. Sutton, 1928), book III; Foot, 178–9; Amery, *Approach March*, 134.
[2] *Point Counter Point* (1928), 114–15.

deception;[1] a reminder that it kept the whole British mainland safe from nazi counter-infiltration, no mean feat; and a mention of the Wandsworth block. For Britain got a great advantage from being an island: the country was far more simple to isolate than, say, Belgium or Czechoslovakia. Ulster apart, there were no land frontiers. Everyone who arrived by sea or air had to go through some form of passport control; and, unless vouched for personally by one of the services (open or secret) or covered by a diplomatic passport, had to pass through an interrogation centre in the requisitioned Royal Victoria Patriotic School at Wandsworth, in south London.

The school was run jointly by MI5 and MI19 (refugees): while MI5 cleared arrivals for security, MI19 cross-questioned them about their journey, and about ordinary life where they had come from. It was all quickly and courteously done; an honest man or woman had nothing to fear. It provided a starting test of sincerity for those who had come to Britain to help resistance from outside; and the meshes of its net were tight enough for MI5 to be able to catch enemy agents who tried to slip through it.

When the war began MI5 was still under its original head, Sir Vernon Kell, who was by then sixty-six; too old to be a proper match for opponents a generation younger than his own. He was succeeded in the autumn of 1940 by Sir David Petrie, who though only six years younger than himself had had thirty-six years' continuous service in the Indian police to sharpen his wits in matters of security, and to teach him knowledge of men. Petrie was able to modernize both the personnel and the methods of a service of which, again, the least said the better.

As for MI6, the British intelligence service had a tremendous reputation when the war began. Though the department was only then some thirty years old, the reputation of the British government for possessing excellent information went back long before. It could be traced back far behind the pandits' operations in the Himalaya and the Hindu Kush, familiar to millions through Kipling's *Kim* (1901). A century before *Kim*, the younger Pitt had been operating covertly against revolutionary France. Thurloe had kept Cromwell informed in the mid seventeenth century; in the late sixteenth, Walsingham had unravelled Mary Queen of Scots' and Philip II of Spain's plans against the great Elizabeth, in the early days of the modern state.

In the war of 1914–18, the service had brought off some remarkable *coups*; particularly in association with NID, Admiral Hall's deciphering teams in room 40 of the admiralty.[2] The welding of field intelligence, decipher, press, postal, and secret intelligence into a single war-winning weapon had been thoroughly well done; even if weak liaison between the intelligence and operations

---

[1] pp. 29–30 above.
[2] The fact that Barbara W. Tuchmann's *The Zimmermann Telegram* (1959) is almost as exciting to read as a thriller in no way detracts from its value as a history book.

branches of the admiralty had prevented Jutland from being an immediately convincing victory. But, since then, there had been some decay.

The selfless ideals of service to one's country, on which an organization of this sort must rest, were a good deal blown upon by the middle 1930s. Sir Mansfield Cumming, the original head, died in 1923 (it was in his memory that his successors signed their minutes 'C', and were so known by their subordinates and by those who dealt with them in Whitehall).[1] Hall lived another twenty years, Compton Mackenzie another fifty; but none of the surviving wartime operators was growing any younger. Sir Hugh Sinclair, C when the war began, was an admiral like Hall, but without Hall's imaginative insight; a less versatile and less commanding personality. The depth to which the service had sunk is shown by the ease with which – within a week of his death – the Germans arrested two of his officers, one of them rather senior, at Venlo. This utterly unprofessional event[2] suggests that SIS was infected at the start of the war with that fatuous over-confidence in British superiority which was endemic in other parts of the imperial structure at the time; notably, as the course of the war showed two years later, in the colonial service in south-éast Asia.

Sinclair's successor, (Sir) Stewart Menzies, was also a regular officer by training and a gentleman by birth; he had served in the household cavalry before entering SIS.[3] He had energy, brains, tactical sense, and political flair; some of his flair he used in the politics of Whitehall, some against his country's enemies. The passion for the devious was strong in him – hence a good deal of feeling in other departments that he was not quite straight; but secret services can seldom be both straight and efficient.

The service he took over had been largely staffed in peacetime by men whose careers had started in the Indian police, such as his deputy Valentine Vivian; this early work as members of a tiny, all-powerful minority had marked them for life. During the war there was a large influx of dons, more flexible in their outlook and decidedly more intelligent. How many of them there were, and how they were organized, remain and are likely to remain secret: this, like the running of escape lines, is one of the fields in which governments feel intelligibly enough that secrets need to be kept for ever, or at least for a very long time, in case past *coups* can be repeated. Most of what we know about SIS's wartime organization comes from a tainted source: Philby the defector, whose object in writing his book was to sling as much mud as he could at the service he had penetrated.[4]

His version is that it was divided broadly into two halves; one under Dansey of operational sections working into various parts of the world, the other under Vivian that assessed what the operations turned up. Between the two halves hovered his own section, V (Roman five, not Vee), which dealt with security;

[1] Eg. Masterman, xix.
[2] See L. de Jong, *Het Koninkrijk der Nederlanden*, ii. 80–115 (1969).
[3] *Times* obituaries, 31 May, 14g, and 6 June, 12g, 1968.
[4] Kim Philby, *My Silent War* (New York 1968).

provided of course a spacious arena for dispute with MI5; and gave him his postwar opportunities for trouble-making. As John Le Carré once put it,

A secret service, in designating its intelligence targets, declares its own ignorance and thereby points to the areas in which it is most easily deceived. A penetrated secret service is not just a bad one: it is an appalling liability. In place of an all-seeing eye, it becomes a credulous ear and a misleading voice, innocently deceiving its own customers in every sphere of the national security; diplomatic, strategic and economic.[1]

Secret services need, if they are to be efficient, to plan a long way ahead of current events. MI6's planning for the war, before it broke out, was inadequate to the challenge with which it had to deal. Preparations for work into north-west Europe suffered from two radical defects. They all assumed the survival intact of France as a combatant ally in control of her own territory; and all the details were arranged from the Netherlands, in so incompetent a fashion that the nazis were able to unravel the whole prearranged spy structure in June 1940.

MI6's man in The Hague was rash enough to summon almost all his proposed agents to meet him in an office, with suitable commercial cover, in one of the central *grachten*; and did not know that every daylight arrival and departure was photographed by a nazi agent through the porthole of a nearby houseboat. Nor did he take in that his accountant, who fled in May 1940, left behind him notes of all sums paid out and when and to whom, over several years past.[2] And MI6 used to accuse SOE of being unprofessional.

Improvisation was the only resource left; MI6 was flexible enough to rise to this challenge, at least.

Philby does not make clear the relation, at which the outsider can only guess, between SIS and two vital and equally secret parts of the intelligence machine: the Government Code and Cypher School at Bletchley and the Radio Security Service. For our present purposes, we hardly need do more than note that they existed. Their importance in securing an Allied victory was clearly great; but their impact on resistance was usually indirect, apart from one matter of technical importance.

Watch was kept on every known wireless wavelength, and presumably an attempt was made to analyse all the clandestine traffic: this is likely to be the practice of any state that can command the equipment, and RSS's name suggests that it was the British service concerned. From a practical resister's point of view, this meant that London would probably be aware of the fact at least of any wireless message, unless sent on a very short-range set; with the skills of GCCS, London could probably become aware of the content also, given an adequate volume of traffic, a breakable cipher, and someone with the time and energy to pursue the point.

[1] Introducing B. Page, D. Leitch, and P. Knightley, *Philby* (Deutsch 1968), 22.
[2] De Jong, ii. 80–115, iii. 161; cp. pp. 259–62 below.

Exactly the same applied to Berlin – that is, wireless traffic was virtually certain to be known to both sides in the end; but German decipherers do not appear to have been quite up to the standards of GCCS. Unless actually dealing with a particular case, Gestapo officers seldom seemed to have mastered previous messages.[1]

The impact of GCCS and RSS, then, on resistance was marginal; that of MI9 and still more of SOE was direct.

MI9 was set up in September 1939, and expanded in the summer of 1940, as the war took a turn wholly unexpected by the British. Large occupied areas within easy air range of the United Kingdom presented much wider opportunities for escape organization than had been foreseen; and the presumed presence on north French and Belgian soil of thousands of evaders who had neither reached Dunkirk in time, nor been taken prisoner, presented a challenge worth taking up. The *ad hoc* arrangements made in Marseilles by Ian Garrow and others were taken in hand and systematized by a small, highly secret, highly efficient staff. Its head, Brigadier Crockatt, and his deputy Lieutenant-Colonel Langley, were both commanding personalities in their own right; and in A. J. Evans and Airey Neave they had among their staff two of the most distinguished escapers of either war.[2]

MI9 did so much to help the air ministry by rescuing trained pilots that it was suspected, no doubt unfairly, by other British and American services working from London of having undue pull with the special duty squadrons. Crockatt seldom had trouble, weather apart, in securing aircraft for drops or pick-ups when he needed them; he needed many fewer of them than other claimants on those squadrons' time. By keeping his organization small, he helped to keep it secret.

SOE, on the other hand, was engaged in a constant struggle to remain secret, although military necessity compelled it to expand, and by 1944 to make itself much more widely known to the rest of the fighting services than it would in security theory have desired.

The Special Operations Executive was a British secret service formed *ad hoc*, in the crisis of July 1940, 'to co-ordinate all action, by way of subversion and sabotage, against the enemy overseas'.[3] It fused together EH, a propaganda branch of the foreign office; a research branch of the war office, called MIR; and a new but lively part of MI6, section D. This section had been formed in March 1938 'To investigate every possibility of attacking potential enemies by means other than the operations of military forces'; as its head put it with characteristic

---

[1] David Kahn, *The Codebreakers* (1966), esp. ch. 14 and 15, summarizes all earlier published work.

[2] Evans's *Escaping Club* (1921, often reprinted) is deservedly a classic. Neave's *Saturday at MI9* (1969) is not far behind it in interest.

[3] Quoted in Foot, 8–9, from a most secret cabinet memorandum by Neville Chamberlain of 19 July 1940.

force, 'one felt as if one had been told to move the Pyramids with a pin'.[1] He was
L. D. Grand, a regular engineer officer by origin, a man of imagination, originality, and driving power, who did not stay with the organization long.[2] His
opposite number from the war office, J. C. F. Holland, another regular engineer,
who had fought with Lawrence in Arabia – thus winning a distinguished flying
cross – had conceived of some such body as SOE when in Ireland during the
troubles of the early 1920s. Researching on methods of irregular warfare, he
projected among other innovations the escape and deception services; and, SOE
once safely founded, went off to command an engineer battalion.[3] He was clearly
the best type of unobtrusive, self-effacing public servant, on which such greatness
as Great Britain had was founded.

Unluckily for resistance, SOE's work for it was hampered for over a year by
an intricate inter-departmental quarrel in London, involving several separate
government offices, about the control of propaganda. The original concept of SOE
would have put every instrument of sabotage, subversion, and political disruption under the one directing body. This rational solution was too coldly
rational to be accepted at that time by all those concerned; who included too
many people less self-effacing than Holland. In August 1941 these wrangles
came to an end with the removal from SOE of its main propaganda element, to
form the Political Warfare Executive under Leeper. (Leeper later went back to
diplomacy, and was succeeded by Bruce Lockhart.) PWE's main offices were
housed in the splendours of Woburn Abbey; it worked in incessant contact with
the BBC.[4] SOE got on with organizing resistance where it existed, and if
necessary creating it where it did not.

Constitutional responsibility for it was accepted by the minister of economic
warfare – Hugh Dalton till February 1942, Lord Selborne thereafter; and from
time to time it received directives from the chiefs of staff. Selborne and Churchill
were personal friends, and their friendship was now and again important to
resistance, for it gave Selborne a chance to put Churchill's weight as well as his
own behind purposes of SOE's that mattered; unluckily for SOE, 'Butch' Harris
was as close a friend of Churchill's as Selborne and a country neighbour in
Buckinghamshire as well. But SOE's work was necessarily too intricate for
ordinary ministerial control to apply; and parliament was given no chance to
discuss it. A succession of executive heads – Gladwyn Jebb the diplomat, Sir
Frank Nelson an India merchant and former conservative MP, Sir Charles
Hambro, and Sir Colin Gubbins – did have some direct personal control over
policy, and a little over operations. Jebb, Nelson and Taylor between them set SOE
up, and forced recognition of it in Whitehall: Jebb then returned to his foreign
office career, which led him ultimately to the Paris embassy and the House of
Lords. Nelson had burned himself out in two years' unremitting struggle, and
died – miserably poor, but not forgotten by anyone who had served close to him

---

[1] Quoted from Foot, 2.       [2] He died in November 1975.
[3] *Who Was Who 1951–60*, private information.  [4] Cp. pp. 58–9 above.

– in 1966. Hambro, of the banking family, who was appointed to succeed him on the ground that a man who could run the Great Western Railway was fit to run anything, and who had managed SOE's work in Scandinavia with much success, had to resign in September 1943 on a difference of opinion with Selborne about the proper chain of command in the near east.[1] The last executive head – known as CD, an inheritance from Grand's days – was Colin Gubbins, who had earlier used the symbol M, as chief of SOE's operations division, from November 1940.

Gubbins, a small, spare, wiry highlander with a keen brain, was forty-four when he joined SOE. He had been through Woolwich – and Dublin – with Holland, whose ideas he shared: the two had run MIR together in the months leading up to the war. He had earned his military cross as a field gunner in France in the Great War; had served under Ironside at Murmansk, an experience he never forgot; had spent some time in the early 1930s in war office intelligence; was one of the few people to emerge with credit from the Norwegian campaign, where he earned a DSO; and had spent the summer of 1940 organizing stay-behind parties in southern England, to make trouble along the communications of the German army of invasion that never arrived.[2] He had a fiery personality, under firm control, considerable gifts of leadership, and some for making enemies.[3]

He and his predecessors stood in turn at the head of a staff pyramid. Next below them, and meeting with them once a week at least – every day, in times of crisis – at SOE's main headquarters at 64 Baker Street, was a council of some sixteen people, the most senior officers in SOE and advisers to it from outside: a working committee that prepared most of SOE's main policies and had a perceptible influence on resistance strategy.[4] SOE was *sui generis*, had a flavour all its own: much of this flavour stemmed from its council. Beneath council, sometimes with intervening controllers, came what were called 'country sections', each responsible for work into a particular occupied country, and technical sections, dealing with security, clothing,[5] forgery, cipher, armament, air liaison, and so on. The organigrams in the French book give an accurate, though incomplete, picture of SOE's organization and how it fitted into the rest of the British war machine.[6] Large intermediate staffs existed at Cairo, Delhi, Kandy,

---

[1] Cp. p. 159 below.

[2] Details in David Lampe, *The Last Ditch* (1968).

[3] His was another death after this book went to press: see *Times* obituaries, 12, 17, 19 February 1976, 16 gh. See also his remarkable articles in *RUSIJ* xciii. 210 (May 1948) and in M. R. Elliott-Bateman ed. *Fourth Dimension of Warfare* (Manchester 1970), 83.

[4] See the account of it, from another and more perceptive pen, in Foot, 27.

[5] The clothing section included two refugee continental tailors, who were able to provide agents with clothes of impeccably continental cut. One of them had brought over to England with him two bolts of continental pyjama cloth; so all the men agents had two pairs of continental pyjamas. One, newly arrived in occupied territory, was staying his first full night with a longer-established colleague; who looked into his room, last thing, to make sure he was comfortable; saw what his guest was wearing; and said with a rueful smile, 'Ah, *pyjamas maison*. I'd get some others if I were you. Good-night.'

[6] Foot, 36–8.

and New York, later at Algiers, and later still at Bari; besides offices on neutral territory, under business or journalistic or diplomatic cover (or all three), in such centres as Ístanbul, Tangier, Lisbon, Bern, and Stockholm. At the pyramid's base, besides the clerks, drivers, cooks, and batmen without whom no unit could survive, and the hundreds of wireless and cipher staff who were indispensable to this particular group of units, were the actual operative secret agents: whether still under training, waiting their turn to go, or already at work on some occupied spot.

SOE's exact total size remains unknown, and may now be irrecoverable. It probably reached a maximum of about 10,000 men and 3,000 women in the spring of 1944; something like the strength of a single fighting division. The influence it exercised on the war was disproportionately very much greater.

Recruiting for it was haphazard; necessarily founded on whom the people already in it happened to know and to trust. Holland's and Gubbins's acquaintances in the service world, and the many people Grand knew in the City of London, provided a start. Half of the Council were regular officers, a quarter senior business men; most of the staff were youngish business men or professionals, with a sprinkling of regulars and of people who had spent their lives in secret work. Gubbins's chief of staff, R. H. Barry, was a regular light infantryman who had been through the staff college. Some of his colleagues affected to despise drills, staff tables, all the donkey-work of organization; this did not always make SOE efficient, or endear it to staff officers in other services with whom its sections had to work. But there were very few *embusqué* or skrimshanker types in SOE, however unsoldierly some of SOE's manners and mannerisms were. The outstanding characteristics, both of the staff and of the agents, were vigour, originality, and enthusiasm. Everybody in SOE felt themselves to belong to a special kind of élite, a picked body called on for vital, unusual, significant tasks; and they were no more 'amateurs' than their opposite numbers in SIS – or in the SD.

They none of them claimed to know everything. For preparing agents to work in the field, they had a series of training schools, in southern England and on the wild west coast of Scotland. The subjects taught included paramilitary training, in small arms of several nations' makes, sabotage, unarmed combat, boating, parachuting, propaganda, and – in a special school at Beaulieu – the elements of clandestine behaviour: how to change identity (be thorough), how to follow a suspect (be inconspicuous), how to be interrogated (be silent), how to escape (be quick).

Be quick in fact was a constant motto for SOE; overshadowed only by Be secret. The organization found it necessary to work in a dense cloak of security: so dense as to create confusion and misunderstanding among people who might have helped, as well as diverting or at any rate diffusing suspicion. 64 Baker Street had a plaque outside that read 'Inter-Services Research Bureau'; four or five other cover names, such as AI10 or MO1(SP), were in use simultaneously.

People in the body were expected not even to tell their own parents or wives what they were doing, even in the barest outline. Officers on small boats in Cornwall, for instance, let it be known locally that they were engaged in signals training, thus accounting for the festoons of radar aerials on their craft; one was told by his wife it was time he went 'to do something dangerous like other boys'.

Strains spread well outside the family: SOE's relations with the other British secret services were often rough. This was due in part to difficulties of personal jealousy and suspicion, which seem to be endemic in that world. More important was the simple, profound fact that SOE's agents went abroad to make trouble – to promote unrest, disquiet, ill feeling, riot, even revolution. The troubled life SOE was trying to create provided the worst conditions conceivable for escape or intelligence agents, who needed quiet streets and lanes patrolled by somnolent police forces, or not patrolled at all.

SOE represented an acknowledgement by the British government that war was no longer entirely a gentleman's affair. A raffish, amateurish, disreputable air has stuck to it. At the time, people in it welcomed being thought disreputable; it made excellent cover for efficiency.

### American

The United States Federal Bureau of Investigation was founded in 1908, even before MI5; its wartime head, J. Edgar Hoover, was appointed in 1924 when Schellenberg was still at school, and held office till his own death forty-eight years later.[1] He had been in charge of American security for the better part of twenty years, in fact, before ever the USA became involved in the war; and remained, unruffled if sometimes surly, in charge of it till long after that war and several others were over, irrespective of which party was in power.

The FBI was set in its ways, but it had also plenty of practice: prohibition's criminal fringe, and the gangster aftermath, made sure of that. As late as 1940 a secretary of the interior could inform Hoover that 'gentlemen do not read each other's letters'; and a visitor from SOE in 1942 saw, with a touch of *Schaden-freude*, a large sign in a Washington side street near the White House: NO PARKING: U.S. SECRET SERVICE ONLY.[2] Hoover was also notoriously no lover of communists.

He was no lover of nazis either; and whatever else he was, he was no fool. Necessarily, the Japanese danger preoccupied him at times more than either the nazi or the communist one; and against it at least he did protect his constitution and his president. But he suffered from that feeling common to people who have long been in the same post, the feeling that he was in complete control of his subject and no one else could come near it without making trouble. This, combined with his long experience and strong personality, made him a formidable

---

[1] *Times* obituary, 3 May 1972, 12g.
[2] Sweet-Escott, 126.

opponent in inter-departmental wranglings in Washington, which were no less acute than those in London, on the problems of how help to resistance in particular and secret warfare in general were to be organized.[1]

Even Hoover was not going to gainsay a direct order from his president; Roosevelt like Churchill was interested by the secret war and ready to dabble in it. The president read, not always with full understanding, the 'Magic' products of the extremely competent American deciphering service;[2] befriended an American hero, 'Wild Bill' Donovan; and directed him to take charge of overseas intelligence in July 1941. Donovan had already joined with 'Little Bill' Stephenson, the Canadian steel millionaire who headed the British secret organizations in the USA, in persuading Roosevelt to agree to the destroyers-for-bases deal in the autumn of 1940;[3] and had visited Britain, Egypt, and the Balkans in the winter of 1940–1, attracting adverse notice from Goebbels, who read his cipher telegrams home. As 'Coordinator of Information' he headed the first body ever formed in the USA for the systematic collection and collation of strategic intelligence.

On 13 June 1942 a military order of Roosevelt's transformed it into the Office of Strategic Services, placed it under the joint chiefs of staff, and re-nominated Donovan as its head.[4]

OSS had three principal branches: intelligence, operations, and research; to which were added departments for security, black propaganda, sabotage by sea, operational groups (much the same as SAS), and training.[5] The head of its research branch, William L. Langer the diplomatic historian, stood so high in American academic circles that he could command some outstanding intellects for OSS work; the young Arthur M. Schlesinger, for example, was one of the advisers on French politics. Donovan kept as close a control as he could over intelligence and operations; he was a friend of Mountbatten's and had been shown round a number of British establishments for training in secret and irregular warfare well before Pearl Harbor.

To give his operational groups a better chance to cooperate with the resisters among whom they were to work, he ordered that they should acquire a grounding at least in the language of whatever country was destined to be the scene of their work. This was a sensible preparation; not one that SAS ever dreamed of taking. But SAS worked largely with British Tommies; while OSS had the immense linguistic resources of the USA behind it. These were used extensively.

Just as SOE had to clear all its agents with MI5, OSS had to clear everyone in its employ with the FBI: a fruitful source of bickering. Hoover was always on the watch to make sure no one else infringed his department's prerogatives, and was frankly jealous – his enemies said, to the point of paranoia – of OSS. He got

[1] But see the attack on him in *Time* magazine, 22 December 1975, 30–5.
[2] See Kahn, *The Codebreakers*, ch. i.
[3] Corey Ford, *Donovan of O.S.S.* (1971), 88–94.
[4] Text ibid. 127–8.    [5] Details ibid. 168; organigram ibid. 338–9.

a ruling for example from Roosevelt that Latin America fell within his preserve rather than Donovan's: a ruling that OSS and SOE later combined to ignore.[1]

OSS's exact strength is no more known than is SOE's. Harris Smith, its unofficial but painstaking historian, does give a total figure of over 13,000 Americans. This would leave out citizens of other countries who worked in it; but it would seem to have been of almost exactly the same size as SOE.[2]

With Stephenson of BSC, as we have just seen, Donovan found it easy to cooperate, and the two got on excellently at their exalted level: not so their underlings. SIS and SOE did what they could to give OSS seniors the benefit of such wartime experience as they had gained; SOE was after all by two years the older body, and SIS was a good deal more senior still. Once it was possible to set up a combined staff, with excellent results: in north-west Europe the SO branch of OSS was fused with the relevant operational directorate in SOE, under the joint leadership of David Bruce – formerly Donovan's head of SI, later a leading American diplomat – and a quiet British regular gunner, E. E. Mockler-Ferryman, who had been in the same gunner brigade as Gubbins in Dublin twenty years before.

Elsewhere conditions varied. In Thailand, to take a fierce and distant example, a series of political and personal accidents almost put SOE and OSS at daggers drawn; they infiltrated the country separately with rival bands of agents.[3] As a rule things were not so bad; one service would take the lead and make most of the running, the other would chime in in support. In French North Africa in the early autumn of 1942, for instance, OSS did most of the clandestine preparation for the 'Torch' landings; while SOE engaged in cover operations in Greece. Later, in Greece, there were some unfortunate tensions between SOE and OSS men on the spot; caused mainly by the political accidents that the Americans there saw sneaking British imperialism lurking under every parachute, and the communists believed they saw a chance of dividing two capitalist powers from each other and thus accelerating the collapse of world capitalism.[4]

Such powerful myths apart, the main trouble was traceable back to an almighty staff muddle, precipitated between Washington and London in October 1942. SOE's mission in the US proposed to OSS a common staff in north Africa, after 'Torch' had succeeded, to work into Italy, France, and the west Mediterranean islands. Baker Street was informed, by a personal cipher cablegram to a staff officer who was fool enough to say nothing about it to anyone; so strong was SOE's obsession with security. Simultaneous talks with Donovan's man in London reached the opposite conclusion; their result was reported back to Washington; and Donovan was naturally livid. 'I was never quite clear', one of the British negotiators later wrote, 'whether they suspected our integrity or doubted our competence. Whichever it was it did not help us.'[5] This incident,

---

[1] R. Harris Smith, *OSS* (1972), 6, 19; henceforward: Harris Smith.
[2] Ibid. 3, 22.      [3] Ibid. 291–308.
[4] Cp. p. 180 below.      [5] Sweet-Escott, 139–40.

small in itself, had consequences of weight for the 'special relationship' the British believed themselves to enjoy with the Americans.

### Russian

The Russians, like the French, have a long tradition of government by police; unlike the French or the British or the Americans, they are used to living in a closed rather than an open society. The survival of the majority – bolshevik – wing of the social-democratic party in the second revolution of 1917, the body now known as the communist party of the Soviet Union, which still holds power nearly sixty years later, was originally due almost as much to Dzerzhinsky the chief of secret police as to Trotsky the military commander or to Lenin the presiding genius. It was Dzerzhinsky who provided the soviet agents' motto, 'Clean hands, cool head and a hot heart'.[1] It was he who organized the Cheka, on the lines and with the methods of the tsarist Okhrana, to hold the country down, and first supervised its expansion abroad, to suit the aims of the comintern.

By the late 1930s the organization, often re-named, had achieved considerable power the world over, and within the USSR had a position of tremendous authority, comparable to – interlaced with – that of the ruling party. Under Stalin's orders, it carried out the great purge which Russians call, after its then head, the *Yezhovshchina*.[2] Yezhov, having served his turn, was one of the purge's victims as it burned itself out in 1938.

So closed was soviet society that the extent of the purge was surpringly little known at the time outside the soviet borders. If foreign governments knew about it, they kept quiet, in order not to compromise their sources. Newspaper reporters, unless sympathetic to the régime, were unlikely to stay long; and if sympathetic to the régime, would not send abroad stories to its discredit. The great show trials of 1936 indicated that something very odd was happening; a credulous newspaper-reading public in the west was more interested in sport and holidays than in politics and cruelty. Arthur Koestler's *Darkness at Noon*, a singularly powerful political novel, appeared in 1940, when the left press could shrug it off as an anti-soviet tract and the right press had other problems to worry about: such as national survival. Weissberg's *Conspiracy of Silence*, direct testimony by a leading scientist, did not appear till 1952 and, again, could be presented by those who could not or would not believe it as an operation in the cold war. Evgenia Ginzburg's still more harrowing *Into the Whirlwind* was not published till 1967.

In short, the Russian secret police forces had, by a deft mixture of secrecy, propaganda and terror, secured themselves a fairly clear field for work. There were two of them, the NKVD and the GRU.

The *Narodny Komissariat Vnutrennich Dyel*, the people's commissariat of

---

[1] 'Rudolf Abel' in *Molodoi Kommunist*, February 1966, cited [and tr.] by D. Wise and T. Ross, *The Espionage Establishment* (1968), 77.

[2] Cp. p. 8 above.

internal affairs, was the successor body to the Cheka, and the ancestor of today's KGB. Yezhov's successor as its head, appointed in November 1938, was Lavrenti Pavlovitch Beria, a Georgian like Stalin but twenty years younger, born in 1899. A squat, tubby, baldish man in rimless spectacles, he has left a considerable reputation as a lecher – virgins in their mid teens are supposed to have been his speciality – but, whatever his private life or lack of it, he was no more of a fool than Hoover was. He had been a secret policeman since the early 1920s, and having spent so long in the work was as cruel and as sly as his exacting post demanded: he held it for all but fifteen years, far the longest tenure of the post, till his colleagues had him shot soon after Stalin died.

It was then alleged that he had been a British agent all along. No evidence to support so wildly improbable a charge has ever been published; that it was levelled at all represents a curious kind of back-handed compliment to MI6.

Important though Beria's post was, his own political standing was not particularly high during the war. Not till after it was over, in 1946, was he admitted to the governing committee of his committee-run state, the politburo; a promotion that may be taken as some sign that his new colleagues and his chief were pleased with the work he had done. Not much is known about such political life as there was near the summit in the USSR during the war. Most of the day-to-day work seems to have been done by a committee of half-a-dozen under Stalin, which did include Beria. Important points of policy were all no doubt referred to the politburo; but the politburo's members were inclined, as were those of the British war cabinet in the same years, to hang on the lips of their leading personality. Stalin in fact can be supposed to have acted as Beria's overseer.

So dense, and so long-lasting, is the fog of security about how affairs are really conducted, in the nominally democratic USSR, that the existence of the other soviet secret service is never officially acknowledged. This body, the *Glavnoye Razvedyvatelnoye Upravlenie* (GRU) or chief intelligence directorate of the general staff, was meant to handle strictly military intelligence, rather than state security. It was by no means immune from NKVD interference: General Berzin, who had built it up in fifteen years' assiduous if not always effective work, and his successor Uritsky – also a general, and the son of a friend of Lenin's – both disappeared in the great purge, and presumably their senior subordinates spent a few months at least in prison. Their successor was General Ivan T. Peresypkin, alias Fedor I. Kuznetsov (which means Smith). These arrests made a poor preparation for work against the German invasion; about which the service had been surprisingly under-informed in its preparatory stages[1] – let alone the crisis of June 1941, when it received sound reports but could not get them believed by Stalin.[2]

Beyond the fact that the GRU was then a good deal smaller than the NKVD, not much is known – or at any rate published – about the size of either. At the

---

[1] Cp. F. Moravec, *Master of Spies* (1975), 69–70.
[2] Cp. p. 288 below.

time of the war, the NKVD may have been roughly comparable in size to SOE or OSS; plus several thousand concentration camp guards. (The KGB, the name under which the NKVD now goes, was supposed to have a private army of as many as 300,000 men in the late 1960s.)[1] Both services could call on the world-wide mass of communists, open and secret: secret communists of course very much more useful to them than open ones, particularly if they could be fed as Maclean and Philby were into the official and even the secret staffs of potential opponents.

The GRU had one technical advantage over the NKVD: most of the material it needed to handle was itself technical, and therefore remote from a difficulty that is troublesome for political intelligence services under a dictatorship. The GRU did not need as a rule to slant the intelligence it transmitted to suit any particular whim of the political leadership; while the NKVD quite often did. On the other hand, the GRU needed to make sure that it employed politically reliable officers; and no doubt, like every other branch of soviet life, it was inter-penetrated by undercover agents of the NKVD, who reported back to their own superiors about anything they thought in any way subversive or even odd.

A section in the NKVD handled propaganda and disinformation; with a good deal of skill. Goebbels himself could envy the propaganda treatment 'our gallant soviet ally' received in the British and American press, all through the second half of the war. Such awkward corners as the discovery of corpses at Katyn were dexterously skated round, and as little as possible was done to shake the hopes that working masses in western Europe had placed in the soviet union since 1917. Everybody could see with half an eye that it was on the Russian front that the nazis were expending the bulk of their effort and their men; on the Russian front everything else depended. A devout marxist does not allow gratitude as a virtue; hundreds of millions of people felt grateful to the Russians, all the same, to the benefit of marxist world policy.

Marxists do not approve any kind of softness or sentimentality, either; except as a weapon of propaganda. Those who worked for the NKVD or the GRU were not always perfectly clear-headed or rational: their marxist beliefs prevented that. But they were always tough: with a toughness that makes the work even of SAS or SOE look more like a scouts' or schoolboys' field day than a world war. From this toughness, again, much of the communists' undoubted success in resistance derived.

### Governments in exile

A word is needed about the various refugee governments, recognized and unrecognized, with which Britain, Russia, and the Levant were dotted during the war. Each will call for special notice in the relevant section of the next chapter, but they are worth a brief collective note as well.

[1] Wise and Ross, *The Espionage Establishment*, 15.

Most – not all – had their main base in London; most – not all – depended to some extent on British financial help. Most – not all – brought with them the shreds at least of legitimacy: the prewar head of state, a flag, a code of constitutional law, duly appointed ministers; most had diplomatic representatives, accredited to the court of St James and to each other. From this arose an oddity of diplomatic history. During the early years of the war, the age-long distinction between ambassadors, in embassies, accredited between great powers, and ministers, in legations, accredited between lesser ones, vanished. It hurt the dignity of these governments in exile, affrontable already by an ill-timed sneeze, to bear any kind of mark of inferiority. The British, American, and Russian diplomatic services joined in the game; and 'legation' is a word that is now already verging on obsolescence.

Most, again, of these exiled bodies had, or quickly created, uniformed bodies of fighting men, often dressed in British battledress, but decked out with national signs and symbols as well. These forces of external resistance were all specially anxious to operate back in their homeland; this occasionally produced startling results. The sole survivor of a dozen Norwegians who had set out to try to organize north Norway, with SOE's help, in the spring of 1943 unexpectedly found himself skiing along a road, early in the morning, through a platoon of German soldiers shambling across it to breakfast; he was wearing a naval jacket, with the Norwegian flag and NORWAY bold on each shoulder; 'they stood back to right and left to let him pass'.[1]

All these forces of external resistance longed, naturally enough, to get back to their homelands and fight there. Most of them had regular officers, easy prey for the concept of a national redoubt. Their anxiety to form or to join such a redoubt featured prominently in their talks with Allied general staffs and with the relevant secret services.

These secret services' staffs often also found themselves in embarrassingly awkward relation with the secret services in exile of some of the occupied countries; for reasons easily enough understood. The British view of the British as naturally the kindest, gentlest, strongest, and wisest people in the world, is – strangely enough – not widely shared abroad, where we are regarded as a gang of wily imperialist oaves, seeking our own profit and our neighbours' downfall from behind a screen of honeyed words. A slogan that 'Great Britain will fight – to the last Ruritanian' could easily get credence among junior Ruritanian officers, torn already between loyalty to the Elphbergs and the need not to antagonize too far the growing power of organized labour in the homeland, or of the great victorious neighbour to the east. Secret services of conquered powers, temporarily based in London or Cairo, were bound to stand continually on their dignity, and to be suspicious that the British (for example) might nourish ultimate designs that

---

[1] David Howarth, *We Die Alone* (1955), 95, the tale of Jan Baalsrud's escape: a story not to be missed, that earns its *credo quia impossibile*, and proves that toughness was not confined to the communist camp.

conflicted with their own object: to re-establish full control over their sovereign territory. No evidence to bear out such doubts has been, or even needs to have been produced: of course there is no trace of such plans in the British war cabinet's records, and – again, carpers will say, of course – such plans would never be written down where an historian could find them. The American record is as clean as the British. The Russian record is unavailable, for impartial inspection; and no one who has read Orwell's *1984* would trust it, even if it were.

### German

A little needs to be said as well about the German secret services whose task it was to suppress resistance, indeed to root it out: not because they were staffs that directed resisters, but because they necessarily took up a good deal of resisters' attention. Their existence was prominent among the data resistance planners, internal and external, had to bear in mind when making plans; their methods, by an irony their chiefs had not foreseen, served in the end to swell the ranks they were trying to disband.

There were two main services; both known popularly by the name of a part of one of them, the Gestapo. As we have seen already with SIS and SOE, FBI and OSS, NKVD and GRU, it seems to be common – to the verge of inevitability – for two secret services of the same power to be each other's rivals. The Germans' rivalry was unusually sharp: so sharp indeed that in 1944 one service swallowed the other up, and its head was executed a few days before the war's end on the orders of his supplanter.

Of the loser, Admiral Wilhelm Canaris, we know a little;[1] of his service, the *Abwehr*, not much. There is a straightforward popular outline of its work by a former member of it;[2] and a very detailed study by an American expert of the efforts of two of its out-stations to plant agents in Great Britain, from which a good deal of general significance can be inferred.[3] The *Abwehr* was the German armed services' intelligence and security authority, responsible for protecting them against resisters' attacks and for discovering what their enemies were going to do next. The German army included a corps of military police, the *Feldgendarmerie*, of which the policemen wore shiny brass breastplates, as deliberately conspicuous as the red caps of their British, the blue caps of their Russian, or the white helmets of their American opposite numbers. The *Abwehr*'s *Geheime Feldpolizei*, secret field police, might operate in field-grey or in plain clothes, as they chose. In the end, this service organization was elbowed out of the way by the party organization of the SS; into which its staff were absorbed *en bloc*.

[1] See Ian Colvin, *Chief of Intelligence* (1951).

[2] Paul Leverkuehn, *German Military Intelligence* (1954).

[3] Ladislas Farago, *The Game of the Foxes* (1972); an interesting book to read, because the author's preconceptions can be seen to alter under the weight of the evidence he unearths.

The SS, originally Hitler's personal bodyguard, became under Heinrich Himmler a state within the nazi state, operating outside the bounds of the nazi constitution; with its own administration, its own factories, its own armed force – the *Waffen-SS*, the very toughest troops under Hitler's command. On the *Waffen-SS*, Stein's book is definitive.[1] Resisters who had the bad luck to encounter them could expect, and normally received, no mercy.

Of the security and political side of the SS we now have an exceptionally full and scholarly account, prepared for the Auschwitz trials in Frankfurt in 1963; it touches the SS troops as well. Anybody who wants to pursue the intricacies of the overlaps and distinctions between the imperial security headquarters (RSHA), the security service (SD), the criminal police (Kripo), and the secret state police (*geheime Sta*atspolizei, Gestapo) can do so, led by an expert hand, in the six hundred learned pages of Professor Krausnick and his colleagues.[2]

For one thing above all the SS are, and will remain, notorious: they ran the concentration camps. To these the least fortunate resisters were consigned; and in them hundreds of thousands of resisters, as well as several million Jews, were as a deliberate act of government policy put to death. Anybody who believes, in the opinion mistakenly attributed to Governor Wallace,[3] that the USA fought on the wrong side in the war of 1941–5 should look at Reimund Schnabel's *Macht ohne Moral*[4] and think again. So should anybody who believes that the frightful but minor atrocity at My Lai was an atrocity of a comparable kind: this is a case where Lenin's dictum about quantitative leading to qualitative change must be remembered.

---

[1] George H. Stein, *The Waffen-SS* (1966).
[2] Helmut Krausnick, Hans Buchheim, Martin Broszat, and Hans-Adolf Jacobsen, *Anatomy of the SS State* (1968).
[3] As reported in the London *Times*, 9 May, 9bc and 10 May 1975, 4f.
[4] Frankfurt-am-Main 1957: why never translated?

# 6 WHAT HAPPENED

Of the secret services we have just surveyed, those of the governments in exile were all necessarily much interested in and concerned with resistance, but almost all of them were technically weak: Moravec's Czechs in London, the dozen best men from one of the brightest prewar services,[1] and Gano's London Poles the outstanding exceptions. The NKVD on the other hand was technically strong; and SOE, SIS, MI9, and OSS all built up technical strength quite fast. Of them all, only the Russians and MI9 attempted as a rule any close control of operations; the Russians in frequent three-sided interactions between partisans, secret police, and Red Army staff; and MI9 by direct wireless contact with a few chosen organizers. OSS carried out one or two particular concerted drives, especially in the Maghreb in the autumn of 1942; so did SOE in attacks on the Gestapo in western Europe a year later. As a rule, in fact as in fiction, secret agents were out on their own; so were the resisters with whom they tried to work.

Fiction has to stress the excitements of the clandestine life. Those who have experienced it know that though it is, rarely, exciting, and now and again terrifying, a lot of it is exceedingly dull. Monotony, loneliness, boredom, even more than fright, were the resister's bugbears. A Tommies' proverb says, War is 99 per cent boredom and 1 per cent fright. A resister might encounter as much as 2 per cent of fright; 98 per cent is still an awful lot of boredom.

The stories that follow are bound to be episodic and incident-ridden. Till near the close of the occupation, an incident or at best a series of incidents was the most that any given group of resisters could hope to produce, however highly organized they were. Some incidents did carry almost Sarajevan weight: the assassination at Sarajevo, that sparked off the great war of 1914, was only after all a students' plot in a secular Balkan resistance context. (A society in which 'student' is becoming a new rude word would do well to remember this.) More-

[1] See p. 204 below.

over, much of what was known outside occupied Europe about life inside it consisted of reports of incidents, more or less garbled; on these, and only on these, people trying to devise policies to help and stimulate resistance had to make up their minds.[1]

There was not in fact any single consistent pattern that occupation followed. What the Germans (and their occasional allies) did, or wanted to do, in any country, was a function both of how they arrived there, and of who had been living there in the first place. Austria got different treatment from Alsace, very different treatment from Aquitaine or Attica. What was suitable in Rotterdam or Rouen might be unsuitable in Fiume (now Rjeka) and out of the question in Sebastopol. The Germans let their occupation policies be guided by their prevalent racial myth. This meant, in the first instance, comparatively favourable treatment for the supposedly aryan peoples of Denmark, Norway, the Netherlands, and Flemish-speaking Belgium; some respect on cultural grounds for France, Italy, Hungary, and Greece; and out-and-out contempt for any area that used the cyrillic script, thus proclaiming itself to be Slav and so foredoomed to subordination.

Stresses of occupation quickly upset these prearranged and in any case fanciful notions. The Dutch, the Norwegians, even the Danes who had hardly fired a shot at the critical moment of invasion, soon showed themselves reluctant to accept the nazi new order, or to accept the Germans as blood brothers. Unexpected allies turned up in south Russia; unexpected enemies in Paris, the Piraeus, Maastricht, Antwerp, a thousand and one other occupied places where the nazis had anticipated, if not welcome, at least acquiescence.

In every country they overran, the proportion of resisters varied with time. People often ask, Did many people resist in such-and-such an area? – a bad question, because history is founded on time as well as space, and if time is left out of its questions the answers may get twisted awry. Some occupied countries did at first almost capitulate: Austria for example or Denmark, or even deserted Czechoslovakia. The Dutch, Belgians, French, Greeks were overwhelmed by the speed of their military catastrophes, and most of them needed a few months at least to recover their breath and consider what they had best do. Even Aragon wrote of drinking that summer, like a dessert wine, in a country château: till the voice of necessity could be heard, louder than the fall of rose-petals, and he went to look for somewhere to fight.[2]

Others were more difficult from the very start. The Germans' troubles in Norway began the day they arrived, and did not cease till they surrendered over five years later. The Albanians, the Yugoslavs, above all the Poles made trouble: bad trouble: fast. Russian communists were, after 22 June 1941, irreconcilable; so were a growing number of ordinary Russian peasants, and peasants of (then minority) subject nationalities in the USSR. Everywhere there

[1] Cp. Foot, x, and Sir C. Parrott, *The Tightrope* (1975), 161.
[2] L. Aragon, *Crève-Cœur* (1944), 46.

were collaborators from the start; everywhere there were resisters also; the numbers of both combined were hardly ever, for the first few months of waiting and seeing, as high a proportion as 5 per cent – one in twenty – of each occupied population.

In some places people got thoroughly used to having the Germans there, and even accepted the nazi régime as permanent. If the reader thinks back to the state of world politics in the winter of 1940–1, with only the British empire and the kingdom of Greece in action against the hitherto irresistible Axis avalanche, with the USA still predominantly isolationist and the USSR positively engaged on the Axis side, the belief that the nazis had won will not seem absurd. A great many more people held it then than were prepared to admit it three or four years later.

For the impact of nazi occupation policy was everywhere the same: everybody came to detest it. This was almost true within Germany itself:[1] the number of convinced nazis grew smaller, if more fanatical, as the splendours of early victory clouded over into the downpour of defeat. The fighting services continued to fight; that was their job. Of the civilians, a devoted few hung on to the end, which was very bitter; millions of others had by then seen their mistake, but were terrified into tagging along with the rest. Elsewhere in Europe, in every country that had been occupied there came a moment when anti-nazi feeling became almost unanimous, and almost everyone was delighted to see them go. This hatred of nazism was the sole factor common to every resister; and in places, above all the places that had suffered much, it was (and in a few remains) intensely strong.

Such feelings were most nearly universal in areas which could welcome the liberating armies unaffectedly: Provence, the Netherlands, Norway, central Russia provide examples. Yet changing one occupier for another was not universally welcome. The Parisians were delighted to see the Americans – provided they were there *en touristes*, not to stay. The people of Prague felt the same about the Russians. As for the people of Warsaw, the few who survived – but it is time we went into detail.

The sections that follow provide a thumbnail sketch of the present state of published knowledge, of a very rough-and-ready kind. They first survey the world outside Europe; then, starting at Constantinople, move round the continent clockwise, by the Balkans, southern, western, northern, and eastern Europe; to end where the troubles began, in Germany.

Although each occupied area, and it is hoped each really significant resistance movement, is covered at least in outline, this is not an encyclopaedia of resistance activity – it is far too small a book to be that. This chapter aims simply at providing specimens to illustrate the chapters before it.

[1] See pp. 300–4.

## Outside Europe

Ever since the modern age began, great powers under great leaders have taken turns at envisaging world domination. Philip II's Spain, Louis XIV's and Napoleon's France, Wilhelm II's and Hitler's Germany and Stalin's Russia are examples that occur at once to Englishmen; others may probably want to add Victoria's England and Truman's America to the list. Every Chinaman has, since Europe was in the dark ages, grown up with the belief that control of China is much the same as control of the whole world; Mao's still unknown successor may yet be the first person on the list to achieve the aim.

World power must be a serious ambition to any follower of Nietzsche. Hitler was too clever a politician to say much about it in public before the time was ripe, and died before time could ripen that plum for him; the few people who knew him well had no doubt that he nursed the policy in secret. His secret services therefore necessarily worked on a world-wide basis. So did Stalin's; marxists being quite sure (among many other points) that their system is of universal accuracy and applicability.

SIS also worked the world over, a task facilitated by British control of so large a proportion of the world's cable network. SOE felt it necessary to operate at a similar range; and OSS also was determined not to be left behind. Some of OSS's most significant work, and a good deal of SOE's, was done in east Asia; and when one tries to assess the performance of the high command of either service in a European context, it is worth remembering that much of that high command's attention may at any given moment have been centred on some still remoter area.

We need not linger over these more distant outposts long.

### The Americas

The importance of south and central America to resistance in Europe was that, if the war spread to the Iberian peninsula, they might provide a lot of agents who could pass themselves off as Spaniards or Portuguese. The solitary practical gain was an excellent organizer, of Argentinian origin, for one of SOE's escape circuits that ran across the Pyrenees; who later married one of his passengers, a Scandinavian girl who had been working in France. It was nevertheless a necessary precaution for SIS, SOE, the FBI, and (as it turned out) OSS to place people here and there across the continent, in case the war took some unexpected turn; and even the NKVD may have made some acquaintances useful many years later, in Castro's or Allende's day.

In north America, the NKVD was engaged in its secular struggle with the FBI and the RCMP to plant agents inside the American and Canadian governmental machines; Gouzenko's revelations after the war was over, and some celebrated later spy trials, indicate with how much success.[1] Whether this helped the war against nazism is quite another thing.

[1] Eg. Report of the [Canadian] Royal Commission, 27 June 1946 (Ottawa).

The Americans' arrangements were reviewed a few pages back.[1] The British had an interesting combined headquarters in Rockefeller Center in New York, called British Security Coordination. The head of BSC, (Sir) William Stephenson, accepted the post on condition that he was in charge of all British secret activities north of the Mexican border; a condition that London accepted. This almost unique arrangement – secret services, as will have been noticed, tending to proliferate, and politicians tending to mistrust holders of secret power – worked remarkably well: thanks to Stephenson's lack of political ambition and the efficiency with which he worked. He was a Canadian steel magnate and financier, with a distinguished record as a fighting pilot in the previous war and many friends in high places. One of his former subordinates has written a highly informative account of his work.[2]

Most of what BSC did was remote from our subject, of resistance in Europe; there were occasional connexions. SOE's team set down to work out how South America might be protected, through demolitions and left-behind parties of saboteurs, against a Japanese attack included (Sir) A. J. Ayer the logician, later political adviser to SOE's gaullist country section, and (Sir) F. W. D. Deakin the historian, who later led the first British mission to Tito.[3] There was a big SOE paramilitary training school in Canada, on the shore of Lake Ontario near Oshawa, some thirty miles east of Toronto. This school was extensively used by OSS as well, both for training agents likely to be sent to the Balkans and for explaining to staff officers, in weekend courses, what clandestine operations could and could not do. These courses were the more popular with the Americans, because they involved service outside the United States and thus earned a campaign medal.[4]

BSC's most spectacular triumph was achieved in two embassies in Washington, under the noses of some FBI patrols who would sternly have disapproved, had they known what was going on, by the most successful woman agent of the war, the irresistible Betty Pack (later Madame Brousse), better known by her codename of 'Cynthia'. By apt seduction, she managed to obtain the loan overnight – long enough for photocopies to be made – successively of the Italian and of the Vichy French naval ciphers; with important results for the naval war in the Mediterranean. Without her work, the victory off Cape Matapan could never have been secured. This was only an indirect help to resistance; but it was a substantial one.[5]

Much the same can be said of the rest of BSC's work, and of that of the FBI. Stephenson began his career in America by making friends with Hoover, and offering the FBI every technical facility – well before the USA had entered the war. Equally he made friends with Donovan; and the combination of

[1] At pp. 141–3.  [2] H. Montgomery Hyde, *The Quiet Canadian* (1962).
[3] Sweet-Escott, 131.  [4] Ibid. 142–4.
[5] See H. Montgomery Hyde, *Cynthia* (1966); and her obituary in the *Manchester Guardian*, 9 December 1963.

'Wild Bill' and 'Little Bill' did a great deal for the common cause. They were able, with Hoover's help, to checkmate Axis efforts to interfere with American war production. Stephenson conducted a sustained pro-British, anti-fascist, and anti-Pétainist propaganda through acquaintances in American journalism, written and spoken. Above all, and this outshone even 'Cynthia's' dexterities, they prepared OSS for action.

### Australasia, East Asia

The epic successes and failures of Australians and New Zealanders on special operations in south-east Asia still await their historian. Their home countries do not affect this story either. A few of them took part in clandestine work in Europe; ranging from Norman Hinton, then an art student, who parachuted into France late in 1942, failed to reach the target he was to have blown up because it was too well guarded, and got away without being caught, to Tom Dunbabin the classical archaeologist who built up a tremendous reputation, both on the spot and in Cairo, while in charge of resistance in Crete. John Mulgan's book is a memorial to all those clear-headed and upright Antipodeans who came back to the old world to help to settle its quarrels, and like himself never saw the Pacific again.

Europeans most of them remember, or reflect on, the war too narrowly in European terms. It was even more of a world war than any of its predecessors; and if history is still being written in half-a-dozen centuries' time, it may well be the Asiatic rather than the European half of the war that seems the more significant in the long run, when all of us are dead. A few perceptive strategists in Moscow, London, Washington may have divined this at the time; particularly in Moscow, always inclined since 1917 to pursue Canning's doctrine of calling in a new world to redress the balance of the old. But Muscovites needed, during the war, to look west where imminent and deadly danger lay; the USSR was only at war with Japan for ten convulsive days, 9–20 August 1945, after the Hiroshima bomb had broken the remaining Japanese will to resist.

One soviet circuit in east Asia is worth mention: Richard Sorge, press attaché in the German embassy in Tokio, had been converted to communism at an early age, and in that atmosphere met nothing to lead him to change his mind. He ran an efficient intelligence network, informing Moscow *inter alia* of the date of Hitler's impending attack and of the certainty that the Japanese would not join in it: two pieces of information of exceptional value. In the end, an indiscretion by a sub-sub-agent put the Japanese police on his track, and he was caught and executed. A generation later, his head appeared on a USSR stamp: a rare admission by a government that it had actually engaged in espionage.[1]

Sorge's diplomatic posting got over the great difficulty that confronts everyone from outside who wants to operate clandestinely in eastern Asia: how account for skin colouring, hair colouring, face, so utterly unlike those of the

[1] See F. W. D. Deakin and G. R. Storry, *The Case of Richard Sorge* (1966).

locals? One strong and simple way round this difficulty was to ignore it: a course taken, with shattering success, by Spencer Chapman whom SOE left behind in Malaya. He emerged over two years later, leaving a trail of over a thousand dead Japanese behind him; but he was a man in ten thousand.[1]

In Burma as well as Malaysia SOE had some striking successes; which culminated in persuading the Burma Defence Army to change sides in the spring of 1945 and help throw out the Japanese.[2] In Thailand on the other hand SOE and OSS were almost disastrously at odds with one another.[3] Further east, in what had been French Indo-China, SOE frankly supported the French, who were anxious to get their colony back, while OSS operated in aid of the Viet Minh. Indeed by a splendid irony it was an OSS team that saved Ho Chi Minh's life when he was stricken with fever in July 1945.[4]

And in the great sub-continent of China, SOE and OSS were little more than spectators of the many-sided war that was in progress between the Japanese, the Chinese nationalists, the Chinese communists, and several local war-lords. The NKVD were hardly, if at all, better placed: the Chinese were working out their own salvation. Among them was the man shown by his achievement to be the leading theoretician of guerilla: Mao Tse-tung.

During the war, he put into action again the theories he had worked out during the long march of 1934-6, and before; above all his concept, now world famous, of the guerilla living among a friendly population as a fish lives in water. No one in Europe had the time or the space or the hundreds of millions of peasants necessary for the practical proof of Mao's theories; Tito came nearest to it, among European resistance leaders.[5] While Europeans were adjusting old scores, the Chinese were moving on to something new.

Mao had foreseen this. As far back as March 1927, just before he had to go on the run when the Kuomintang turned against the communists, he had produced this apocalyptic passage in a report on Hunan:

> The present upsurge of the peasant movement is a colossal event. In a very short time, in China's central, southern and northern provinces, several hundred million peasants will rise like a mighty storm, like a hurricane, a force so swift and violent that no power, however great, will be able to hold it back. They will smash all the trammels that bind them and rush forward along the road to liberation. They will sweep all the imperialists, warlords, corrupt officials, local tyrants and evil gentry into their graves. Every revolutionary party and every revolutionary comrade will be put to the test, to be accepted or rejected as they decide. There are three alternatives. To march at their head and lead them? To trail behind them, gesticulating and criticizing? Or to stand in their way and oppose them? Every

---

[1] F. Spencer Chapman, *The Jungle Is Neutral* (1949); *Times* obituary, 10 August 1971, 14g.     [2] Sweet-Escott, 243–9.
[3] Harris Smith, 291–318.     [4] Ibid. 332–3.
[5] See some further discussion on pp. 190–7 below.

Chinese is free to choose, but events will force you to make the choice quickly.[1]

## Africa

The African Mao, who will lead another horde of peasants into a new world, has yet to emerge. Most of the events in Africa that affect this story concerned Europeans visiting Africa, in one kind of imperial context or another.

A little was done by SOE in Madagascar in 1942 to countervail Vichy's influence in the island, before and during the British invasion. One of the agents concerned, France Antelme, a Mauritian who spoke perfect French but had never set foot in France, distinguished himself enough to be picked out for a delicate and important mission to Paris in the summer of 1943; which he survived, only to be dropped by inadvertence slap into the hands of the Germans some months later. A broader illustration of how the war was won came from one of the results of the Madagascan invasion: local labour supplied, unwittingly, the very pure graphite, essential to the making of the first atomic bombs.[2]

Orde Wingate, who could be relied on to be the exception to any rule, did make some real contact with Africans, on the right wing – which he led – of Wavell's advance into Ethiopia in the spring of 1941. His mixed force of Ethiopians and Sudanese, under British officers, and accompanied by the emperor himself on his return from exile, took 15,000 Italian prisoners in two months, and returned Haile Selassie to Addis Ababa. This was of importance in Europe for the depressant effect it had on the Italians; besides giving a good precedent for what to do with fascist or nazi invaders. 'Gideon Force', as Wingate was delighted to call it, was the distant precursor of several armies of liberation to come. Whatever Haile Selassie's ultimate fate – at the moment of writing he is deposed and under house arrest[3] – he was for years one of the symbols of the free world's hope that those who are merely brutal should not always have things their own way.

The only other special operation known in Africa, south of the Mediterranean and Moroccan coastlines, is the raid by a Brixham trawler called *Maid Honor* and a couple of tugs, crewed by British and Free French officers under the brilliant Gus March-Phillips, who in the spring of 1941 cut out an Italian liner from Fernando Po.[4]

Along the northern coastline there was much more of importance for resistance. Cairo was a vital centre of the British war effort, and had corresponding attention from SOE and several other services; and the coast from Tunis to Casablanca was in turn the scene of a large operation by OSS, and the springboard from which hundreds of agents later took off into Europe.

[1] *Quotations from Chairman Mao Tse-Tung* (Bantam Books, New York 1967), 65–6; tr. anon.   [2] Fragments in L. Grafftey-Smith, *Hands to Play* (1975), 49–74.

[3] Like Franco, he died while this was in the press: *Times* obituary, 28 August 1975, 12d.

[4] Sweet-Escott, 59, and J. E. A[ppleyard], *Geoffrey* (1946), 66–78.

Cairo's importance for the clandestine war, particularly in the Balkans, was great. MIR, one of the immediate parents of SOE, had a large and busy branch in GHQ Middle East,[1] known as GS(R); while section D, the other parent, took over the title of the body that had supervised Lawrence: MO4. The inter-departmental wrangles that were the curse of SOE's first year in London were reproduced on this more heated Egyptian stage, with the extra acerbity that comes from working on the edge of a great desert, twenty degrees closer to the equator. Sweet-Escott tells us that 'Nobody who did not experience it can possibly imagine the atmosphere of jealousy, suspicion, and intrigue which embittered the relations between the various secret and semi-secret departments in Cairo during that summer of 1941, or for that matter for the next two years.'[2] It is indeed astounding, to those who have never been exposed to the temptation, that grown men in responsible posts should behave in this way; it is equally astounding, to those who have never felt Cairene heat, that no official work of any kind was ever normally transacted in Cairo between two and five o'clock in the afternoon. Once, in July 1942 when the Germans were wrongly believed to be about to arrive, people worked all day, burning archives; while Auchinleck and Dorman-Smith were winning the decisive first battle of El Alamein, in reward for which they were both dismissed.

Within and around these hothouse headquarters SOE, SIS, and PWE wrangled with each other and with the service departments, with the foreign office, with governments in exile and with governments in embryo. Peter of Yugoslavia held tenuous court at Jerusalem before retiring via Cairo to London. George II of Greece preferred London to Cairo, but his exiled government preferred Cairo to London, and stayed in Africa. It was in Cairo that talks were held with Romanian and Bulgarian emissaries, seeking to make peace; and to Cairo as well as to London that the Jewish Agency in Palestine looked to forward its political and military aims. It was indeed in Cairo that their main rivals, the Arab League, held their foundation meeting in March 1945.

To strengthen the illusion that GHQ Cairo was like a dinosaur's subsidiary brain, lodged in the spinal cord to manage the beast's back legs, the British war cabinet kept a minister resident in the city – successively Lyttelton, Casey, Moyne, and Grigg – to resolve as many inter-service and policy questions as he could on the spot. The British embassy to Egypt, under a strong ambassador, Killearn, provided another political *point d'appui*.[3]

All these bodies produced, as may be imagined, a tremendous volume of wireless traffic between Cairo and London; sometimes much more than the signals staffs could manage. On one occasion at least, when even cipher messages bearing the highest priority were having to wait two or three days to be de-

---

[1] GHQ Middle East was located, to the annoyance of geographical pundits, in the near eastern city of Cairo. Near east and middle east became hopelessly confused, in the public mind, during the war, and now seem conflated for good.

[2] His p. 73.          [3] See Trevor Evans, *The Killearn Diaries* (1974).

ciphered, SOE had to call on army signals for help; which raised some awkward problems in security.[1]

Large possibilities were open to the nazi secret services in the way of sabotage, espionage, and subversion in the Delta; of which they do not seem to have made much use.

The degree of warmth in Anglo-Russian relations in 1943 can be gauged from the fact that when the Maiskys, en route from London to Moscow, were staying with the Maitland Wilsons they kept their rooms locked, so that the servants could not even get in to make the beds.[2] The nearest to an NKVD interest that has emerged was the presence, in a senior post in SOE's Balkan section, of a particularly senior British communist. More of that Balkan section shortly.[3]

The basic problem was the same as Humpty Dumpty's with words: who's to be master? The service authorities at GHQ Cairo had got used, over the years, to ingesting intelligence which reached them through accustomed channels, and to coping with security; but what was SOE? Was it just another of those proliferating private armies? In that case, it had better be firmly under the command of GHQ, as they were. Maitland Wilson was not alone in voicing the complaint that SOE could communicate with London behind his back, so that no one in Cairo really knew what it was up to.[4]

Personal difficulties made this formal awkwardness worse. Several successive heads of SOE's Cairo office included Arthur Goodwill, (Sir) George Pollock, Terence Maxwell, Lord Glenconner, his former chief of staff the forceful Brigadier Keble, and General Stawell who had Brigadier Barker-Benfield under him.[5] All this chopping and changing on the spot was not fully compensated for by the retention for four years on end by J. S. A. Pearson of the middle eastern desk in Baker Street.[6] Liaison officers kept moving to and fro between London and Cairo, at best a tiresome and often a dangerous journey – one more proposed head of the Cairo mission was shot down on the way there. In the end, in September 1943, the whole problem was taken to chiefs of staff level; and SOE was formally subordinated thereafter to the commander-in-chief, middle east (this was the point on which Hambro parted company with Selborne). By then, the main clandestine part of SOE's work was over, and the working problems were more concerned with arming existing groups, than in getting resistance under weigh at all. The aircraft available were by now more than the half-a-dozen Halifaxes based at Derna; sea landings in the Adriatic began to be promising; the time in fact for SOE to remain independent of the local force commander was passing, if not past.

Who MI6's and MI9's heads in Cairo were is not known; nor is it known whether their rate of change of head was as high. Both services were necessarily much more concerned with the fighting in the western desert than was SOE, of

---

[1] [H. Maitland] Wilson, *Eight Years Overseas* (1950), 164–5.
[2] Ibid. 171.        [3] pp. 168, 197–8 below.        [4] Ibid. 164.
[5] Sweet-Escott, 43, 71, 155, 186–8.        [6] Ibid. 56.

which the responsibilities there were nil: resistance to the Italian occupation of Tripolitania and Cyrenaica was not worth the stimulating. MI6 had a mass of material from combat, prisoners, and the Y service to consider, some of it to process; MI9 had hundreds of thousands of fighting men to train in techniques of evasion; neither service could give almost its full attention to occupied Europe in the way that SOE could.

MI6's and MI9's staffs in Cairo seem to have remained on speaking terms, at least, with their opposite numbers in OSS; this was not always the case with SOE, with which OSS's relations were often strained. OSS had three heads there, in three years: a West Point colonel till late summer 1943; then a Boston banker, John Toulmin, till early 1945; and another regular soldier, Harry Aldrich, till the end of the war.[1] The strains in OSS–SOE working derived from climate, personalities, and above all politics. OSS officers were prepared, preconditioned even, to believe that SOE must be a tool of the British imperialism of nearly two centuries earlier, against which their own revolution had been fought. Many of them had no need of evidence, for or against; they could no more see any other view, than they could see red as blue. Some of SOE's officers were no less prejudiced in opposing directions. Had there been many NKVD officers in Cairo as well, a third diverging view would have been present, but the days of Russo-Arab collusion lay in the future.

OSS's objections to some of SOE's work, though strong, were not at this point pressed to the hilt. A formal understanding left it to SOE to take the lead, in work from north-east Africa into Europe; while in north-west Africa, in the Maghreb, it was OSS that held the predominant stand. This was part of a wider division of 'spheres of influence' in undercover work, by which the Americans were to make the running in east Asia, the Pacific, and Finland, while the British were to be ahead in India, the Balkans, and west Africa as well as the middle east. 'West Europe was considered joint territory.'[2]

Robert Murphy, Roosevelt's political representative in Algiers, was in charge of work in the Maghreb; under him came his nominal superior, Colonel William Eddy at Tangier, and a dozen American vice-consuls scattered along the coast between Tunis and Casablanca. These vice-consuls were provided in 1941 by the war department, and secured valuable intelligence; in spite of a Gestapo comment that 'all their thoughts are centred on their social, sexual, or culinary interests'.[3]

The Gestapo had plenty of agents in north-west Africa, most of them under cover so transparent that they were quickly spotted by their enemies. They were particularly thick on the ground in Tangier, where section D had had a man from an early stage – at first, Hugh Quennell of Slaughter and May, the city solicitors,[4] who later moved to Balkan affairs. Gradually, as happens everywhere,

[1] Harris Smith, 124, 128.     [2] Ibid. 52.
[3] Ibid. 39. Murphy's *Diplomat among Warriors* (New York 1964) is useful.
[4] Nearly all their partners under 50 were absorbed into SOE early on. A wag complained that the organization was originally 'all May and no Slaughter': the effect of starting from scratch.

people fell into routines. The Germans once noticed some parcels lying on a Tangier quay, with a too inattentive guard in British pay; and out of mere devilment, to revenge a minor slight, planted a small bomb among them, with a short delay fuse. That week, the parcels in transit happened to be full of explosive; a dozen people were killed, and SOE had a lot of explaining to do.

'Torch', the invasion of the Maghreb in November 1942 by a large Anglo-American force under Eisenhower – the Americans playing the more prominent part, to butter up the local French – provided a dress rehearsal for the invasions of Europe to come.[1] A great many mistakes were made, some – perhaps all – of them unavoidable, all useful as warnings of what might be avoided next time.

The Americans had learned one lesson already, from the bitter British experience in Syria:[2] they took care to keep the gaullist French out of the landing force. This they did the more willingly, because of the intense hostility to de Gaulle and gaullism in the state department; which derived in turn from the contemptible bickerings of the French exiles in New York, and from Roosevelt's personal distaste for the Free French leader. De Gaulle, the most independent of men, was still late in 1942 regarded by the Americans – few of whom knew him – as a puppet of the British.

They had maintained close relations with Pétain's régime at Vichy, through Roosevelt's friend Admiral Leahy as ambassador.[3] The accident that Pétain's deputy Admiral Darlan happened to be in Algiers at the moment of the landing got them out of a military difficulty, at the cost of plunging them into a political one. Darlan talked his way out of the arrest in which some young resisters had tried to hold him, on the night of the invasion; and agreed to order the French forces in north Africa to lay down their arms. This saved Eisenhower casualties, but the tacit – indeed the explicit – admission of the legality of the vichyste administration was a fearful shock to resisters inside France. They could at least be glad that General Giraud, brought out of France by submarine to arrive at Gibraltar on the eve of 'Torch', proved a broken reed; and that Roosevelt put out a statement on 18 November insisting that the arrangement with Darlan was transitory. Stalin approved the arrangement wholeheartedly: it suited Russian interests best.[4]

Darlan's assassination on Christmas Eve by a young French royalist, who had been chosen by lot from a sealed knot of five friends for the task, cleared the political air. Giraud promptly had the assassin shot; but was then outmanœuvred, and elbowed out of the way, by de Gaulle, who established his French committee of national liberation at Algiers, and got on with many of the tasks – such as releasing Jews and political prisoners – that pétainists and darlanists had left undone.

---

[1] Harris Smith, ch. ii, 'The Torch of Reaction'.    [2] See next section, p. 164 below.
[3] An unfriendly critic said of William D. Leahy's autobiography, *I was there* (1950), that on the evidence it provided, he must have been somewhere else.
[4] Feis, *Churchill Roosevelt Stalin*, 92.

Roosevelt had strong sympathies with the nationalist aspirations of the western Arabs, who were restive at the continuance, even under the gaullists, of French colonial control; but that is a separate story.[1] Meanwhile the Arabs benefited, on the whole, from the presence of large occupying armed forces who needed base staffs. OSS's attempts to make more active use of them came to nothing.[2]

SOE set up a base, called 'Massingham', with the cover name of Inter-Service Signals Unit 6, at Guyotville just west of Algiers, under (Sir) Douglas Dodds-Parker, formerly of the Sudan civil service. OSS had a larger working headquarters in Algiers. Both bodies undertook thence, from the spring of 1943, active operations into France, Italy, and various west Mediterranean islands, a few of which will be noticed below. But we need to begin our circuit of Europe from the other end of the inland sea, for which the Italians were trying to revive the Latin name of *mare nostrum*: a title they lost off Cape Matapan.

### West Asia

In Palestine, the war of 1939–45 was spent by most politically conscious people – that is, by most of the population – in preparing for quite another war, the first Arab–Israeli war that broke out in 1948. The area, conquered by the British, Australians, and Arabs from the Turks in 1917–18, had been a British mandate from the League of Nations since 1922. Successive British governments had wrestled since November 1917 with the intricacies of the Balfour declaration, that had committed them to the setting up of a national home for the Jewish people in Palestine without prejudice to the rights of non-Jews who were there already.

By the late 1930s, race rioting and skirmishing between Arabs and Jews was common, and each had begun some degree of paramilitary organization. Wingate's first Gideon Force was indeed raised before the war, round Gideon's home at Ein Harod; composed of special night squads of counter-terrorists, to keep Arab raiders in check.[3] It was from the success that these small bodies of desperate men secured that the British conceived the idea of the commandos.[4] Later, a substantial number of Jews, amounting eventually to a brigade, were armed and trained in Palestine during the war by the British, and fought with some distinction in Italy.

Palestine's main wartime interest to the British was as a security headache. The Jews, already a third of the population, were ready to help anyone who would fight the nazis, who were recognizably by some way their worst enemies; but they knew that after the nazis were done for, they would have to fight for their lives against the Arabs. They therefore extrapolated from the special night squads into their own secret underground army, the Haganah. They seized every

---

[1] Cp. P. Calvocoressi and G. Wint, *Total War* (1972), 370–4.
[2] Harris Smith, 49–50.
[3] Christopher Sykes, *Orde Wingate* (1959), 135–60. Cp. Judges vi. 14, viii. 23.
[4] H. St G. Saunders, *The Green Beret* (1949), 21–2.

opportunity – and there were hundreds, thousands of opportunities – of arming themselves; by searching the desert for abandoned arms and ammunition; by stealing them from dumps; by buying them outright from venal storemen. This gave security officers all over the Levant plenty to do.

On the other hand, the Jewish Agency – the principal zionist body, till the state of Israel sprang again into existence in 1948 – had several links with section D, through which a number of more or less desperate enterprises were put in hand. If ever the clandestine history of the war gets treated in the detail it deserves, it will be found that many Jews who, like Horace's Regulus, well knew what the barbarous torturer had ready for them,[1] were ready to go back into Europe on secret missions; some of them did astounding things.

A feature of the Palestinian political ulcer worth remark is that it was a weak point in Anglo-American relations. Though nazi newspapers wrote a lot of rubbish then, as Arab newspapers do now, about Jewish influence on United States policy, such influence did exist: was indeed still more considerable in Roosevelt's day than in Ford's. British official policy in Palestine, which sought to limit the influx of Jewish refugeees, was not popular with rich American zionists whom Roosevelt sometimes needed to conciliate.

The limit was not popular with the Jewish community in Palestine either; and as a protest against it the British minister resident in Cairo, Lord Moyne, was assassinated on 6 November 1944 outside his private house by two young Jews.[2] They were arrested, and subsequently hanged; and two hundred members of the Stern gang, to which they belonged, were deported to Kenya. This did not stop the run of attacks on Palestine police and even (to secure their arms) on small bodies of British troops, which went on all through 1944–5: effort that might have been better expended against the common enemy, as such responsible leaders as Weizmann appreciated.

The mufti of Jerusalem, Haj Amin el Husseini, once called by Churchill 'the deadliest enemy of the British empire', was always ready to make trouble for the British from the opposite or Arab quarter. He slipped clandestinely out of Palestine in 1937, escaped from Iraq in turn when Rashid Ali's pro-German rising was put down in May 1941, and ended the war in Italy and Germany; whence, again, he got away, full of anti-British bile he had not yet had time to discharge.[3] The Germans' organization of anti-British feeling in western Asia was handled with a less sure touch than when Enver had been encouraging Wassmuss in the war before.[4]

The Allies seemed almost to be capable of making trouble enough between themselves. The British had committed themselves, by a secret pact made with

[1] Odes IV. v. 49–50.
[2] Weizmann expressed 'deep moral indignation and horror' to Churchill next day: see his *Trial and Error* (1949), 437–8.
[3] See his obituary, *Times*, 6 July 1974, 14g.
[4] Christopher Sykes, *Wassmuss* (1936), 50.

the French as far back as 1916, to giving the French a share in their Levantine conquests from the Ottoman empire, and France had held mandates for Syria and Lebanon for as long as the British had held them for Palestine and Trans-jordan. Like most of the French colonial governors, those of Syria and Lebanon declared for Pétain; thus removing themselves from active aid to the Allies. When the troubles began in Iraq, the British discovered from their intelligence sources that Luftwaffe aircraft on their way to help Rashid Ali were being serviced and refuelled at Syrian airports. An invasion of Syria, which carried with it an invasion of Lebanon, was at once mounted; and, there being not enough others to send, Free French troops were used against the troops of Vichy France. Five weeks' bitter fighting, ending on 14 July 1941, ensued; driving even deeper the wedge between pétainists and gaullists, and making a national resistance move-ment in France even more difficult to coordinate, or even to conceive, than it had been before.

Less important than this nasty confrontation, a personal incident is worth a passing word. An Air France pilot, overrun at Aleppo, was offered similar work by the British; and accepted on the condition that he could revisit France first. He did so; got married; settled his wife near Paris; and was brought out to England by Guérisse's escape line in August 1942. He was snapped up by SOE, in spite of the warning by MI5 that he might have been in touch with the Germans; his name was Déricourt.[1]

The gaullists, placed in power in Syria and Lebanon by this campaign, took a more liberal attitude to Arab aspirations than their colonial predecessors. Constantly prodded by the British and Americans, they gradually conceded both countries' independence.

The case of Turkey provides a convenient bridge to join these extra-European complications up with the main narrative survey for Europe; Constantinople is a traditionary starting- and finishing-point for adventures of espionage. The city bears still the marks of having been the capital of the known world for a thousand years; but in the early 1920s it ceased even to be the capital of Turkey. Kamal Atatürk's national republican revolution, that abolished the sultanate and the caliphate, re-named the city İstanbul and moved the capital away to Ankara.

In Ankara, the government of İsmet İnönü – who had taken over on Kamal's death in 1938 – long preserved Turkish neutrality. The Turks had no wish to fight alongside the Russians, their secular enemy, or against the Germans, their allies of 1914–18; nor did they want to fight for nazism. They were one of Germany's principal sources of chrome on which armour-plate production, and indeed all alloy-steels for armament depended.[2] The British needed Turkish chrome as well, and maintained a steady pressure on the Turks to make them reduce their exports to Germany; without success till 1944, when the Turks did

[1] pp. 19, 245, 249.
[2] A. S. Milward, *The German Economy at War* (1965), 184.

agree to a fall. They went further, and broke off diplomatic relations with Germany, when they could perceive that 'Neptune', the landing in Normandy, had succeeded; and at the end of February 1945 they at last entered the war on the Allied side, to make sure of a place at the founding conference of the United Nations. No operations resulted.

Meanwhile there had been a good deal of secret activity; including one world-famous case, the 'Cicero' affair.

'Cicero' was the German codename for Elyesa Bazna, a Turkish subject – born at Priština, in southern Serbia – who was valet successively to Ribbentrop's brother-in-law Jenke, counsellor in the German embassy at Ankara; then to Busk, his opposite number in the British embassy; and finally to Sir Hughe Knatchbull-Hugessen, the British ambassador. His prewar service with the Jenkes should have made him unacceptable to the British, but seems not to have been known to them; he was just accepted as one more of the unobtrusive Turks who acted as servants in the diplomatic colony of Ankara. Ankara was still in those days, for a capital city, rough and smallish; good valets were hard to come by; Bazna was a good valet.

He was also a good spy. Motivated, by his own account,[1] simply by greed for money, with which he could impress a series of mistresses, he took wax impressions of the keys to his master's safe, copied them, photographed the contents, and sold them – 52 highly secret documents – to the Germans for £20,000. They supplied him with a better camera and unlimited film; and from November 1943 to early April 1944 he provided them with a mass of invaluable material, including the minutes of the Cairo and Teheran conferences. They paid him, all told, £300,000: the highest known sum ever paid to a spy.

Pathetically little use was made, by either party, of the results of this bargain. Bazna's fortune was most of it paid in exquisitely forged Bank of England notes, which passed a Swiss bank's scrutiny, but not that of the bank of issue: hence the disappearance of those beautiful old £5 notes on fine white paper, all withdrawn. Eventually he sued the west German government, but died before the case came to trial.[2]

In Ankara, the German ambassador – that same Franz von Papen who had supervised German sabotage in the USA in 1916,[3] and had been one of the last Chancellors of the Weimar republic – left all the details to his RSHA man, an honest Austrian called Moyzisch who has published a straightforward account.[4] The main trouble was that Ribbentrop and Kaltenbrunner quarrelled so long and so bitterly about which of them should lay 'Cicero's' revelations before Hitler, who alone was competent to take action on them, that Normandy D-Day came and went before any counter-measures could be attempted. The 'Cicero' material

---

[1] Elyesa Bazna and Hans Nogly, tr. Eric Mosbacher, *I Was Cicero* (1962).
[2] *Times* obituary, 28 December 1970, 8h.
[3] See F. von Rintelen, *The Dark Invader* (1933), 82–95.
[4] L. C. Moyzisch, tr. C. Fitzgibbon and H. Fraenkel, *Operation Cicero* (1950).

did not in any case reveal much about 'Neptune': no one was going to pass naval detail out to a distant embassy. What it did reveal was the size, strength, solidity of the Allied war effort.

Moyzisch suspected a plant. There is no doubt Bazna passed over genuine material: was he allowed to do so? If he was, in an indirect effort to frighten the Germans into making peace by a show of overwhelming strength, the effort failed, because it never got onto Hitler's work-table. More probably, Bazna was a genuine spy, who benefited from the attitude to servants of the Knatchbull-Hugessens' class (it was Lady Knatchbull-Hugessen who nearly caught him in the act).[1] But he was not a perfectly efficient one: when preparing to flee, for instance, he forgot to dispose of his duplicate keys.[2] Nor was Moyzisch a perfectly efficient security officer: when carrying his first batch of photographs across his embassy's grounds, he dropped one, and it blew away.[3] Both of them in fact were human beings, not automata.

Moyzisch moreover discovered, too late, that one of his secretaries (he calls her 'Elisabet', Bazna calls her Cornelia Kapp), whom he knew to be a moody girl, had defected to OSS; bearing with her the news that there was a German source in the British embassy, called 'Cicero'. Bazna at this point saw the red light, and closed down.[4] 'Elisabet' was only following the example of other German diplomats. Early in 1944 a senior *Abwehr* agent, Papen's nephew, Vermehren, had defected to the British, with his wife:[5] a considerable sensation.

İstanbul remained all through the war a centre for undercover activities of innumerable kinds. Rashid Ali and the mufti, for example, were both smuggled out of Turkey through it by the *Abwehr*.[6] Sweet-Escott, visiting it on SOE's account in the summer of 1941, found it pullulating with his own side's staff and agents, let alone the enemy's; not to speak of journalists from both sides and from the neutrals.[7] His business was with Gardyne de Chastelain, then SOE's head in Turkey, who had spent many years in the Romanian oil industry and was at that time mainly occupied in trying to work back into Romania. İstanbul's proximity to German-occupied Europe gave it great advantages over Ankara, as well as exposing the people there to some slight danger of being snatched into enemy territory.

It was there that Helmuth von Moltke several times, with Canaris's connivance, gave the Allies some indication of the hopes of the anti-nazi Germans with whom he worked. This is a rare example of an item of political intelligence in transit. Nothing came of it; Roosevelt would not deal with Junkers.[8]

---

[1] Bazna, 116–19.   [2] Ibid. 166.   [3] Moyzisch, 57–60.

[4] I am grateful to Dr David Kahn for drawing to my attention an error in my *RHDGM* article (April 1973, p. 43): most of the material Bazna handed on was in one-time-pad cipher, and therefore useless to German cryptographers. I should have remembered Kahn's *Codebreakers*, 451–2.

[5] Cp. Paul Leverkuehn, *German Military Intelligence*, 25.

[6] Ibid. 16–19.   [7] Sweet-Escott, 82.

[8] Allen Dulles, *Germany's Underground* (1947), 87; Peter Hoffmann, *Widerstand Staatsstreich Attentat*, 276–9.

On the escape front, again, Stamboul offered large advantages; and there were also extensive escape line operations on the west Turkish coast, mainly in the gulf of Smyrna (İzmir). The MI9, Special Boat Section, OSS, and naval people concerned did their best to be inconspicuous; some of the Turkish police did their best to look the other way. Either the Germans never found out, or they judged it inopportune to try to interfere.

## The Balkans

This rugged and traditionally turbulent area, overrun successively by Romans, Goths, Avars, Slavs, and Turks, was divided at the end of the 1930s among five states successor to the vanished Ottoman empire – Albania, Bulgaria, Greece, Romania, and Yugoslavia – and a remaining fragment of Turkey-in-Europe, that lay between Edirne (Adrianople) and İstanbul. Much of the area is mountainous, much of the soil is poor; railway and industrial development were then little advanced. Indeed in large areas of the Balkans the Middle Ages had not ended; had hardly even begun. Family and tribal groups clung to the loyalties their ancestors had brought from the steppes. Personalities counted for more, and 'iron laws of history' for less, than in the more elaborately organized societies of western Europe.

The triangle Trieste–Odessa–Matapan, roughly 1,200 kilometres each side, encloses the Balkan peninsula; which is skewered, rather than soldered, to inventive Europe by the Danube. Where the Danube forces its way through the Carpathians there is a sabotage target of continental importance: the Iron Gate, the deepest gorge in Europe. Here, midway between Orsova and Turnu Severin, the river is cramped for three miles into a channel only a furlong across; sometimes, narrower still. The eastern cliff is in Romania, the western in Yugoslavia.

Section D reconnoitred the Iron Gate in the first winter of the war. Its leading Balkan expert on the spot, well known in such business circles as there were in Belgrade, was Julius Hanau, known of course as 'Caesar'. He got as far as assembling some explosive; but the problems of transporting it to either side of the gorge, laying, tamping, and eventually firing it turned out greater than even his assiduity could overcome; nor could he explain away some tunnellings near the cliffs to the Yugoslav police. He turned his attention instead to barge pilots, and at least persuaded some of them to go slow at work; thus hindering, but not by much, the upstream flow of corn and oil to Germany in the summer of 1940. A more elaborate plan – to fill a large steamer, which the Jewish Agency was to provide and section D to crew, with concrete and sink it athwart the Iron Gate – also came to nothing; and Hanau had to leave, rather hurriedly, before the Germans arrived.[1] Buying barges and sailing them to Turkey proved more useful.[2]

---

[1] Some further details in Elisabeth Barker, *British Policy in South-East Europe in the Second World War* (1976), 35–40, which rests mainly on foreign office archives; and in Merlin Minshull, *Guilt-Edged* (1975), 156–94, by one of the river raiders.

[2] Sweet-Escott, 26.

In its earliest stages, section D's Balkan office 'was under the control of a brilliant but ruthless Australian called George Taylor', an ex-rancher and oil magnate, who 'had a mind of limpid clarity and knew exactly what he wanted'.[1] Having run it from London so far, Taylor flew out to Cairo at the end of May 1940, and thenceforward D's, and later SOE's, Balkan affairs were run from there; usually under Taylor's strategic guidance, transmitted as we have seen through Pearson in London;[2] till the great shake-up of the autumn of 1943.

The Italian change of sides, and the establishment of Allied forces in southern Italy, enabled British – and, conformably, American – support for resistance all over the Balkans to be reorganized to suit the new facts of military geography. Cairo continued to be in charge of most operations into the peninsula; but work into Yugoslavia, where the most German forces were pinned and the greatest possibilities of subversive expansion seemed to lie, was detached from the commander-in-chief, middle east, and placed under the supreme commander, Mediterranean theatre – that is, under Allied Force Headquarters at Algiers, with advanced headquarters at Caserta, near Naples. So much work was done by AFHQ on subversion that it added to its four conventional branches – G1 troops, G2 information, G3 operations and G4 supply – the novelty of G5 special forces. Stawell was installed at Bari; and a complicated signals operation transferred the SOE and OSS clandestine home stations, to which sets in the Balkans worked, from Cairo to the heel of Italy. For convenience and proximity's sake, Albania also was transferred from Cairo's to Bari's bailiwick: though, as we shall soon see, no part of Albania or indeed of Yugoslavia was responsive to control of a close kind by any foreign authority, unless that of the CPSU(B).

The Greek government-in-exile remained in Cairo, the Yugoslav government-in-exile in London; and one of the troubles with which Allied commanders, at several levels, found they had to cope was that the foreign office and the state department were slow to keep pace with these changes in the clandestine headquarter layout.

The Soviet Union was officially informed, through Donovan's and Gubbins's missions in Moscow; there was no reaction.

Soviet policy towards the Balkans was dominated by the national questions involved: Russia's national interests first, then those of the slav cousins. The comintern sometimes preached a communist federation, sometimes south slav unity; without ever defining a south slav, so that Albanians, or Macedonian Greeks, could be included in or excluded from calculations as convenient. Everyone agreed that neither Romanians nor Greeks were slavs; and the peoples of each of the five Balkan states were more conscious of differences from their neighbours than of common interests with them.

Only on one occasion had they ever acted in concert: in the first Balkan war of 1912. Servia, Bulgaria, and Greece were secretly combined, by the agency of J. D. Bourchier, the *Times's* Balkan correspondent, into an anti-Turkish alliance,

[1] Sweet-Escott, 21.                    [2] p. 159 above.

fought a successful war against Turkey, only to fall out with each other and Romania next year over the division of the spoils.[1]

## Romania

In spite of having a Hohenzollern king, whose family had reached the throne by an almost operatic adventure during the German civil war of 1866, Romania had chosen the Allied side in the war of 1914–18; had chosen it late and clumsily; but had emerged at the war's end as a main beneficiary of Woodrow Wilson's doctrines of self-determination. Bessarabia, the Bukovina, and Transylvania were transferred to her from the defunct Romanov and Habsburg empires; and the southern Dobrudja, taken from the kingdom of Bulgaria which had fought on the opposite side and lost in 1913, was confirmed Romanian, as Bulgaria had just done the same thing again. Between the great wars, Romania had been a client state of France, joining with Czechoslovakia and Yugoslavia in a Little Entente under French patronage.

Schacht, the nazis' financial wizard, had already by 1938 secured for Germany the bulk of Romania's most important export, oil; in exchange for such goods as aspirin. People used a lot of aspirin in Bucarest, a joyous, frivolous, miniature Paris-and-Vienna rolled together, with a rich spending class of aristocrats, courtiers, and businessmen, three categories with extensive overlaps. There was also a strong tradition, left over from centuries of Turkish occupation, that any difficulty could be resolved by a bribe.[2] Illiteracy was high, perhaps as high as three-fifths of the whole population; a good deal less high in Bucarest than among the peasantry, the largest class in the country.[3] Iuliu Maniu's national peasant party, strong in the 1920s, commanded widespread secret support; but had been put down by Codreanu's dictatorship, which dissolved in Codreanu's violent death in 1938. Royal dictatorship followed under Carol II.

Romania was among the countries to which the British and French offered guarantees in the following spring. By midsummer 1940 these were clearly worth little; and Romania, wealthy and defenceless, suddenly became her neighbours' whipping-boy. In rapid succession Bessarabia was reoccupied, and the northern Bukovina occupied, by the USSR (June), part of Transylvania by Hungary (August), and the southern Dobrudja by Bulgaria (September). Carol II, who had long since left his wife, now left his kingdom also, abdicating it to his son Michael, a boy of eighteen. The new king – Mihai, his subjects called him, but English was his nursery language, as it was of his cousin and contemporary Philip of Greece – was the virtual prisoner of Ion Antonescu, the self-appointed

---

[1] This war has made its mark in propaganda – contrast Hermengilde Wagner, *With the Victorious Bulgarians*, with Lionel James, *With the Conquered Turks* (both 1913). It also provided curious analogies with the south-east Asian wars by proxy of the 1960s and 1970s.

[2] A. G. Lee, *Crown against Sickle* [1950], 29–30.

[3] H. Fainaru, *Wall Street's New Darling* (Detroit 1948), a prejudiced source but a credible statistic.

Conducator. Antonescu ruled Romania dictatorially through Codreanu's old party, the Iron Guard, subordinated to the army by armed action in January 1941.

Though he forced a fascist party into submission, there was nothing that could seriously be called a resister in Antonescu; and his arrival in power signalled the moment for refugees who had escaped as far as Romania from Germany or Poland to move on if they could. For in October 1940 twelve German divisions, coming with Hungarian acquiescence on the heels of some invited military experts, occupied Romania; and in November both Hungary and Romania joined the Tripartite Pact. Michael's enemies have blamed these steps on him; but he had as yet no base from which to counter his over-powerful subject.

Section D, MIR, and SOE had all had some staff in Bucarest; attracted by the two prime sabotage targets of the Iron Gate[1] and the great Ploeşti oilfield, some 40 miles north of the capital. Colonel Norton-Griffiths had set it on fire in 1917, just before von Mackensen's troops reached it; and no doubt there was a report laid up somewhere of how he had done so. Burning up an oil well is not all that hard, for someone who has plenty of time, a little technical knowledge, and free access to the site; but access was far from free. The oil companies, Standard Oil and Royal Dutch Shell prominent among them, were understandably reluctant to have their production, and therefore their profits, abolished or even badly interrupted. The bulk of the Romanian spending class, from the king downwards, got a sizeable slice of their incomes from oil: oil and land were the twin props on which their wealth and power rested (Michael owned, palaces apart, over 200,000 acres of his country). So local enthusiasm for inactivating the Ploeşti oilfield was limited; and from October 1940 it was closely guarded by the Germans, whose war effort hinged on its product.[2]

German advances deeper into the Balkans in the spring, and into the USSR in the summer, of 1941, were in no way hampered by any resistance activity. SOE's people in Bucarest turned out unable to generate anything more memorable than a bar-room anecdote.[3] When the British diplomatic staff were formally withdrawn in February 1941, the undercover men withdrew also; leaving behind a wireless set and a lot of well-intentioned but ill-organized friends.

There was plenty of pro-British feeling; but for the time being it was silenced. There was plenty of anti-soviet feeling, which had full scope during the Russo-German war; in which Romania participated from the start on Antonescu's order (he forgot to tell the king).[4] With anti-soviet feeling there joined anti-Russian feeling, an ordinary nationalist desire to repossess Bessarabia. And there was another strong current of feeling in wartime Romania that favoured

[1] p. 167 above.          [2] Cp. E. Barker, *British Policy in S-E Europe*, 32–4..

[3] The anecdote is worth a footnote. One of them, on his way to a friend's wedding, was trapped in a stuck lift for quite a time with a ravishingly pretty girl; with the consequence that might be expected in Bucarest. When the lift re-started, he said he didn't even know her name? 'Oh, I'm the bride.' (D. E. Walker, *Lunch with a Stranger* [1957], 87).

[4] Lee, *Crown against Sickle*, 31.

the nazis: dislike, even detestation, of Jews. While Antonescu ruled, the 800,000 Jews in Romania were reduced by half: most were massacred. There was a small communist party, about a thousand strong, carrying no political weight; many of its leaders were Jewish. Its head, Lucreţiu Patraşcanu, escaped concentration camp, but was placed under nominal house arrest by Antonescu's police force, the Sigurantza.

SOE's wireless set, called Z4, made intermittent contact with Cairo and was frequently moved. Maniu was among those who housed it, as was Prince Barbu Ştirbey. It was operated by a few ardent young Romanians, who were impatient at their elders' caution. It went off the air on 23 June 1941; but de Chastelain was able later that autumn to send another set in.[1]

Occasional touch with Maniu was maintained by messenger also; but nothing solid emerged except messages and assurances of support. Not till August 1943 did SOE send in a mission: Major David Russell, who was dropped in Yugoslavia, crossed the Danube into Romania successfully with his wireless operator Turceanu, met a representative of Maniu's; but was murdered a few days later, apparently by a bandit. De Chastelain, back from a recruiting drive in north America, parachuted into Romania (at the third attempt) just before Christmas. He was accompanied by Ivor Porter and a Romanian called Meţeanu; they landed several miles from their peasant reception committee. De Chastelain, walking into the nearest village to find out exactly where they were, was spotted as a foreigner by an alert village woman, who denounced them to the gendarmerie. They spent the next eight months in prison in Bucarest. Turceanu reported their whereabouts, and they could occasionally transmit themselves; but they could do little good.[2]

Bucarest teemed with café-conversationalist resisters; and with secret policemen, German and local. No one trusted anybody else. Maniu, also under nominal house arrest, was in occasional touch with the western Allies, as Patrascanu was in intermittent touch with Moscow. The bulk of the army had disappeared into the USSR; where several thousands deserted, and were eventually formed (October 1943 and January 1945) into two divisions of the Red Army.[3]

A Patriotic Front was set up in June 1943, communist-inspired and composed mainly of left-wing activists; production at Ploeşti was not pressed forward vigorously, and peasant youths throughout the country were reluctant to present themselves for call-up. There was also some sabotage: not at Ploeşti.[4]

When the Red Army drew close to the Romanian frontier, its partisan staff judged the moment ripe for stirring the country up. A wireless set for Patrascanu was dropped in the spring of 1944, with a small mission; several attempts were made in the spring and summer to raise bands *en maquis* in the hills.[5] On 2 April

[1] Sweet-Escott, 51n, 84. Cp. E. Barker, op. cit., 223–4.
[2] Ibid. 228; Lee, *Crown against Sickle*, 62; Sweet-Escott, 195.
[3] N. Goldberger, *ERM* ii. 200.     [4] Ibid. 201, 196.     [5] Ibid. 203–4.

1944 the soviet government announced that it would approve the return of Transylvania to Romania after the war; an eloquent silence covered the fate of Bessarabia. SOE meanwhile pinned its trust in Maniu, who continued unable to make up his mind.

In May 1944 Maniu sent an emissary to Cairo, who left quite openly, by train for İstanbul under his own name; this suggests a degree, though not a wide one, of German complicity in, or at any rate assent to, the mission. For the emissary was a considerable personage, Ştirbey, aware of his princely rank and his direct descent from the elected ruler of mid-nineteenth-century Wallachia. SOE housed him as discreetly as could be in Cairo, and he negotiated peace terms with a committee of British, American, and soviet diplomats: that is, terms on which Maniu would guarantee to overthrow Antonescu. Even air raids on Bucarest did not make Maniu realize that chaffering could not go on for ever.[1] He asked for an Allied airborne division to be flown to Bucarest airfield on the day he seized power; not realizing that none was available, and not appreciating that you cannot order an airborne division as you can order a taxi. SOE brought out a further emissary, the diplomat Constantine Visioanu – this time quite clandestinely – in late May;[2] he joined Ştirbey; the talks went on. So did the communists' preparations. On their initiative, a national democratic bloc was formed in secret on 20 June, comprising the peasant, liberal, and socialist parties as well as themselves. Their leader, Gheorghiu-Dej, escaped from camp on 9/10 August.[3]

In the end the young king cut the Gordian knot. On 20 August the Russians, who had paused since April on the Dniester, attacked, and broke into the Romanian front. On the 23rd the king sent for Antonescu; told him to sue for peace; and on getting a refusal, had him quietly arrested – with his namesake the prime minister – and locked away in the closet where Carol used to keep his stamp collection. Under the noses of the German and Romanian secret policemen in the ministry of the interior opposite the palace, the king's attendants disarmed Antonescu's bodyguard; and a new government was formed that evening, headed by Sanatescu, with seats in it for Maniu and Patraşcanu. The two last-named took care, during the critical twenty-four hours, to be wholly unavailable.[4]

De Chastelain, released from prison, hastened to the palace – still in British uniform. The king sent him that night to Istanbul to announce Romania's surrender; he promised to return at once, but was forbidden to do so by the foreign office, who knew that his return would be suspected by the Russians – evidence or no evidence – as some sort of intrigue.[5]

The new government's first act was to declare, without conditions, that Romania was no longer at war with the Allies. Michael retired for a few days to the country. The Germans bombed Bucarest, but made no attempt to hold

---

[1] Sweet-Escott, 207–8.     [2] Ibid. 210–11. And cp. E. Barker, op. cit., 230–3.
[3] *ERM* ii. 210, 214.     [4] Lee, *Crown against Sickle*, ch. vii; E. Barker, op. cit., 237–41.
[5] Cp. Churchill's outburst, ibid. 234–5.

Romania. The partisan bands, by now numbering 14,000 round Bucarest, claimed over 5,000 prisoners from them as they withdrew; and over 50,000 more, throughout the country, in the last week of August.[1] In this they were helped by the rear area troops of the Romanian army, who promptly changed sides, and proved a fair match for their German opposite numbers.

The soviet authorities peremptorily forbade any attempt by SOE to send in a mission to seek out and reward its supporters.[2] Romania had been placed by informal agreement between Stalin and Churchill firmly in the soviet zone of influence; and the communists, once given a foothold in the government machine, did not take long to secure power. Sanatescu's successor Radescu was replaced in March 1945 by Groza, who was more acceptable to them; and on the last day but one of 1947 Michael gave up the attempt to be king of a communist state.

## Bulgaria

Before England was a kingdom, Bulgaria was an empire, which momentarily contested the power of Byzantium; but these early mediaeval glories were distant. After several centuries' Turkish domination, the Bulgars fought their way back to independence late in the nineteenth century. The once famous 'Bulgarian horrors' of 1875–6, a massacre in which fewer than 20,000 people were killed, convulsed the consciences of the British, brought the recently retired Gladstone back into politics, helped to overturn a British cabinet, and established strong Anglo-Bulgarian friendship;[3] but Russo–Bulgarian friendship, stemming from cousinhood, was and remains much stronger.

The country's frontiers fluctuated a good deal; in 1939 they were at their present state, making a territory a little smaller than England, and with a population of some seven millions. The forms of constitutional monarchy and orthodox Christianity were observed. There was little industry. One living Bulgar was world-famous, Georgi Dimitrov who had outfaced Göring at the Reichstag fire trial, and secured his own acquittal. Since 1934 he had been living in Moscow, as secretary to the communist international, and had indeed become a soviet citizen. The comintern's following in Bulgaria was estimated at about 12,000.

There is no published evidence at all about either British or American espionage or escape activity; though there are indications that most Bulgars were less anti-semitic than their government, and might hide Jews.

Militarily and economically, Bulgaria was too weak to think of standing alone. In March 1941 the king, Boris III, made no difficulties when the *Wehrmacht* occupied his country, and it was used by the Germans as a springboard from which they could mount their invasions of Yugoslavia and Greece. In mid-May 1941 Hitler allowed the Bulgars to occupy eastern Thrace, thus regaining

---

[1] *ERM* ii. 218, 220: a propaganda claim.          [2] Sweet-Escott, 220.

[3] R. T. Shannon, *Gladstone and the Bulgarian Agitation, 1876* (1963): contrast the lesser stir made nowadays by greater killings, such as those in Biafra or Bangladesh.

the Aegean seaboard they had lost in the second Balkan war, of 1913; they also occupied the middle Vardar valley, in the south-eastern corner of Yugoslavia. When, at the second great turning-point of the war, Germany attacked the USSR, the Bulgarians refused to join in; they declared war on Great Britain (and, six months later, on the USA) instead. The help they afforded to the Germans was thus limited to securing the right rear of the 'Barbarossa' attack; and thereafter to reducing the number of divisions the Germans had to divert to the Balkans from fronts more important to them.

As the Russians were not at war with them, the soviet union could retain a large diplomatic mission in Sofia, already suspected by the *Abwehr* of containing a sizeable intelligence element early in 1940. From it, they were able to direct specialist agents, parachuted in or put in on the Black Sea coast by submarine or infiltrated over the Romanian or Yugoslav frontier; such as the three elderly Hamburg communists, disguised as members of the Organization Todt, who after ten years' training in the soviet union killed two German sailors in a Sofia park late in 1942.[1] Eighteen communists were executed in July 1942; thus making the Russians shy of direct intervention in the Balkans.[2]

Many more Bulgarians, in fact, were involved – in 1941–3 – in repressing resistance than in conducting it; and for the time being the Bulgarian communists held back. Nicholas Petkov, head of the Agrarian Union – a peasant grouping – was the main leader of such resistance as there was. His main committee was penetrated by the police; only he and two others survived raids in April 1942. When the main tide of the war on the eastern front turned, at Stalingrad in the winter of 1942–3, communists began to adhere to Petkov's union, and began the familiar process of 'boring from within'. Michel records a rise in the number of recorded sabotage operations from 12 in January to 280 in November 1943.[3] The communists set up a 'Fatherland Front' late in 1942; it was, again, penetrated by the police, and there were many arrests in April 1943. Next month, all the same, a 'National Committee' of this front was proclaimed:[4] later in the year, the communists settled down to organize a Popular Liberation Army.

Suddenly, on 28 August 1943, the king – who had just returned from a visit to Hitler – died: his death remains a mystery, and the fact that no secret service ever claimed credit for it is some indication that it may have been due to natural causes. Simeon II, then only six, succeeded without a hitch; with a council of regency to act for him. OSS hardly ever, if ever, had any agents on Bulgarian soil; and all SOE's few attempts to lodge some there petered out. Mostyn Davies, a major in SOE, was dropped into Serb Macedonia in the summer of 1943 to try and make contact with Bulgar partisan bands, who were believed to be operating between Skoplje and Sofia.

In January 1944 OSS's agents in İstanbul got some peace feelers, via a travel-

---

[1] Leverkuehn, *German Military Intelligence*, 141–51, esp. 147–8.
[2] E. Barker, *British Policy in S-E Europe*, 213.
[3] Michel, *SW*, 214.                    [4] Ibid. 294.

ling banker, from the council of regency; these produced nothing but a row between OSS and SOE.[1]

In the same month, Frank Thompson – who would have been well known as a poet, had he survived – was dropped to work under Mostyn Davies before joining Deakin. Davies was killed in action against Bulgarian regulars in March; whereupon Thompson and the wireless operator who had come with him, K. A. V. Scott, crossed into Bulgaria with two hundred Bulgarian communist partisans, the 2nd Sofia Brigade. They had a heavy spring, on the run from frequent German attacks, seeking some mountain fastness where they too could create a national redoubt.

Thompson was an able linguist – McLachlan had started him on Russian at school and he had taught himself passable Bulgarian; he showed warm sympathy with the Bulgars' secular struggles against oppression, and almost everybody liked him. But in May, when his party was surrounded, he and Scott (who was wounded) were taken prisoner: there are indeed indications that Thompson was sold to the Germans by somebody who wanted to save his own skin. He was brutally interrogated; gave nothing away; and, though in uniform, was shot on 5 June 1944.

His family received an official telegram from the war office, notifying them of his death. A few days later they received another, purportedly signed the previous day, thanking his mother for her latest letter and sending his love: some staff officer in Cairo having forgotten to cancel SOE's 'good news letter' system.[2]

Sergeant Scott survived, and received a distinguished conduct medal; the Germans' attempts to play his set back foundered on correct use of security checks. Thompson, a strong romantic radical libertarian, had a mining town named after him, and was posthumously awarded the Bulgarian Order of the People's Liberty, first class. What he would have made of Dimitrov's rigid state capitalism is another question.[3]

For the Fatherland Front's rotting away of the solidity of the Bulgarian régime's hold on the people could hardly have been more deft. On 26 August 1944, three days after Michael's *coup* in Romania, a group of ministers proclaimed – now that there was an Allied army within striking distance – that Bulgaria was at peace with Britain and America, and would welcome a Russian invasion. The Russians – without forewarning the British or Americans, of whose every important diplomatic move they continued to wish to be told in advance – thereupon declared war on Bulgaria, just to make sure of what they thought to be the proprieties. On 2 September a well-coordinated Fatherland Front insurrection took place all over the country; Sofia fell to the insurgents on 8/9 September; the Bulgarians made peace with the Russians, and war upon the Germans. 450,000

---

[1] Sweet-Escott, 193–4; and cp. E. Barker, *British Policy in S-E Europe*, 217–18. Her pp. 55–61 and 212–22 deal with Bulgaria.          [2] Cp. Foot, 42–3.

[3] T. J. T. and E. P. T. – his mother, and his brother who became the historian of the English working class – *There Is a Spirit in Europe* . . . (1947); private information. Stowers Johnson, *Agents Extraordinary* (1975), appeared while this book was in the press.

Bulgar troops joined the Red Army in the pursuit up the Danube during the following winter and spring.

The communists meanwhile ousted everybody else from power. There was a purge of regents, ministers, and resisters of the wrong political complexion in February 1945; scores were shot. Dimitrov returned in November 1945 to supervise affairs; he died near Moscow in 1949. The boy king was allowed to go into exile, with the queen mother, in September 1946. Petkov struggled for the semblance at least of free elections, but was no match for Dimitrov, who had him executed in 1947. The people's democratic republic of Bulgaria now lives in part on tourist earnings from the forgetful west.

## Greece

The iron limits of this book's chronological frame press particularly hard in this section: so little of any period of Greek history is comprehensible without reference back to the past and forward to the future. In the country of which the language has provided us with most of our political terms – starting with politics, aristocracy, oligarchy, democracy, tyranny – the political complications in 1940–5 were nothing short of frightful: we must abbreviate as best we can.

Of the glories of ancient Greece, from which so much of our own culture – east and west alike – derives, there is no need to write here; nor of the Greek-speaking empire of Byzantium, of which the fall to the Turks in 1453 is generally taken to mark the start of the modern age;[1] nor of the centuries of Turkish occupation. A war of independence in the 1820s freed the Peloponnese and Attica at least from Turkish rule; by 1913 the Greeks, victorious in both Balkan wars, were nearing Constantinople again. Yet during the 1914–18 world war their history was unhappy. Their monarch, Constantine, happened to be married to Kaiser Wilhelm II's sister, and therefore could not follow the bulk of his subjects in supporting the anti-Turkish cause. Greek politicians divided into royalists and republicans; and successive kings were driven into exile, recalled by plebiscite, and exiled again. Constantine's eldest son, George II, had spent much of his life in England and was well known and well liked by the English court and ruling classes.

Unhappily for whatever role he could play in the war, before it reached Greece he had compromised himself – unforgivably, in the eyes of a great many of his subjects – by assenting to the dictatorship of Metaxas. John Metaxas, a great Greek patriot, had been chief of staff during the war of 1914–18; but had never been able to see eye to eye with that other great Greek patriot, the Cretan Venizelos, who led the anti-monarchists, and died in March 1936. On 4 August that year Metaxas, to avert a communist-threatened strike, proclaimed a dictatorship: which endured till his own death in January 1941. The dictator hoped to save Greece from the wilder eccentricities of a parliamentary system which had, in his view, run to seed; and because he was a professional soldier, at least

[1] Modern history at Oxford begins in the reign of Diocletian; but Oxford likes to be different.

he did something to prepare his country for the attack from outside he thought inevitable. But a régime that censored Pericles' funeral speech, as Thucydides reported it, did not take up a strong stance for any kind of freedom. He had a phobia of communism, and locked up all the communists he could catch; other vocal opponents he deported to the islands. Only the king could readily have overturned him; and the king let him be.

The first attack came in October 1940, from the Italians in Albania; the army, as Metaxas had had it trained and armed, was able to throw the invaders back promptly behind their starting line. The Greeks' presence so early in the battle-line against fascism, highly honourable to them, is too often forgotten; but their early successes led only to a stalemate in the mountains.

Metaxas thought the presence of British troops on Greek soil would only provoke the Germans, and forbade it. His successor Koryzis, a blameless figure-head who did what the king told him, changed the policy: a small British, Australian, and New Zealand force arrived in the spring of 1941, just in time to be bundled unceremoniously out of the mainland by the *Wehrmacht* in April and out of Crete in May.

All Greece was occupied by German or Italian troops. The Italians took the Ionian islands, which had been in British hands from 1815 to 1864; the Albanian puppet province was given a slice of Epirus; the Bulgarians took Thrace and eastern Macedonia (except for Salonika, which the Germans kept for them-selves); there was talk of a Wallachian republic in the Pindus. And as if the Greeks' cup of despair was not full enough already, the British murmured about a Turkish occupation, for safety's sake, of Lesbos, Chios, Samos; perhaps the Greeks would like eventually to join the British commonwealth?[1]

SOE had a few demolition parties with the expeditionary force; they were not there long enough to do much, indeed a scintillating broadcast of Peter Fleming's explains how little they could do at all.[2] They seem to have made no elaborate arrangements about stay-behind parties, either. MI6 and MI9 both managed to leave behind a few wireless sets in trusty hands in Athens. What messages they sent we do not know, but Cairo seems to have been regularly fed with intelligence from Athens all through the three years and a half that the Germans were there: at a sharp price in arrested agents.

Clearly there is an interesting book waiting to be written one day about this; and there must be dozens of unwritten or at any rate unpublished adventure stories of escapes across the Aegean. The bare bones of several have been men-tioned already.[3] A few people who were in the Special Boat Section, the mari-time offshoot of SAS, have given some idea of what these journeys, dodging

---

[1] C. Pyromaglou in *ERM* ii. 306–7. Miss Barker, who handles Greece lightly in her *British Policy in S-E Europe*, 154–7, 164–72, omits this.
[2] 'An Ammunition Train in Greece' in Patrick Howarth ed, *Special Operations* (1955), 1.
[3] pp. 47–8, 59.

from island to island through the Sporades or the Cyclades, felt like.[1] It is worth remembering, as well as these spectacular adventures, the amount of sheer grind that went into conveying and hiding the escapers before they could ever set foot in a caïque: the men and women, bitterly poor, who risked their lives over and over again to help Australians, New Zealanders, Englishmen, each to get away once.[2]

The naval effort involved was not negligible, either. Small boat and submarine crews took substantial risks; sometimes to be rather cavalierly treated by their passengers, or potential passengers. One rather odd case is worth quoting from Crete, whence a great deal of escape work was done. A young naval officer, working for MI9, went ashore from a submarine at a deserted spot on the south coast, and climbed to a cave where he found, as anticipated, two Australian army privates. Each of the two had a drink in his hand; each had his arm round a good-looking peasant wench. He ordered them to come with him; they told him, in words it would be offensive to print, what he could do; he went back alone to his submarine, which had risked mortal danger for no useful purpose.[3]

Most evaders had better sense; all were supported by a tough and long-suffering peasantry, who acted on long-standing loyalties, to the British and to people in trouble, rather than on any instructions from any political or social or administrative authority.

For when the Germans invaded, the central government of Greece withdrew. The king, having acted briefly as prime minister when Koryzis killed himself, appointed the Cretan banker Tsouderos, and retired with him to Crete; whence they were lucky to escape straightaway in a British warship to Egypt. The Greek government-in-exile shifted between Alexandria, Cairo, and Johannesburg; the king shifted between Cairo and London. The cabinet were in a constant state of political disagreement, even among themselves: they were Greeks. Part of the Greek army managed to escape also, and was encamped in the Nile delta, pending discussions between its government and the British about how and where it could be used.

The Germans installed a puppet prime minister, a general who had changed sides, in Athens; and left a small occupation force to hold the main north–south railway line and the ports. They had more important business on their hands in Russia.

The population was left to eke out its life as best it could. The British blockade was at once clamped down; the Germans were not interested in whether the Greeks had enough to eat; their puppet government commanded no more confidence in neighbour countries than it did at home. Country people were used to subsistence agriculture and to going short of food; townspeople had to learn.

[1] Eg. John Lodwick, *The Filibusters*.

[2] Cp. Mulgan, *Report on Experience*, 128–37, on the old man who travelled thirteen times from Euboea to Athens and back, and lost an eye when the Germans questioned him. He accepted a drink as a reward.

[3] Conversation with one of the five, 1972.

Thanks to United States and Vatican intervention, a little help was provided through the international red cross. All the same, many thousands starved to death, especially in the winters.

In Athens, a highly civilized city with highly politicized people in it, abnormally interested in current affairs, there was a great deal of talk; but the chances for action were sparse. The Germans saw all the classical sights, in large numbers; but were always armed, and always vigilant. Metaxas's police force remained ostensibly on the side of law and order; though Evert, its chief, was secretly in touch with the British agents who soon began to visit Athens, to collect intelligence and to arrange escapes. There were thousands of evaders left behind from the British withdrawal in April for whom something had to be done. And SOE had managed to leave a wireless set with a left-wing colonel, Bakirdzis ('Prometheus'), who spied out possibilities of action for a year before he escaped by sea. He organized some sabotage of ships at the Piraeus with limpets.

As the German invasion took place while the Molotov–Ribbentrop pact was still running, and only the German high command knew how soon the pact was to be dissolved by 'Barbarossa', one of the first things the German police authorities did was to release the communists whom Metaxas had had arrested; all except the secretary-general of the Greek communist party (KKE), Zakhariadis, whom they took away to a German concentration camp. George Siantos, a great believer in 'boring from within', acted as his deputy for the rest of the war. These communists soon all hurled themselves into the business of resistance, and set up a National Liberation Front (EAM) in September 1941.

Up country there was a lot more freedom from the Germans than in Athens or Salonika, and groups of resisters (*andartes*) proliferated. For the first winter, there was not much more than talk; and plenty to talk about. Talk centred – these were Greeks talking – round the role of the king, and the rival merits of the British, the Americans, or the Russians as external sponsors. A group of officers, called the Six Colonels, were in touch by wireless with the king, and could relay his instructions to the officer corps; George II ordered his officers to do nothing that might provoke reprisals. The EAM proliferated, in the way that a vigorous front organization is supposed in marxist theory to do. As few as 10 per cent of its membership may have been communist; the KKE provided the main drive, and looked after where it was going.

In the spring of 1942 the movement, vigorous already on a national basis, sprouted a military wing, the Greek Popular Liberation Army (ELAS); one of several small armies to appear in the mountains, all the rest of which at one time or another it attacked. Its main resistance rival was the National Republican Greek League (EDES), under a retired colonel called Napoleon Zervas: at 5,000 men, about a quarter the size of ELAS. ELAS looked nominally inward to the Greek people to provide its own salvation, actually outward to the unresponsive USSR: Stalin in 1942 was busy saving his own country, and later promised Churchill he would leave Greece alone; a promise that, on the whole, he kept.[1] EDES looked, nominally again, to General Plastiras, an eminent exile, then living in occupied France, who had led a right-wing revolution in 1922–3. Several of Zervas's army colleagues – Saraphis, Psaros, Bakirdzis – raised bands of their own. Psaros for example collected all he could of his own old regiment, in his home neighbourhood round Parnassus; and was supported from the towns by EKKA, National and Social Liberation, a body of liberal republicans.

SOE's manifest duty was to try to bring some degree of concerted anti-German effort out of this motley orchestra. Several fleeting visits in the late summer of 1941 brought information, but no decision. On 10 October 1942 a party of eight parachutists under E. C. W. Myers landed near Delphi;[2] and succeeded – this was the only occasion on which this was done – in getting ELAS and EDES to cooperate in a military operation. A force of some 150 men, commanded by Zervas, blew up the viaduct of the Salonika–Athens railway in the Gorgopotamos gorge,[3] south-west of Lamia, on 25 November 1942. This was an important *coup*; it severely interfered with the Afrika Korps' supplies, during their retreat from El Alamein.

Some indication of the political complexity of Greek resistance is given by the fact that Athanasios Klaras – alias 'Aris Veloukhiotis' – who had distinguished himself under Zervas in this attack was a communist so acrid and vehement that he later had his thugs murder Psaros, whom he had made prisoner; and at the tail end of the war repudiated even the agreement his party colleagues had made with the Allies, took once more to the hills, and ended with his head on a stake.[4]

More routine difficulties are brought out by the fact that Myers' party missed their submarine on the Epirus coast, and had to winter in Greece; and that their reports made it clear to Cairo and London that there was plenty of mobilized and mobilizable resistance in the Greek mountains, but that almost all of it was anti-monarchist.

This raised a whole hornet's nest of political difficulties. Churchill personally felt himself bound to George II and was inclined to put the king's restoration as a *sine qua non* for continued British help to Greece. Eden, ill and busy, was prepared to accept short-term arguments from SOE about operational necessity and military advantage, without deep reflexion on the consequences.[5] In Cairo, ministers and staff officers – British, Greek, American alike – were deep in plots and counter-plots. No one in OSS was in principle likely to support any King George, if any viable alternative offered; and in 1943 there were distinct signs that EAM was trying to play OSS officers off against SOE ones, appealing to the Americans' anti-imperialist instincts and painting the British as merely rapacious.[6]

[1] Cp. E. Barker, *British Policy in S-E Europe*, 142–7.
[2] Myers' *Greek Entanglement* (1955) is valuable. On this particular point, see C. M. Woodhouse – his second-in-command – in *ERM* i. 381–2.
[3] Photograph of the viaduct in Myers, op. cit., at 65; account of the operation ibid. 69–87.     [4] C. M. Woodhouse, *The Struggle for Greece* (1976), 140–1.
[5] Sweet-Escott, 160–1.     [6] Eg. Harris Smith, 126–8.

Moral difficulties were added to political – if indeed there is any fair disjunction to be made between the two – in the summer of 1943. As part of the cover plan for 'Husky', the invasion of Sicily, Greek resistance activity was warmly encouraged in May and June. So much sabotage resulted that the Germans sent two more divisions to Greece, one of them armoured. When the armoured division had reached the Peloponnese, the Salonika–Athens line – by which alone it could withdraw, without wearing out its tank tracks – was again blown up, this time at the Asopus viaduct, a little nearer Athens: a fortnight before 'Husky' began. The line was closed for four months.[1] Sensitive people might feel that this created some sort of obligation towards the Greek saboteurs: most but not all of whom belonged to ELAS. (ELAS had held aloof from the previous big bridge bang till it was clear that EDES were involved; ELAS then joined in, lest EDES get all the credit. In the Asopus attack ELAS took no direct part at all: six British members of SOE did all the work themselves.)[2]

Sensitivity was not the leading characteristic of ELAS' governing men. They provided four of the delegation of six resistance leaders who were flown out of Greece, with Myers and Woodhouse, on 9 August 1943 for discussions in Cairo. (EDES and EKKA provided the other two.) Tzimas, the leader of this body, plunged headlong into an attack on the king, demanding an undertaking from George II not to return to Greece unless a plebiscite summoned him to do so.[3] He was supported by all his colleagues and by some of the ministers in exile; the king was indisposed to agree; the British government supported the king; and the angry delegation flew back on 16/17 September, minus Myers (but, unexpectedly, plus Bakirdzis, on his way to raise his private army). They had achieved nothing but dissension – Tzimas's aim, it would appear, all along.

They arrived back to meet a substantial military crisis: the Italian surrender. ELAS, convinced that the war was about to end, secured most of the arms of the Italians in Greece, outwitting Germans, British, and other Greeks with equal dexterity; and used them for a massive onslaught on EDES, which Zervas and his men only survived with difficulty. Zervas thenceforward was confined to north-west Greece; where on SOE's orders he bided his time, receiving occasional supplies of arms by sea and waiting to attack the Germans when they withdrew.[4] This attack on EDES demonstrates the main object towards which EAM was always working: control of Greece in the interests of international communism. To be fair, this was only the object of its hidden leadership – most of its members simply wanted, like any other resisters, to get rid of the Germans.

Let us turn aside for a moment from high politics to comedy, to mention in passing a *coup* brought off by SOE on Crete: conceived by George Jellicoe, and executed by Patrick Leigh-Fermor and Stanley Moss late in April 1944. Wearing

[1] Myers, op. cit., 169–86; photograph at 192.
[2] Ibid., and C. M. Woodhouse, *Apple of Discord* (1948), 141–2.
[3] The king had returned in just this way in 1935; but by a plebiscite manifestly rigged in his favour. See C. Pyromaglou (who was on this delegation), in *ERM* ii. 298 and iii. (ad rem) 10.     [4] Woodhouse, *Apple of Discord*, 158–68.

German uniforms and carrying German army regulation red lights, they stopped the German divisional commander's car on a lonely road; coshed the driver; and drove the general, through a score of his own control posts, up into the mountains, and so out to Cairo by submarine. It was a model minor operation;[1] but we must turn back to major ones.

ELAS/EAM had miscalculated when the Germans were in fact going to go. A soviet mission reached them from Yugoslavia in July 1944, and seems to have had some moderating impact.[2] In September 1944, when the Germans did in fact pull out, ELAS and EDES – the only two surviving guerilla organizations; ELAS much the larger – harassed them to useful military effect. British troops came in hard on their heels. In December 1944 EAM, as in October 1943, again attempted to seize control of the entire country; and the troops who had expected to fight Germans found for some uncomfortable weeks that they had to fight communists instead. Superior armament, on the British side, and total lack of support for EAM on the Russian, soon had their effect. Plastiras, the nominal head of EDES, became prime minister; Damaskinos, archbishop of Athens, became regent for the king, who had at last to agree to a plebiscite before he returned. This agreement saved ELAS's face, and the civil war was suspended by a truce on 13 January 1945: where we must leave it.

This section has necessarily had to deal with politicians, leaders, ministers, officers; let it close with a reminder from John Mulgan.

The real heroes of the Greek war of resistance were the common people of the hills. It was on them, with their bitter, uncomplaining endurance, that the German terror broke. They produced no traitors. We moved freely among them and were guided by them into German-held villages by night without fear. They never surrendered or compromised, and as a result the Germans kept five divisions guarding Greece all through the war. The Greek people paid a terrible and disproportionate price for this resistance.

On a particular occasion, near Lamia in 1944,

They had the look of all peasant Greeks, of men who don't expect much fun but are prepared to endure. They didn't ask us to stop sabotaging the railway line, but requested modestly that if we did anything it would be on a scale comparate to the reprisals that would follow.[3]

## Albania

Albania is much the smallest surviving Balkan independent country, and was long notoriously the least developed. Mineral wealth is there – lignite, iron, and nickel are all now worked; in the 1940s, there were appreciable quantities of copper and chrome. It was as a source of chrome that Albania was important to the Germans. It was sparsely inhabited, by a population of little over a million,

---

[1] W. Stanley Moss, *Ill Met by Moonlight* (1950), a clear participant's account.
[2] But cp. Woodhouse, *Struggle for Greece*, 64.
[3] *Report on Experience*, 99, 115; cp. Myers, op. cit., 11.

85 per cent of them living in a congeries of peasant villages among the limestone mountains, or scattered along the 150 miles of Adriatic coastal plain. Five centuries of sharply resented Turkish occupation had converted about three-quarters of the population to Islam.

Albania was created as an independent kingdom, with a German prince imposed as king by the great powers, after the Balkan war of 1912. Its frontiers were too small for the ambitions of its few political figures, and too large to suit its Greek and Montenegrin neighbours. Tribal divisions remained important; the chief being between the Ghegs of northern Albania, who still lived in clans – like the Scots clans before 1745 – and held their lands on feudal tenures,[1] and the Tosks of the south, who held by a different sort of moslem feudalism from a few large landlords. The Ghegs were much taken up with problems of family, relationship, obligation; the Tosks were nearer something a marxist could recognize as a proletariat. Such industry as there was, was in Tosk rather than Gheg territory. A few Tosk young men had been educated abroad, part of the large Albanian diaspora over southern and eastern Europe.

Mussolini coveted Albania, for the purposes of imperial greatness he thought necessary. On Good Friday, 7 April 1939, the Italians suddenly invaded it. King Zog capitulated quickly, and retired abroad. At first, there was no resistance: everyone was too surprised. Besides, in a country with weak communications, few schools, few newspapers, the central authority was in any case not highly regarded, and played no prominent part in people's thinking. The railways, that had transformed so much of peasant Europe, have still got no farther than connecting Tirana, the capital, with Durazzo, the nearest port.

Fascist Italy did what little it could to wake up the inhabitants of its newest province to their imperial destiny; this annoyed the Albanians, a thoroughly independent-minded lot. From April 1940 there were occasional guerilla attacks on fascist policemen and officials, in the remoter mountain areas, and when six months later the Italians attacked the Greeks, their supplies – difficult enough to deliver, on poor roads, into mountainous country – were occasionally interrupted by hostile local bands. Though other local bands cooperated with the Italians against the Greeks, many of their members on second thoughts deserted.[2] In midsummer 1941 the Germans added to Albania part of western Macedonia, and also the Kosovo region, largely Albanian in population though regarded by the Serbs as Serb, because they lost a battle there in the fourteenth century. Balkan peoples have memories as tenacious as the Irish.

The Albanians remained dissatisfied: SOE, following section D – which had done some work from Belgrade – tried to canalize their unrest against the occupiers. Colonel Oakley Hill, who had visited northern Albania once for section D,

[1] I have shaken hands with a man, born an English speaker, whose parents held a few acres of Connemara bog at a feudal rent, of fourteen man-days of labouring work a year: a tenancy forcibly ended during the Troubles. That is to say, English speakers need not feel they are all that far 'advanced' on Albanians.

[2] *ERM* ii. 125.

went back again in April 1941, with a group of Gheg leaders who called themselves a United Front; but they had few arms, there was no serious clandestine organization, some prominent men were captured, and the rest retired to their own hill forts to wait.[1]

It was not till the autumn of 1942 that an initiative, originating perhaps from Yugoslavia, stirred resistance up thoroughly. The Albanian communist party, formed in November 1941, was small but well disciplined, and in Enver Hoxha[2] it had a Moscow-trained young leader of unusual vigour and toughness: even for an Albanian. His party, pursuing the comintern's popular front doctrines, summoned a meeting in September 1942 from which there emerged a National Liberation Movement (LNC). This had the usual broad anti-fascist democratic programme suitable for a wide appeal.[3]

Soon thereafter, a body of more conservative Albanian chieftains set up a rival organization, the Balli Kombëtar or National Front. Early in 1943 a strong SOE mission under Billy McLean[4] entered Albania from northern Greece, and made contact successively with the LNC and the Balli Kombëtar. One important chieftain, a northern royalist, Abas Kupi, belonged to both movements, and was the sort of man to whose opinion people deferred, in a predominantly deferential society. He proposed a conference between delegates of the two movements, which was held near Tirana in July 1943; full of euphoria on hearing of the fall of Mussolini, they agreed to sink all differences for the sake of driving the Italians out.

The agreement did not last long. When the Italians changed sides, a lot of arms were available; there was a premature national rising; and the Germans, in a few characteristic swift strokes, took the country over. They had to have the chrome, and the coastline. So they flew troops to Tirana airfield, made sure of Valona Durazzo and Scutari with motorized columns, and shot everybody suspicious they met.

They made some attempt to track down the Balli Kombëtar and the LNC leaders in their mountain lairs, burned a lot of villages, and killed a lot of civilians.[5] Surviving resisters spent the winter mulling over old mistakes, contemplating new policies, and looking round for arms. The Gheg leaders were tempted by the idea of retaining the new provinces the Germans had provided; the Tosks were being regimented more and more strictly under Hoxha's discipline.

SOE withdrew Maclean for a rest, and sent in Brigadier E. F. ('Trotsky') Davies to head an enlarged mission; but Davies was captured by Albanian quislings in January 1944.[6] Maclean and Julian Amery returned, by parachute, on 19/20 April 1944 with the tasks of reorganizing and coordinating the British

---

[1] Cp. E. Barker, *British Policy in S-E Europe*, 47–54.
[2] Pronounce Hodja, with two short vowels.                                   [3] Cp. ibid. 175.
[4] Distinguish from (Sir) Fitzroy Maclean, of whom more in the next section.
[5] *ERM* ii. 133–5.
[6] E. Barker, op. cit., 179.

teams in northern and central Albania, of raising the Ghegs against the Germans, and of getting Ghegs and Tosks to cooperate. In this last aim they failed. The Balli Kombëtar and the LNC remained even more suspicious of each other than of their occupying power. Each resented the slightest favour shown by SOE to the other; and each accused the other of secretly collaborating with the nazis.

There was certainly an occasion, in May 1944, when an LNC force found itself engaged against a mixed body of some 2,000 Germans and Balli Kombëtar, acting jointly. Amery on the other hand gives a graphic and almost simultaneous account of an attack on a German artillery unit mounted by Abas Kupi and some Zogists and a platoon of Tadjik deserters from the Russian and German armies successively, commanded (with no common language) by himself.[1]

SOE pursued its usual policy of arming whichever party provided the most satisfactory proof that it was killing Germans; irrespective of longer-term political consequences. From Amery's account, it certainly looks as if SOE Bari promised Abas Kupi more than it intended to perform. In spite of repeated requests and promises, he only got a single drop of arms; none were sent to his group by sea, though other Balli Kombëtar parties got some arms by sea and the LNC got a lot. There would seem to have been some strong influence inside SOE which determined to back the LNC's National Liberation Army – so named, that summer, after Tito's – against the field. It seems to have had a maximum fighting strength of about 13,000 men, plus unnumbered supporters in the villages; till the closing stages, when its supporters claimed for it over 60,000.[2]

Michel lists Albania as a complete failure by SOE, and among the territories acquired for the USSR's postwar zone of influence by the Red Army.[3] This is perhaps to mis-appreciate both SOE's aim, and the Red Army's reach. Elements, or an element, in SOE certainly supported Hoxha's LNC and gave it both money[4] and weapons: believing it to be the strongest lever for removing the Germans from Albania. The Germans did in fact pull out, chrome or no chrome, when their left flank was turned by the capture of Belgrade in October.

In spite of all the talk, not much was done to chase them away. The LNC, instead of hunting Germans, used SOE's weapons to hunt Abas Kupi. Amery was just able to get away; as could the old man, alone, by boat: all having been lost, save honour, and even of honour not a great deal was left.[5]

Next day in mess at Bari, a provost-marshal reproached Amery for daring to wear a beard while in army uniform: he was back in the sort of system SOE existed to destroy.

---

[1] Julian Amery, *Sons of the Eagle*, 124. His *Approach March* (1973), 333–421, embodies his later reflexions.

[2] *ERM* ii. 142. And cp. E. Barker, op. cit., 179–83.          [3] Michel, *SW*, 124, 338.

[4] Gold sovereigns bearing Victoria's unveiled face were unacceptable to Moslems: an extra difficulty for SOE's Q branch, in Albania and elsewhere.

[5] An obituary of Abas Kupi, who had just died in New York, by Amery appeared in *The Times*, 16 January 1976, 16 fg.

## Yugoslavia

In Yugoslavia the racial, social, and political complications of Balkan life were even denser than in Albania. It was a new country, only twenty-one years old in 1939; its component parts were still shaking down together. Its formal title was till 1929 the Kingdom of the Serbs, Croats, and Slovenes; the royal family of Serbia, which owed its position to a savage palace revolution as recently as 1903, held a constitutional throne on no very certain tenure. The population, of some fifteen million, consisted of the three races named already, plus substantial minorities of Germans, Magyars, Albanians, and Turks; and a few thousand Roumans, Greeks, Bulgars, and Italians; leaving aside the question whether Macedonian counted as a separate nationality or not. There was a great deal of inter-marriage between the races; and racial statistics varied enormously, because the allegiance one expressed when asked to state one's nationality hinged partly on the facts, partly on who asked the question, and partly on how heavily the inquirer was armed.[1] A century earlier, the whole country had been part either of the Habsburg or of the Ottoman empire; not till both empires vanished could a large south slav state emerge.

Serbo-Croat was the official language. Among the three main races, the Serbs were sometimes inclined to assert themselves as the leading group, and Croat separatism was strong; fed by a myth that the Croats, who were Roman catholics and wrote Serbo-Croat in Roman script, were culturally a cut above the Serbs, who were orthodox in religion and used cyrillic.

From 1929, when he was forty, the Croat leader Ante Pavelić had led a terrorist group called the Ustaše,[2] usually from exile in Italy. An Ustaša group, trained in Hungary and paid for out of Italian secret funds, killed the king of Yugoslavia, Alexander, in Marseilles in October 1934; they also shot the man beside him, who wandered in the crowd for half an hour, half-stunned, unrecognized, and bleeding quietly to death. He was Barthou, the French foreign minister. Barthou, like Baldwin, had read *Mein Kampf*; unlike Baldwin, he had been determined to do something to block Hitler. The nazis, therefore, had him on a list; and would have gone gunning for him, had the Croats not saved them the trouble.[3]

Alexander's son and successor, Peter II, had only just turned eleven; his cousin Prince Paul was senior regent. The prince was a reluctant realist; he could perceive Germany's power, and Yugoslavia's weakness; and the Germans worked on him accordingly. An interesting, indeed typical, divergence of view arose, among the British representatives in Belgrade, between the diplomats who could appreciate Paul's gentlemanly qualities and applaud his realism, and the

[1] Conversation with R. W. Seton-Watson, 1947.
[2] Pronounce to rhyme with Worcestershire.
[3] Conversation with (Sir) John Wheeler-Bennett in 1946. He had been shown the list in 1933; everyone on it was dead before 1936.

The partition of Yugoslavia, 1941

1  annexed to Germany
2  occupied by Germany
3  administered by Germany
4  German sphere of interest
5  annexed to Italy

6  occupied by Italy
7  Italian sphere of interest
8  annexed to Hungary
9  occupied by Hungary
10  annexed to Bulgaria

Z, L = Zara, Lagosta; Italian since 1920

All the Adriatic islands were occupied by Italy late in 1941; all were
also annexed, except for Pag (NW of Zara) and Brac and Hvar (SE of
Split).

187

emissaries of section D and later of SOE who could see that being realist amounted, by the winter of 1940–1, to being pro-nazi: and was therefore from the British point of view a pity. Masterton, 'a wise and most impressive old man' of about sixty,[1] who had helped Norton Griffiths damage the Romanian oilfield in 1916, was made head of SOE's Yugoslav office on the spot, with the cover of a first secretary's post in Belgrade; among those who helped him were S. W. Bailey, a young mining engineer, and the even younger Julian Amery, originally the press attaché.

Amery has given a vivid picture of the embarrassments of being formally on a minister's staff, while pursuing policies directly opposed to those he favoured; and of the extreme poverty of some of the Yugoslav peasantry, living in droves in earthen huts below ground level, on whom SOE's peasant party contacts depended for support.[2] The contrast must have been all the more striking for someone who came from his father's house in Eaton Square, and from the white-tie-and-tails atmosphere of the prewar Oxford Union.

When German pressure finally persuaded Prince Paul to adhere, on 25 March 1941, to the tripartite pact, there was an explosion of popular wrath in Belgrade. SOE undoubtedly had a hand in this explosion, though few reliable details of what it did are published. In any event, Paul's régime was overthrown two days later by a *coup d'état*, of which the supporters ranged from the air general staff to a faction in the communist party. General Simović became prime minister, Peter was declared of age, and Paul was allowed to go into exile.[3]

The Yugoslav military attaché in Berlin, Vauhnik, had sources so good that he had already reported the Germans' intended attack on Russia; the defeated cabinet had not credited the report, but had passed it on (via London) to Moscow. On 1 April he reported that the Germans would attack Yugoslavia within a week.[4] Yugoslav mobilization was still incomplete when seven panzer divisions marched in on the 6th, and air raids on Belgrade inflicted 10,000 casualties. The Serb army had held out for two years against Austria-Hungary; the Yugoslav army held out against the *Blitzkrieg* for ten days.

The military disaster was followed by a political one. Germany, Italy, Hungary, Romania, and Bulgaria all took adjacent strips of Yugoslav territory; the Italians' largest gains, including most of Montenegro, across their Albanian frontier. What was left was cut in half: a small Serbia, smaller than the Serbia of 1914, and a large Croatia. Independent Croatia was handed over to Pavelić, and the Ustaše were let loose.

The massacre that followed had, air bombing apart, only two parallels during the war: the hundred thousand people shot in an afternoon at Kharkov, and the three million and more sent to their final end at Auschwitz. It was directed initially against Jews and Serbs; then against everyone who was neither Croat

[1] Sweet-Escott, 52.
[2] *Approach March*, 152–74.
[3] Cp. E. Barker, *British Policy in S-E Europe*, 78–95.
[4] Phyllis Auty, *Tito* (1970), 157, 160.

nor catholic. Some Serbs converted to catholicism were spared; the rest were slaughtered, over 500,000 of them. In some villages, catholic priests were the ringleaders, the organizers of who was to live and who to die; in others the Ustaše did all the work. A few ineffectual attempts to interest the Vatican in what was being done in Christ's name got nowhere.[1]

Against this reign of terror, as frightful as Armenia in 1915 or the Punjab in 1947, only the insensately brave or desperate were likely to be ready to resist; many Serbs were nevertheless to be found to meet even this challenge.

Even more than in Greece or Albania, resistance in Yugoslavia took on the form of civil war; not only because the country was carved up into so many fragments, but also because the two principal resistance movements, which walked warily side by side at first, soon came to active hostilities against each other.

Draža Mihailović, the colonel in charge of the operations bureau of the general staff till just before the lightning struck, was already something of an expert on guerilla;[2] of which there were long-standing traditions all over the Balkans. Instead of fleeing the country with the king and the government that went into exile, or surrendering to the new authorities, he took to the hills, and used his knowledge and personality to weld into a fighting force such elements of the dissolving Yugoslav army as he could find and persuade to join him.

The forces he raised were called četniks, after the Serb bands who had fought the Turk in earlier times. He was himself a Serb, and always put Serbian interests (as he saw them) first; he was also continuously aware of his duties as an officer and his responsibilities to his king. Most of his original četniks were Serbs, officers and men who had evaded German capture and kept their small arms at least. They first collected in the heart of Serbia, in the mountainous country between Belgrade and Užice.

The name of četnik had such historical resonance in Yugoslavia that it was also used by a collaborationist force that supported the puppet government of Nedić which was supposed to govern Serbia from Belgrade. These 'legal' četniks, roughly comparable to Vichy's *milice*, had existed since 1918; they were an armed extension to the civil police force, and more dangerous to resisters than German occupying troops because, being natives of the country, they understood its ways much better, and might know something of the character of individuals as well. They were a considerable brake on operations in towns. They have also become an obstacle to historians, for their use of the same name as a resistance movement has sometimes led to confusion. That is, not all the reports to which we shall come in a moment of 'četniks cooperating with the occupiers' necessarily referred to Mihailović's četniks; they might refer to Pećanac's or to other collaborators.

[1] See Branko Bokun, *Spy in the Vatican 1941–45* (1973), for the diary of a young Yugoslav intelligence officer sent to Rome to pierce, if he could, the carapace of hierarchs' complacency. He had no success, and hid in the city till the Allied armies arrived.

[2] Amery, *Approach March*, 179; cp. E. Barker, op. cit., 154.

Mihailović's bands were raised with the serious intention of resisting the Germans, and the Italians, and the Ustaše; and the fact that their leader came to a sticky end at the hands of his rivals in the civil war should not blind us to their original aims. He failed to achieve these aims; but the failure was imposed on him by circumstance. It did not arise from any malice aforethought in his upright mind; it arose from his upbringing, his character, and the times he had to fight in. His loyalties were always to the crown and to Serbia; it was not difficult, in the end, to pillory him as the lackey of the vanishing old régime, which a modern people's republic had elbowed out of the way to progress. Strictly, 1946 (the year of his trial) is outside these pages' scope; but it is hard to think of Mihailović's life without recalling the firing party that concluded it. In his earliest days as a resister, that dismal end was out of sight and out of mind.

His first difficulty was the simple, basic one of communications. Yugoslavia and Greece once subdued, the *Wehrmacht* roared off eastward on 'Barbarossa'. The Danube and Vardar valleys alike were virtually closed to clandestine traffic; the Italians and the Ustaše divided the Dalmatian coast between them. The military disaster seems to have come so suddenly that SOE only managed to leave a single wireless set behind; those of its staff who were overrun in Belgrade had the odd experience of being interned in Italy for some weeks while their admissibility to diplomatic status was mulled over between the Italian and Swiss foreign offices.[1] In Serbia, in fact, one was shut in.

Secondly, he was reluctant to embark too soon on active operations; judging, correctly, that the war would go on a long time yet, and knowing that the nazis whom he detested would lose it, he wanted to spare the Serbs whom he loved any avoidable casualties from reprisals. His hand was shortly forced: by his rival and eventual supplanter, Tito.

Tito is the cover name of Josip Broz, at that time the general secretary of the communist party of Yugoslavia (CPY). He was rising fifty; the son of a middling peasant Croat father and a Slovene mother; trained as a metal-worker, seasoned already in warfare, and extensively experienced as a communist and clandestine. He had been a prisoner-of-war in Russia when the revolutions of 1917 took place, and sympathized with the second, more extreme of them. From trade union work in Yugoslavia he graduated successively to prison, a responsible job under the comintern – running clandestine communications between Paris and Barcelona early in the Spanish civil war – and training in Moscow; where he escaped arrest during the great purge, by dint of doing what he was told and never pushing himself forward. His party in Yugoslavia was illegal, and the regular object of police counter-action.

He already knew all he needed to know about how to fight, how to survive, how to conspire; he detested nazism; but he was no mere apparatchik. He was a good south slav, who wanted to get all the south slavs together in a single working state, in which no particular race predominated: he had seen more than

[1] D. E. Walker, *Death at my Heels* (1964), ad fin.

enough of predominant racism in the Habsburg army (in which his military talents had quickly raised him to the rank of sergeant-major). Croat separatism and Croat pretensions to superiority left him quite unmoved; Pavelić he found as unacceptable as Hitler.

As a comintern agent, he had learned the indispensability of keeping his mouth shut; his taciturnity had been his surest shield in Moscow, where he fully appreciated the perils among which he had to walk. 'When I went to Moscow,' he said long afterwards, 'I never knew whether I would come back alive. And while I was there I never knew that I would not wake up in the middle of the night to hear the fatal knocking at my door.'[1] No one in the west in the 1940s had fully taken in what Stalin and Yezhov had done to Tito, and thousands of his companions among the world's leading communists, in the late 1930s.

His capacity for making up his mind promptly, that great military gift, and his control over the CPY gave him two great advantages over enemies and rivals alike. Mihailović still had in the summer of 1941 to make the mental transition between being a staff officer, dependent on his general for guidance, and being a commander himself; Tito had made the transition beforehand. The CPY was only some 8,000 strong, and then consisted of town workers and of intellectuals, rather than peasants; but it had had years of experience already of illegal work. 300 of its members had heard the call to go to Spain, had been passed there by Tito (before he became their general secretary), and had survived; he knew them all, and summoned them all to join him. The party had cells all over Yugoslavia, and a large following among the very young,[2] and working courier links with its centre; this gave him a further start.

In accordance with the comintern policy of the popular front, the CPY offered cooperation to any other anti-fascist bodies with whom it could make contact. The first success was in Montenegro as early as 13 June 1941; communists and nationalists worked together to produce a sudden widespread anti-Italian outburst, which had a momentary success, but was promptly put down by an incursion of Italian troops and police.

Fifty attacks on German soldiers in the ruins of Belgrade, and thirty of them killed at Niš, are recorded for the month of July 1941; and west of Niš, in southwestern Serbia, Tito himself began active operations in September. A great many infuriated peasants were prepared to help him, and he organized them formally into bodies of troops, who took the name of partisan: already used for guerilla forces in the campaign of 1812 in Russia that ruined Napoleon's Grand Army.[3] The partisans captured several towns; the Germans were inclined for the moment to let them be, so long as the Morava and Vardar valleys remained clear.

In one of the captured towns, Užice, the partisans found a rifle factory, in which they stepped up production; and a printing press; and the entire note

---

[1] 1967? Phyllis Auty, *Tito*, 146.     [2] See Casterman, s.v. Yougoslavie.
[3] H. Seton-Watson, *East European Revolution* (2 ed. 1952), 119n.

reserve of the Yugoslav National Bank, which they appropriated. This was not a matter of bandits lining their own pockets; they needed the money to pay for what they ate, and they ate as sparingly as they could.

An important feature of the partisan army was that the whole of its command structure, from Tito at its head down through brigade and battalion to company commanders, was in the hands of communists: non-communists, however talented, however brilliant, could command nothing stronger than a platoon. Stalin indeed reproved Tito for such strict party control over his force, which might inhibit bourgeois patriots from joining it.

Tito, on the spot, believed he knew better, and ignored the reproof. He would have been the more inclined to do so, had he known then that Stalin had proposed to send a mission to Mihailović: a proposal that the Yugoslav government-in-exile turned down.[1] Stalin had made this proposal, to a government which in the previous May he had declared defunct,[2] as a result of a propaganda outburst from which Mihailović benefited in the autumn.

The colonel managed to get a message out of Yugoslavia, which got to London in September 1941; it gave some account of the preparatory steps Mihailović was taking to set up četnik bands in the hills. This news, arriving at a time when there was little other news that was good, made a sensation. Mihailović was hailed, by the BBC, in the English, American, and Russian press, as the first of those resistance heroes and heroines who were to be staple journalists' fodder for so long. He was at once promoted general; in January 1942 he was appointed minister of national defence in the exiled cabinet, and commander-in-chief of all resistance forces under the Yugoslav crown. He never sat round a cabinet table with his colleagues; and the partisans eluded his grasp.

He and Tito met, on 19 September and on 26–27 October 1941, to discuss their future policy.[3] Each was promptly disillusioned about the other. Mihailović saw in Tito the godless, lawless apostle of a doctrine that would abolish the crown he served, and all it stood for. Tito saw in Mihailović the incarnation of the bourgeois régime he and his companions in arms sought to overthrow as soon as they had got the nazis out of the way. As he put it to an SOE visitor, he had 'nothing against the Old Man personally, but the Yugoslav Officer Corps as a whole was compromised';[4] that corps had indeed disgraced itself in the April campaign, and its members bothered too much about points of personality and protocol, too little about actual power. Mihailović for instance resented the partisans' incursion into western Serbia, uninvited by himself, as an unwarranted incursion into 'his' territory.

The Germans resented it also, for straightforward military reasons, and

---

[1] Michel, *Mouvements clandestins*, 98–9.

[2] Stalin, on becoming prime minister in May 1941, had told the envoys of the Belgian, Norwegian, and Yugoslav governments who were in Moscow that, as their governments had ceased to exist, they had better go: I. Deutscher, *Stalin* (1949), 454.

[3] Casterman, s.v. Yougoslavie.

[4] (Sir) F. W. D. Deakin, *The Embattled Mountain* (1971), 135.

mounted in November 1941 the first of the seven separate full-scale offensives, all Pyrrhic victories, they put in against the partisans. These seven offensives would by themselves provide a justification for the partisan effort, for they were each mounted by several divisions of good troops – on one occasion at least, led by a *Waffen-SS* division specially trained in mountain warfare. They were backed by armour and by air support; they represented a substantial diversion, of resources, petrol, and emotional effort, from the main fronts on which the *Wehrmacht* was engaged.

**Table 2** AXIS OFFENSIVES AGAINST YUGOSLAV PARTISANS[1]

| | Date | Place | Notes |
|---|---|---|---|
| 1 | November 1941 | Serbia | Occasion of Tito–Mihailović split; SOE witness on hand |
| 2 | Early 1942 | Bosnia | |
| 3 | June 1942 | Montenegro | |
| 4 | January to April 1943 | Hercegovina, Montenegro, Dalmatian hinterlands | |
| 5 | May–August 1943 | Montenegro | SOE witnesses on hand |
| 6 | Spring 1944 | Most of Yugoslavia | OSS and SOE witnesses |
| 7 | Summer 1944 | Most of Yugoslavia | OSS and SOE witnesses |

Tito's forces met all these offensives in roughly the same way: by resolute opposition to start with, and then by a controlled disappearance, as soon as it was clear that the main attack could not be mastered. Knowing their own country better than the Germans or Italians could, they were skilled in tactical withdrawals, even with the handicap they felt they had to impose on themselves: they took their wounded with them. Early experience, in the first offensive, showed them that wounded who were left behind were massacred; thereafter, wounded preferred to be killed by their own side, or carried away by it.

Deakin's book contains some startling examples of the severity of this struggle. One, from the fourth offensive, may give the tone. The German First Mountain Division was clearing a large area, with instructions to shoot all those possessing arms, and to burn their houses; the troops went well beyond these orders, already fierce enough. Ninety old men, women, and children were hiding in a cave; as a German patrol neared the entrance, a new-born baby started to cry. As there was nothing else to do, its mother strangled it. The Germans glanced

[1] Based on Seton-Watson, *East European Revolution*, 122n.

into the cave, shot dead the people in sight from the entrance, and went away. An empty cradle still marks the spot.[1]

*The Embattled Mountain* lacks what one might call the social graces of popular resistance literature, but among its many countervailing virtues one stands out: it conveys the authentic confusion of irregular war, in which to the usual fog of battle are added extra doubts about who is who and what is what. The fighting in Yugoslavia was both savage and confused; to the wild terrain, poor roads, rough tracks, few railways, the variegated population added many further doubts for the travelling soldier – on any of the several combatant sides. Germans, Ustaše, Bulgars, Italians, partisans, two sorts of četnik, Greeks, Albanians – here already are nine distinguishable groups, and there were several more; though none but the Germans and Italians could be distinguished at a glance by their clothes. Any of these groups might, not necessarily waiting to be provoked, open fire on almost any of the others. Some armed parties, Ustaša in particular, were inclined in some areas to open fire on any moving biped, and ask questions later, if they bothered to stop.

Given their divergent beliefs, it was hardly surprising that Mihailović's followers and Tito's soon came to blows. Mihailović understood that he had orders from his government-in-exile to soft-pedal activity against the Germans for the time being. These orders reached him in the autumn of 1941 through two Yugoslav majors, returned from brief exile, called Ostojić and Lalatović. Julian Amery saw them ashore on the Montenegrin coast from a British submarine on 20 September;[2] they were accompanied by a wireless operator, Dragićević, with two sets, and by D. T. Hudson, of SOE.[3] It was a joint British–Royal Yugoslav mission; but Hudson's companions had some orders of which he was not aware. Though he had his own ciphers, they had the wireless sets; one of which promptly went out of order.[4]

Bill Hudson, a vigorous and independent-minded mining engineer, knew Yugoslavia and spoke fluent Serbo-Croat. He was the unwilling spectator of the first main dispute between the četniks and the partisans, which broke out during the first German offensive. Mihailović decided that his duty to Serbia's future compelled him for the moment to side with the German against the communist intruder – he was reluctant to accept the internationalist Tito as a fellow country-man. Hudson, who depended on him for access to a wireless set, could remonstrate, but could not affect the course of battle. The četniks attacked Užice; without success, but weakening the partisans, who then gave way before a German onslaught. They withdrew westward; richer, by 21,000 rifles, with over 1,000 rounds each, which they had made[5] and by several million dinars, but sore at heart at being attacked by Serbs as well as Germans and Italians.

[1] Deakin, *The Embattled Mountain*, 29–30.
[2] Amery, *Approach March*, 252–6.
[3] Snapshot of Hudson in Harris Smith, 141.
[4] Deakin, *The Embattled Mountain*, 126–9.          [5] *ERM* i. 308.

After being, in their belief, driven out of Užice by Mihailović's četniks working hand in glove with the nazis, the partisans were determined never to trust a četnik of any kind again.[1] Their rising was far from over; it was only just beginning.

With Tito's nation-wide CPY contacts, the partisans could get news and find friends everywhere; at the tempo imposed by an unindustrialized society. Throughout Yugoslavia's prewar frontiers, except perhaps for the Slavonian plain, the ground provided cover for small groups of outlaws to subsist; and the main force of outlaws, the partisan army with the central committee of the party at its head, moved round from group to group. It would be fanciful to press an analogy with a mediaeval potentate making a round of his vassals in troublous times; an analogy that every left-winger would vigorously repudiate. Nevertheless, there were some points of resemblance.

Much more important, there were sharp distinctions. The partisans appeared everywhere not only as opponents of nazism, but as heralds of a new order. They had not let the presses in Užice stand idle, and bore quantities of pamphlets away with them. Among their members were many intellectuals, who were prepared in the intervals of fighting to teach in village schools, ot to set up schools in villages too little sophisticated to have any so far. Their leaders were all impregnated with marxist-leninist thinking, and quick to denounce the prewar ruling classes as well as the invading hordes.

They were driven from Bosnia to Montenegro by the second offensive, and back from Montenegro to Bosnia by the third; their political cohesion, and their tactical efficiency, improving with time. Mihailović in effect confiscated Hudson's wireless set for several months, so that SOE's operations in 1942 were hampered by lack of news; no one was going to parachute many agents blind at this stage into what was clearly a bubbling cauldron of difficulties. Terence Atherton, who was sent to find out what had happened to Hudson, disappeared; probably murdered for the gold he was carrying.[2] In November 1942, in a respite between attacks, the partisans protected a meeting at Bihać in Croatia at which the Yugoslav National Anti-fascist Liberation Council (AVNOJ) was set up, and the movement began to clothe its insurrection in legal forms: an assembly, courts, legislation. Eastern Croatia and western Bosnia formed a loose republic; for which Tito promised eventually a federal structure. Meanwhile, the republic had no fixed capital: there was a peripatetic revolution, moving round the mountains in its supporters' minds, resting on their fire power and their will. They numbered, at this time, about 20,000; including quite a thousand young women, who fought alongside the men. Tito thought he was leading something entirely new. Mao's Eighth Route Army might have provided a precedent; but the publications of the Left Book Club were not widespread in Yugoslavia.[3]

[1] Cp. E. Barker, *British Policy in S-E Europe*, 160.
[2] Deakin, *The Embattled Mountain*, 156, 172–4.
[3] Cp. Deakin, op. cit., 100; and Edgar Snow, *Red Star over China* (1937).

The great now began to take an interest in him. The NKVD set up a black broadcasting station near Tiflis to support him; it was called 'Free Yugoslavia'. Bill Deakin, a young officer in SOE who happened to be well known to Churchill, was parachuted to Tito's headquarters in late May 1943, and arrived in the middle of a battle: he could see gunfire as he dropped. At the start of the fifth offensive, the Germans had attempted a major encirclement; Tito only just broke through the steel ring, with his new companions, as it closed. He and Deakin were wounded a week later by the same bomb, from a light aircraft's low-level attack; which created a bond.[1]

Deakin was able to report, in much fuller detail than any of his predecessors, on the fighting capacity and morale of the partisans; he could never doubt that, whatever else they were doing, they were hotly engaged in fighting Germans, and he could see that they were pinning down sizeable forces of high-quality German troops, whose services were badly needed by the *Wehrmacht* that summer in Russia.

A parallel mission to Mihailović produced a much less favourable report.[2] He was clearly by this time on thoroughly friendly terms with some of the Italian occupation authorities, could show little in the way of actual sabotage performed, and would not start out on operations against the Germans till he had cleared his own left political flank by subduing the partisans. Bill Bailey had parachuted to Mihailović on Christmas Day 1942, and had regained touch with Hudson; neither could persuade Mihailović of the need for četniks and partisans to cooperate against Axis forces. Several SOE missions were sent in to join him – nine in all; all reported nothing much going on.[3] One agent, Neil Selby, deserves mention: captured by Serb collaborators, and imprisoned and interrogated by the Gestapo in Belgrade, he overpowered a guard while taking exercise; shot him; shot another; but ran up a blind alley by mistake, and was shot down himself.[4]

On the strength of Deakin's messages, a more senior mission was dispatched to Tito on 17 September 1943, headed by Brigadier (Sir) Fitzroy Maclean, a widely travelled conservative member of parliament who was Churchill's personal representative.[5] In the same month, the Italian change of sides transformed the nature of the war in Yugoslavia.

Tito's partisans secured a great deal of Italian armament; and the CPY's nation-wide organization was efficient enough for the partisan army to multiply ten times almost overnight, absorbing a great many Croats – some of them recent deserters from the *Wehrmacht*. By November 1943 Tito had about a quarter of a million available armed soldiers, including a decent proportion of artillery units. This meant that he could tackle the Germans on equal and the Ustaše on superior terms; it also released him from much dependence on SOE for supplies

[1] Deakin, op. cit., 3, 19.
[2] Jasper Rootham, *Miss Fire* (1946), a model of its kind.
[3] Deakin, op. cit., 177–85.
[4] Ibid. 184, and conversation with Deakin, 1969.
[5] Cp. E. Barker, op. cit., 165.

of arms. On the other hand, his troops' needs in blankets, boots, and food[1] were greater than ever.

OSS was by now ready to join in supply. The Allied presence in southern Italy, and the decision at the highest level in Teheran that Tito was to receive full support, transformed the problem as well. Churchill and Roosevelt, Churchill particularly, put their full personal weight behind the business of arming the partisans. Liberators became available in quantity, for drops; so did Dakotas, for pick-ups. Late in 1943 4,000 wounded were flown out of Yugoslavia from BATS landing-strips to hospital in Italy, thus relieving Tito from a crushing moral and tactical burden; a further 8,000, including 2,000 civilians, were flown out in 1944. Naval and SBS operations in the Adriatic, backed by a British commando brigade and a partisan fishing fleet, cleared Vis and some other Dalmatian islands of Italian troops, and provided Tito with a secure summer rear headquarters in 1944.[2]

In November 1943, the second formal session of AVNOJ at Jajce had proclaimed him a marshal, and had set up a national liberation committee as the provisional government of postwar Yugoslavia. By this time he was in somewhat closer touch with Moscow. In January 1944 the British flew in a Russian mission to him from Cairo, commanded by a lieutenant-general, Korneev, and there was presumably some efficient wireless contact. The Tiflis station certainly got from time to time quite prompt news of partisan exploits. He visited Italy once, with Maclean, on a British destroyer and met Churchill; and in the autumn of 1944 vanished altogether for a few days, from a BATS airstrip, in a Dakota with a Russian pilot; spending those days in Moscow, where he saw Stalin.

The government-in-exile, convinced at last that Mihailović was collaborating with the occupiers more than he was opposing them, dismissed him in May 1944; and in June and November the exiled prime minister, Subašić, and Tito concluded agreements envisaging a unified régime. Even after his dismissal, Mihailović continued to cooperate with OSS in rescuing American pilots shot down over central Europe who were trying to escape. Over a hundred were brought away.[3]

OSS had had a difficult time with its Yugoslav operations. Ethnic and political differences on the ground were reflected in the USA; and those rivalries that seem endemic between secret services – or perhaps simply the Cairene atmosphere – bedevilled its relations with SOE Cairo.[4] There were some indications of a tendency by OSS to back Mihailović, in opposition to SOE's growing enthusiasm for Tito; and some of a degree of obstruction by SOE that hindered OSS from operating as amply as it wished by sea from Bari and Brindisi into

---

[1] There is an anecdote worth recall of the package of dried egg, parachuted to a partisan group by the British. They did not think of eating it; and sent a puzzled message, complaining that none of their types of detonator would make it explode.

[2] Many details in Maclean, *Eastern Approaches* (1949), a book that records also his earlier travels in communist Russia.

[3] See photograph in Harris Smith, 132.    [4] Ibid. 129–62.

Dalmatia. What part in all this was played by the intelligence officer of SOE's Yugoslav section in Cairo, the subsequently eminent British communist James Klugman, is unclear; a London political colleague of his was jailed for passing SOE's secrets to the soviet embassy.[1]

On this comparatively petty note we must leave the Yugoslav adventure till the next chapter's summing up.

## Central Europe

All five of the Balkan states had occupations and resistance movements, though some of the five had governments more friendly to the occupier than the others. Next we need to look at the affairs of four countries that had only one historical experience in common besides contiguity: they had all at one time formed part of the estates of the Habsburg family. But the Swiss had thrown out their Habsburg overlords as far back as the thirteenth century; while the other three had formed part of the Austro-Hungarian dual monarchy throughout its existence, from 1867 to 1918. Of these three, Austria had been incorporated in the Third Reich in 1938, Hungary under Horthy was on the whole a cooperative satellite, and Czechoslovakia had been extensively carved up in the year before the war began.

### Hungary

Hungary had been for a thousand years a Magyar bastion, planted in the middle Danube plain between the north and the south Slavs. Hungarian armies had helped to stem the Turks' advance up the Danube; Hungarian great families retained memories of their ancestors' chivalrous exploits, and enormous landed estates. On some of these, as late as the late 1920s the peasants were so backward that they neither possessed chairs or benches, nor knew how to use them; at their midday break they lay on the ground, only the upper classes sat.[2]

There was some industrial development, aided by an extensive railway system, and the Magyars collectively regarded themselves as a people of standing.[3] After the German civil war of 1866, their leaders had forced on the Habsburg emperor the recognition of Hungary as Austria's equal in the dual monarchy of Austria-Hungary; to the Magyars, the monarch's role as King of Hungary outweighed his title of Emperor of Austria. When that monarchy was dissolved by defeat and revolution in 1918, there was for a hectic few months a communist régime in Hungary, under Béla Kun. (This name of terror to the bourgeoisie loses some of its force if translated: as Gutsy Cohen, he sounds less fearsome.)

A brief 'red terror' under Béla Kun was succeeded by a still more sanguinary 'white terror' under Admiral Horthy. (The Habsburg empire, with ports at the head of the Adriatic, had not been a negligible naval power.) Kun escaped to

---

[1] Peter Kemp, *No Colours or Crest* (1960), 77–8.
[2] Elizabeth Wiskemann, *The Europe I Saw* (1968), 106.
[3] See, eg., R. Rhodes James, *Victor Cazalet* (1976), 82.

Russia, to be reprimanded by Lenin for atrocious conduct in the Crimea; he worked for the comintern, and Stalin had him executed in 1939.[1] Horthy became head of state, as regent for the absent Habsburg king; whose restoration was often talked about, but was never likely to be realized, even then. Horthy accepted, as a political fact, the boundaries to which Hungary was reduced by the treaty of Trianon in 1920;[2] like all his compatriots, he hoped one day to expand them.

His régime was not altogether dictatorial: some of the forms of parliamentary democracy were retained, there was a reasonably free press, there were vigorous – though far from influential – socialist and small farmers' parties. Only the communists were persistently persecuted; a small underground organization just managed to stay alive.

A substantial proportion of the country's banking and newspaper industries was in Jewish hands; many of the great families were heavily in debt to their bankers; this did not make the Jews much loved. As an anti-Jewish reaction, there was a small noisy fascist movement, called the Arrow Cross, under Szálasi.

Horthy, being a sailor by training, had a firm grasp of what was possible and what was not; he understood that most Hungarians disliked and resented the country's reduced status in the world, as he did; Hungary was known to be a revisionist power. This led him into cooperation with Mussolini; though neither of them needed to have been told about the killing of Alexander of Yugoslavia, and he bears only nominal responsibility for it.[3] But cooperation with Mussolini led inexorably, as Chamberlain discovered, either to cooperation or to a break with Hitler; and Horthy judged Hungary too near to nazi Germany, after the Austro-German Anschluss, to risk a break. Hungary received a slice of dismembered Czechoslovakia after the Munich agreement,[4] and a further slice – Ruthenia, the eastern tip – in March 1939.

Of resistance there had so far been hardly a trace. Poland's relations with Hungary had not always been warm since 1918; Hungary was a 'revisionist', Poland a 'succession' state. The Hungarians at least, mindful of ancient friendship, did all they could for about 140,000 refugees from Poland in the autumn of 1939, of whom two-thirds moved on to fight in the Polish forces in exile. MIR and section D had each got parties in Budapest; there was some serious muddling between them and Sikorski's staffs there.[5] A private individual did as well as any of them: a Polish countess in her early twenties, Krystina Gyzicka (née Skarbek), better known by her later SOE codename as 'Christine Granville'. She made several frontier crossings over the Carpathians in mid-winter, using her acquaintances among the ski instructors to help her, and brought some scores of Poles back with her across Slovakia: so many that the Polish secret authorities felt sure, quite wrongly, that she must be working in with the Germans.[6] Many thousand Poles stayed in Hungary, and helped to keep lines to their homeland open.

[1] Conquest, *The Great Terror*, 579–80.  
[2] *BFSP* cxiii. 486.  
[3] p. 186 above.  
[4] *BFSP* cxlii. 529.  
[5] Sweet-Escott, 28.  
[6] See p. 114 above.

Hungary was much more hostile to Romania, and reoccupied another *irredenta*, northern Transylvania, in August 1940.[1] By this time German influence in Budapest was becoming strong. It looked as if Germany was winning the war, and in November 1940 Hungary acceded to the tripartite pact. Thereafter the steps to co-belligerence were unavoidable.

In April 1941, the Germans gave orders to the Hungarian army, and insisted on troop transport facilities for their own; the Hungarians were by now in no state to protest.[2] Two results followed. The British broke off diplomatic relations; to the regret of many anglophil Hungarian notables.[3] And Hungary received, as part of the carve-up of Yugoslavia, the province of Bačka, lost in 1919. The army general staff, pro-German for the most part, persuaded the cabinet to join – a little late – in the attack on the USSR, on which Hungary declared war on 27 June 1941. A small force fought in the Ukraine. It was increased to about 150,000 men in 1942, and was cut to pieces at Voronezh; whereafter Hungarian troops were used mainly to try to hold down partisans, both nationalist and communist.[4]

None of the British agents in Budapest in 1939–40 had been able to organize any sort of stay-behind parties or to leave behind any wireless sets; unless the intelligence service left a set for a well-placed spy, to whom we come in a moment. Whatever the Russians were able to do there, they had to do clandestinely. As the Hungarian economy had gone over to war production – making arms for the Axis armies – and unemployment had consequently almost vanished, there was not much working-class discontent.[5]

The communist party, following the example of the CPSU, appealed to patriotic rather than proletarian sentiment, and helped organize on 1 November 1941 a demonstration in favour of a free and independent Hungary at the tomb of Kossuth, one of the heroes of the rising of 1848–9.[6] A crowd of several thousands demonstrated in mid-March 1942 at the statues of Kossuth and Petöfi. This was something; but it was not much. In September 1943 there were some protest strikes in munition factories.

By this time Horthy was thinking of reinsuring with the Allies. Badoglio's example impressed him. He had already put out one feeler through a Hungarian who worked with SOE in Istanbul;[7] he now sent his minister in Berne to get in touch with Allen Dulles. The upshot was an OSS mission, parachuted into Hungary in mid-March 1944; which may have been notified beforehand by leftists in OSS to the Russians, and by them (but how?) to the Germans. In any

---

[1] p. 169 above.
[2] E. Wiskemann, *The Rome–Berlin Axis* (1949), 256.
[3] Cp. E. Barker, *British Policy in S-E Europe*, 60–70.
[4] Seton-Watson, *East European Revolution*, 98–100.
[5] István Pintér in *ERM* ii. 170.
[6] Ibid. 178. Kossuth was received in 1850 by one of the largest crowds that has ever assembled at Southampton.
[7] Cp. E. Barker, op. cit., 248.

event, on 19 March the Germans took over complete control of Hungary; and the Hungarians obligingly handed the mission over.[1]

SOE's effort seemed on a less exalted level than OSS's. Dalton had dared to claim a train wrecked in Hungary, back in 1941, when he had not got a single agent there; MI6, aware of this, took care he was found out.[2] In fact, by contrast with western Europe, there seems to have been little railway sabotage. SOE attempted to organize the peasants of the Bačka, through the mission of Basil Davidson who was parachuted to Deakin in Yugoslavia in August 1943, and has put his adventures into a stirring book;[3] but their strategic effort was on the slight side.

Their most promising channel worked through the young Dr László Veress, a Hungarian diplomat who made touch with them in Lisbon early in 1943, and regained it in Turkey that August, meeting the ambassador. He soon took two transmitters back to Budapest, worked for him by the political police. He had support in even higher quarters, including Szombathelyi the chief of staff and Miklos Kállay the prime minister; but confusion, crossed wires and misunderstandings combined to bring Veress' efforts to nothing. Eden, egged on by Beneš, was deeply suspicious of any Hungarian offers to change sides. And of six small SOE missions, parachuted during 1944, five fell promptly into the wrong hands and the sixth withdrew. Veress himself escaped, via Croatia and a BATS aircraft.[4]

MI6 did rather better than SOE at the start of the war; what happened later is uncertain. It had a great stroke of luck: the Hungarian chief of military security, Ujszászi, had previously been military attaché in Prague; while there, a routine operation by the Czechs had unravelled a large spy network of his; sooner than be exposed, he had agreed to work for the Czechs; and the Czechs, on closing down their Prague office, simply handed him on to the British.[5] He must have been an interesting source. Unluckily for MI6, he was reported killed in an Arrow Cross brawl in the second year of the war. His cover was always that of a genial *flaneur*, and he may have done nothing about a replacement for himself: few people do. In fact the report of his death was false; he simply detached himself from work he no longer wanted to perform. Possibly even the report of his death was planted on the Czechs by MI6, who continued to work with him.

What the Russian intelligence sources were in Hungary, beyond newspapers and routine party contacts, we also do not know. One of their very best wartime agents was a Hungarian, Sándor Radó; but he had fled his country when Kun's régime collapsed, and worked in exile; where we shall meet him again shortly.[6]

The German occupation of March 1944 brought Hungarian resistance into

[1] Harris Smith, 104–5; to which I owe the reference to Florimond Duke – the mission's leader – *Name, Rank and Serial Number* (1969). The book seems unavailable in England.
[2] Private information.                                    [3] *Partisan Picture* (1946).
[4] E. Barker, op. cit., 245, 251–9.
[5] F. Moravec, *Master of Spies* (1975), 96–105.
[6] S. Radó, *Sous le Pseudonyme 'Dora'* (1972), 30–6; and pp. 213–16 below.

sharper focus, and provided a much wider popular backing for it. It also spelled doom for 700,000 out of Hungary's 800,000 Jews, whom Eichmann came to remove to his camps. There were a number of escapes, but none systematically arranged. The extraordinary German proposal to swap a million Jews for ten thousand lorries, and some soap and coffee, came up at this time: the British in Cairo simply could not believe it.[1]

Horthy retained the shadow of power; slightly more than the shadow, indeed. In the late summer, encouraged by Anglo-American successes in France and by Michael's *coup* in Romania, he entered into secret talks with the left underground. These were conducted, on his side by Ujszászi, long chief persecutor of the communists, who 'seems to have got on excellently with Rajk', the leader of the small communist group in Budapest, 'both showing an aptitude for sentimental and dramatic phrase-mongering'.[2] But Horthy, like Maniu, was slow to make up his mind. By the time he did so, suddenly announcing Hungary's surrender on 15 October 1944, the Germans were ready for him. He was bundled off to a concentration camp, Szálasi's fascists took power that day, and 'the last and most horrible chapter in Hungary's war-time tragedy' began.[3] The country was fought over bitterly; Budapest was sacked by both Germans and Russians. The Russians carried behind them to the western borders a provisional government formed from left-wing politicians; from which the stern régime of the early 1950s derived.

## Czechoslovakia

Though Czechoslovakia has only appeared on the political map in the present century, Czechs and Slovaks have been settled in the heartland of Europe since the dark ages, and like most Slavs have memorable traditions. The saintly Wenceslas, the central European monarch[4] best known to English carol-singers, had ruled Bohemia in the tenth century; Hus was martyred in 1415 because his views were indistinguishable from Wycliffe's; Charles I's beautiful sister Elizabeth was the 'winter queen' of Bohemia; it was at her court that the 'defenestration of Prague' triggered off the thirty years' war in 1618. That war brought Bohemia more firmly than ever under the Habsburgs; but both Czechs and Slovaks remained aware that they were Slav, not German, even under Francis Joseph's dual monarchy. And the area that produced Smetana, Janáček, Dvořák, Kafka, has made a sizeable contribution to recent culture.

During the 1914–18 war, a great many Czech and Slovak troops deserted to the Russians. In 1918, as Russia and Austria-Hungary were both disintegrating, these deserters formed themselves into a Czech Legion which fought its way home eastabout along the trans-Siberian railway to Vladivostok, disposing of

---

[1] Calvocoressi and Wint, *Total War*, 232.
[2] Seton-Watson, *East European Revolution*, 104.     [3] Ibid.
[4] In fact he refused the crown the emperor offered him, and was only a duke (J. F. N. Bradley, *Czechoslovakia* [1970], 11).

Admiral Kolchak on the way. Thomas Masaryk, already professor of philosophy in Prague, had fled via Switzerland in 1915 to England and the United States; and with the help and advice of R. W. Seton-Watson secured allied agreement to the establishment of the Czechoslovak republic in 1918.[1]

The new state reproduced in miniature some of the vices of the Austro-Hungarian empire. There were many minorities; a lot of inter-marriage between races softened but did not remove the races' cultural and political divisions. In particular, over three million Germans close to the northern, western, and southern frontiers – known as the Sudeten Germans, after one of the mountain ranges along which they lived – were restive at no longer belonging to a great power.

The Czechs, the dominant race so far as there was one, took their defence problem seriously. The republic had an excellent armaments factory, the Skoda works at Brünn (Brno) – the Bren light machine gun was invented there, though mass produced (hence the second pair of letters in its name) at Enfield in Middlesex. Its army, fully mobilized, had thirty-six divisions; and the Czech youth movement, Sokol, ensured that their physical fitness was high.

Moreover, the republic had a remarkable military intelligence service, of which the effective head from March 1934 was Frantisek Moravec (on no account to be confused with Emanuel Moravec, an out-and-out collaborator with the nazis), who had been a pupil of Masaryk's at the university when war broke out in 1914. Starting pretty well from scratch, Moravec in four years built the Czech security and intelligence systems up to an unusual degree of competence. His unmasking of Ujszászi's spy network in Czechoslovakia, and turning-round of Ujszászi to become an agent of his own, was a small masterpiece of routine police work combined with aggressive information-seeking. He had troubles enough with his eastern neighbours; and still more troubles with the Germans – in the Sudetenland and beyond.

He also had luck. In the spring of 1937 he received an offer of information from inside the *Abwehr*. All his chief assistants warned him it looked like a trap. He followed his own judgement, and found himself in touch with a quite senior *Abwehr* officer, known in his book simply as A-54.[2] A-54's original motive was money, but after he had received about £100,000 he continued to provide information – excellent, plentiful, strategic information – free, because he had ceased to support his nazi masters.[3] He provided for instance vital data on *Waffen-SS* wireless drill, and their current cipher codes;[4] he provided the exact dates of the invasion of Bohemia and of France and of the USSR – in this last case, nearly four weeks before it happened; he predicted the break-through at Sedan. This last was the occasion for Menzies' remark, 'A-54 is an agent at whose word

[1] R. W. Seton-Watson, *Masaryk in England* (1943): some pages of history not admitted n the current Czech version of the state's origins.
[2] J. Piekalkiewicz, *Secret Agents, Spies and Saboteurs*, 132–49, identifies A-54 as Paul Thümmel, following J. F. N. Bradley, *Lidice* (1972), 40.
[3] F. Moravec, *Master of Spies*, 77–94, 151–5, 182.     [4] Ibid. 124.

armies march'; but the French did not believe the report, any more than Stalin believed his.[1]

Moravec did take the reports seriously; more so than his own cabinet at first. After the Munich conference of 29–30 September 1938, the Czechs found themselves bereft of the Sudetenland, and of the slices of Silesia taken by Poland and of south Slovakia by Hungary; they also had to suffer the trauma of being abandoned by all the great powers – France, England, the USSR – on the help and friendship of which they had depended. Russia could not help, because the great purge rendered her armed forces unfit at that moment to take the field. France would not help, because of weakening will to resist, and growing dependence on England. England neither would nor could: her forces were still pitiably weak, and Chamberlain the prime minister, with a conceit that seems endemic in Birmingham businessmen, thought he knew better. For Czechoslovakia, worse trauma lay ahead: for in mid-March 1939 the country was entirely disrupted. The Slovakian half of it was declared 'independent', and became the first nazi satellite; while the Czech half, declared a 'protectorate', was swallowed up in the Reich.

A few hours before this happened, Moravec – with help from MI6's man in Prague – brought off a singular manœuvre. He and his ten most competent assistants, and all their essential files, moved *en bloc* from Prague to London by air (across Germany, by an interesting irony; in a snowstorm almost too severe for the Dutch aircraft that carried them). Moravec maintained touch, from his new base, with his wide existing networks of agents. In return for the chance to work from British soil, he made the material that reached him available to MI6, and hence – after the general war he had foreseen broke out – to the British war machine; though always scrupulously careful to pay his own way.

He did not simply run a private intelligence organization. He felt responsible to Masaryk's successor, and former assistant, Edvard Beneš; who left Czechoslovakia after Munich, for a visiting chair of sociology at Chicago, but returned to London early in the war and established a Czech government-in-exile. Beneš, Moravec, and a few other far-sighted Czechs had made some preparations for long-term, large-scale resistance: the moment had now come to see whether they would work.

Beneš could not give his full time to this; he was necessarily preoccupied in working, with Thomas Masaryk's son Jan his foreign-minister-in-exile, towards the acceptance of his government's legality by the principal powers that might be able to restore it at the end of the war. He had responsibilities also towards the non-political Czechs in exile, in such bodies as the Czechoslovak squadrons in the RAF or the Czechoslovak parachute brigade in the USSR. Moravec too was primarily concerned with maintaining his intelligence networks.

Lack of firm detailed leadership was not necessarily a handicap for Obrana Naroda (Defence of the Nation), as the left-behind movement was called: such

---

[1] F. Moravec, *Master of Spies*, 190.

bodies frequently do better on their own assessments of what can be done on the spot than distant controllers can do for them. It was probably an advantage to it that its thirteen divisions were all under the command of regular officers. There were two serious obstacles: the body was too large for efficiency, and it was too insecure. Michel calls it indeed the largest clandestine organization of the war:[1] size almost necessarily brings insecurity. It made attempts in the autumn of 1939 at bomb attacks both on Hitler and on Himmler: neither succeeded.

Josef Mašin, its head of sabotage, brought off a few useful *coups*; and an extensive popular following was available to support it. Large student demonstrations on independence day, 28 October 1939, led to a death; larger ones at the funeral led to the occupation on 16/17 November of all Czech universities and polytechnics by the SS. Nine students were shot; 1,200 were imprisoned; and all institutions of higher learning were closed down. None reopened till the war was over.

The puppet prime minister, Eliáš, was a friend of Obrana Naroda's commander Josef Bily – both had been generals before the war – and did what he could to help, in the necessary deadly secrecy. But in the teeth of German repression, it was hard to do much.[2] Mašin himself was arrested, wounded, during a clandestine transmission to London; his two companions shot their way out.[3]

In Hitler's and Himmler's view, on the other hand, repression was still not severe enough: they wanted to make sure the Czechs knew how heavy the hand of the aryan master could rest on a non-aryan race. In late September 1941 the comparatively gentle and diplomatic Neurath was replaced as imperial governor (Reichsprotektor) of Bohemia and Moravia by Reinhard Heydrich, the second man in the SS. Heydrich, still under forty, was Hitler's ideal of the new man: tall, blond, virile – he had been cashiered from the navy for immorality – and devoid of ethical inhibitions of any kind.

He began by having Bily shot and Eliáš arrested. Arrests and executions became daily, almost routine affairs. Meanwhile his protectorate was filling up with missions from abroad: four Czechs had been parachuted in on 10 September 1941, from the USSR, but one of them promptly changed sides. 160 arrests and a wireless game resulted; but A-54 notified the wireless game to London, who tipped off Moscow, and it came to nothing.[4] SOE sent in a dozen missions by parachute during the winter; one of them, 'Anthropoid', with the task on Moravec's order of assassinating Heydrich.

Heydrich never normally moved without an armed escort; like everybody else, he eventually lowered his guard because nobody had attacked him. On 27 May 1942 he stayed rather longer at home than usual before driving to the office; saying goodbye to his family, as he was to fly to Berlin that night. Instead of keeping his bodyguard hanging about, he told them not to wait for him; and

[1] Michel, *SW*, 146.          [2] Moravec, *Master of Spies*, 176–80.
[3] Bradley, *Lidice*, 25.          [4] Ibid. 41.

set off in an open Mercedes with a single chauffeur. At a hairpin bend in a Prague suburb, Gabčik of 'Anthropoid' suddenly leapt in front of his car and levelled a sten at him. The sten jammed, but the car slowed down further; and Gabčik's companion Kubiš was able to toss a bomb into it, which burst: wrecking the car, and wounding Heydrich, who nevertheless, pistol in hand, gave chase. Kubiš, also wounded by the bomb, got away on a bicycle; Gabčik got away in a crowded tram. A third man, their lookout, walked quietly away. Heydrich was taken to hospital, where he died (of blood poisoning from a fragment of dirty uniform) on 4 June.

K. H. Frank, the nazi state secretary, proclaimed martial law by a broadcast on the evening Heydrich was shot, and buckled down on Hitler's orders to exacting an unforgettable revenge. The assassins had vanished. They were betrayed, for the sake of a large money reward, by Karel Čurda, another SOE agent; who survived the war, to hang separately.[1] They committed suicide after a gun-battle with the SS. Their deaths were nothing like enough to satisfy the nazis; who arrested everybody of the same surnames they could catch (Gabčik was a Slovak; that made some more trouble) and exacted over 2,000 dead for their murdered Reichsprotektor. These included almost the entire populations of the villages of Lidice and Ležáky. 143 women and 16 children, out of 203 and 104 deported, returned in the end to the ploughed-up site of Lidice; almost all 197 of the men had been shot on one June afternoon.

The atrocity got world-wide publicity, and Lidice like Oradour remains a name of horror; like Oradour, again, it had no real connexion with the atrocity for which vengeance was exacted. (Its name had come to Gestapo attention because of a note found on a Czech agent of SOE's arrested earlier: that for Gestapo purposes was reason enough.[2]) Less publicity attended the deaths of those already in German hands, which were far more numerous; and included everyone traceable who had been arrested for membership, or even suspected membership, of Obrana Naroda.

This repression, combined with the remoteness of Czechoslovakia either from English or from Russian bases, did have a deterrent effect. Czech resistance was forced underground; German police persecution went on. Between March 1939 and May 1945, some 350,000 Czechs were deported to German camps; of whom only 100,000 returned.[3] Kaltenbrunner was Heydrich's successor at the head of the RSHA; and from a resister's point of view was no improvement on him. He was hanged at Nuremberg as a war criminal in 1946; and nobody outside their families is likely to be sorry that both of them are dead. Himmler could indeed be pleased about Heydrich's end: it removed from the scene his own most dangerous rival. Moravec for one held, of 'Anthropoid' and its result, 'Given the circumstances in which we were placed at the time, it was a good try. It was the largest resistance operation in the country and it is a good page in the history

[1] Moravec, 220–2.    [2] Bradley, Lidice, 41–2.
[3] J. Doležal and J. Křen, La Tchéchoslovaquie en Lutte (Prague 1961), 146.

of Czechoslovakia in the Second World War. The Czech people should be proud of it. I am.'[1]

Repression forced the Czechs back on the techniques already glanced at, of their compatriot in fiction the *Good Soldier Šveik*.[2] With decades of tradition of struggle against Vienna behind them, they were able to apply the techniques with equal ease against Berlin; from which no part of Bohemia, at least, had ever been governed before 1938. They were able to go through the motions of being complaisant to the Germans, whom they secretly detested; but no one should deceive himself into thinking they had an 'easy' war.

Though the Czech communists were not involved in the killing of Heydrich, they suffered like everybody else from the aftermath. Not for the first time, their central committee were all arrested by the Germans; this time they were all executed. It was nearly two years before the party's organization recovered from this blow.[3]

Nationally and internationally, the Lidice massacre had a considerable impact. Čurda had made no secret of Heydrich's assassins' training in England, for he had taken part in it. This became generally known within the protectorate; and even in spite of the price exacted for the killing, Beneš's standing there improved, because people felt it had been carried out with his approval. It certainly helped him and Jan Masaryk in their efforts to get their policies and their government-in-exile accepted as the future rightful government of Czechoslovakia. The massacre also made more generally acceptable a policy to which they had already begun to incline: after so savage a stroke, it was manifestly going to be more difficult than ever for Czechs and Germans to live side by side, and the case for deporting the Germans from the Sudetenland was correspondingly strengthened. Stalin in 1941 had had a million Germans deported from the middle Volga to Siberia at a few hours' notice, and made no difficulty. Nor, after Lidice, did Eden or Hull. It was Lidice that provided the impetus for organizing the international military tribunal that sat in judgement on the nazi leaders in Nuremberg after the war.[4] And it was of course a superb gift to Allied propaganda services: it showed what nazi domination actually meant.

Life in Czechoslovakia meanwhile went on as best it could. SOE sent in several more missions, after an appalled interval; but all (according to Bradley) for intelligence work only, since the conditions for active subversion hardly existed.[5] Possibly MI6 and SOE arranged a sharing of functions; MI6, getting plentiful intelligence from Moravec, may well have left it to SOE to use available resources, instead of starting up a third set. The communists were able to start a few small partisan bands in the Moravian hills in the last winter of the war, but

---

[1] *Master of Spies*, 224.
[2] See p. 44 above. V. Mastny, *The Czechs under nazi rule* (1971), 160, finds this view of Šveik 'superficial'; we must agree to differ.
[3] Bradley, *Lidice*, 156; Heinz Kühnrich, *Der Partisanenkrieg in Europa 1939–1945* (2 ed., Berlin 1968), 200.
[4] Cordell Hull, *Memoirs* (1948), ii. 1184–5.　　　　　[5] Bradley, *Lidice*, 147–56.

they had not the arms or the training to effect much: even when stiffened by some Red Army parachutists and some escaped British prisoners-of-war.

Late in August 1944 there was a serious uprising in Slovakia, which had hitherto lain comparatively passive: the Slovaks did not enjoy satellite status much more than the Czechs enjoyed being a protectorate. Moravec's intelligence system operated there too; with his customary degree of security. The satellite régime, under the fascist people's party, started red-hot in favour of the nazis, but grew no more than lukewarm; by 1943 it was shutting its eyes to communist and agrarian party activities. Some senior army officers, remembering the precedent of 1914, thought of taking their troops over to the other side *en bloc*.

The Germans decided to occupy Slovakia, just in case; arrangements to counter them were not perfectly ready, and they took western Slovakia with no trouble on 29 August 1944. But in the centre, a Free Slovakia was proclaimed, round Banska Bystrica, and defended against the Germans by part of the Slovak army under Colonel Golian. The Russians flew in the Czechoslovak exiled airborne brigade, under Colonel Přikryl, to help; partisan bands and a body of escaped French prisoners-of-war joined the struggle; the Red Army itself was understood not to be far away.[1]

The Slovak rising was simultaneous with the rising in Warsaw,[2] to which it has evident similarities; but, as is usual with historical analogies, the parallels are not quite exact. Slovakia was closer to Bari, SOE could therefore, and did, send in a mission by air, under Major Sehmer, who fell into German hands; and although as was usual for SOE's own agents in eastern Europe, he wore uniform, he was executed. The Russians had not clinched arrangements proposed in mid-August to coordinate the rising; but their sending in Přikryl's brigade is a proof that they did not want to pretend it was not taking place, as seems to have been their attitude to Warsaw. They maintained their usual refusal of airport facilities for SOE's or OSS's supply planes; nor, having once sent Přikyl's brigade in, did they exert themselves unduly to keep it supplied.

Free Slovakia had one further, temporary advantage over Free Warsaw: a friendly, or at least a neutral neighbour. Its southern marches ran with the northern border of Hungary, while Horthy was in the throes of indecision about changing sides. But after Horthy's arrest and Szálasi's seizure of power (15 October 1944) this advantage for the Slovaks disappeared; the Germans moved in from the south for the kill. They captured Golian, and shot him; they captured, and shot, General Viest, sent in by Beneš to take command.[3] A large OSS mission, dropped into the Tatra mountains on 25 September, never made proper contact with the rising, and was betrayed at Christmas: all but two of its members were shot.[4] Those who survived, of Golian's and Přikryl's units, and of the

---

[1] H. Seton-Watson, *East European Revolution*, 146–9; Kühnrich, op. cit., 267–71.
[2] pp. 299–300 below.
[3] Kühnrich does not mention Viest; or Přikryl.
[4] Harris Smith, 107-8.

partisans, melted away into the mountains; a very few, very tough ones survived till the Red Army was able to renew its advance and overrun them in the spring.

Beneš and most of his ministers visited Moscow early in 1945, and came to an agreement with the Czechoslovak communists in exile there; so that it was from Russian soil that this government-in-exile returned home. At Košice in eastern Slovakia there was set up, on 4 April 1945, a government of the national front of Czechs and Slovaks – the Slovaks having got themselves this far dissociated from the Czechs – under the social democrat Fierlinger, with the communist Gottwald as his second-in-command. Hailed by a modern conformist historian as the first Czecho-slovak government in which the bourgeoisie did not have the upper hand, this body put out a programme of social reform that included confiscation of collaborators' goods.[1]

The Red Army swept across Moravia in the second half of April 1945. The inhabitants of Prague, as of several other Bohemian cities, could not bear to wait for them to arrive: on 5 May 1945 there was a spontaneous popular insurrection. The tone that the nazis were upholding, even in the Reich's death-throes, can be gauged from a Prague commander's proclamation only three days before:

> In the present situation every means is legitimate to prevent a rebellious movement flaring up. The only thing is not to show any weakness now. Ruthless action against every hotbed of unrest is to be taken. Participants must be decimated. In the same manner action must be taken against those who are soft and tardy in our own ranks, who fail in this hour.[2]

That this was not treatment a free people would endure indefinitely, the insurrection proceeded to prove. Here as in Paris[3] the Germans had tanks; here they used them; here, tank-proof barricades were built against them. In less than five days' fighting, nearly 2,000 citizens were killed: not by the standards of an infantry battle a severe rate of loss, not for a city of some 900,000 inhabitants an enormous percentage, but an honourable one. A decisive influence was exercised by a division of Red Army renegades, hitherto in German pay, who changed sides back on 7 May, and attacked their former masters.[4] On the morning of 9 May – two days after the Germans had surrendered, the day even their land forces on the Biscay coast gave in – Red Army tanks entered Prague from the north to mop up such corners as were still in arms, and the fighting was over.

Three years later, another defenestration of Prague killed Jan Masaryk, and Czechoslovak history took another turn; but that is a separate story.

### Austria

Austria, the first foreign country to be taken over by nazi Germany, had well within living memory been one of the world's great powers. Its greatness had

---

[1] František Kavka, *La Tchécoslovaquie Histoire lointaine et récente* (Prague 1960), 155–6.
[2] V. Kŕal, *Lesson from History* (Prague 1961), 161; his tr.
[3] p. 253 below.
[4] Littlejohn, *Patriotic Traitors*, 330–1.

been inextricably intertwined with the family of Habsburg.[1] They had been counts of Habsburg since the eleventh century, dukes of Austria since the thirteenth, kings of Hungary and Bohemia from 1526, and Roman emperors from 1438 to 1806, with dozens of other ramifications of grandeur: all swept away in 1918. Francis Joseph, who became emperor of Austria, aged eighteen, in 1848 did not die till 1916; and always looked on the empire as a family estate. During his lifetime, Austria ceased to be the principal Germanic power. The second German Reich, the empire that Bismarck created for the king of Prussia in 1871, had been meant to settle for good the arguments between the *grossdeutsch* and the *kleindeutsch* schools of German nationalism – that is, between those who wanted all German speakers in one vast agglomeration, and those who wanted a smaller, more manageable state – firmly on the *kleindeutsch*, the smaller side. Yet that empire too foundered in 1918.

Among the wreckage of both, there emerged an Austrian-born corporal of the dissolved German army, full of fanatical beliefs and with mesmeric powers of oratory: Adolf Hitler. Hitler, born at Braunau-an-der-Inn in 1889, the son of a minor customs official, had spent his adolescence and young manhood in imperial Vienna as an art-school drop-out; and loathed it. Having survived the great war, he determined to devote his fanaticism to reversing Bismarck's decision, and setting up a Great Germany to eclipse every other power on earth.[2] Once he had power, Austria was his first foreign target.

As early as October 1933, a young nazi put two bullets into Dollfuss, the Austrian catholic dictator;[3] on 25 July 1934 the job was done properly, and Dollfuss was killed by SS gunmen in the course of a bungled nazi attempt at a *coup d'état*. Dollfuss had put himself out of court beforehand with the Austrian left, and with all progressive opinion; because he had sent troops against a working-class district of Vienna in the previous spring. Austria hung on to independence for nearly four years after his death; but the country was deeply divided, and subversive attacks from across the German border were incessant.

Eventually, in the spring of 1938 the chancellor, Schuschnigg, announced a plebiscite which would give the Austrians a chance to say that they were determined to remain independent. No one doubted they would give a large affirmative vote. Lest they should do so, Schuschnigg was terrorized into

[1] C. A. Macartney, *The Habsburg Empire 1790–1918* (1968), xi, records that he mentioned over forty years earlier to A. F. Přibram the hope that he might one day write the empire's history. 'Yes,' Přibram replied, 'we all start with that ambition. I did myself, but gave it up because I did not know fourteen languages.' Přibram's implied rebuke applies more strongly to the present writer than to Macartney; whose book will hold the field for many years, unless we have a holocaust.

[2] T. Ravenscroft, *Spear of Destiny* (1972), presents a view of Hitler that is startling to the dryasdust type of scholar, but deserves more serious attention than the learned world seems yet to have given it. Hitler's own *Mein Kampf* (tr. James Murphy, 1939) is important for his views; as is Hermann Rauschning, *Germany's Revolution of Destruction* (tr. E. W. Dickes, also 1939).

[3] G. E. R. Gedye, *Fallen Bastions* (1939), 81; an angry book by the *Daily Telegraph's* Vienna correspondent, later in Prague; later still in SOE.

resignation; and the Germans occupied Austria on 15 March 1938, wiping its very name off the political map for seven years. The incoming nazi police made 60,000 arrests on the day they arrived;[1] there were several hundred suicides as well.

Austria provided the Gestapo with its second exercise – the first, in 1935, had been in the Saarland – at taking over a new area: rehearsals had clearly been thorough. They had the advantage that they had long had informers lodged in Austria to prepare the way for them; and there were no difficulties about language. Overcrowding in the concentration camps resulted: relieved to some extent in midsummer by the opening of a new camp, which became one of the most notorious, at Mauthausen near Linz, a couple of days' walk from Hitler's birthplace. There was workable granite at Mauthausen, worked for the profit of an SS firm, Deutsche Erd-und Steinwerke; thousands of resisters were worked to death in that quarry.[2] Hitler's and Himmler's hands lay in fact so heavily on Austria that there was little anybody could do against them, except hope and pray that their régime would not last for ever.

There was one political difficulty that Germany took over by absorbing Austria, of which some propaganda use might have been made to drive a wedge between Germany and Italy: the problem of South Tirol. Italy had insisted, at the peace settlement of 1919–20, on getting not only Istria but also the Adige valley above Trent from defeated Austria-Hungary: the frontier was fixed, for strategic reasons, at the summit of the Brenner pass.[3] This left 200,000 German speakers as a minority in Italy; about whose fate many German and all Austrian nazis had continually complained.

Hitler, with his usual dexterity and Gladstonian accuracy of timing in politics, played this issue down at first; secured an agreement with Mussolini in 1939 that those who wished to leave South Tirol for German territory could; arranged, after he had defeated France, for them to be settled in the reconquered *Reichsland*, formerly Alsace and Lorraine; and then, after Mussolini's power was broken, simply annexed South Tirol to the Reich in October 1943, throwing in Istria as well, the old Austrian *Küstenland*.[4]

The culturo-historico-political hot potato was too hot for PWE ever to try to hold it: this opportunity for trouble-making between the Axis partners was muffed. Some advice might have been taken from Baron Franckenstein, once Aehrenthal's private secretary, who had had charge of the Austrian legation in London till the Anschluss, and had preferred exile to life under nazism; he was at once naturalized British, and knighted[5] as a mark of the court's favour. His time was taken up instead with a foreign office committee that prepared the case

[1] Leopold Voller in *ERM* ii. 569.

[2] H. Krausnick *et al.*, tr. R. H. Barry, *Anatomy of the SS State* (1968), 456–7; Evelyn le Chêne, *Mauthausen* (1971), with photographs.

[3] *BFSP* cxii. 338.    [4] E. Wiskemann, *Rome–Berlin Axis*, 313, 316.

[5] He had received an honorary knighthood, a grand cross of the Royal Victorian Order, in the previous year's coronation honours.

– accepted by everybody concerned – for restoring Austria's independence after the war.[1]

There was indeed virtually nothing that could be done to help the Austrians, apart from a few Scarlet-Pimpernel-like efforts to get Jews out in the earliest days of occupation, made by disinterested citizens who could not bear the spectacle of oppression.[2]

SOE had a small Austrian country section, and sent at least one mission into Austria – walking in from Yugoslavia – in 1943; but its organizer never felt safe, felt he was doing no good, and soon came out again.[3] MI6 had at least one Austrian agent, a major on the staff of German army headquarters in Paris, who must have provided some useful intelligence, besides acting as intermediary between Parodi and Choltitz during the Paris rising.[4] OSS sent in Franklin Lindsay, a young lieutenant-colonel, during the war's last winter; but even a briefing from Allen Dulles could not provide him with much in the way of achievement.[5]

The Austrians had to do what they could for themselves. A small, banned communist party, a large social-democratic party, a few brief years' experience of parliamentary life counted for something; bravery, charity, culture, humanity counted for more. 170,000 of them were arrested for activities alleged by their nazi jailers to be resistance activity of one kind or another; of whom some 35,300 – half a per cent of the total population – were killed.[6] Most of the organized activity developed in the last eighteen months of the war, in Styria and Carinthia particularly; there was some direct contact with Tito's partisans. In Vienna, as in Paris, the coup against Hitler of 20 July 1944 worked well, with disastrous results for those who had worked it after the collapse in Berlin. A survivor among them expanded the work of a secret socialist-and-communist committee, already formed, called O-5, and had some clandestine touch with the Russians about the eventual shape of post-war Austria. Austrian gallantry in the cause of freedom from tyranny is beyond question.

## Switzerland

The Helvetian republic is the world's oldest free state. Some of its cantons secured their independence in the thirteenth century, and in a few of them all full citizens can still assemble together for debate. It is also the world's oldest federation; and has an intricate and effective military system. This is derided by staff officers of the *ancien régime* who have never looked into its undoubted efficiencies: for instance, its rate of scoring against German fighters which violated Swiss air space in May and June 1940 – flying exactly the same aircraft,

---

[1] *Times* obituary, 15 October 1953.
[2] Cp. Sir M. Bruce, *Tramp Royal* (1954), 228–35.    [3] Conversation with him, 1966.
[4] Cp. pp. 252–3 below.                           [5] Harris Smith, 161, 224.
[6] Erika Weinzierl and Kurt Skalnik, *Österreich* (Graz 1972), i. 127.

the Me 109E – was over four times as high as that registered a few weeks later by the RAF in the battle of Britain.[1]

Both sides would willingly have controlled Swiss territory, in 1940–5 as in 1915–18: neither side was able to do so, as the Swiss were so clearly ready and able to defend themselves. Ground helped them, obviously enough, but the valley Konstanz–Olten–Solothurn–Yverdon–Geneva is quite as passable to armour as the Ardennes: it is a mistake to think of Switzerland as wholly mountainous, or indeed wholly pastoral. The country has long been industrialized, with high levels of skill, and particularly well-developed railway and banking systems.

It also has an ancient and honourable tradition of hospitality to political refugees; one from which Lenin and his friends benefited in 1915–17. Its political tone in the early 1940s was solid, bourgeois, conservative; it was rich; it contained also some of bourgeois culture at its best.

The Swiss made clear to all inquirers that by international law they were neutral; and that, at the first serious breach of their neutrality, they would destroy the principal strategic advantage that a hold on Switzerland offered to a belligerent – the Alpine tunnels.[2] Without the Simplon, the St Gotthard and the Albula tunnels open, Switzerland was not worth the having; so no one invaded it. They stuck to their rights as well as their duties as neutrals; continued to trade with anybody who would accept their goods; and allowed no overtly military activity to take place on their territory. They were also as skilled as Nelson at turning a blind eye.

In return – it may be supposed – for not examining too closely the contents of the frequent trains sent across Switzerland between Germany and Italy, they took little or no notice of clandestine wireless traffic; unless forced to do so by diplomatic pressure from an aggrieved power. The British would dearly have liked to add *Soldatensender Friedrichshafen,* working from the opposite shore of the lake, to their effective *Soldatensender Calais;* but the Gestapo was too fully equipped to take incriminating cross-bearings for any attempt to be made. The Swiss police were good at taking cross-bearings too; they were also good at minding their own business. If we can believe 'Alexander Foote' – and much of his book[3] carried conviction – he transmitted intermittently to Moscow from the same flat for two years on end, sometimes several times a week, before the police came to interrupt him.

He was one of several wireless operators, in a formidably able GRU intelligence circuit, operated by the Hungarian Radó from 1937 to the autumn of 1943. Radó might be described as a natural clandestine; apart from some conversations with Uritsky in Moscow, he had no schooling as a spy at all. But he had been on the run, one way and another, since his teens; his wife had worked with Rosa

[1] H. Guisan, *Bericht an die Bundesversammlung über den Aktivdienst 1939–1945* (1946) iii. 47.

[2] Sir David Kelly, *The Ruling Few* (1952), 277–8.     [3] See *Handbook for Spies.*

Luxemburg, and was a founder-member of the German communist party (KPD); and he was a professional scientist, with a scientist's passion for exact information. He worked in Geneva as a cartographer: excellent cover, and a respectable source of income.

Most of his information reached him at first through a German–Swiss journalist, Otto Pünter ('Pakbo').[1] He had contacts with Trepper's subsequently ruined group, that centred on Brussels, but his own circuit was secure enough to survive Trepper's disaster intact.[2] His chief initial difficulty was money. He could easily slip from Switzerland into France, without showing a passport, through the free customs zone near Geneva; an area full in any case of foreigners, because the dying League of Nations' headquarters were there. But as the war developed, this frontier was closed, and the Germans overran his source of supply and point of contact in Paris. For some months he accumulated material he had no means of passing on; for though he had a transmitter, he had neither ciphers nor prearranged wavelengths and call signs. Through a messenger, he got word he was to visit a church in Belgrade, where a courier would meet him with money. He went there, with his wife, in the spring of 1941; the church had long since been demolished, the courier was a fortnight late.[3]

He was not the sort of man to be deterred by such routine accidents; and from the late summer of 1942 he was in touch with another refugee, equally tough, less devotedly communistic in his views, startlingly well informed: Rudolf Roessler, known as 'Lucy'.[4] Roessler, who had kept a bookshop in Lausanne since 1934, had been a German officer in the war of 1914–18; and said, after the next great war was over, that he had then formed a close friendship with a group of some ten colleagues, who sent him out of Germany when Hitler became powerful, and fed him with information intended in the end to lead to Hitler's downfall. One of them, it appears, rose high on the operational and another on the signals staff of the *Oberkommando der Wehrmacht*, the principal German defence staff below Hitler's personal headquarters.

There has long been, and there is likely to remain, a good deal of mystery about Roessler. Radó himself did not know where Roessler got his information from; he knew only that it repeatedly turned out to be exceptionally valuable, high-level military intelligence about German order of battle and strategic intentions. We need not linger over Accoce and Quet's story of a couple of sergeant-wireless-operators in the OKW's main transmitting room, who handled all the passing of secret messages to and from Roessler; unnoticed in the perpetual

---

[1] 'Pakbo' is the Russianized spelling of *paquebot*, the little mail-steamer of which Pünter's manner reminded Trepper: *Sous le pseudonyme 'Dora'*, 104. Radó constantly complains in that book of the errors in (*inter alia*) Pünter's *Der Anschluss fand nicht statt* (Bern 1967).

[2] p. 256 below.     [3] Radó, 123–9.

[4] Ibid. 209 ff. Till Radó's book came out, the best source on this network had been P. Accoce and P. Quet, *The Lucy Ring* (1967); Radó repeatedly exposes errors and exaggerations in their book, in his own.

rush of signals traffic.[1] This agreeable story would carry more conviction if there was any hard evidence that Roessler had a transceiver of his own. Radó's best guess was that his material did originate in the OKW, was telephoned to Milan, and then sent on to Lausanne by courier.[2] The same careful source observes that Roessler's information was usually between three and six days old, not, as even Allen Dulles seems to have thought, less than twenty-four hours old; this would fit the transport scheme Radó suggests.[3]

Roessler made it a condition of providing information that no attempt was to be made to uncover his sources' identity; and died, not before being grilled by the Russians at leisure, in 1958. Those who dealt with him must often have feared they were about to be the victims of some colossal deception (a normal state of mind among intelligence officers); but he never, ever, passed false coin.

At first, in the late 1930s and for the opening years of the war, he let the Swiss know what he found out; dealing with the Bureau Ha, an ostensibly semi-independent, semi-clandestine organization, based near Lucerne and named after its head, Hans Hausamann.[4] There were some contacts between the Bureau Ha and MI6; exactly how much of Roessler's information thus got through to the British neither the Bureau nor MI6 have ever announced.

Nor, according to Radó, was he in touch with 'Dora's' circuit until well on in the war. Radó once went to call, as a cartographer, on Roessler at the Vita Nova Verlag at Lausanne; summed up his man; and approached him through an intermediary late in 1942. Roessler by this time was enthusiastic enough about the soviet military effort – which attracted almost the whole world's admiration at the time – to be prepared to join in helping it. His enthusiasm may have waned when he met the torrent of questions Radó's anonymous Director hurled at him; but he worked steadily on.

About this time, Radó began to have troubles with the Swiss police. On 27 October 1942 they called on one of his Geneva operators, Hamel, during a transmission. Mme Hamel burnt the telegrams and hid the transmitter.[5] The police found an incomplete spare transmitter, which Hamel was able to persuade them was a medical oscillograph which he had bought to treat his own visibly precarious health; and they released him.[6] This is a good indication of the circuit's professional devotion. So is the fact that when most of them were arrested a year later, the few admissions they did eventually make indicated that they had been working for MI6;[7] not for the GRU, a body that Radó never even names. He describes himself simply as dealing with 'the Centre'.

He lays the arrests at the door of Colonel Roger Masson, then Swiss head of intelligence and security, whom he accuses of acting in too friendly a fashion

---

[1] Op. cit. 73-4.  [2] Radó, 217-18.  [3] Ibid.

[4] For what it is worth, Accoce and Quet, 76, have Hausamann owning a photographer's business at Zürich in the late 1960s. He died in the middle seventies.

[5] Mme Hamel was his second operator, 'Foote' the third; hence the Gestapo's name for the circuit, 'Rote Drei' (red three).

[6] Radó, 199-200.  [7] Eg. Radó, 377.

towards the RSHA. Possibly Masson only arrested the operators because he knew that the RSHA was preparing to kidnap them: there are indications of a proposed raid on 'Foote's' flat a few days after his arrest on 19/20 November 1943. There were certainly Gestapo agents enough in Switzerland: one, her hairdresser, became the lover of Radó's reserve Geneva operator 'Rosie', and so put the whole circuit in further danger, from which Radó's meticulous system of keeping everything and everybody in separate compartments saved it.[1]

In the end the organizer had to go to ground, with his wife, for eleven months in a tiny flat in Geneva; till they were able in September 1944 to make an ingenious escape on a milk-train to Annemasse.[2] What they had done while the circuit was flourishing to its full extent Radó's book, with its wealth of dispatches exchanged between Moscow and himself, amply demonstrates.

All its members used book-codes, and the Swiss did manage to capture Radó's own code, though they never laid hands on him. Their efforts to play a wireless game with Moscow, on one of 'Foote's' several frequencies, did not succeed: Moscow was too wily for them.[3]

'Dora's' was not the only group of clandestines in Switzerland during the war, by any means; it just happens to be the one about which we have a long, authoritative book, written by the man in the best position to know. In the previous great war, Switzerland had been the base for extended clandestine activity, immortalized in fiction by Somerset Maugham;[4] the diplomatic stage was crowded with latter-day Ashendens.

(Sir) David Kelly, the British minister to the Swiss republic in 1940–2, was a man of rare imperturbability, even for a British diplomat, and took his virtual imprisonment calmly. His successor (Sir) Clifford Norton was no less impressively calm. The military attaché, Cartwright, had been a celebrated escaper of the earlier war,[5] and had the presence to overawe exuberant escapers who gave way too readily to high spirits and careless talk when they reached the haven of Switzerland from a prisoner-of-war camp: as several score did.[6] He handed the more promising of them on to MI9's 'Victor' at Geneva, who had ways of getting them moving on across France towards England; with the direct help, in the early days at least, of Swiss police.[7]

Hardly anything is known of the personnel, and little of the work, of the British secret agencies in wartime Switzerland, but the listening post was too important to be left unmanned. Philby says MI6's head there was called Van Der Heuvel. Harris Smith names Edge Leslie, of MI6, and John McCaffery, of SOE, as especially helpful to OSS;[8] it was presumably Leslie who talked to the

[1] Eg. Radó, 201–5.  [2] Radó, 393–7.  [3] Ibid. 388.
[4] Ashenden (1928).
[5] See M. C. C. Harrison and H. A. Cartwright, Within Four Walls (1930).
[6] See Neave, 39–42.  [7] Ibid. 42–5.
[8] Harris Smith, 211; Philby, My Silent War, 80.

Bureau Ha and thus provided the British link with Roessler.[1] It was certainly McCaffery who was in charge of Geoffrey Parker, the surgeon, and many other characters' smuggling operations, through the barbed wire of the Jura frontier, that provided one of SOE's most significant contributions to the war effort, and justified its connexion with London's ministry of economic warfare.[2]

Of one British service we do happen to have some news, because one of its members wrote a discreet autobiography that her brain prevented her from making dull: Elizabeth Wiskemann of PWE.[3] Her book gives an accurate idea of what the business of collecting political intelligence is like; of how indispensable it is to have a wide range of friendships, and to collate systematically the data that spring from them, without having so much system that you lose your friends. It shows also how a dedicated anti-nazi and a superb scholar can attain the objectivity indispensable to sound appreciations. She had herself been for a few hours a prisoner of the Gestapo in 1936, when her dispatches to the *New Statesman and Nation* had been too frank for German taste;[4] not an experience she could ever forget, though she was not even severely cross-questioned.

Her cover at Berne was that of assistant press attaché. The legation's press department had plenty of ordinary press work to do, because it produced a bulletin – originally duplicated in eighty copies or so for the information of its own staff, who were cut off from English newspapers – of news of the course of the war, as received over the BBC's ordinary broadcasts. Word of its existence leaked out, demand for it snowballed, and by the spring of 1941 it was being printed twice a week at 80,000 copies a time: more than the circulation of any Swiss newspaper. Great care was taken to put nothing in it that could offend the Swiss desire to remain neutral, and no charge was made for it, though Kelly let it be known he would accept gifts to British service charities: several thousand pounds were subscribed. Economy enforced from London kept the bulletin down to two issues a week, and to a size which did not exhaust demand.[5]

It was an interesting propaganda exercise; the legation had more important parts to play in the secret war as well. Elizabeth Wiskemann, for example, was a friend of Adam von Trott, whom she could never cure of saying 'It's Adam speaking' whenever he rang up;[6] but his visits to her had little political effect.

More, and more important – though still not, till right at the end of the war, more effective – contact with the forces of German resistance was made through the OSS mission in Switzerland. The head of this mission, Allen Dulles, was an experienced diplomat – his brother John Foster was later a world figure as

[1] Radó, 306, is frankly contemptuous of Malcolm Muggeridge's suggestion that Roessler got his information from MI6, who got it from 'Ultra', and used Roessler to feed it to the Russians (*Observer*, 8 January 1972).
[2] p. 26 above; and see Sir John Lomax, *Diplomatic Smuggler* (1965).
[3] *The Europe I Saw*, 129–205. Obituary tribute in *Times*, 6 July, 14gh; 9 July, 14h, 10 July, 14g, 15 July 1971, 18h.
[4] *The Europe I Saw*, 48, 55–60.       [5] Kelly, *The Ruling Few*, 274–5.
[6] *The Europe I Saw*, 168–9, 188.

Eisenhower's secretary of state, and indeed he was a world figure himself as head of OSS's successor body, the CIA. He reached Switzerland by the last train before the Germans sealed the frontier with Vichy France, in November 1942; and was soon at the centre of a large web of intelligence and subversive networks. As has been noted above,[1] it was to him that Horthy sent his minister in Berne to find out how Hungary could escape the nazis' clutches. It was to him that Italian resisters repeatedly appealed for arms and other support; and he had several lines of communication to the German resisters, of whom he wrote one of the earliest sound accounts.[2] He said himself that it had been in Switzerland, during the previous war, that he had acquired his own taste for intelligence work:[3] for two and a half years he could indulge it to the full.

He had some links to the German extreme left through the Quaker communist, Noel Field, who entered Switzerland when he did,[4] and with the industrial right through Gero von Schulze-Gaevernitz, the son by a Jewish mother of an eminent Weimar politician, whose wife was a Stinnes. Gaevernitz had become an American citizen; his parents lived in Switzerland; he could do a good deal.[5] Still more could be attempted by Hans Bernd Gisevius, a German vice-consul in Zürich who was a friend of Canaris, and still more important a friend of Beck: Dulles had advance information of the plot to kill Hitler, though he was able to do nothing to further it.[6]

Some complications have been added to the study of OSS's work in Switzerland by turns in postwar history: when Dulles became the first head of CIA, the soviet authorities seem to have found it necessary to try to discredit him by doctoring versions of talks he had with Germans during the war:[7] an exercise in disinformation that must surely have earned his professional approval, even if he found it politically inconvenient.

Gisevius had originally been in touch with MI6, who dropped him as unreliable;[8] and were perhaps professionally alarmed at having an agent who stood six feet four in his socks. They were equally suspicious of an independent German diplomat who offered Colonel Cartwright in Berne a suitcase-full of German foreign office documents – rejected unopened, as an obvious Gestapo plant – but got them accepted by Dulles. This diplomat, Fritz Kolbe ('George Wood'), produced several more invaluable loads: his task was to see to the distribution of incoming cipher telegrams round the office, and he was occasionally used also as an official courier. No one thought of searching courier bags he had sealed up himself.[9]

Kolbe was of course an ideal agent. Dulles could not send his material intact

---

[1] p. 200.      [2] *Germany's Underground* (1947). And see pp. 300–4 below.
[3] Harris Smith, 204.
[4] Flora Lewis, *The Man Who Disappeared* (1965), 147.
[5] Harris Smith, 212–13, 230.
[6] H. B. Gisevius, *To the Bitter End* (1948).
[7] Harris Smith, 214–15.      [8] Ibid. 213.
[9] Ibid. 218–19; A. W. Dulles, *The Secret Surrender* (1967), 22–5.

out of Switzerland, lest the Germans could read his ciphers and thus unravel his source; the compressions he sent were interesting enough. They included Papen's original report to Berlin about 'Cicero', and it says much for 'Cicero's' skill as a spy that he was able to survive the consequential tightening of security in the British embassy in Ankara.

For OSS loyally passed on all Kolbe's material to the British; whose scepticism was appeased, if we may believe Philby, by the help they gave to Denniston, the head of the diplomatic section of GCCS, in breaking German and Japanese ciphers. In London, as Philby gleefully explains, Dansey at MI6 at first pooh-poohed the source, and then took all the credit for MI6; and gave Philby a good mark for not having revealed that the material came through OSS. This incident helped towards Philby's eventual promotion within the secret service.[1]

Through Kolbe, Dulles was able to open up some touch with German socialists; and it may have been through Kolbe that at the tail end of the war he made contact with the celebrated Richard Gehlen and the files of *Fremde Heere Ost*, foreign armies east, that were destined to play so prominent a part in the cold war.[2]

On the action side, Dulles's German activities could not amount to much; Gisevius and his friends had a spectacular failure on 20 July 1944.[3] After that, the nazi machine of terror plunged into the horrors of the worst winter of the war. A few OSS agents attempted missions from Switzerland into Germany, some even reaching Berlin, but in that pile of terrorized rubble there was hardly anything they could do.

The action side of French resistance took up a lot of OSS's time;[4] indeed Americans in Berne had been busily engaged in talks with French resisters before ever OSS had been formed. Several eminent Frenchmen, who mistrusted the British and distrusted de Gaulle, turned to the Americans instead; and the strong hostility to de Gaulle evinced in Washington made them the more wel-come. In the winter of 1941–2 some gaullists even got the impression that the Americans were trying to buy their friends away from them with a flood of dollars.

Giraud's failure to impose himself over de Gaulle brought an end to most of these manœuvrings, and Dulles's contacts with French resistance though plentiful were more routine. OSS supplied plenty of resistance funds, and from January 1944 the USAAF was available for supply drops to the maquis;[5] some of which were arranged through Berne, with the help of constant messenger traffic across the frontier. Coordination of resistance effort with 'Overlord' could

---

[1] Philby, *My Silent War*, 102–9. But can we here believe Philby? GCCS would need the exact texts of Kolbe's messages for accurate decipher. Were they brought out by a clandestine land crossing into France, and thence by air pick-up?

[2] Harris Smith, 239–40. But Heinz Höhne and Hermann Zolling, *Network* (1972), 49–59, do not tell quite the same story.

[3] pp. 302–3 below.   [4] Dulles, *The Secret Surrender*, 20.

[5] Foot, 473.

be forwarded through the same channel; and the double success of 'Overlord' and 'Dragoon' freed Switzerland from isolation in early September 1944.

Dulles ended his wartime career with a spectacular success; it was through his agency that the fighting in Italy was brought to an end. Of this he has left so full an account[1] that a summary in a paragraph is all that is needed here. It was well enough known – had indeed been in the newspapers when he arrived – that he was present in Berne as Roosevelt's 'special representative', and no one in senior posts in Swiss or German or Italian intelligence had any doubts about who he was or what he did. The Swiss arranged for most dealings with the Germans to be conducted through Masson, and with the Allies through Masson's colleague Max Waibel, a member of a Lucerne family with military traditions ranging back for several centuries.[2] Early in 1945, Waibel was approached by Karl Wolff, the senior SS commander in Italy,[3] with an indication that Wolff was prepared to contemplate organizing a surrender by all the German army and air force units in that theatre of war. As a guarantee of good faith, Wolff handed over both an OSS intelligence agent[4] and Parri, an important Italian resistance leader who was being held in Verona jail. (Parri, with perfect honour, insisted on being sent back into captivity before operations were over.[5]) A series of hair-raising adventures followed; including the arrest of Wolff's family by Himmler, apparently on mere suspicion, and Wolff's rescue of them; and the sending into SS headquarters in Milan and then in Bolzano of an OSS clandestine wireless operator, Vaclav Hradecky ('Little Wally'), who having passed through Dachau – he was one of the few people ever to escape from it – seemed to feel there was no room left for fright. Late in April 1945 the negotiations were almost complete when the combined chiefs of staff ordered their cancellation; in response to a personal protest by Stalin.[6] By this time Wolff himself and other emissaries with full powers to treat were already on their way into Switzerland; Dulles was able to persuade the combined chiefs to change their minds. On 29 April the instrument of surrender was signed at Caserta, in the presence among others of Kislenko, a senior officer of the GRU; and on 2 May 1945 it came into effect.

Switzerland thus justified the role it had played all through the war: a haven of sanity, culture, common sense, and civilization.

---

[1] *The Secret Surrender* (1971).
[2] *The Secret Surrender*, 27; personal knowledge.
[3] Not the Karl Wolff who was commandant of the death camp at Treblinka.
[4] F. W. Deakin, *The Last Days of Mussolini* (1966 ed.), 269–70.
[5] Dulles, *The Secret Surrender*, 94.
[6] Deakin, op. cit., 273.

## Italy

Mussolini appealed, in the country where fascism originated,[1] to the imperial traditions of a Roman empire that had expired beneath barbarian attack some fifteen hundred years before he came to power. There were strong counter-traditions alive in Italian popular consciousness; not only in the north, where the Habsburg dominion that succeeded the renaissance flowering of city-states had lasted in Lombardy till 1859 and in Istria till 1918, but in the south, where the Bourbon kingdom of the two Sicilies – 'the negation of God erected into a system of Government'[2] – had lasted till 1860. The grandsons and great-grandsons of men who had fought with Garibaldi, Manin, Mazzini against tyranny were ready to fight tyranny again: if given the chance and the lead.

Unhappily for Italy, parliamentary life there did not run smoothly. The combination of procedural ineffectiveness and military setbacks in 1915–22 brought out the energies of Mussolini, once a socialist agitator; and of his bands of thugs trained in street fighting, the *fasci di combattimento*, from which his followers became known as *fascisti*. He became prime minister in October 1922, after a bogus 'march on Rome' – he arrived there in a railway sleeping-car – because the king wanted to try this among other combinations. During the next four years he gradually acquired power for himself and his party over the whole state machine, and Italy became a single-party dictatorship.[3] Even in the earliest stages, a man who was ready to stand up and say Bo to the fascist goose could make it run away;[4] but as is usual the cowards outnumbered the brave men, and there were plenty of old women to murmur that geese had once saved the Capitol, and might again.

Mussolini's power rested, as so much Axis power in occupied territory did, on daring, a competent police force, and a few startling examples of terror. The OVRA was a professionally more than adequate body; and the thugs who did the dirty work got some cheap laughs, and made their enemies undignified and ridiculous, by lavish use of laxative castor oil. Really serious opponents were bumped off: Matteotti in 1924 in Italy, Alexander of Yugoslavia in Marseilles in 1934, Rosselli in Normandy three years later. Automatically, the OVRA sought to penetrate foreign missions in Rome. Equally automatically, the British

[1] The word comes from the Latin *fasces*, the bundle of rods with a beheading axe in the middle, carried by the police bodyguards of leading officials of the Roman republic; long a symbol of authority. There is such a bundle above Gambetta's tomb in the Panthéon; topped with a cap of liberty.

[2] W. E. Gladstone, *A Letter to the Earl of Aberdeen* (1851), 9.

[3] Since the war, Elizabeth Wiskemann, *Fascism in Italy* (1969); Adrian Lyttelton, *The Seizure of Power* (1973); D. Mack Smith, *Italy. A Modern History* (Ann Arbor 1959); and C. Seton-Watson, *Italy from Liberalism to Fascism* (1967) provide the indispensable background. Theory can be traced in an essay by Gentile, signed by Mussolini for the *Enciclopedia Italiana* (1930), and reprinted by Michael Oakeshott in *Social and Political Doctrines of Contemporary Europe* (1939). Gentile was killed by partisans in 1944.

[4] Several instances in Emilio Lussu, *Enter Mussolini* (1936), hailed by Wickham Steed when it appeared as far the best account of fascism in English.

ambassador trusted his servants; Perth's major-domo had the run of his safe and was an OVRA spy. Hence Mussolini's sureness of touch in the international crisis of 1935-6.[1]

Many good Italians were prepared to struggle even against so well equipped an enemy, but most of their struggling had to go on abroad, with the usual fissiparous ineffectiveness of *émigré* politics. Baldwin and the Chamberlain brothers cherished the illusion that Mussolini would be a useful counterweight to Hitler, and should not be antagonized; as late as 1938 the British were still seeking and even signing Anglo-Italian accords. Mussolini's sense of imperial destiny had meanwhile drawn him into Ethiopian and Spanish adventures that overtaxed his country's meagre economic strength – Italy has no coal – and over-extended his momentarily excellent air force, which in the middle 1930s was the strongest in the world. From being Hitler's inspiration and model, he gradually became his jackal.[2] Protesting his unreadiness for war, he nevertheless joined in on 10 June 1940, hurrying to the conqueror's help lest all the spoils be swallowed up before Italy had a share.

Silence swallowed up the resisters who survived: silence, discretion, hope for better times. Even children had to begin each day at school by chanting the fascist ten commandments, one of which ran '*Mussolini ha sempre ragione*', Mussolini is always right.[3] From the age of eight, they were encouraged to join the *Balilla*, and to wear fascist uniforms, salute their nine-year-old superiors, and inform on their parents as well as their schoolmates. It was not a promising society for resisters, outside the proletarian areas of the large towns where a skeleton, illegal communist party eked out a skeleton existence. But there was no persistent, perpetual hunting out of those who only disapproved of the régime, as there was in Germany: when Mussolini and his system toppled, many more people were ready to come forward and take a hand in public life than were left at the comparable stage in Germany, after a reign of much fiercer terror, half as long.[4]

Elderly, educated people who could not abide fascism, but could not emigrate either, kept their thoughts to themselves till the course of the war released them. Peasants were more outspoken; out of earshot of the village carabinieri. Over and over again Allied evaders got help, willing and immediate help at frightful risk to the helpers, as soon as they revealed that they were not German.[5]

[1] Knatchbull-Hugessen fell into the same trap in Ankara later. Compare pp. 165–6 above.

[2] Elizabeth Wiskemann, *The Rome–Berlin Axis* (Oxford 1949), though written before many documents were available, contains a wealth of historical and psychological insight into the relations between the two dictators.

[3] I heard this myself through the windows of a village primary school in Tuscany on a beautiful June morning in 1938. The fact that Dante had mentioned the village (*Inferno*, xxxi. 40–1) made the sound no more agreeable.

[4] Wiskemann, *Fascism in Italy*, 20–1.

[5] See for instance John Verney's account, *Going to the Wars* (1955), 162–202, of an SAS raid on Sardinia; but his party met in the end a group of peasants who made sure they were made prisoner.

As the war ground on, and Italy's unreadiness for it and incompetence at it became clear for all to see, resisters grew more vocal. In March 1943 there were some important protest strikes in Turin; and in Sicily in July and August an Italian army of nearly a quarter of a million was quickly outfought by a less numerous Anglo-American expedition ('Husky'). The surviving Germans present cut their way contemptuously out to the mainland.

Sicily provided the Allies with their first opportunity[1] to occupy any part of Axis home territory. By a startling political turn, the new régime upset one of the few positive benefits of the old.[2] Mussolini, alone among rulers of Italy, had mastered the Mafia. The American occupation régime was largely staffed by *mafiosi*, whose excellent Italian fitted them for the task and whose cover was good; they soon had Sicily back under the corrupt domination of their secret society.[3]

By an equally startling, and much better known, political turn, the bungling over the invasion of Sicily brought Mussolini down, as the bungling over the invasion of Norway had brought down Chamberlain. He was felled by a palace revolution, in the strict sense: his fall was concerted between the king, who had at last lost confidence in him, and the Roman chief of police, who by an unlucky accident was killed in an Allied air raid; a loyal subordinate replaced him. Mussolini, who could not refuse a summons to an audience with Victor Emmanuel, was quietly removed from it under police guard in an ambulance on 25 July 1943.[4]

Marshal Badoglio, the new prime minister, engaged at once in a negotiation with the Allies: muddled from the start, because the Allies thought he was seeking to surrender, while what he was seeking was their help against the Germans. An inconspicuous but essential part in the negotiation was played by a captured SOE wireless operator, whose set and ciphers provided Badoglio with a confidential channel of communication the Germans could not tap.[5]

On 8 September, simultaneously with the first Allied landings on the Italian mainland, it was announced over Allied broadcasts that Italy had surrendered. Badoglio made a mess of the Italian announcement; he had not been quite ready for it. The Germans beat him to the draw, and seized the airfields round Rome on which an Allied airborne landing had been planned. Nearly twenty months' heavy fighting followed.

The Allies were prepared to admit Italy, reluctantly, as a co-belligerent, but not as an ally. Badoglio's original cry, on coming into office, had been that the war was to go on; and while secretly he was determined to get out of the Axis alliance, he had for a while to go through the motions of maintaining it. Signs of

---

[1] Pantelleria and Lampedusa deserve a word of exception.
[2] The quasi-proverbial benefit of fascism, that the trains ran on time, was not even true.
[3] Calvocoressi and Wint, *Total War*, 376.
[4] Details, and full political analysis, in Deakin, *The Brutal Friendship* (1966 ed.), ad fin.
[5] See Dorothy Barlow, 'From Enemy to Co-Belligerent: Italy mid-July to mid-October 1943', unpublished Manchester MA thesis (1972), 126.

communist-inspired unrest in northern Italy were promptly put down at the end of July.[1] Neither the king, nor the new prime minister, nor the Allied generals with whom they dealt, nor even the 'big three' leaders Roosevelt, Stalin, and Churchill, appreciated that extensive swathes of the people of Italy – not by any means confined to the urban working class – were longing for a change from fascism, and prepared to fight for it.

But they were not organized to fight for it, yet. Neither SOE nor OSS had succeeded in getting any extensive resistance cells organized so far, in town or country; and the NKVD had hardly done better. The first SOE party did not arrive till December 1942, and thanks to Italian police efficiency was soon arrested.[2] Resistance in Italy was about to explode into frenzied activity, but the explosion was self-generated. The Allied high command, even among the secret services, had been too much obsessed so far with duly constituted authorities.

This was not unexpected; both on account of the conservatism that seems the almost unavoidable concomitant of high office, and on account of the presence at the edge of Rome of the temporal seat of the Papacy. Roman catholicism permeated practically all Italian life – even communists married in church and had their children christened; nobody could divorce; outside a few traditionally protestant corners, Italy was still a profoundly catholic country, and in nineteen centuries people had had time to forget whatever resistance elements lay at the origin of Christianity.[3]

There has been much controversy about the church's role, and the pope's role in particular, during the war; into which we do not need to go here beyond two or three remarks: that the pope had an extensive knowledge of Germany and of nazism; and that he like all the Roman hierarchy was trained to think in centuries and in millennia, and about eternity. Working on that time-scale, the war is not seen in the perspective in which it appears to, say, an air staff officer or a railway saboteur.[4]

The Vatican was just as much neutral territory as Switzerland; like Switzerland, it contained legations from many powers (excluding, in both cases, the USSR); but size as well as suitability prevented it from playing any extensive role as a watchtower or a point from which clandestine expeditions could set out. OSS ran a 'liberated' enclave of Italian territory, Campione on the western side of Lake Maggiore, a village of 600 souls that became a small OSS springboard, and financed itself by issuing rare stamps;[5] the Vatican was far too small for even such minuscule operations (and was in the stamp business itself already, come to that). Harris Smith does have one odd and evidently incomplete tale, for which he gives no printed source, about an OSS contact with Cardinal Montini, the future Pope Paul VI; and an odder one about a senior Vatican official who

[1] F-K. von Plehwe, *The End of an Alliance* (1971), 49, 108–9. This book is an interesting eyewitness account by the chief of staff to the German military attaché in Rome.

[2] J. M. Stevens, 'Britain and Italy', in *ERM* iii, 7.

[3] See S. G. F. Brandon, *Jesus and the Zealots* (1967).

[4] Cp. also p. 80 above.     [5] Dulles, *The Secret Surrender*, 18–19.

secured data through diplomatic channels about strategic bombing targets in Japan.[1]

The NKVD is not likely to have had many, if any, agents in the Vatican; nothing about them is known. An equally complete discretion covers anything MI6 may have been able to arrange.

Of MI9's activities a little is known; and that little, interesting.

At the moment of changing sides, the Italians held perhaps 80,000 British prisoners in camps: almost none of whom had so far succeeded in making an escape that carried him outside Italian territory.[2] In this moment of total military confusion, many commandants simply opened their gates, and let the prisoners move out. The quicker-witted, tougher, and more resolute of them got clean away into the Apennines; where some joined the partisan bands that soon sprang up, a few hid, many were recaptured, and some thousands walked out south-eastward towards the battle line. One of them had the leisure to write, in odd moments, two of the most powerful English novels to come out of the war; and never lived to revise them, because he got involved in a gun battle with a Gestapo agent who tried to break up the escape line he ran.[3]

Some hundreds of prisoners tried their luck in Rome; arriving in clothes they had been given by peasants in the hills, and attempting to get to the British mission in the Vatican. One gunner battery commander, who had survived the double risk of jumping from a guarded train in motion that was taking him and his camp companions off to Germany – Germany was the fate of all those prisoners who did not make tracks promptly in the second week of September – found himself taken in hand by an Irish priest in the Vatican, Monsignore Hugh O'Flaherty. O'Flaherty had no particular reason to love the English, but he was a good enough Christian to hate the nazis; and was a tremendous pillar of the escape structures that centred on Rome. This gunner officer, Sam Derry, has written a vivid account of how the Monsignore dressed him also in a cassock, and strode past the papal sentries – who all knew him well – into the Vatican with Derry beside him; there to meet Sir D'Arcy Osborne, the British minister. Osborne took care that nothing was done that infringed papal neutrality; he took care also that everything possible was done to supply Derry with clothes, money, communications. Derry found himself in charge of keeping the escaped prisoners in and near Rome out of the wrong hands, and organizing them into parties to meet naval rescue ships at suitable spots on the coast. Figures are sparse, but the adventures were real.[4]

None of these or any other escapes in Italy would have been conceivable without the self-sacrifice and cooperation of hundreds of thousands of the Italian rural poor: small peasants, charcoal-burners, shepherds, old women tough as the soil they tilled. Even the names of most of them are lost to history.

---

[1] Harris Smith, 84–6.  [2] Cp. pp. 39–40 above.
[3] Dan Billany, *The Cage* (1949) and *The Trap* (1950).
[4] Sam Derry, *The Rome Escape Line* (1960).

Their achievement is the more memorable as a tribute to the impact of twenty years of fascism on popular feeling.[1]

They had no doubt what would happen to them if they were caught. Mussolini was rescued, by a brilliant *coup de main* of Otto Skorzeny's,[2] from the hotel in the Abruzzi where he had been ineffectually hidden, as early as 12 September 1943; and was settled by Hitler at Salò on Lake Garda, in charge of a nominal republic. The Italians refer to it in the diminutive, as a *repubblichina*; it had little information and less authority; but it was fascist, so it had some atrocity in its manners. The Germans ruled all of Italy that had not been conquered by the Allies; and they were atrocious enough, killing off Italians at moments of exasperation as readily as they killed off Slavs. The Italian garrison of Cephallonia, for example – politically at that moment a part of Italy – tried to change sides with Badoglio, and were all killed: over 8,000 of them. Massacres less severe in quantity, but memorably revolting in form, took place repeatedly on the mainland. The 335 hostages shot in the Ardeatine caves near Rome on 30 March 1944, though less than a tenth – perhaps less than a twentieth – of the Serbs shot at Kragujevac in October 1941, have also never been forgiven.[3] A smaller killing of hostages in the Piazzale Loreto at Milan had a macabre sequel in the following spring.

The most spectacular atrocity, too diffuse to be as sharply recalled, took place at Naples. In the last four days of September 1943, as the Allied armies drew near, the people of Naples rose to meet them as their ancestors had risen to meet Garibaldi in 1860: with shatteringly different results. The troops of King Bomba, outfaced by Garibaldi in person, held their fire; Hitler's troops did not. Spontaneous insurrection brought on spontaneous massacre.

The Allied armies arrived on 1 October, in time to succour the less severely wounded. They brought with them the cumbrous apparatus of AMGOT, prepared at leisure by military bureaucrats in Washington, London, and Algiers.[4] Administrative generals were even less inclined to trust Italians than were operational ones. AMGOT officers took over the whole business of food supply, drainage, health, currency supply, traffic control, the maintenance of public order: only gradually did AMGOT take in that the Italians were looking forward to a chance to govern themselves again, had not loved dictatorship much, and were trying to shed their bureaucracy, not longing to be directed – either by it or by anybody else's.

As Parri and Venturi have put it in a powerful article, the true reply of the

[1] Tony Davies, *When the Moon Rises* (1973), an account – mostly written in the late 1940s – of his journey down the Apennines with Toby Graham (later ski champion and Fredericton history professor) and Michael Gilbert the novelist, is filled with readable examples.
[2] Skorzeny might be called the German David Stirling. He ran SAS-type raids; and after the war struck up a friendship with Yeo-Thomas. Obituary (brief and inaccurate) in *Times*, 8 July 1975, 16g.
[3] See Casterman, s.vv.
[4] See C. R. S. Harris, *Allied Military Administration of Italy 1943–1945* (1957).

Italian people to the fall of Mussolini and the king's change of side was shown in the partisan movement.[1] Parri was too modest to add that the maturity of judgement shown by the principal resistance politicians, himself included, had a lot to do with the partisans' success. The fissions of exile politics were healed, for the time being; Stalin declared himself disinterested; and liberals, socialists, communists, conservatives could all be patriots together, seeking to get rid of the Germans.

In Italy in the autumn of 1943, as in France in the autumn of 1944, there was a temporary feeling that the war was almost over; and something like 100,000 people took to the hills in hope. Most of them had to creep back to the towns and villages they came from, as the hills held little shelter and no food; but in the spring and summer of 1944 they were back, in still greater strength. There were plenty of young and very young men[2] who were ready to die for their idea of liberty, if they must; and a few regular soldiers who were prepared to join them. In quantity and quality alike, they made up for their late start. The British Eighth Army trained several brigades of Italian volunteers, who fought a great deal better than their cousins had done against the same army in the Libyan desert; the American Fifth Army remained too suspicious to give Italians a place in their own lines though they made wide use of Italian labour.

Alexander, the commander-in-chief, gave a great deal of unintended offence in a proclamation in November 1944, in which he in effect ordered those partisans who were still holding out to hide for the winter: they felt they took their orders from the CLNAI, not from him, and realized far more keenly than he did how all-but-impossible it was going to be to hide.

> The toad beneath the harrow knows
> Exactly where each tooth-point goes.
> The butterfly upon the road
> Preaches contentment to the toad.

Kesselring, Alexander's opposite number, had just held an anti-partisan week, from 8 to 14 October; having heard Alexander's order broadcast, he stepped up his operations to put down the partisans. But in the spring, up they sprouted again: irrepressibly.

The grand total of partisans was probably nearly 300,000; of whom 45,000 were killed in action. Some 3,000 tons of supplies were parachuted to them, two-thirds by British and the rest by American aircraft. SOE sent in 48 missions to help them train, organize, and fight.[3] With one of these, in August 1944, there parachuted General Raffaele Cadorna (son of the commander-in-chief of the previous war) to exercise some degree of command on the spot. But the nature of

---

[1] *ERM* ii. xiii, with a useful set of notes, ibid. xl.

[2] Not many young women: Italians being socially much more conservative than Yugoslavs.

[3] Parri and Venturi, *ERM* ii. xlii, put the total figure of missions as high as 150. The figure in the text is from J. M. Stevens in *ERM* iii, 7; it only covers SOE. OSS and CLN missions presumably divided the rest.

partisan war is such that lack of communications prevents a commander on the spot from exercising control over a much larger area than he can see.

By the spring of 1945 almost everybody on special forces staffs who had not yet been on a mission, wanted to go; hence an Italian complaint that there were embarrassingly many by April, when the war was clearly drawing to an end.[1]

SAS, SBS, and PPA were busy also. SBS did a lot of work shifting escapers from the German side of the battle line. Of one SAS mission Parri and Venturi remark that it is a perfect model of how a highly intelligent fighting man can pick up the importance to partisans of incessant action and of a political content to their action.[2] And Peniakoff ('Popski') earned the gratitude of everybody who loves beautiful things by driving to and fro through the main battle, with a white sheet tied to his jeep aerial, while he persuaded the commanders on both sides to spare the churches of Ravenna.[3] His small, highly trained, uniformed force, a sort of modern light cavalry, cooperated closely with partisans on the Adriatic coast, and on its commander's impulse five of its jeeps drove seven times round the Piazza San Marco in Venice to mark the impending end of the war.[4]

In the final offensive of April 1945, the partisans more than proved their worth. In the words of the secret report to Allied Force Headquarters of Colonel Hewitt, commander of the British Special Force No. 1, the partisans took in that month alone 40,000 German and fascist prisoners, and liberated over a hundred towns before the Allied armies reached them. 'The contribution of the partisans to the Allied victory in Italy was a very considerable one, and far surpassed the most optimistic forecasts. By armed force, they helped to break the strength and the morale of an enemy well superior to them in numbers. Without the partisans' victories there could not have been an Allied victory in Italy so fast, so complete, and with such light casualties.'[5]

The most famous partisan victory was a small and squalid one. Mussolini, left in the dark by everybody, realized the war was lost, and set out from Salò with Clara Petacci, his last mistress, for the Swiss border. Near it the convoy in which they were travelling, in German uniforms, was stopped by a communist partisan band. Mussolini was recognized. They were both arrested, and shot next day. Their bodies were exposed, hanging upside-down from meat hooks, in the Piazzale Loreto at Milan.

This is too gloomy a note on which to end: return a moment to Venice.

Beside the Ponte de la Cortesia stands a plaque, one of those plaques you see so often in towns where there was stiff resistance fighting:[6]

[1] Parri and Venturi, loc. cit.
[2] *ERM* ii. xxxi: see Roy Farran, *Operation Tombola* (1960).
[3] Monument to him in San Apollinare in Classe; V. Peniakoff, *Private Army* (1950), 490.
[4] Ibid. 474 ff., 499.     [5] Quoted by M. G. Vaccarino in *ERM* i. 93; retranslated.
[6] Tr.; *Vidi.*

ON THE NIGHT OF 18 NOVEMBER 1944
## LUIGI GIACOPINO
WHO FELL HERE TO GERMAN BULLETS HASTENED
THE HOUR OF ITALY'S LIBERATION FROM
INTERNAL AND EXTERNAL TYRANNY

The plaque faces across the square the statue of Daniel Manin, who led Venice's fated republican rising in 1848–9.

## Iberia

The Iberian peninsula contained two right-wing, indeed near-fascist, régimes, of which Spain preserved a precarious neutrality right through the war, and Portugal – allied to England since 1373 – preserved it till bullied into collaborating with the Allies in October 1943. There was also the rock of Gibraltar, in British hands since 1704.

Gibraltar was a key point in the clandestine, as in the open, naval war in the western Mediterranean: SOE's feluccas were based there, so were some other light craft usable for beach landings, so for a short time was *Fidelity*; as the civil population had been evacuated to England, there was staging-room also for parties passing through. A small airfield was built between the harbour and La Linea, with one runway, just long enough to take a Liberator. This made Gibraltar still more important as a staging-centre, and no doubt offered MI6 facilities for investigating other powers' diplomatic bags.[1]

We need not spend much time on the pretence that the Polish General Sikorski's death on 4 July 1943, when the Liberator carrying him crashed on take-off from Gibraltar, was anything but an accident. SOE was the only body competent to fake an accident; and did not in fact do so.[2] Sikorski was a personal friend of Gubbins as well as Churchill. Gubbins could not have failed to know of an SOE plan to kill Sikorski; and as certainly would have blocked it. The truth was that a fitter maintaining the aircraft overlooked his empty haversack, which had contained a snack meal; the haversack slid aft on take-off, and jammed the elevators. A postwar dramatist, looking for evidence incriminating a British secret service, misread in Mason-Macfarlane the governor-general's appointments diary 'Swear Carrara' as 'Sweet Escott'. Sweet-Escott was in fact in London, not in Gibraltar, at the material time: collapse of dramatic theory.

Gibraltar's main importance to resistance was as an escape line terminal: not only for SOE's sea escapes by felucca, but for several lines set up by MI9 in the winter of 1940–1. Their originator, Donald Darling, settled at Gibraltar with the pseudonym of 'Sunday', enlivened his head office with frequent reports, and

---

[1] See Philby, *My Secret War*, 63–5, 79, 111–12.
[2] Private information.

satisfied himself of escapers' good faith before passing them on to Britain by air or sea.[1] Alternatively, escapers could go to Lisbon.

The clinching arrangements for the original line were made by a highly conspicuous agent, whose work was rendered the more secret because he was so conspicuous, and therefore beyond suspicion: Nubar Gulbenkian. He happened to hold a neutral passport; his father Calouste Gulbenkian the oil magnate happened to be in Vichy; what more natural than a visit by a son to his parents? His valet perhaps pushed their luck a little when he dropped an iron on a very senior German officer's toes.[2] Two visits to Vichy by Gulbenkian, via Lisbon, Madrid, and Perpignan, in the autumn of 1940, sufficed to set up an adequate line. Michel Pareyre ('Parker'), a Perpignan garage-owner, handled all the contacts with the smugglers, and received £40 for every officer and £20 for every other rank he passed over the Pyrenees. (Sir) Michael Cresswell ('Monday') in the British embassy in Madrid looked after the Spanish side.[3] Gulbenkian brought back some useful intelligence from Vichy, as a bonus, as well.

Some intelligence from Spain was handled by Hillgarth, the naval attaché, who had a special dispensation from Churchill to go outside the usual diplomatic drill. Philby, reporting this, indicates that Hillgarth's information while accurate was a good deal less complete than his own (he was in charge of the English end of secret intelligence work in Spain at the time): an odd example of how contagious the pride in one's sources can be among professional handlers of intelligence material.[4] McLachlan gives a better informed and more favourable account of Hillgarth's work.[5]

The main clandestine importance of Iberia during the war, apart from its value to the escape services, lay in the fact that it was from here that the Germans mounted most of their attempts to plant agents in Britain: it therefore played a central part in the war of deception. Beyond Masterman's and Delmer's inside accounts of this, referred to above,[6] it is worth mentioning Lily Sergueiev's *Secret Service Rendered*,[7] an unaffected account by one of the intermediaries of what she went through. McLachlan mentions also considerable local success with a deception plan to confuse the enemy about 'Torch'.[8]

The *Abwehr* maintained large and varied staffs in Portugal and in Spain, and thought they were doing useful work for the Reich; in the first half of the war, at any rate, while the Reich seemed to be winning. Little could be done by ordinary people in either country against them; they had to be endured. The civil war had

---

[1] Neave, 55, 71, 75–8, &c; Darling, *Secret Sunday* (1975).

[2] N. Gulbenkian, *Pantaraxia* (1965), 192–3.

[3] N. Gulbenkian, *Pantaraxia*, 199–206; Neave, 77–9, &c; Langley, *Fight Another Day*, 167.

[4] Philby, 65–7. Many people have leapt to the conclusion that, as Philby had something to do with Iberia where Sikorski was killed, and it was to Stalin's interest to obliterate Sikorski, and Philby was Stalin's agent, therefore Philby must have arranged the crash. Capable as Philby was, in his field, this lay outside it.

[5] *Room 39*, 186–206.  [6] p. 30.

[7] 1968. She figures as 'Treasure' in Masterman, *Double-Cross System*, 143, 149, 161, 169.

[8] *Room 39*, 196.

made it painfully clear, in Spain, which side was on top; it had also left the Spanish nation economically and emotionally exhausted.

That war, which raged from July 1936 to March 1939, had been an exercise in disillusion for the left intelligentsia of Europe and north America; many of the best of whom were killed in it, fighting for a cause that, as it turned out, hardly existed outside their imaginations. The survivors discovered with George Orwell that great powers only go to great trouble to suit their own interests.

The causes and course of the civil war fall outside this book's range.[1] It provided plenty of lessons about the main struggle that impended; few of them learnt. The Luftwaffe's failure in the battle of Britain, for example, was due in part to faulty deductions about a bomber's needs in defensive armament, drawn from untypical experiences in Vizcaya and Catalonia. The NKVD was busy in Spain, as we have seen:[2] Catalonia was the anvil on which it broke anarchism and tried to break trotskyism too. Card-holding communists played a leading part in the international brigades. Most of the survivors were then summoned to the USSR, obeyed the summons without hesitation, and were disposed of in the great purge.[3] As Conquest said of Cornford, who was killed near Cordoba late in 1936, 'not even high intelligence and a sensitive spirit are of any help once the facts of a situation are deduced from a political theory, rather than vice versa'.[4]

Another man of high intelligence and sensitive spirit, from a cultural background differing sharply from Cornford's Cambridge, visited Spain during the greater war: Wilfred Israel. His father's department store in Berlin was sacked in the *Kristallnacht* of November 1938. Having secured compensation and apology, and done what he could for his staff, he had gone to England in the following spring. (He had dual nationality, British and German.) He was in touch both with PWE and with the Jewish Agency, and at the end of March 1943 began a visit to Spain on the Agency's behalf. The Franco government was much less passionately anti-semitic than the German, and he made some progress in organizing the transport of young Jews to kibbutzim in Palestine.[5] His identity, mission, and appearance very probably became known to German agents in Madrid and Lisbon; and at Lisbon, anybody who cared to take a drink in the airport café could see who boarded the plane for England. Perhaps it was on his account that on 2 June 1943 the Germans shot down the England-bound Dakota; which also carried the actor Leslie Howard. There were no survivors.[6]

Pusillanimity by the Spanish republic's western friends, and the tough lines taken by Hitler and Mussolini – particularly Mussolini – had made Franco's

[1] Among shelves of books on them, three stand out: Gerald Brenan, *The Spanish Labyrinth* (1943) for the origins; and Hugh Thomas, *The Spanish Civil War* (1961, 1965, revised ed. 1976) for the military and Gabriel Jackson, *The Spanish Republic and the Civil War 1931–1939* (Princeton 1965) for the political struggle.

[2] pp. 92–3 above.  [3] Robert Conquest, *The Great Terror*, 316, 588–92.
[4] Ibid. 665.  [5] See p. 312 below.
[6] Ian Colvin, *Flight 777* (1957), 117–24, and H. G. Reissner in *Leo Baeck Institute Yearbook 1958*, 245–56.

victory in the civil war pretty straightforward: as soon as it was clear that the full weight of the USSR was not going to be put into the balance against him. He must fully have expected a British defeat, particularly after the fall of France; but when the British refused after all to give in, he was grateful enough to them for their policy of non-intervention to apply it himself in return.

Three years of savage and bitter fighting had left the Spaniards in no state for more. The whole country seemed, to foreign visitors, desolate: burned-out churches, bombed houses, untilled fields, hungry faces, surly policemen everywhere: a land wasted already by war. Strangers were discouraged; large prison camps awaited those who could give no coherent and visaed account of how they entered Spain, and passengers even on the best escape lines sometimes found themselves accidentally held up in such noisome places for months. Yet the régime was not an entirely closed one; as we saw a moment ago, for instance, it was not inordinately anti-semitic, and it was open to conventional diplomatic pressure.

Churchill, by one of his deftest appointments, sent Hoare, a leading appeaser, to be ambassador in Madrid; and Hoare succeeded in persuading Franco not to join Hitler.[1] Hoare had been head of the British Secret Service mission in Russia during the 1914 war,[2] and so understood some fundamentals of intelligence work. This strengthened his hand in the spring of 1941; carefully briefed by NID, he called on Franco in state and exposed an *Abwehr* plot to set up a radar station to monitor the straits of Gibraltar ('Bodden').[3] This plot was cancelled; as a counterpart, Sir Samuel set his face like flint against efforts by SOE to operate in Spain, and did all he could to limit the work of MI6 and MI9.

Two operations of any size were prepared by SOE; we know of each from an intended participant. Peter Kemp got as far as Gibraltar, after an intensely uncomfortable voyage in *Fidelity*, in the spring of 1941 with a party who were supposed to counter 'Bodden'; and were stood down when the Germans tackled the USSR instead. Kemp remembered most vividly how much he disliked the staff officer who came out by battle-cruiser to brief them.[4] The operation was called 'Goldeneye', a name lifted for his house in Jamaica by Ian Fleming.[5] Donald Hamilton-Hill had no more action with 'Skiddaw', a highly trained party of eighteen Spanish-speaking officers who stood by in the winter of 1942-3 to disrupt any German invasion of Spain as a riposte to 'Torch'; but the main German forces stayed north of the Pyrenees.[6]

More useful work for the war effort was done by Hillgarth, and by his assistant Gomez-Beare, in looking after British ships that used Spanish ports. The Germans made numerous attempts at sabotage, most of which the British were

---

[1] Lord Templewood (Sir Samuel Hoare), *Ambassador on Special Mission* (1946).
[2] McLachlan, *Room 39*, 199.    [3] Ibid. 204-6.
[4] P. Kemp, *No Colours or Crest*, 18-38. Philby, 40, identifies the staff officer as Hugh Quennell.
[5] McLachlan, *Room 39*, 195, 404.
[6] D. Hamilton-Hill, *SOE Assignment* (1973), 42-9.

able to frustrate by stimulating the local police into some sort of vigilance; and by persuading ships' crews to keep a proper lookout. Italian frogmen made two damaging attacks on Gibraltar from a well-hidden base in Algeçiras bay; but only damaged merchantmen. The Spaniards were also on the whole persuaded to keep to their duties of neutrality over the refuelling of U-boats; of which a little was arranged by the Germans on the north coast of Spain, in thorough secrecy.[1]

Of the most famous secret operation of the war that affected Spain, the floating ashore near Huelva at the end of May 1943 of the body of 'Major Martin, R.M.', a word has been said already,[2] and we only need to add here that Gomez-Beare showed his customary skill in making it clear to the Spanish authorities at Huelva that 'Martin' was carrying important papers, while not letting them, or the Germans with whom they were promptly in touch, suspect a plant. It remains a small masterpiece of deception.

OSS had an even more rugged time in Iberia than SOE. The head of its Portuguese station, Robert Solborg, quarrelled both with George Kennan, the *chargé d'affaires*, and with Donovan, who eventually dismissed him. The American ambassador in Madrid, the historian Carleton J. Hayes, took an even sterner line than Hoare: he forbade OSS activity of any kind in Spanish territory unless he had approved it in advance, indicated that he would approve very little, and wished both to see all OSS wireless traffic with Washington and to have the right not to pass on messages of which he did not approve. There were less pro-Franco elements in OSS. They recruited a number of the surviving members of the Abraham Lincoln battalion of the international brigades, and looked for a chance to employ them actively. They also got in touch with the exiled Spanish republican government, and infiltrated a few armed parties into southern Spain to work with such opposition as they could find. But even the communists in Spain had by now been counter-infiltrated by the Spanish police; the OSS parties were betrayed; there was an awkward incident between Spain and the USA, an equally awkward one between Hayes and Donovan; and thereafter Hayes had his way.[3]

Many thousands of good Spanish republican soldiers, who had survived the civil war, crossed the Pyrenees into France as the republic foundered. Most of them were clapped by the French police into internment camps of which Arthur Koestler has given an unforgettable, if ostensibly fictional, impression.[4] A few escaped, or stayed at large; they were the backbone of several maquis, three or four years later, when these bands of outlaws began to assemble in the remoter French hills to escape the call for compulsory work in Germany.[5] Correctly, they regarded themselves as having been first in the armed resistance field;[6] and

---

[1] McLachlan, ch. ix.     [2] p. 29 above.
[3] Harris Smith, ch. iii.     [4] *Scum of the Earth* (1941).
[5] Cp. pp. 251–2 below.     [6] Cp. Pierre Bertaux, *Libération de Toulouse* (1973), 90.

their customs were seldom soft. The British foreign office showed some nervousness, in September 1944, that some of those liberated Spanish maquisards might be in such a mood of elation that they wanted to re-start the civil war: nothing important in fact came of this.[1] The fall of France to Eisenhower's and Patch's armies left the German missions in Spain and Portugal cut off from home leave, but still in touch with Berlin by wireless; and a certain amount of deception work still went on through their unwitting agency.

This section need not end on quite so conformist a note. At the end of the war, there were a great many small fast landing craft, and a few lively young officers – some men, some women – in the western Mediterranean; and a few people put in a highly adventurous (and lucrative) spell smuggling, till the syndicates moved in.[2]

## North-west Europe

France, Belgium, the Netherlands, and Luxembourg were joined by no political bonds, apart from the bonds of German occupation, in the summer of 1940 (always excepting their membership in the Universal Postal Union); but contiguity did bring some bonds of common interest, on the economic front, and of tactical importance for the war. All four lay between England and Germany, and were liable to witness air interceptions; the Netherlands especially, which lay between RAF bomber command's main airfields and the Germans' main industrial base, the Ruhr. All four necessarily lay athwart the Germans' route to England, and the British route to Germany, and were therefore certain to be full of prime sabotage targets in the case of an invasion, either way. All four had an elaborate railway system, running on a common gauge, with regular international services. Their climate and terrain were similar; Mediterranean and mountain France apart. And they all had highly educated, lively enterprising inhabitants: an ideal stamping-ground, in fact, for resisters.

The British secret services treated the area accordingly. There was a north-west European section of MI9, headed by Langley, assisted – after his escape from Colditz – by 'Saturday', Airey Neave. MI6 had a north-west European section, run from a forward base in Holland: with disastrous results.[3] SOE grouped its several sections working into France, and its Belgian and Dutch sections, under a coordinating officer called D/R, who was in turn subordinated to a director who handled the training section and some other country sections as well. It had a small efficient escape section, DF, which covered all north-west Europe and Iberia as well, in the group under D/R. To this 'London group' under the director, Gubbins's friend Mockler-Ferryman, was also welded the OSS operations branch in London, under Joe Haskell.[4] Haskell

---

[1] Cp. Pierre Bertaux, *Libération de Toulouse* (1973), 106–7
[2] D. E. Walker, *The Modern Smuggler*, 191–7.     [3] Cp. pp. 136, 259–62.
[4] Brother of the John Haskell who was OSS commander with the American Fifth Army in Italy (Harris Smith, 94–5).

worked happily in double harness with Mockler-Ferryman, under two masters –
Gubbins of SOE, and the overall OSS commander in Europe, David Bruce.[1]
This arrangement, which looks improbably imprecise on paper, worked in
practice rather well. Let us see how.

### France

Let us skip thirteen centuries of history, that should be known to every school-
child,[2] and turn to some points of wartime political geography after June 1940
that affect our theme, and may be less familiar.

Alsace and Lorraine, the *Reichsland* of 1871–1918, were in 1940 again annexed
from France to Germany, and some efforts were made to settle in them Germans
from southern Tirol.

Two more *départements*, Nord and Pas de Calais, were administered, to suit
German convenience, from Brussels.

Till autumn 1942, the Germans only officially occupied the northern and western three-fifths of France: all France north of a line from Nantes to Belfort,
and the whole Biscay coast. Between occupied and unoccupied France there
ran a demarcation line,[3] which nobody was supposed to cross without a permit:
an obvious starting-point for escape workers. After 'Attila', the German takeover
of the unoccupied zone on 11 November 1942, the demarcation line was kept in
existence, as one more police obstacle to control free movement.

Under their armistice with France, the Italians exacted Mussolini's prewar
claim to Nice and Savoy; after 'Attila' they took Corsica; after the Italian armistice of 1943, the Germans quietly disarmed the Italian garrisons and took over
themselves.

Even before 'Attila', German missions, some more and some less secret, into
the unoccupied zone were frequent. The *Abwehr* had some influence over the
numerous French police forces, and from September 1942 German radiogoniometry teams were given free range all over France. A few had been active
there already.

There were constitutional as well as geographical hitches.

The third republic, founded in the aftermath of the Franco-Prussian war of
1870–1, did not long survive the Franco-German war of 1939–40. Marshal
Pétain replaced it in July 1940 by what he called, simply, the French State; of
which he was the Chief.[4] He ran his state from the watering-place of Vichy; in
his own frail, upright, elderly person he incarnated those doctrines of established
order that had long formed the political aims of French conservatives, of every
party.[5] Though not himself a person of particularly pious life – his wife was, for
example, a divorcée[6] – he attracted to his régime a degree of devotion from the

---

[1] Bruce was, much later, a greatly liked American ambassador in London.
[2] Alfred Cobban, *A History of Modern France* (3 v 1965), is the most recent scholarly
summary in English.           [3] Map in, eg., Foot, maps 1–3.
[4] Robert O. Paxton, *Vichy France*, is decisive.           [5] Cp. p. 79.
[6] Obituary of Mme Pétain, *Times*, 31 January 1962, 15a.

French episcopate that might have been consecrated to more sacred objects.[1] Roosevelt dealt amiably with Vichy, usually through Admiral Leahy his ambassador there,[2] till November 1942; the American diplomatic bag carried a good deal more than Leahy wanted to know. The Canadians maintained a legation at Vichy, under the highly cultivated *chargé d'affaires* Dupuy, who was also accredited to the Belgian and Dutch governments-in-exile in London, and could therefore travel openly between the two cities till he was withdrawn in November 1942;[3] he provided a safe channel for verbal messages, but hardly for more, as he was naturally kept under constant watch.

Churchill was privately and publicly short with Pétain, but was kept in touch with him by a series of unofficial missions; was himself a proponent of established order, having outlived his radical youth; and felt some glow of mutual feeling with Pétain's naval chief, Darlan, whom he believed – correctly – to be set against letting the Germans lay their hands on the one remaining French military asset, the fleet at Toulon. Darlan could feel no reciprocal glow of affection towards Churchill after the lamentable affair of Mers-el-Kebir, which both the French and the Royal navies detested: as bad a start as could be to four years' indispensable working together between the British at war and the French in resistance.[4]

The difference of view between internal and external resistance, which has already been noticed as wide in Greece and Yugloslavia, was particularly wide in France; in 1940 the external leader was hardly known, even by name, within the country that he felt he *was*. As Pétain the hero of Verdun was the most senior, de Gaulle was the most junior general officer in the French army; Pétain was a world figure; de Gaulle was a nobody. He was so dim that the BBC did not bother to record his original broadcast of 18 June 1940, which gaullists now revere as the starting-point of resistance. A few professional friends, and a handful of politicians, knew him; a few people had read his books on military theory, one of them dedicated to Pétain under whom he had served.[5] His name sounded like a magniloquent pseudonym. It was in fact an old one – a Sieur de Gaulle had fallen at Agincourt – and one of his grandmothers was a MacCartan of Lille, descendant of an Irish soldier who had preferred Louis XIV to William III. It was not an ancestry to predispose a man to love the English.

Like Tito, de Gaulle had been taken prisoner when severely wounded; the two men shared characteristics of bravery, loneliness, charm in private, powers of leadership, self-confidence, even a sense of destiny; but their professional training, one as a revolutionary and the other as a soldier, had given them wholly different casts of mind. Tito was a good south Slav patriot, but he always looked at Yugoslavia as an arena in which the world communist movement was at work.

[1] See Louis Allen, 'Resistance and the Catholic Church in France', in Hawes and White, *Resistance 1939–1945*, 77–93; especially 84.
[2] Cp. p. 161 above. [3] Adrienne D. Hytier, *Two Years of Foreign Policy* (1958), 106.
[4] See A. J. Marder, *From the Dardanelles to Oran* (1974), 179–288.
[5] They quarrelled about this: see Brian Crozier, *De Gaulle* (1973), i. 76–8.

De Gaulle's patriotism was no less strong, but was divorced from much thought of party. Republican principle counted for a great deal with him, as much as marxist principle counted for Tito; honour counted for even more.

Many of the searing personal tragedies in resistance history, particularly in France, stemmed from officers' understandings and misunderstandings about where the true path of honour lay. To marxists, then as now, to many reasonable men of other creeds or none today, that phrase is a meaningless noise: to tens of thousands of regular officers, it was the central question of conduct and belief.

De Gaulle and Pétain answered it in opposite senses, and their former friendship passed quickly into rancorous dislike, even hatred. Pétain had de Gaulle sentenced to death *in absentia*; de Gaulle made sure that in the end the marshal was sentenced to death himself, and then commuted the penalty to life imprisonment on an island. (The old man did not die till 1951, aged ninety-five.)[1]

Though Pétain was already eighty-four when he came to power, and sometimes seemed almost gaga, he retained much shrewdness and an iron will; his régime was meant to cure France of the evils of permissiveness and parliamentarism. Government, paternalist and well intentioned, was by decree, and the 'national revolution' proclaimed from Vichy was intended to purify and transform the whole public and private life of France.

At times it has been unfashionable to admit the fact; but there it is, staring any historian in the face: collaboration with victorious Germany was positively popular in France, early in the occupation at any rate, and some Frenchmen remained collaborationists, right through to a very bitter end. Franco sent a whole division to fight in the USSR; France sent a brigade, the Légion des Volontaires Français (LVF), about 3,000 strong. The Waffen-SS abandoned its nordic prejudices in July 1943, and some 3,000 Frenchmen volunteered for that too; the SS and LVF volunteers were ultimately merged into a weak division, some 7,000 strong, called Charlemagne:[2] to distract attention, perhaps, from another Charles the Tall. There was a host of other collaborationist parties and movements as well; from a resister's point of view, one was exceptionally nasty.

This was the *Milice Française* formed early in 1943 from Joseph Darnand's *Service d'Ordre Légionnaire* on a strong hint from Hitler to Laval that there must be an efficient body of counter-terrorists in France. Littlejohn compares them to the Black and Tans who disgraced the British name in Ireland in 1919–21.[3] They were less battle-experienced than the Black and Tans; like them, they included saints as well as sinners; unlike them, they operated mostly in their own home districts. This gave them a large advantage against resisters; they knew

[1] Obituary in *Times*, 24 July 1951.
[2] Littlejohn, *Patriotic Traitors*, 240–51, 262–5, 280–3.
[3] Ibid. 261. J. Delperrie de Bayac, *Histoire de la Milice* (1969), is full.

many faces already, could spot strangers and oddities, and therefore could exploit one of the main weaknesses of resistance workers: loneliness.

One of the earliest of resisters was for a long time one of the loneliest: de Gaulle himself. Fewer than one in five of the French troops staging in Britain on their way back from the Norwegian expedition decided to follow his call, and join fighting France: different views of duty and honour, different estimates of the future course of the war took them back to their homeland. He got one important early recruit, André Dewavrin ('Passy'), who headed his nascent secret services, and has published three volumes of memoirs less well known, but hardly less astonishing than the general's own.[1] All his appeals to his seniors to come and take over the Free French movement from him fell on deaf ears; he had to struggle on alone.

It is fair to mention that a still earlier resister than de Gaulle, Robert Mengin, has put it on record that he cannot believe the general's proposals to hand over his movement were sincere. Mengin shares to the full the age-long suspicions of the French and English left about generals in politics – suspicions that go back, behind the Dreyfus case and the Boulanger case, to Bonaparte and what he did to the great revolution of 1789; for him, de Gaulle was the saviour of de Gaulle, rather than the saviour of his country. His voice is a lone one; but his book is undoubtedly sincere.[2]

The general had had some contact with politics in June 1940, as Reynaud's under-secretary for war; his voice and hand carried to France the proposal for a complete fusion of Great Britain and France into a single state, the 'spectacular irrelevance' of 15–16 June.[3] He tried to remain above politics, as the symbol of France that had been and was to be; a position too grand even for his capacities of grandeur. The price that the politicians of internal resistance exacted for accepting his leadership was his admission that politics and parties had a part to play, even in external resistance.

The national liberation committee (CFLN), of which he and Giraud were the co-presidents when it was set up at Algiers in June 1943, was from the start a body with governmental pretensions and a political character; and indeed the whole story of the relation between de Gaulle and Giraud, both professional soldiers by training, shows that when it came to politics the junior could dance rings round the senior.

De Gaulle was brighter than Giraud: that was not difficult. He also turned out, more surprisingly, to be a defter politician than the astute and case-hardened leaders of the PCF, the French communist party; who gave in their adherence

---

[1] *Souvenirs du Colonel Passy*: i *2ᵉ Bureau, Londres*, ii *10 Duke Street, Londres* (both Monte Carlo 1947), iii *Missions secrètes* (1951); iv was projected, but never appeared. De Gaulle's *Mémoires de Guerre* (3 v 1954-9) are already a classic.

[2] R. Mengin, *No Laurels for de Gaulle* (1967); contrast D. Grinnell-Milne, *The Triumph of Integrity* (1961). The latest full treatment in English is Brian Crozier's *De Gaulle* (2 v 1973).

[3] P. M. H. Bell, *A Certain Eventuality* (1974), 72-6.

to him in January 1943, no doubt with private reservations, and never managed to unseat him. They had had, and continued to have, a difficult war. Their party was outlawed in October 1939; Thorez their leader fled to Moscow, where he spent the next six years. They entered into arrangements to re-issue their newspaper, *L'Humanité*, legally in Paris after the Germans arrived there; which were blocked by the Paris police, because formally they were still outlaws.[1] Some of them began anti-German activity during the following winter, and in May 1941 launched the Front National, which became the party's main stalking-horse for the rest of the war. After 22 June 1941,[2] the PCF devoted itself wholeheartedly, and at enormous sacrifice, to the business of resistance, but there can be no doubt that there had been dubious passages in its history beforehand, or that, in 1944, de Gaulle and not Thorez took power: perhaps because the general had read Trotsky, or at least 'Malaparte', more carefully than had the communists.[3]

Though the communists were busy and effective resisters, neither were they first in the field, nor did they dominate it anywhere except in a few particular areas: the 'red belt' of factories round Paris, where they organized some telling strikes, and some maquis zones controlled by the military wing of the Front National, the *Francs-Tireurs et Partisans*.[4] Another, contrasting body of comparable importance to resistance consisted of senior civil servants, in central and local government, who ran a movement with the untranslatable title of *Noyautage de l'Administration Publique* (NAP), intended to rot the vichyste régime right through with resisters who would take over control of civil life at the appropriate military moment.

NAP was only one of a score of important movements of resistance, some of them like the Paris group centred on the Musée de l'Homme dating right back to the late summer of 1940. The internal problem was, how to coordinate their efforts; the external one, to arm them as necessary and to give their efforts a strategic point. It will be clear already to the reader that French resistance was highly politicized, as one might expect in so sophisticated a nation; it will also be clear that everything depended on timing. As time passed, the régimes of occupation and of Vichy that ninety-nine Frenchmen and Frenchwomen out of a hundred had accepted in July 1940 became less and less bearable, till by July 1944 those figures were not far off being reversed.

In between, an extraordinary effort of double fusion had succeeded: most resisters had combined, and almost all had agreed to accept as their leader Charles de Gaulle.

[1] See J. L. Vigier in Henri Noguères and others, *Histoire de la Résistance en France* (4 v 1967–76), i. 447–51: an awkward book for me to cite, since swathes of it are paraphrased without acknowledgement from *SOE in France*.

[2] Noguères, i. 410, puts 'Barbarossa' on 21 June and Churchill's offer of support to Stalin on 23 June; 22 June is the correct date for both.

[3] See p. 253 below.

[4] See Charles Tillon, *FTP* (1962), an excellent if prejudiced account by their commander-in-chief.

The main architect of this fusion was his first delegate-general to enter France, Jean Moulin. Hundreds of thousands of visitors to Chartres have seen his monument there, a great clenched fist holding a broken sword; fewer know his story, which bears a moment's recall.[1] He entered resistance early; during the war in Spain, while in the French air ministry, he caught a subordinate smuggling an aircraft to the nationalists, and as the price of his silence, made the wretched man smuggle a dozen to the republicans.[2]

In 1939 Moulin, at Chartres, was at the age of forty the youngest prefect in France; and there he quarrelled with the Germans next summer. They wanted him to blame some atrocities on the wrong people; he refused, and tried (on 17 June) to cut his throat; soon after, he was dismissed, and retired to Provence. He rapidly got into touch with the main movements in south-east France, which were called *Liberte, Libération nationale,* and *Libération*; the first two fused late in 1941 into a group called *Combat.* By then Moulin, a man of resource, had organized his own journey to London to put their views before de Gaulle.[3]

He might have supplanted the general; instead, he gave him total loyalty. He was parachuted back into France on new year's day 1942, with a wireless operator, and spent almost all the following eighteen months there: travelling, arguing, cajoling, persuading. By March 1943 he had persuaded the non-communist groupings in the formerly unoccupied zone to unite in the *Mouvements Unis de Résistance.* Two months later, with the help of Dewavrin, Brossolette and Yeo-Thomas, who came over by parachute to join him, he secured a national link-up: a *Conseil National de la Résistance* which fused politicians, trade unionists, churchmen, soldiers, and anti-politicians into a single national body, pledged to evict both Hitler and Pétain and to bring in de Gaulle. He took the chair at the CNR's first meeting, at 48 rue de Four in Paris on 27 May 1943; in six weeks' time he was dead.

He attended another large meeting at Caluire, a suburb of Lyons, on 21 June; it was held in a doctor's house, with every possible clandestine precaution but one – there was no way out at the back. The Germans became aware, somehow, that the meeting was going on; eight of them arrived, armed, and led the assembled company away. One man ran for it, and escaped wounded; to run into much trouble and suspicion later. Moulin's identity eventually emerged, possibly from himself; he gave nothing else away at all, and, horribly tortured, died in German hands. Neither the exact place, nor the exact date, nor the exact cause of his death are known; nor is it even quite certain that the ashes now buried in the Panthéon under his name are his. What is quite certain, is that he earned his place among France's national heroes.

Several attempts to rescue him failed. One of his youngest companions, Raymond Aubrac, was rescued instead, from a Lyons hospital, by a particularly

---

[1] Henri Michel, *Jean Moulin l'unificateur* (2 ed. 1971).
[2] Conversation with his sister, 1967.
[3] See his report of October 1941, in SOE translation, in Foot, 489–98.

daring *coup*; in which Madame Aubrac took part, tommy-gun in hand. A Lysander brought them both out of France a few weeks later; she went into labour on the journey, and had her baby at Tangmere.

The Caluire arrests dislocated the whole gaullist system for concerting the actions of resistance. Moulin's successors *ad interim* lacked his experience and his capacity. Brossolette and Yeo-Thomas had to undertake another mission to France to sort the resulting difficulties out. One was accidentally arrested, the other was caught while trying to arrange a rescue. Brossolette jumped out of a fifth-floor window, to make sure he did not talk under torture; Yeo-Thomas brought off the hardly less gallant feat of an eventual escape from Buchenwald. The gaullists listened at last to repeated British counsels about the need for decentralization, and in the spring of 1944 organized resistance through regional military delegates (DMRs), a dozen of whom were on the spot, in touch with London and Algiers, with plenty of arms ready stocked, when invasion came.

Political action, aiming at an eventual insurrection, has so far preoccupied us; a great deal else was going on as well.

On the side of strictly military intelligence, the British encountered a double shock in the summer of 1940. No one had made contingency plans to cover the complete, immediate military collapse of France; and such few very long-term contacts as MI6 had, were all mopped up as a matter of routine by the *Sicherheitsdienst*, because their names and addresses had been written down by that fool accountant in The Hague.[1]

The Poles had a working intelligence system in France, brought with them in the autumn of 1939, and one large and lively circuit under Roman Garby-Czerniawski soon came on the air from Toulouse, and then moved to Paris. It had plenty of naval intelligence, of which the British were in desperate need; unfortunately it also developed touch with the *Abwehr*, which proved fatal to it early in 1942. The Germans were able to use it to deceive the British about the seaworthiness of *Scharnhorst* and *Gneisenau* before London took in how much had gone wrong.[2]

Much more formidable was an eventually huge circuit called 'Alliance', set up by an extreme right-winger almost as soon as France fell. The catastrophe of defeat left almost everybody stunned: if one has known from early childhood that one's country has the world's most splendid military tradition, it is inconceivable that it can be beaten in a six weeks' campaign; and when the inconceivable happens, it takes time to get used to it. But Georges Loustaunau-Lacau ('Navarre') was not stunned: he buckled down to work.

The intelligence branches of the Vichy armed forces continued, from force of habit, to amass intelligence; but they pigeon-holed it all. It would be most improper to pass it on to any foreign power.

[1] p. 136 above.
[2] See Garby-Czerniawski, *The Big Network* and M-L. Carré, *I Was the Cat* (both 1961).

Loustaunau-Lacau soon changed that: he made use of his widespread friendships to ferret out this excellent information, went to Lisbon, and met there Kenneth Cohen (Dewavrin's 'Commander Clam'), head of the French section of MI6. They rapidly came to terms. Loustaunau-Lacau was soon arrested (he survived the war); his secretary Marie-Madeleine Fourcade, who had been doing much of the donkey-work already, simply took the circuit over. It had, eventually, some three thousand contributing members; of whom nearly 500 were killed. They knew each other by the names of beasts and birds: hence the Germans' name for the circuit, which Madame Fourcade adopted as the title of her account of it: *Noah's Ark*.[1]

A service like this, run by fanatical friends who knew and trusted each other, was far more productive than what the odd visiting agent could produce. MI6 nevertheless sent a few visiting agents, from August 1940 onwards; it is always as well to check and double-check every report, if time and chance allow.[2]

The French stayed well in front of the British, in this intelligence field. Dewavrin was sending people over to France even before MI6 was; such as his friend the huge Maurice Duclos ('Saint-Jacques') – on no account confuse him with Jacques Duclos, Thorez' deputy in charge of the PCF: 'Saint-Jacques', like 'Navarre', had been on the far French right before the war. His first mission, to Normandy in August 1940, communicated by carrier pigeon.

Another body, almost as large as 'Noah's Ark', was Renault-Roulier ('Rémy')'s 'Confrérie de Notre-Dame'. As its title suggests its head and many of its members had strong religious leanings; no bad equipment for work against so aggressively pagan a system as Hitler's, or in conditions of danger and difficulty in which one sometimes needed a miracle, and always needed faith, to survive. 'Rémy's' own accounts of his friends' work are fresh, clear, and lively;[3] and a well-known English supplement describes an accidental yet brilliant by-product, the detailed plans for Hitler's Atlantic wall, which were in London before a single post on it had yet been built.[4]

There were incessant alarums, excursions, dangers, difficulties for all the people working in these and similar circuits; not least over cipher. London and Algiers often felt the people in the field were being wilfully obtuse, or impossibly rash; in the field, people often thought the staffs in London and Algiers idle or obscurantist or both; the work went ahead all the same.

And some work of exceptional quality was being done by the French in France, unprompted by London or Algiers; with some results quite as striking as the Atlantic wall affair.

---

[1] 1973. The original French version, *L'Arche de Noé* (1968), includes the roll of honour.
[2] 419 Flight, 1419 Flight, and 138 and 161 Squadron operational record books; Hugh Verity's impending book on pick-up operations.
[3] Eg. *The Silent Company* (1948), *Courage and Fear* (1950), *Ten Steps to Hope* (1960).
[4] Richard Collier, *Ten Thousand Eyes* (1958). I can testify to the invaluable nature of these plans, of which I used a well-thumbed copy when helping at CCO's headquarters to plan raids on the Channel coast.

Consider the case of 'source K'. French postal workers welcomed the Germans sourly; nevertheless, as part of Vichy's plan of submissive collaboration, they found themselves providing long-distance telephone facilities. These included two large coaxial cables from Paris, one via Metz and the other via Strasbourg, which went through ultimately to the main German defence headquarters in Potsdam and Berlin. The cables were under particularly heavy guard; every French operator had an armed German at his elbow. Yet from the autumn of 1940 a group of linesmen under an engineer called Keller worked on the problem of interception; and in April 1942, by a combination of technical skill and luck, they succeeded in tapping the Paris–Metz cable at Noisy-le-Grand, near Paris. They took down every word said on it till December; when, a fortnight after they had broken in to the other cable as well, they were caught in the act.[1] Almost all of them were killed; but meanwhile they had passed on a vast amount of material of the highest quality.

They sent their material to Vichy; where Gustave Bertrand collected it, and passed it on by wireless to London.[2] Bertrand had been in French army intelligence for many years, and was currently in charge of an even more astonishing body of intelligence, called 'source Z'.

During the 1930s, as he had discovered from a secret defector in a German cipher department, the Germans had gone over from one-time-pad to a machine cipher, a variant on the commercial 'Enigma', which they believed to be unbreakable.[3] The Poles succeeded, by sheer mathematical genius, in breaking this cipher and imitating the machine, and in July 1939 presented two copies – one each – to Bertrand and to his British opposite number, 'Dilly' Knox.[4] The Germans, it turned out, had just changed their coding wheels; but there was plenty for skilled cryptographers to work on, and by the turn of 1939–40 Bertrand's team at least was able to read much of the traffic it heard. All through the Battle of France, indeed, the French high command was supplied with an enormous quantity of information, including the entire German land and air order of battle and a mass of tactical data: with what lack of result, is notorious.

Bertrand managed to hide, in a château in Provence, with a team of thirty cryptographers – half of them Poles, and a quarter of them Spaniards – and to remain at work. In March 1941 he went to Lisbon, where his friend Bill Dunderdale of MI6 gave him a transmitter; the Vichy diplomatic courier took it back to France for him. Thenceforward he could let London know what his team found out; on a condition, imposed by a Vichy chief still smarting from Mers-el-Kebir, that he passed nothing 'operational'.[5]

In November 1942 the Germans closed in on his château. He sent his team out to England by Spain – a few were sold to the Germans by intermediaries on the way, but most ended up at GCCS where they were invaluable. Bertrand himself

---

[1] Noguères, i. 215–17, ii. 414–15, iii. 123–5.   [2] See his *Enigma* (1972), 128–9.
[3] Ibid. 20–33.   [4] See p. 292 below.
[5] Bertrand, *Enigma*, 110–11.

tried to continue resistance work; was arrested; found himself staying with Delfanne ('Masuy'), the chief collaborationist torturer in Paris; and was able to escape, to hide for six months, and to be brought to England by Lysander in early June 1944, with his wife, through a plan made by 'Jade Amicol', then MI6's largest circuit in the Paris area.

It may have been worth spending a little time on General Bertrand's story, for it is important as well as unfamiliar: it illustrates the professional capacity of the French intelligence services, even when working under a degree of strain that few people, in or out of uniform, could endure for long.

Enough of intelligence: let us turn to escape.

Thousands of escapers and evaders were left behind in France when the British expeditionary force was rescued from Dunkirk. Some settled down quietly on farms and learned French, some were recaptured; most of the rest found their way to Marseilles. There, a few hid, most were nominally interned in a fort but could wander where they liked by day; and two determined Scotsmen set to to get them away. Donald Caskie, formerly pastor of the Scots Kirk in Paris, ran a seamen's mission near the harbour which succoured hundreds of strays,[1] and Ian Garrow, a Seaforth Highlander who had evaded from St Valéry, looked after the business of moving them on.

Garrow did not look in the least French, was half a head taller than those round him, and did not speak French well. The Vichy and German police took for granted that Caskie and Garrow were front men, acting for some secret service agent of such skill that they could get no other evidence of his presence:[2] in fact the two Scots were following where their consciences and their abilities led. Garrow's calm courage impressed everyone he met, and he gradually built up an efficient route through Perpignan to Barcelona; no doubt, though the sources are not quite explicit on this, working through Pareyre.[3]

In the spring of 1942 Garrow received a powerful reinforcement: the Belgian doctor Albert Guérisse ('Pat O'Leary'), who got left behind by accident on an operation *Fidelity* conducted for SOE, passed himself off as a Canadian trying to evade, got quickly out of an internment camp, and set up the 'Pat' escape line, which handled over six hundred passengers in a year.[4] The main trouble about the 'Pat' line was that most of its leading members knew each other well, they all trusted each other, and it was therefore only too easy for the Germans to penetrate it. A subsidiary difficulty was lack of prompt communications: not till July 1942 did 'Pat' receive MI9's first wireless operator in the field, and it took several months' more experience to awaken high authorities outside MI9 to the value of clandestine W/T for this purpose.[5]

'Pat' was also in touch with Harold Cole ('Paul'), one of the secret war's

[1] See his *The Tartan Pimpernel* (1957).
[2] So Langley was told by the security head of the Marseilles police, when the latter came to England in 1942: *Fight Another Day*, 104.
[3] Neave, 79.     [4] Vincent Brome, *The Way Back* (1957), unofficial but exciting.
[5] Neave, 86–7.

shadier characters, who had a police record as a con man; showed great gallantry and ingenuity in the early days of escape; changed sides; sent some fifty helpers to their deaths; and was in the end shot himself in Paris, while resisting arrest, in the autumn of 1945.[1] Too many dubious sub-agents, and too much activity for perfect safety, cost Guérisse his liberty in March 1943, at the hands of another double agent. He survived over two years' imprisonment, much of it in concentration camps; his thirty-two decorations include a George Cross.

A separate, equally fearless escape line organizer, who worked on a smaller scale, was Mary Lindell, Comtesse de Milleville; who habitually travelled in red cross uniform, wearing English medals in front of French ones which she had earned in the war of 1914. Her principal weapon was the air of command that sits naturally on upper-class Englishwomen; when she told German or French officials to do things for her, their instinctive reaction was to do them. Reports of her methods used to make Neave's flesh creep on his scalp; but they worked. It was she for example who got 'Blondie' Hasler away after 'Frankton', his successful canoe-born limpet raid on shipping at Bordeaux; at their first meeting, bringing her own nail-scissors for him to cut off his moustache before she would let him go out of doors. Hasler, exceptionally, had been given a hint about how to get in touch with her line; as a rule, MI9 kept its agents' locations a deadly secret. Not even Ravensbrück could terrify her; she saved several companions' lives there, and still lives in Paris.[2]

In parallel with such main escape lines as these and as 'Comet', which will be touched on in the next section, there were a number of smaller and supposedly more secret lines, run by SOE for the benefit of its agents. One of these, 'Farrier', an air line worked by Déricourt between the central Loire valley and Tangmere, carried over a hundred passengers; and turned out, long afterwards, to have been managed in consultation with the SD, who sent French gangsters to watch most operations and to attempt (usually without success) to follow the incoming passengers.[3] The others were more secure, but not so busy.

One large SOE line, called 'Vic' after Victor Gerson its commander, ran for two years from Brussels to Barcelona via Paris, Lyons, and Perpignan, carrying in the spring of 1944 up to a passenger a day. Gerson had been meticulously trained by Leslie Humphreys, section D's expert in escape and clandestine technique; made seven secret missions into France himself; and still lives quietly at his flat in the rue de Lisbonne, which the Germans (who had discovered his real identity) repeatedly searched without avail: he kept clear of it during the war.[4] Many of his helpers were Jews, who were brave enough to stay and see the war through on territory where both the occupying and the local

---

[1] Neave, 82–5, 97–102, 307–11.
[2] Ibid. chs. xv and xvi; B. Wynne, *No Drums . . . No Trumpets* (1961).
[3] Foot, 289–307.
[4] Thérèse Mitrani ('Denise'), *Service d'Evasion* (1946), includes some telling details. Others in Foot, 94–100.

régimes were anti-semitic.[1] Their Jewishness was in one way a positive advantage for secret work, because it gave them a sense of privacy, of being in a group apart; and thus helped to keep them from boasting about what they were doing for resistance. His line – or lines, rather; he kept three available in parallel – were securely enough run to survive two penetrations by the Gestapo (as a spill-off from 'North Pole', SOE's troubles in Holland) without disastrous casualties. Another line, called 'Var', ran in 1943–4 between Paris and London via the coasts of Brittany and Cornwall with comparable smoothness and low rate of casualty.[2]

Everyone was anxious to avoid in France in 1944 what Langley frankly calls the fiasco of Italy in 1943, when seven-eighths of the prisoners in enemy hands failed to get away. A joint Anglo-American force called IS9 was set up, to look after the interrogating and repatriating of escapers and evaders in the 'Overlord' area (if they were not interrogated, the Germans might try and slip some agents in among them; and those who were not really evaders, but deserters who had changed their minds, might reap unfair advantages). IS9 went farther: it tried to establish camp areas, near Rennes, north of Vendôme, and in the Ardennes, to which escape lines could direct their passengers, who could lie up there till their camps were overrun. In the event, the Belgian Jean de Blommaert ('Rutland') looked after over 150 escapers and evaders in the Forêt de Freteval near Vendôme. Neave took charge in person of the rescue expedition, when the battle turned fluid in the second half of August; Langley, one of the first British officers to re-enter Paris in uniform, was not far away.[3]

Whatever the relations were between MI6 and MI9 – neither Neave nor Langley is quite explicit about this in print – 6 could presumably call on 9, or even instruct 9, to move its agents to and fro when necessary.

Relations between MI6 and OSS were strained, to start with at least; 6, Sir Claude Dansey in particular, taking an attitude the Americans can hardly have failed to find offensive, treating them as brash and ignorant newcomers, while OSS felt that they had quite as much to contribute as an organization which had been left at the post, as MI6 had been in June 1940.[4]

By the spring of 1944, these early resentments had worn off and intelligent cooperation was well established. At 'Rémy's' suggestion, MI6 and OSS joined with the BRAL (the London link of de Gaulle's secret services, by now centred on Algiers) to form two- and three-man teams called 'Sussex' parties, whose task was to provide tactical intelligence from the impending and actual battle area.[5] Some fifty of these teams were spread out, from May 1944 onward, in a great arc from Brussels to Rennes; all were supposed to have working transmitters and to report frequently.

They were able to reinforce London's already extensive knowledge about the

[1] See Paxton, *Vichy France*, 173–85, for a depressing record.
[2] Details in Foot, 69–73.
[3] Neave, part vi; Langley, ch. xiv.     [4] See Harris Smith's rather oddly titled ch. vi.
[5] See Rémy, *Les Mains Jointes* (1948), 127–30.

ski-shaped sites in Normandy and Picardy from which the Germans launched in mid-June their attacks on London by pilotless aircraft (VI). This knowledge had been built up in part from air photographs, in part from agents' reports from other areas; the indispensable elements in it had come from a French circuit called 'Agir'. Michel Hollard, the originator of 'Agir' – like Radó a virtually self-taught natural clandestine – had by this time begun his tour in Himmler's concentration camps, which by a miracle he survived; his circuit's work, his own above all, earned him the title of 'the man who saved London'.[1]

To close this section, we need a word on subversion: a subject well to the fore in the mother country of the great revolution of 1789. As was noted above,[2] there were more than a thousand separate clandestine newspapers in circulation, at one time or another, in France between the late summer of 1940 and September 1944. They covered most conceivable aspects of anti-nazi feeling, from a wide variety of standpoints. There is a thorough and useful analysis of them, from a politico-literary angle of sight, in print already, to which we need do no more than refer the interested reader.[3] Historians of French politics need to weigh the varied impact of various newspapers; a problem beside our present purpose. The point we need to take is that the combined weight of the clandestine press and of the various programmes broadcast into France from abroad – particularly 'Les Français parlent aux Français' from London – had by the summer of 1944 created strength enough of anti-nazi and pro-gaullist feeling, all over France, to sustain a mild national uprising from mid-August till the Germans' withdrawal was all but complete in mid-September.[4]

How was this uprising articulated?

It had been among SOE's main aims from the start: much of the war revolved round the question of who was to control France, a cardinal question in English strategy ever since England emerged from the heptarchy. Unfortunately the high command of SOE was far too busy ever to be able to concentrate on the French problem for long; and as often happens in large organizations matters of real importance sometimes got overshadowed by points of office politics and even personal pique that seemed no doubt vital at the time, but cannot help looking ludicrous, at best, in retrospect.

SOE had not one country section working into France, but six. DF the escape section, whose 'Vic' and 'Var' lines were described just now, AMF the branch of ISSU6 that worked from Algiers, and EU/P which worked in intense secrecy among the half-million Poles who lived in France, can be put on one side.[5] So can the 'Jedburgh' parties, SOE's equivalent to 'Sussex', international

[1] See the biography of him, *Agent Extraordinary*, by George Martelli (1960; republished with the title in the text, 1963).
[2] p. 136.  [3] C. Bellanger, *Presse clandestine 1940–1944* (1961).
[4] Not quite complete: some of the Biscay coast ports held out till 9 May 1945.
[5] One operation in which AMF cooperated is worth a footnote at least: the liberation of Corsica (20 September–4 October 1943). Gubbins's son took part in this action, and was killed at Anzio soon afterwards. (Another son survives.)

teams of three, 93 of which operated as local stiffeners of fighting resistance in June–September 1944. The other two, called F and RF, need more than a few words' explanation.

F section, amalgamated from MIR's and section D's experts in France when SOE was founded, was first commanded by Humphreys; then, for nearly a year from December 1940, by H. R. Marriott, formerly Courtaulds' man in Paris; and for the rest of the war by Maurice Buckmaster, who came from the publicity side of Ford's.[1] Its existence was for a time concealed from de Gaulle, some of whose entourage were regarded by the British as insecure: he was furious when he found out that it was at work, and he continually took the line that no one had the right to operate into France without consulting himself first. F section was not anti-gaullist; it was not pro-gaullist either. It was an independent body, seeking at first to inquire what the subversive possibilities in France were; de Gaulle's primacy, after all, only emerged slowly, and up to about midsummer 1943 was far from secure.

Many of F's agents became his ardent supporters, and did more to bring him control of France than he ever cared to admit. All RF's agents were his supporters from the start, and took as well that oath to him personally that so much affronted Mengin's republicanism.[2] RF section of SOE was a sort of administrative hyphen, connecting de Gaulle's secret services to SOE and to the special duty squadrons. No one ever spelled out precisely where the division of duties between it and the BCRA, or later the BRAL, lay; the officers at GSO2–GSO3 level who did the actual work of getting parties off to France knew and liked each other, and a sound enough system resulted.

There was rivalry between F and RF staffs, and even occasionally between their agents in France;[3] no worse, no better, than the rivalry between SOE and SIS, OSS and FBI, GRU and NKVD; better at least than that rivalry between Himmler's *Sicherheitsdienst* and Canaris's *Abwehr*. By the summer of 1944 F and RF had come to understand their common interests, and all worked together in a multi-national staff commanded by General Koenig: the *Etat-major des forces françaises de l'intérieur*, EMFFI. Even then, F's intelligence officer, Vera Atkins, stayed behind in Baker Street to keep an eye on the personal files of Buckmaster's agents; lest political or personal enemies made trouble.[4]

Let us try to get away from these staff perplexities to what was actually done in France: an equally perplexing subject, and one to which many specialized scholarly studies have been devoted. Pre-eminent among them is the collection

[1] People still sometimes describe Thomas Cadett, long the BBC's excellent Paris correspondent, as once head of F section. SOE's files do not bear this out: cp. Foot, 20, 179.
[2] R. Mengin, *No Laurels for de Gaulle* (1967), 115–21.
[3] The story that the head of one section ordered the shooting (which never took place) of a leading agent of the other – the principal witness for which is long dead – is, the witness's widow assures me, a pure fiction. (Conversation in 1975.)
[4] Foot, 32–3, 47.

edited by Henri Michel, called 'Esprit de la Résistance', among which three volumes deserve particular mention: his own book on strands of political thought, for a wealth of insight into feeling, René Hostache on the CNR for the institutional framework, and Paul Durand on the railways for a practical exposé of what could be done.[1]

Arms from the armistice army were often enough promised, but hardly ever available when it came to the point. Under SOE's arrangements, the British, and from January 1944 the American, air forces sent in arms by parachute instead: a total of perhaps half a million weapons, of which – perhaps, again – about three-fifths were in useful hands at the critical period, July–August 1944. At this stage the USAAF made some big drops by day.[2]

Their distribution, as dangerous and complicated a business as their storage, was effected through a wide variety of networks and movements. F section floundered at first. It had trouble finding agents; and the first one it sent to France by air, in November 1940, was brave enough to refuse to jump. What set the section up was the work of the three de Vomécourt brothers, Jean (whom the Germans killed), Pierre, and Philippe. Pierre got embrangled with the Polish intelligence circuit of dubious affiliation we have already met,[3] and spent the second half of the war in Colditz; Philippe survived to lead an important circuit in central France, and to write a colourful war autobiography.[4] Between them, the three had shown by the autumn of 1941 that circuits depending ultimately on the British general staff for orders were feasible. In the next three years, F section's agents managed some ninety different circuits, ranging in size from the purely notional quarter-million of 'Carte' – the mirage of 1942 that dazzled Buckmaster, Bodington his brave and wayward second-in-command, and many more senior people who might have known better – to the half-dozen or so trained agents and their friends of some tiny circuits that never got started at all.[5] Fifty F circuits were still at work when the Allied armies overran them in France. About half of these were fairly newly formed, but in many cases the new formations had been put together by people who had themselves been active in resistance since the early days.

F section's failure with the illusory 'Carte' in 1942 was followed by the 'Prosper' disaster in 1943, when too many agents congregated in Paris in defiance of their orders, and fell into the hands of the SD: partly because their air movements officer, Déricourt, allowed the Germans to read their inadequately coded correspondence; partly because they inherited some points of contact from 'Carte', such

---

[1] H. Michel, *Les courants de pensée dans la résistance* (1962), R. Hostache, *Le conseil national de la résistance* (1958), and P. Durand, *La SNCF pendant la guerre* (1969); all Presses Universitaires de France.
[2] See Foot, 470–7.                                                    [3] p. 241 above.
[4] *Who Lived to See the Day* (1961).
[5] 'Carte' inspired a great many people outside F section too: cp. Guillain de Bénouville, *Le sacrifice du matin* (1946), passim, and A. Gillois, *Histoire secrète des Français a Londres* (1973), 146–64, for examples.

as the Tambour sisters;[1] partly because they formed a sort of dining club, eating excellent black market meals and talking English together: riding for a fall.[2] The wireless expert of the SD's IVF section, Jozef Götz, succeeded in bluffing F section, through played-back wirelesses, into dropping eighteen agents smack into the Germans' hands in the spring of 1944.[3] There has been some fuss in print about this, some of it deserved; it was a mistake, and a bad mistake, on F section's part, but it was not a catastrophe. Was it not Turenne who said, the general who has made no mistakes has commanded in remarkably few battles?

It is necessary to look at this wireless game in its proper proportions. The wireless game in Holland, as we shall soon see,[4] was all but fatal to SOE's work there; for a time, it absorbed almost all N section's effort, to no avail at all. The French wireless games caught fewer than a twentieth of F section's 400-odd agents dispatched, who in turn were less numerous than those sent by RF. Even if all the people arrested in the wireless games in France had been people of outstanding capacity – which was not the case – they represented something under two per cent of SOE's effort into that country. People can still be sad and angry about it; but within measure.

And F section did learn from its mistakes. All the wireless game howlers were compressed into two short periods, one in the late summer of 1943 when by a stroke of luck the Germans got an entire bogus circuit set up in Lorraine, to which the British trustfully dropped arms and money through the winter; and one in the early spring of 1944, when they started to drop men as well, till an S-phone operation to an unmistakably German accent brought them to their senses. By the time of the amalgamation, with RF, into the EMFFI, they had numerous well-found and secure circuits: such as Tony Brooks's small but deadly efficient 'Pimento', which controlled the main railway lines southward from Lyons and northward from Toulouse; Seailles' 'Farmer', which exasperated railway authorities round Lille; Claude de Baissac's 'Scientist' in southern Normandy, or Sevenet's 'Detective', which armed an important maquis in the Montagne Noire between Castres and Carcassonne.[5]

The strain involved for some of the agents was severe. Maurice Southgate, who ran a large F circuit ('Stationer') south of the main Loire bend, recalled long afterwards that the effort of receiving and passing on, clandestinely, twenty-seven fellow agents by the April moon had been almost too much; and that his first reaction on being accidentally arrested was, '*at last I can sleep*'.[6] His circuit was quietly taken over, divided into two, and run with high combatant efficiency, by Maingard, his wireless operator, and Pearl Witherington, one of

---

[1] Photographs in *Simone et ses compagnons* (1947), 121–2, a memorial to Simone Seailles of F's 'Farmer' circuit.
[2] Foot, ch. x.
[3] Ibid., and 368.
[4] pp. 264–7 below.
[5] The *Journal de Marche du corps franc de la Montagne Noire* (Albi 1963) repays study.
[6] Conversation with him, 1968.

his couriers: she had a private army nearly 3,000 strong in the northern half of the Indre.[1]

Beside the British-run circuits and the gaullists, there were two other large fighting bodies on the side of resistance: the communists and the Poles. The communists dominated the FTP, whose commander Charles Tillon has written an interesting – if, necessarily, a biassed – account of their work.[2] They pursued, as communists like to do, a double aim – based perhaps on the principles of the fork and the skewer, as they apply on the chess-board: both the aim of getting the nazis out of France, and the aim of pinning as many of them down there as possible, in order to relieve pressure on the USSR. The last-mentioned line of reasoning may help to account for the communists' tendency, here as elsewhere, to press on with a policy of assassination without bothering overmuch about reprisals.

The Poles were much more painfully conscious of the danger of reprisals, and took endless trouble about security: no one in the fields of resistance can regard Poles as amateurs. They had two large networks in France, 'Nurmi' round St Etienne and Lyons, and 'Monica' round Lille, both of which passed a good deal of information – 'Monica', like 'Agir', was exceptionally useful on the V1 – and prepared innumerable sabotages.[3] There was an efficient Polish secret army, with its own espionage, counter-espionage, and escape links laid on for it by Zdrojewski ('Daniel'); it lacked only the opportunity to fight. Care about reprisals delayed any unleashing-signal from London until the Polish-occupied areas were about to be overrun.

One party of a hundred Poles, codenamed 'Bardsea', provides an interesting example of administrative friction. They had been trained à point in Britain as underground fighters, parachutists, saboteurs; they were to reinforce 'Monica' as 'Jedburghs' reinforced resistance movements all over France. The London Poles, determined they should not be wasted, got an undertaking that 'Bardsea' would only go to areas likely to be overrun within two days; not understanding that mounting such an operation – getting the men, the stores, the maps, the parachutes, the target details, to the right place at the right time – took almost three days. So Lille fell into Allied hands while 'Bardsea' were still near Peterborough; and an attempt to divert them to Warsaw failed as well.[4]

The French were more successful than the Poles – in the very short run – in their pursuit of the mirage of the national redoubt. The injection of many giraudist staff officers onto gaullist staffs in the winter of 1943–4 strengthened the hold of this conventional idea. Many efforts were bent towards creating one, or several, among the maquis – groups who had taken to the hills and were living rough there, to escape forced labour service in Germany. As early as March 1944

---

[1] See Georgette Guéguen-Dreyfus, *Résistance Indre et Vallée du Cher* (Montluçon 1970), another leading example of the detailed local histories available in many parts of France.
[2] *FTP* (1962).
[3] Conversations with Generals Kukiel, 1968, and Zdrojewski, 1969.      [4] Foot, 400.

the maquis on the Glières plateau in Savoy, of which the members regarded themselves as liberated already, was broken up by a set-piece attack by several thousand troops. A party of fifty Spaniards on a hillock held out literally to the last man and the last round: magnificent, but not irregular war. Members of the *milice* who joined in the attack, and were captured by the maquisards, later pointed out to the Germans those who had saved their lives: a touch of jungle life in what used to regard itself as the world's most civilized country. A muddle about an order from Algiers produced a still bloodier disaster in the Vercors south-east of Grenoble, in July: again, a large German force overwhelmed the area, and troops who would have done better tactically to withdraw held on, in the vain hope of sparing their womenfolk rape and massacre.

A similar disaster, at Montmouchet in the Massif Central, was mitigated by a regular British officer, Freddie Cardozo, who was there with an EMFFI mission called 'Benjoin'. He persuaded the maquisards, after a couple of days' battue – in which nevertheless they inflicted, as well as receiving, severe casualties – to scatter, hide, re-form, and re-emerge a month later. In the end they liberated Clermont-Ferrand. Sevenet, and Despaigne his wireless operator, who took over when a Ju 88 killed him in action, had a similar success with their *corps franc* near Castres; getting their people to ground without the casualties that have made Montmouchet notorious, and then bringing them out again.

The SAS party in Brittany also persuaded the Bretons not to congregate, not to set themselves up as free until they really were. SAS worked, over most of northern France, as an invaluable stiffening to resistance; a party of ninety of them in the Vosges distracted an entire SS division from the main battle. Four jeep-loads of them once took on a German force 3,000 strong, near Chalons-sur-Saone; all but two of the SAS were killed, but they took 400 Germans with them.

SAS worked directly, if at several removes, under the orders of Eisenhower, the supreme commander of 'Overlord'. Practically, resisters of all kinds were by midsummer 1944 all more or less working in the same direction: even Stalin wanted 'Overlord' to succeed, because if it did his own task on the eastern front would be made that much more easy. There is a delicate and difficult calculation, waiting to be made one day, about the degree of tactical help that resistance provided for 'Overlord's' advance: through the total disruption of the French and Belgian railway systems (950 rail cuts in France on the night of 5/6 June 1944, the night of 'Neptune'), the dislocation of long-distance telephones, and the perpetual ambushes on the roads. The Germans came to feel they no longer controlled their own lines of communication: unsettling.

'Dragoon' was still more visibly helped by resistance, in two disparate ways. Small but vital parties of French naval officers were put into Marseilles, Toulon, and Sète to preserve the port installations which the Germans wanted to blow up: Marseilles harbour was too big for five men to manage, but they baffled German plans to block the other two ports, and thus made supply for 'Dragoon' much more feasible.

A still more important role was played by the mountain maquis, prepared for this task by RF's 'Union' mission under Fourcaud and Thackthwaite and by F section's 'Jockey' circuit under Francis Cammaerts. 'Dragoon' planners had reckoned on reaching Grenoble by D+90. The commander was persuaded to risk a few American armoured cars on the mountain road from Nice through Digne and Gap; and Grenoble surrendered to them and their maquis guides on D+7. This turned the Germans' left flank in the Rhone valley and levered them out of all southern and western France.

By this time every French town of any size wanted to liberate itself, and many did so.[1] Parisians believed they ought to have an insurrection; café-conversationalist resisters, there as in Athens, had been gossiping about one for years. One did take place: after a fashion. More French people were killed in the Paris rising than had been killed at Valmy. And yet – and yet: more than thirty years after the event, the historian may be allowed a note of faint scepticism. The barricades the Parisians built were not tank-proof. The Germans had tanks; but hardly used them. The title of liberator of Paris is given, by political acclaim, to Colonel Rol-Tanguy, the communist, or to Alexandre Parodi, the gaullist leader on the spot, according to the giver's political leanings; or to Leclerc, the commander of the French armoured division of which some troops entered the city on 24 August 1944. The man who really has a stronger claim to have liberated Paris is General von Choltitz, the German commander there: who disobeyed his orders to set the city on fire, because – in spite of what he had done at Rotterdam and Sebastopol – he had some instincts of humanity, could not bear to destroy anything so lovely, and knew the war was lost.[2]

Even before Choltitz surrendered, gaullist agents had taken over some of the essential key points in Paris, such as the Hôtel Matignon, the prime minister's official residence, occupied by Yvon Morandat (who had been trained in clandestinity by Philby, during Philby's spell with SOE[3]), or the minister of the interior's room in the Place Beauvau, held by Lazare Racheline, once a pillar of the 'Vic' line. The NAP's arrangements worked very smoothly. In many parts of France, young men and women of the MMLA arrived in towns before the fighting was quite over, went to the mairie and the post office, and secured the stocks of unissued ration cards: the real levers of civil power in a wartime society. The gaullists had made a special study of the seizure of power, and secured it without much trouble.

[1] P. Bertaux, *La libération de Toulouse*, in a series edited by Michel, is gently scathing on this point: as a rule, as in Toulouse, the resisters arrived after most of the Germans had gone.

[2] Adrien Dansette, *Histoire de la libération de Paris* (1946, constantly revised) remains the leading account. (I have used the 67th ed., 1966.) L. Collins and D. Lapierre, *Is Paris Burning?* (1965), add some recollections.

[3] Conversation with Morandat, 1969. And see *Times* obituary, 11 November, 18h, and 15 November 1972, 19g.

The communists made no difficulties: they seem to have been told not to. Stalin, in Taylor's view at least, did not want communists in power out of his own reach, and instructed Thorez to hold the PCF in check.[1] The excuse Thorez gave later, that the Americans would promptly have put down a communist rising astride their lines of communication, was probably true as well.

There was a greater danger from sheer anarchy. Where the gaullists' MMLA did not penetrate, or even where they had not the force of personality to impress themselves in the name of the State on a riotous population, people did for a while just what they chose; drank a lot, slept around, danced in the fields and the streets, paid off old scores. About one in a thousand of the whole population vanished: executed, with or without trial, in a liberationist purge. Emmanuel d'Astier, supposedly a minister, has left a splendidly vivid account of a momentarily ungovernable corner of the Ardèche.[2]

Yet the war was not over, after all; and the iron hand of government closed, by late October, even on areas as remote and joyous as that.

## Belgium

Belgium is by European standards a comparatively recent state; it broke off in 1830 from the kingdom of the Netherlands. The area, heavily industrialized and densely populated by 1940 in its north-western half, and with excellent communications, was only too used to foreign occupiers. Prolonged spells under Spanish and Austrian dominion gave way to the revolutionary French, then to the counter-revolutionary Dutch. Seventy-five years after Belgium's independence had been placed under international guarantee, the German breach of that guarantee brought the British into the great war of 1914; and for over four years most of Belgium had been in German hands.

The Belgians in fact had been here before, well within living memory, and began at once a series of well-drilled responses; in a few cases, the same individuals could pick up precisely the same tasks, and do them again. The clandestine press, abundant in 1914–18,[3] again became abundant and influential; though this took time.[4] The shock of a swift defeat in eighteen days' fighting in May 1940 was severe; there was a great deal of confusion – nearly two million refugees thronged the roads; rumours of betrayal and fifth-column activity were rife; and a few strata of the population did not look on the Germans' arrival with abhorrence. The Flemish national party (VNV) positively welcomed it; so did the Rexists, the small fascist party created by Léon Degrelle in Walloon – that is, French-speaking – Belgium. The Waffen-SS secured 3,500 recruits in Flemish Belgium; about as many more were in various auxiliary units, some of which

[1] A. J. P. Taylor, *Second World War* (1975), 205.
[2] *Seven Times Seven Days* (1958), 179–81.
[3] See for example Jean Massart, *La Presse Clandestine dans la Belgique occupée* (1917).
[4] Ninety-five journals started in 1940; though they only produced 20,000 copies between them, *selon* G. de Lovinfosse, *Au Service de leurs majestés* (Brussels 1974), 132.

had severe casualties on the Russian front. The proportion of the population was tiny: under 1 per cent in some 8,400,000.[1]

There was much more activity on the side of resistance: even if as usual the neutrals heavily outnumbered the combatants on both sides put together.

Walthère Dewé, for example, who had run a highly successful intelligence circuit called 'La Dame Blanche' in the previous war, set up another called 'Clarence' which was soon in contact with the Belgian government-in-exile in London and with MI6. Wireless operators were parachuted in, and for the second half of 1943 the circuit could communicate by S-phone also, from the neighbourhood of Ghent, to a special duties aircraft.[2] Dewé, a particularly ardent catholic patriot, resisted quite as much for religious as for patriotic motives; knew and welcomed the dangers of his work; and expected the martyrdom he received on 14 January 1944. Trying to escape from a party who had arrested him in Ixelles, he was shot down in the street; an officer stood over his body and prevented a passing friar from giving absolution. St Peter will hardly have needed to delay Dewé at heaven's gate; he was by all accounts an unusually saintly man.[3]

'Clarence' may have been the best, it was certainly not the only large intelligence circuit working from Belgium. It specialized in railway information; as Belgium lay athwart the main railway connexions between the north-west German ports and the U-boat bases on the Biscay coast, much of its news was invaluable in London. But there were awkwardnesses about handling information there.

King Leopold III had stayed in Belgium with his army, when he ordered it to surrender; while telling his ministers to go to London and run the legitimate government-in-exile from there. He took no part in Belgian government or administration, save for an unfortunate attempt in November 1940 to get Hitler to do something about the food problem. The fact of his journey to Berchtesgaden became known; its object did not; hence much suspicion and misunderstanding. His ministry reached London piecemeal, during the autumn of 1940; not all of its members rose to the crisis they had to face.[4] For the second half of the occupation, from the autumn of 1942 to the summer of 1944, it ran its secret business through two separate departments. The ministry of defence, headed by Pierlot who was also prime minister, included a 2[e] section under Bernard (and then under Marissal, when Bernard went on his second mission), which handled military resistance in Belgium, in frequent touch with SOE's T section. The ministry of justice under Delfosse dealt simultaneously with T section on points of civil resistance, and handled also relations with PWE, MI9, and MI6.[5] This

---

[1] Littlejohn, *Patriotic Traitors*, 156, 160-1.
[2] Henri Bernard, *Un géant de la Résistance, Walthère Dewé* (Brussels 1971), 168.
[3] Ibid. 205. His circuit's archives for both wars are now in the Imperial War Museum in London.
[4] Lovinfosse, op. cit., 65-90, handles them with barely concealed contempt.
[5] Organogram ibid. 141.

provided ample opportunity for treading on the wrong people's toes. Lepage, Bernard and Marissal's opposite number under Delfosse, was fortunately a man of equal energy, capacity, and tact. He dealt in MI6 with Dansey; in MI9 with Neave or Langley; and in SOE successively with Claude Knight and with Hardy Amies, the dress designer, who succeeded Knight after the Belgians, in a fit of pique, broke off relations with SOE (temporarily) in August 1942.[1]

These squabbles look all the more petty in the light of the event that is supposed by the half-learned to be *the* event of resistance in Belgium: an event of which, as is common with newspaper sensations, the importance has been exaggerated out of all connexion with reality. It was Brussels that provided the occasional headquarters for a big GRU circuit, run by Leopold Trepper ('Gilbert') and known by the Gestapo as *Rote Kapelle*, usually translated 'Red Orchestra'.[2] Trepper, a Polish Jew by origin, almost as much a dyed-in-the-wool communist as Radó, was an extremely competent organizer, short of competent wireless operators and a trifle short of luck. He ran a group of rather junior agents in Berlin, whom we shall meet again later;[3] they were not highly enough placed to tell him the sort of things his Russian masters wanted to know, about German order of battle and intentions. In Belgium, Holland, France he accumulated extensive networks of agents, who were able to tell the soviet authorities a lot about the order of battle and equipment of the German forces in the west: points only of peripheral interest in the Russians' struggle for survival. They would have been intensely interesting to the British and Americans, who were going to have to fight in western Europe; not one identification, not one word of the data provided by Trepper was ever passed to the British by the Russians, who though they had signed a treaty of alliance[4] behaved rather as co-belligerents than as allies. The circuit was unravelled by a combination of decipher, goniometry, and straightforward police work; when arrested, most people talked. Trepper himself arrived at a wireless operator's house during a raid, passed himself off as a harmless commercial traveller, and walked away; was caught later; and walked away again. Like Radó, he surrendered to the Russians after the war;[5] both survived a long spell in prison, and are still alive.

More astounding, if less notorious, adventures took place in the 'Comet' escape line, which ran from Brussels through Paris and Bayonne to Bilbao and Gibraltar. The forty-odd miles of Belgian coastline became, next to the Maginot line, about the most heavily fortified area in the world; sea escapes were not to be thought of.[6] A twenty-four-year-old schoolmaster's daughter, Andrée de Jongh

[1] Organogram ibid. 145–9.

[2] Heinz Höhne, *Codeword: Direktor* (1970, tr. R. H. Barry 1971), supersedes all the rest.

[3] p. 303 below.                                        [4] *BFSP* cxliv. 1038.

[5] Radó escaped, in Cairo, on his way to Moscow; and was traced, recaptured, and handed over by the British security authorities.

[6] Nevertheless two Royal Marine Commando privates, the only survivors of a small raid near Gravelines on Christmas eve 1943, turned up five months later in one of Heslop

('Dédée'), was undeterred by dangers of any kind, and seemed to have an inexhaustible fund of physical energy as well as moral fervour. She turned up at the Bilbao consulate in August 1941 with a British soldier and two young Belgians, and said that if she could have some money for their fares, she could provide a regular supply. The 'Comet' line ran for three years, and carried over 700 people; sustained by the fervour of the de Jonghs and their friends far more than by secret service funds or methods. They moved the line's headquarters from Brussels to Paris in May 1942; Jean Greindl ('Nemo') undertook the Belgian end of it. In the spring of 1943, he and the de Jonghs and many of their helpers were betrayed and arrested; Andrée de Jongh survived her concentration camp, and now works in a leper hospital in Addis Ababa.[1]

This carried on Edith Cavell's tradition of 1914–15 with glorious devotion. There were several other less ardent, and less readily penetrable, lines from Belgium into Spain, such as Lovinfosse's 'Woodchuck' which he ran from Bernard's mother's country house near Châteauroux. One of their main tasks, in which virtually the whole population of Belgium joined if chance offered, was that of hiding Jews.

There were elaborate arrangements as well for articulating an uprising by a secret army, prepared over several years from the wreck of the army of 1940, and stiffened by SOE-trained agents and missions from England. We do not need to linger over these arrangements; the course of battle in the main war rendered most of them unnecessary. The Allied armies raced across Belgium in September 1944 even faster than the German army had done in May 1940: almost the whole country was freed in a matter of days. One main task for the maquis was to try to keep delirious crowds in enough order for fighting men and supplies to get forward towards the enemy.[2]

The other main task was that of 'counter-scorching': keeping the Germans from demolishing too much as they retreated. Here again the speed of the Allied advance was a great help; the Germans did not have time to do as much damage as they might have liked. The Belgians had already made some impromptu experiments in urban guerilla,[3] and in Antwerp they were able to make an exceptional contribution to the war.[4] Elaborate arrangements had been made by the Germans to destroy the port installations; almost all of which were frus-

---

('Xavier')'s maquis in the Ain; having walked there, armed and in uniform, and knowing no French. (Personal knowledge: I had briefed them for the raid, and had to help identify them from afar.)

[1] Langley, *Fight Another Day*, 165–71; Rémy, *Réseau Comète* (3 v 1966–9); Neave, part iii; Cecile Jouan, *Comète* (Furne, 1948).

[2] See Foot, 423, for an account of how a resister of long standing was saved from execution by a former colleague in Spain.

[3] H. Bernard, *Un maquis dans la ville* (Brussels 1970), describes in detail the clandestine organizations in Schaerbeek, the north-eastern quarter of Brussels.

[4] Details in H. Bernard, *Guerre totale et guerre révolutionnaire* (3 v, Brussels 1962–5), iii. 72–96.

trated, by a combination of bravery, intelligence, and engineering skill. Long before Montgomery had cleared the mouth of the Scheldt, this great port was ready to supply his army.

And swiftly though, in the end, Belgium had been overrun, its resistance effort had not been made on the cheap. 17,000 people were killed in action, or executed, or died in concentration camps, because they had been or were suspected of having been Belgian resisters:[1] over twice as many as had put on German uniform.

### Luxembourg

The grand duchy of Luxembourg, supposedly the site of the strongest fortress in Europe after Gibraltar, was guaranteed neutral in 1839 and 1867;[2] which did not preserve it from German occupation in 1914 or in 1940. The grand duchess escaped to London with her family and her government; leaving behind over 250,000 inhabitants, mostly peasants or metal-workers, almost all Roman catholics, and almost all trilingual in French, German, and Letzeburgesch. They were not many, but there were enough of them to make a mark on resistance history; they no more welcomed the nazis than did any other occupied country. (The Prussian garrison that had held their fortress from 1816 to 1867 had been a quite different and much less inquisitive body.) They did indeed something no other occupied area achieved. Their nazi *Gauleiter*, Simon, announced a plebiscite in favour of the occupation on 10 October 1940: a 97 per cent hostile vote was the result.[3]

Escape lines were promptly and spontaneously set up, to run westward and southward towards freedom. Some young citizens, conscripted into the German army, did what they could to supply information about it to the Allies: a party of nine were shot at Lyons, in February 1944.[4] Four landed in Normandy with the commando brigade on the easternmost beach of 'Neptune'. Ten were successfully trained by SOE and parachuted back into occupied Europe, from among the nearly four hundred Luxemburghers who volunteered to serve after reaching England; most of the others served in the Belgian army. Forty-four members of the maquis bands raised by these SOE agents, and spontaneously on the spot, died in action or in German hands.[5] A few carried out missions for SIS. Among the survivors, one man might be picked out: the broad-shouldered Jules Dominique, a former gendarme. Arrested on suspicion by the Gestapo in September 1942, he escaped, and raised in the Belgian Ardennes a band of 120 freebooters – Belgian, Luxembourg, and Russian by origin; armed them with,

[1] H. Bernard, *La Résistance 1940–1945*, 131.
[2] It gave up neutrality on joining NATO in 1949.
[3] H. Bernard, *Histoire de la résistance européenne* (Verviers 1968), 190.
[4] Henri Koch-Kent, *Sie boten Trotz* (Luxembourg 1974), 333–4; a work to which this section is largely indebted.
[5] Nominal rolls ibid. 248, 393–5, 397–8.

*inter alia,* a heavy machine gun from a crashed American aircraft; and specialized in cleaning out German police detachments.[1]

The grand duchy was liberated in mid-September 1944, apart from a brief irruption of Rundstedt's troops in the Ardennes offensive of December. Luxembourg's recent development as a financial centre of the European community lay ahead; its citizens had worked hard already, and 6,000 of them had been killed.[2]

## The Netherlands

Dr Louis de Jong, the sole member of his family to survive the German occupation, has devoted the thirty years since it ended to compiling a history of the Dutch kingdom during the war; an absolute model, for erudition, insight, and range, of what history should be. It would be impertinent to fail to refer the reader to it; so far it is only available in Dutch, but English, French, and German abbreviated versions are on the way.[3] What follows is largely a summary of those parts of his book that bear on resistance. He would be the first to protest that the history of resistance is a long way from being the whole of the history of the war: quite rightly.[4]

The Netherlands, neutral in the war of 1914, pursued a policy of strict neutrality in the 1930s; extremists, whether of left or of right, were not favoured by the tough and moderate Dutch. Communists and fascists between them secured only 8 per cent of the votes cast in the last general election before the war, in 1937. Government was, as it remains, by constitutional monarchy through a particularly delicate scheme of proportional representation by lists: a scheme so delicate that coalitions are normal, and shifts in their composition almost incessant. Officially, no objection could be taken to the neighbouring nazi régime that seemed abhorrent to most of the Dutch; though there was a small noisy Dutch nazi party, the NSB, under Anton Mussert. Officially also nothing could be, and in hard fact practically nothing was, done in the way of precautionary contact with Britain and France, even after those two powers had declared war on Germany.

MI6, as has already been remarked,[5] ran its north-west European operations from The Hague in peacetime, and saw no reason to make any change when the war began. The Dutch security and intelligence authorities were aware of this; neither providing help, nor raising objections. Unluckily for MI6 the German secret services were aware of it as well. Payne Best, the head of 6's Dutch office, and Stevens, a senior visitor from London, were decoyed in the autumn

---

[1] Ibid. 285–90.         [2] Bernard, as above, 191.

[3] L. de Jong, *Het Koninkrijk der Nederlanden in de tweede wereldoorlog* (The Hague, 8 v in 12 so far out of a projected 10 v, 1969–76). For his personal tragedy see Casterman, s.v Pays-Bas. He now heads the Netherlands institute for research into the history of the war.

[4] See his foreword to W. Warmbrunn, *The Dutch under German Occupation* (Stanford. Calif., 1963).

[5] pp. 136, 234 above.

of 1939 into believing that they were in touch with a quite senior German officer, who was prepared to meet them at the frontier crossing point of Venlo, east of Eindhoven. They went there on 9 November with a subaltern in the Dutch service; and were kidnapped by a handful of SS under Naujocks, the man who had engineered the Gleiwitz incident from which the war formally stemmed.[1] The Dutchman was killed trying to resist the attack.

The Dutch were lucky to escape an immediate German riposte. Payne Best had already provided the Germans he supposed to be his friends with a secret transmitter and a code; which the Dutch broke and read. The Dutch in fact were fully *au courant* with the supposed negotiation: conduct far from neutral. And as if mistakes enough had not already been committed, Stevens had just jotted down on a piece of paper which was captured in his pocket the names of the people he must make sure to get out of Holland.[2] Hitler followed his interrogation closely; it unravelled numerous SIS links in the Netherlands and in Czechoslovakia.[3]

Much worse followed six months later. On 10 May 1940, early in the morning, with no declaration of war, the full weight of the *Wehrmacht* was unleashed on the Netherlands. A cloud of airborne detachments, the updated equivalent of the skirmishers of the peninsular war, operated in advance of the main armoured columns. A parachute company attempted to carry off the queen; her son-in-law Prince Bernhard exchanged pot-shots with them in the palace gardens. She, her immediate family, and her government were brought over to London by the British on the 12th and 13th; and an unobtrusive emissary from section D, M. R. Chidson, removed over a million pounds' worth of industrial diamonds from under the German advance guards' noses in Amsterdam.[4]

The Dutch armed forces fought hard, but were hopelessly outmanœuvred and outgunned. Most of the survivors stopped fighting, by order, on 14 May. A few got away to England. Thousands more refused to hand themselves or their weapons over, and went into hiding: the first of the *onderduikers*, the people who dived under the surface of officially recognized society and spent the war concealed: of whom there were as many as 100,000 by the middle of the war.[5] One *onderduiker* has become world famous: Anne Frank, the German-born schoolgirl, who had lived in the Netherlands since she was four, and was hidden in a house in Amsterdam with seven companions till 1944; when she was found, sent to Belsen, and killed. Her diary is not a book quickly forgotten.[6] Another Jewess's account, shorter but almost as harrowing, deserves to be more widely known: Marga Minco, who was also in hiding, had better luck when her hiding-place was raided, managed to run away down a back lane, and survived.[7]

[1] p. 2 above.   [2] De Jong, op. cit., ii. 106.
[3] Ibid. 110–15.
[4] See his obituary in *Times*, 4 October 1957; and David E. Walker, *Adventure in Diamonds* (1955), for detail.
[5] Bernard, *Résistance européenne*, 217.   [6] Anne Frank, *Het Achterhuis* (1946).
[7] Marga Minco, *Bitter Herbs* (1964).

Dutch feeling was the more inclined to favour the Jews, because well over half the population were protestants, many of them brought up to a strict knowledge of the Bible and so inclined to treat anti-semitism as not merely inhuman, but sacrilegious.[1] Nevertheless, some 105,000 of the 140,000 Jews who lived in the Netherlands in 1940 did not survive the racial policies of the third Reich, which were applied with special severity by Reichskommissar Seyss-Inquart; who had had plenty of practice already as nazi regent in Vienna.

Opinion hardly needed to be mobilized; to sustain it, there was an exceptionally active clandestine press. Printing was one of Holland's largest light industries; there were thousands of small presses and skilled compositors, plenty of paper, and plenty of subjects to write about. On 15 May 1940, the day after the armed forces surrendered, the first illegal news sheet appeared: Bernard IJzerdraat's *Geuzenactie*, which ran for several months. The *Geuzen*, resisters of an earlier time, had taken a notable part in the eighty years' war against Spain (1568–1648) from which Dutch independence derived, and their name was now taken by one of the main paramilitary groups. Among several others were the left-of-centre *Knokploegen*, and two in close touch with the government-in-exile, the right-wing *Ordedienst* and the left-wing *Raad van Verzet* (RVV).

The underground press eventually produced about a thousand separate clandestine newspapers, five more of which are worth particular mention: the calvinist *Trouw*, the communist *De Waarheid*, and the progressive *Parool*, *Vrij Nederland*, and *Je Maintiendrai*.[2] These papers were supplemented by a great many broadsheets and pamphlets, to which the Dutch made an ingenious addition. Their historians, headed – before his arrest in 1941 – by Pieter Geyl, took a sudden interest in republishing documents bearing on the eighty years' war. The occupation authorities, not best pleased with the Spaniards, and aware that the Spaniards were not aryans, were imperceptive enough to allow a lot of this: not realizing that appeals to throw out the old invader would be applied instantly by their readers to the new.[3]

But there was very little prospect of much more than an active clandestine press, and possibly some convulsive mass movement at the moment of an Allied invasion: the hard facts of military geography all told the other way. Such open country as the Netherlands contains is really open – a lot of it *polder*, reclaimed marshland, criss-crossed with dykes, open as the sky. There are no mountains, there is hardly a hill; there are few woods. Round the Rhine estuary there is, there was already in 1940, intense industrial and urban development. Terrain militated against country maquis; time militated against urban guerilla. Van Oorschot, the peacetime intelligence chief – dismissed, hardly before time, after

---

[1] Bernard, *Résistance européene*, 216, points out that the areas where most Jews lived, Amsterdam, Haarlem, and Rotterdam, otherwise had predominantly protestant populations.

[2] Cp. pp. 91–2.

[3] Anna E. C. Simoni, 'Dutch clandestine printing 1940–1945', *The Library*, 5s. xxvii. 1–22 (March 1972), and *Publish and be Free* (1975).

Venlo[1] – had hardly given urban guerilla a thought; nor had section D nor MIR.

Surprisingly – for it was heavily fortified by the Germans – the sea coast of Holland, between the Hook and Den Helder, proved not to be absolutely impermeable. A landing on, or an escape from that strip of straight and level open sand was so improbably brave an action that sentries did not take watching it as seriously as they might have done. Several hundred evaders got safely across to East Anglia from Holland. Whether scores, or even hundreds, of others tried, and were drowned in their canoes or dinghies in the rough North Sea, no one now knows.[2]

A few successful sea crossings were made, in both directions, by Dutch intelligence agents with British naval help;[3] some of them positively melodramatic in their details. One man escaped arrest by lurching past a sentry, singing loudly and reeking of cognac; he had taken the precaution of putting on a white tie and tails before he set out, unconventional wear for his real purpose but effective cover.[4] The main intelligence difficulty, as always, was communication: there were several spontaneous Dutch circuits which assembled a good deal of information about the occupying forces but had no means of transmitting it to London.

MI6's prearranged agents were all cleaned up at the start. Most had called, at one time or another, at the office in The Hague and had been photographed by the Germans from the opposite bank of the *gracht*; and the office accountant had fled, leaving two trunks full of paper including notes of everything he had paid out, and when, and to whom.[5] As Mrs Gladstone would have said, 'Than which'.

Almost as severe a comment is earned by the conduct of an early MI6 wireless operator, a twenty-year-old naval officer called Zomer who was dropped in June 1941. When direction finders closed in on his transmitter on the last day of August 1941, they captured not only him and it, but about a hundred past messages, some both in code and in clear; from which Ernst May, the Germans' cipher expert, could rapidly reconstruct the coding system. Zomer succeeded, by disguising his 'fist', in alerting London to the fact that his set had been captured; Van 't Sant, the Dutch head of intelligence in exile, and Rabagliatti (Cordeaux's predecessor as head of the Dutch section of MI6) were not deceived. May did better next time.

Schrage, the twenty-four-year-old police inspector who had dropped with

---

[1] De Jong, op. cit., ii. 114.
[2] Account of a typical success, preceded by a failure, in Pieter Dourlein, *Inside North Pole* (1953), 20–38.
[3] See chart in front endpapers of E. Hazelhoff Roelfzema *Soldaat van Oranje '40–'45* (The Hague), the war autobiography of an agent who later flew 72 Mosquito pathfinder sorties over Germany, and ended the war as aide-de-camp to Queen Wilhelmina (I owe this reference to Dr A. Bijnen of Breda).
[4] De Jong, op. cit., v (ii). 900.　　　　　　　　　　　　　[5] Ibid. iii. 161.

Zomer and had provided him with most of the information he sent, nevertheless persevered in collecting more; ran into Sporre of SOE, probably a family friend, who was dropped on 9 September; and tried to return with him in mid-November in a flimsy canoe. Both were drowned. Zomer was shot later.[1]

Later in the war MI6 and the exiled intelligence staff were able to retrieve such early failures, and to work with several effective intelligence circuits; aided by the stubborn patriotism of such Dutchmen as Hazelhoff Roelfzema, indeed of the great majority of the Dutch population. The Germans tried to treat the Dutch as favoured nordic cousins; the Dutch were not interested in the least. They had one simple, splendid way of showing this: when a uniformed German entered a bar, all the Dutch present quietly drank up and left.

There was a notable example of the force of popular approval for resistance in February 1941, when the Germans effected their first serious turn of the screw against the Dutch Jews. NSB parties marched through the Amsterdam ghetto, hoping to provoke incidents; they succeeded, at a price in casualties. Several other street scuffles had fatal results. When further restrictions on the Jews were announced, and 400 Jewish men and children were beaten up in public and taken away to a concentration camp, the communist party called for a protest; and on 25–26 February there was a general strike in Amsterdam, which spread to several neighbouring towns. For a moment, vast crowds singing the national anthem felt themselves free from the nazis. German military reaction was prompt; the Dutch police, who sympathized strongly with the strikers, dispersed them gently before there was a massacre.[2]

Almost simultaneously, the dismissal of Jewish professors in the universities was ordered. In Leyden and Delft, professors and students struck, and Seyss-Inquart closed the universities; they remained closed for several weeks. Nevertheless, there was a small but strong Dutch nazi counter-current; and, as in France, as indeed in all occupied countries, there were a fair number of people who were tempted into acting as *V-Männer*, trusties, for the occupying power.

For a year, the Dutch scene was confused by a new party, *Nederlandse Unie* (Netherlands Union), intended as a counterpart to the Vichy régime in France; but without any of Vichy's real if limited political power. A million people joined it, because it was not German. The Germans dissolved it when it proved less than enthusiastic for the attack on Russia, and from 14 December 1941 the NSB was the only party allowed in the country. Mussert helped to organize a Netherlands Legion which fought on the Leningrad front in 1942–3, and played some part in the internal running of his own state through a group of ten leading NSB officials; three of whom were assassinated by resisters, with nearly forty

[1] Ibid. v (ii). 891–3, 1118, 969. Ab Homburg, Sporre's organizer, got away by hiding in an IJmuiden trawler, and forcing its crew at revolver's point to take him to England. His brother Piet, trying to repeat the *coup*, was arrested; with nine companions.

[2] B. A. Sijes, *De Februaristaking* (1954); conversation with Rector Brugmans, a participant, 1974.

other NSB notables, during the year 1943. The legion's survivors, and some 3,000 fresh recruits, were formed into an SS armoured brigade, which fought partisans in Croatia late in 1943 and then went back to the eastern front. All told, some 30,000 Dutchmen entered various kinds of German military service.[1]

The *V-Männer*, not included in these figures, were more dangerous to the resisters' main forces in the Netherlands. As de Jong says,[2] there is little point in speculating on their motives; their depredations were many, and incompetence in London made some of them far-reaching. We can see how if we examine SOE's work into Holland, which provided that service's one major catastrophe.

Its N section, successively commanded by Majors Blunt and Bingham, worked in constant cooperation with a small exiled group under M. R. de Bruijne, a marine lieutenant-colonel who had previously been in the east Indies; it was called the Office for preparing the Return[3] – of Queen Wilhelmina. Both N section and de Bruijne's office were gentlemanly in their approach to war. On some points they were exceedingly thorough; on others, not. They provided their agents sent to Holland, for example, with carefully tailored clothes, bearing no English labels; but absolutely identical (size apart), even to the ties.[4] They provided them also with forged identity cards; with carefully chosen details, but of the wrong colour, and with both supporters of the royal arms facing the same way.

Every secret service dreams of taking over some of the other side's operators, and using their sets, or better still themselves, against the enemy. A combination of skill on the German side, luck, and faulty staff work in London enabled the *Abwehr* and the SD – operating for once fairly smoothly together – to do this in the Netherlands in 1942–3. Giskes, the *Abwehr* colonel in charge of the case, called it 'Nordpol' – 'North Pole'; his SD opposite number, Schreieder, called it the 'Englandspiel', the match against England. Each has written an account;[5] and there was an extensive Dutch parliamentary inquiry in 1949, before which survivors and some SOE staff officers were able to testify.

'North Pole' worked partly because Giskes, Schreieder, and May were clever; partly because of obtuseness in London. On 6 March 1942 a routine goniometry operation pinpointed in The Hague, in a suburban block, the set of H. M. G. Lauwers, an SOE wireless operator who had been dropped exactly four months earlier with his organizer, Thijs Taconis. Lauwers was warned by his protection team, and strolled away; the woman from whose flat he had been working dropped the set out of the window, she supposed into a clump of rose-bushes. But it stuck on the washing line of the flat below; and Lauwers was quickly caught.

---

[1] Littlejohn, *Patriotic Traitors*, 83–129, puts the figure as high as 50,000.

[2] Op. cit. v (ii). 877–8.

[3] *Bureau Voorbereiding Terugkeer*. De Bruijne later moved across to succeed Van 't Sant as head of Dutch intelligence in exile.

[4] Forceful examples in de Jong, v (ii). 914–15.

[5] H. J. Giskes, *London calling North Pole* (Kimber 1953); Joseph Schreieder, *Das war das Englandspiel* (Munich 1950).

Unknown to himself, he had been for some time under watch by the *Abwehr*; through the agency of a *V-Mann*, Ridderhof. He had committed a solitary fault: he had still got in his pocket, when arrested, the already enciphered texts for the three messages he had been about to transmit. He did not know that these in turn had been planted on him via Ridderhof, and was sharply disconcerted when a German seemed able to decipher one quickly. (The Germans had discovered the current coding system from a captured MI6 agent, van der Reyden, who was so shattered at being given away by a colleague that he at once started to talk: May did the rest.) Lauwers was still more disconcerted when he discovered that Taconis had been arrested, three days after himself. He agreed to continue to operate his set to London; confident that London would notice he had left his security check out.

London did not; and from what de Jong rightly calls 'this one capital blunder' protracted troubles followed.[1]

At that time MI6 was still handling SOE's signal and cipher business.[2] The signals clerks did not fail to mark Lauwers' message appropriately; N section ignored the marks. This quite often happened, in the sections that mistrusted the whole security check system, as many did;[3] people felt they knew their friends the agents, who had no doubt been under too much strain – poor brave fellows – to remember; and neither N section nor de Bruijne's Bureau had been sophisticated enough to agree in advance on occasional test questions that might be sent to agents, as a further check.[4] And the passing of messages round via MI6 introduced a little delay. So Lauwers could fancy some accident had caused his first message to be overlooked, when the Germans read him the reply: he and Taconis were to prepare a reception committee for another agent, who duly arrived soon after. The newcomer, Baatsen ('Abor'), was so appalled to find himself handcuffed by his reception committee and taken straight to Gestapo interrogation, that he produced a flood of information; with the help of which the Germans undermined in turn the confidence of his successors.

The process was cumulative; more and more newcomers were more and more informative. A few remembered what they had learned at Beaulieu, and tried at least to prevaricate; others did not. Lauwers, at risk to himself, thrice – under the Germans' noses – transmitted the group CAUGHT as part of a supposedly cipher message; no one in London noticed.[5] He and his cellmate Jordaan, another wireless operator caught on 3 May through another *V-Mann*, van der Waals, smuggled out of their jail a letter to London with a barn code warning in it; by a misunderstanding in Holland, it never got delivered.[6] N section was even foolish enough to remind Jordaan's set, 'You ought to use your security checks': a howler as bad as a notorious one of F section's, and with proportionately much worse

---

[1] De Jong, v (ii). 920, tr.     [2] Cp. Foot, 104.
[3] Eg. ibid. 107, a message from a (then) perfectly safe F section agent containing no checks at all.
[4] Cp. pp. 106–7 above.     [5] Giskes, op. cit., 192–4.
[6] Ibid. 194–6; also in Lauwers' postscript to Giskes' book.

consequences. F section had, at a bad moment, repeatedly reminded operators who were in fact in enemy hands to use both their checks; with unhappy results.[1]

In the Netherlands the results were worse than unhappy: they were disastrous. N section managed to get 51 agents of their own and one of MI9's straight into the hands of German security, between March 1942 and May 1943; during which time they did virtually no other useful work at all. Five escaped; a very few others survived.[2] By May 1943, N section's repeated requests for someone to come back and report, via a contact house of the 'Vic' line in Brussels and one of Déricourt's Lysanders, did produce a sort of response. A German agent travelled down one of 'Vic's lines, and appeared to be arrested in Paris; four more turned up in the autumn, and got as far as the Pyrenean foothills before another fake arrest; there were several real casualties in 'Vic's' line as a result.[3]

The basic trouble was that the brightest people in SOE were too much preoccupied with other things, or with their own immediate work – whatever it was – even to observe that there was danger in N section's habit of sending repeated parties through a single clandestine channel of entry, with no independent check. Nelson, Hambro, Gubbins – all three executive heads in turn while 'North Pole' raged – were, like their Council members, too remote from what went on at country section level to be able or indeed willing to interfere. Country sections were necessarily more or less autonomous. D/R, Robin Brook, had a supervisory interest in N section from directly above it; the bulk of his attention was necessarily taken up with France, where there were always a myriad of problems. It was to him that MI6 confided their fears that all might not be well with SOE in Holland[4] ('all accusations are self-accusations'[5]); and he who eventually brought N section to its senses. Why, one cannot help wondering, was no use made of the S-phone? Too much flak?

Two of the five agents who escaped, Pieter Dourlein and J. B. Ubbink, got clean away to Switzerland, by skill and daring and lavish help from friends; were welcomed by the Dutch military attaché in Berne; sent on clandestinely through France and Spain; and given a chill welcome in London, where they found themselves held in Brixton prison till 'Neptune' had safely been launched. Messages from Holland – originating, it is now clear, from the Germans – had indicated that they had gone over to the Gestapo. All the thanks Dourlein got, in the short run, was to be reduced in rank from sergeant to corporal, as his special mission was over.[6]

The Germans had told their prisoners that they had an agent in London: a deft interrogator's trick, and a tale that people caught in this particular horrible trap could only too easily believe. The tale had no real basis: London's fault was

[1] Foot, 329–30.
[2] Nominal roll in Schreieder, *Englandspiel*, 401–2.
[3] Details in Foot, 312–14, 326–8.
[4] Conversation with him, 1965.
[5] Conversation with W. F. d'E. Anderson, 1966.
[6] Dourlein, op. cit., 167; but cp. ibid. 205–6 for a handsome retribution.

not treachery, it was dumbness, that degree of stupidity against which in Schiller's phrase the gods themselves fight in vain.

The MI9 agent who fell into the 'North Pole' trap deserves a few words to herself. She was Beatrix Terwindt, a quiet, handsome, capable KLM air hostess, who had escaped to London via Belgium and Switzerland and was willing to go back. Neave envisaged her as a sort of Dutch Dédée de Jongh, and thought her strong personality admirable for the running of escape lines from Holland into Belgium. MI6 had, in the winter of 1942-3, no channels for getting her into Holland, having no agents there at all at that time; so Neave turned to SOE. They trained his agent, and took over her dispatch; she left eventually on 13/14 February 1943. She survived the shock of arrest with unusual equanimity; only gave away one point of importance (the address of a man in The Hague); managed to conceal the fact that she worked for a different service from her fellow prisoners; and survived three days' and nights' continuous interrogation, and over two years in concentration camps.[1] In spite of promises to the contrary, made in the Netherlands and overruled from Berlin, 46 of her fellow victims were shot at Mauthausen.

Again, these figures need to be seen in perspective. Over 10,000 Dutchmen and Dutchwomen died at German hands for their part in the resistance struggle.[2] Part of the importance of 'North Pole' lay in the dislocation it caused to Allied plans for creating armed resistance in the Netherlands; though the Germans got much less intelligence out of it than they had hoped. On All Fools' Day 1944 Giskes sent, over the ten sets he still had working, the following message is clear:

> To Messrs Blunt, Bingham & Co., Successors Ltd., London. We understand that you have been endeavouring for some time to do business in Holland without our assistance. We regret this the more since we have acted for so long as your sole representatives in this country, to our mutual satisfaction. Nevertheless we can assure you that, should you be thinking of paying us a visit on the Continent on any extensive scale, we shall give your emissaries the same attention as we have hitherto, and a similarly warm welcome. Hoping to see you.[3]

All that SOE managed to do, in the remaining year or so of the occupation, was to drop in some 30,000 sten guns and a few instructors: not a notably successful record.

SOE, in fact, in Holland holds the wooden spoon among secret services; having managed even less well than MI6. OSS hardly worked there at all; Anton Poelhof, a student in his early twenties, was arrested in February 1945 on its first intelligence mission there, and used in April as one of Himmler's many feelers for a separate peace.[4] The Dutch communists, who sparked off

---

[1] Neave, 205-13.
[2] De Jong in *ERM* i. 149.
[3] Giskes, op. cit., 135.
[4] Harris Smith, 233.

the great February strike in 1941, remained active, but were not numerous.[1] They had some influence in the *Raad van Verzet*, and could provide some intelligence for the Russians.[2]

An interesting raid was carried out by a well-intentioned group in March 1943, on the main civil register in Amsterdam. It was meant to hinder the Germans' search for Jews by destroying the register of births; unluckily the cards concerned were not inflammable enough for the incendiaries used to make much useful mark. Next month there was a great strike, in protest against an order that the Dutchmen who had been taken prisoner in 1940 and released were to go to Germany. The strike covered most of the eastern Netherlands – even the Friesland farmers joined in – and lasted several days. It was forcibly repressed, with 150 deaths; the order was enforced all the same; yet the Dutch remain proud of it as an example of their sturdy desire to be independent, and of their readiness to pay the price.

MI6 eventually, from early 1943, did well in the Netherlands; so did MI9, in spite of the troubles with Beatrix Terwindt. Perhaps as many as 7,000 Dutch citizens escaped, some to England, a few by sea to Sweden, some to Switzerland; compare and contrast the 30,000 French who fled to Spain, or the 50,000 Norwegians – a much larger slice of the population – who made their way to Sweden.[3] So tightly had the kingdom been hemmed in by occupation. But in September 1944 the end seemed near: operation 'Market Garden', the spearhead of the advancing Allied armies, struck at Nijmegen and Arnhem.

The government-in-exile, to help this operation, called for a railway strike which brought the Dutch railways to a standstill. Unhappily liaison arrangements were still somewhat incomplete, and the exiles' fear of reprisals was acute; so though they could set the strikers on, they could not call them off – once out, they stayed out. An internal resistance network supplied the railwaymen, through a network of messengers on bicycles – mainly young girls – with strike pay, including a Christmas bonus; not a florin went astray.

'Market Garden' just failed to carry its last objective, the Arnhem bridge over the Rhine. It is often said that this was because a Dutch resister, Lindemans ('King Kong'), had changed sides, and betrayed the plan to the Germans: an example of how readily people jump to conclusions. Lindemans was an accomplished escape line worker, whose loyalties had been unhinged by his brother's arrest;[4] there is no reason to suppose that he had, or could have had, advance knowledge of the Arnhem drop, though he did know more than he should have done.[5] Moreover Dutch intelligence had provided news of the presence of elements, at least, of two SS armoured divisions in the area; and this was known to the British airborne corps commander concerned. The IO who

---

[1] The Netherlands are not mentioned in Boltin's survey of soviet relations with resistance, *ERM* ii. 3–71.
[2] De Jong, vols. v, vi, vii.
[3] De Jong in *ERM* i. 143.
[4] Cp. p. 97 above.
[5] See Langley, *Fight Another Day*, 226–8.

reported it to him was told he must be overwrought, and should take a few days' leave.[1] The truth was, First Airborne were determined to jump somewhere, and were tired of having successive targets overrun; they went in spite of the intelligence reports.[2] It was just bad luck that a formidable trio of German commanders, Model, Student, and Bittrich, happened to be present in person.

Several hundred airborne troops, many of them wounded, were left in the Arnhem neighbourhood when the battle ended, and provided MI9 with a challenge Neave at once picked up. He already had an efficient line run to Brussels by Dignus Kragt ('Dick'), who had passed out a hundred people since being parachuted blind in June 1943. Kragt, 'Fabian' of the Belgian independent SAS squadron and 'Ham' of MI9 provided him with some chances of communication. When he got to Nijmegen himself, he found a power station telephone circuit in resistance hands that worked from there to Ede, some fifteen miles west of Arnhem; round Ede many parachutists were being hidden by the locals.

Neave and Hugh Fraser of SAS organized two major boating rescue operations across the Waal. 'Pegasus I' on 22/23 October collected 138 men; 'Pegasus II', a month later, only saved seven, because the Germans stumbled on the main body of 120 as they were moving down towards the Waal bank. Kragt hid some thirty more survivors in the marshes of the Biesbos, and brought them over to Fraser in dribs and drabs through the winter; they included Brigadier (later General Sir John) Hackett.[3] Continual minor dramatic incidents, quarrels, misunderstandings could not conceal the grand fact: those of the Dutch who were still under German occupation were by now almost all of them determinedly antinazi.

German reprisals for the continuing railway strike finally brought on famine: in the last, frightful winter 15,000 people died of hunger. The rest survived, on sugar beet, tulip bulbs, and water.

## The British Isles

Of Great Britain almost enough has been said already, particularly in chapter 5; two or three more remarks are all that we need.

Had it not been for the battle of Britain, the only kinds of resistance to nazism that could have had any chance to develop on the continent would have been those, of communist inspiration, that suited soviet Russia. And what the fate of soviet Russia would have been, had the battle of Britain gone the other way, is a question for the speculator rather than for the historian. It was the battle of Britain that let Hitler in for a long war, to which his war-making system was not geared, instead of that series of short wars, *Blitzkriege*, towards which the whole nazi economic system was directed.[4] It was therefore a decisive battle in just the

---

[1] Private information.

[2] Winterbotham, *The Ultra Secret*, 165, points out that there was hardly any 'Ultra intelligence from the area.

[3] Neave, 279–300.      [4] A. S. Milward, *The German War Economy*, passim.

way that the Marne had been decisive in 1914: it did not by itself settle the fate of the war, but it ensured that the war would be long, instead of a German walk-over.

Moreover, had it not been for Churchill's resolute defiance of Hitler, the fate of Europe and of resistance would undoubtedly have been different. Most great men's reputations pass through an eclipse soon after they die; Churchill's is under routine attack while this book is being written. Certainly he made many mistakes; some of them, bad ones, in the field of irregular warfare, for which he had such enthusiasm and about the details of which he was so ignorant. Yet his place in popular memory, that makes men heroes, is as secure as Wellington's or his own ancestor Marlborough's; and every Englishman alive today can say, 'Had it not been for him, I should not now be here.'[1] Much the same debt is owed by many free Europeans, whose freedom he defended in his way.

Britain did provide a *point d'appui* for several governments-in-exile, and air and naval bases important for resistance; and the inestimable services of the BBC; quite apart from the general British contribution to the war, which was far from insignificant.[2]

An embarrassment for an English writer on resistance remains: the Channel Islands. There was virtually no resistance there; the conditions for it did not exist. Most young men left before the Germans arrived; German soldiers comfortably outnumbered the remaining men of military age. With so high a garrison : population ratio, and *nowhere to run away* – the whole group of islands was crawling with concrete and field-grey – resisters had no chance.[3]

Ireland also deserves a word; though for once we do not need to go back to Strongbow's landing in 1169. We do need to touch on the Easter rising of 1916, to which the modern Irish republic dates back its independence; for that dramatic failure, which attracted support from the exiled Lenin,[4] had been prepared in collusion with the German general staff, who used subversion in Ireland as a subsidiary weapon in their struggle with Great Britain in the great war. The links between Berlin and Dublin did not survive the Troubles, as the Irish call them, of 1918–22; or at least did not survive them to any extent that menaced the British empire.

The Irish Republican Army, by that time little more, and little more significant, than an armed gang of city thugs, had shot its bolt in the summer of 1939, in a series of raids on the English midlands that caused some casualties and sent most of its leading men to prison, where they spent the war. It seems likely that the Germans were able, through methods that have never publicly been un-ravelled, to make a few arrangements for the refuelling of U-boats on the wild

---

[1] Cp. H. van Thal ed, *The Prime Ministers*, ii. 311.

[2] Not till July 1944 were more American ground troops engaged than British (Churchill, *Second World War*, ii. 5 [1949]).

[3] See Charles Cruickshank, *The German Occupation of the Channel Islands* (1975), a complete and authoritative survey.

[4] Lenin, *Collected Works* (Moscow 1964), xxii. 357.

west coasts of Ireland: thus aiding their deadliest menace to the survival of Great Britain as a combatant power. Fortunately for the British, who had hampered themselves by giving up in 1938 their naval bases in southern Ireland, this Irish help to U-boats was not extensive.

Probably the Germans got better value out of the daily weather reports they received from their legation in Dublin. This legation stayed open all through the war; it provided the Germans with a good deal of political and a little military intelligence, culled from the London newspapers which were of course available in Dublin on the morning of publication. It also provided the British with a readily available channel for feeding false material to the Germans; used with a good deal of success. Masterman records that the XX committee was able to run agents the Germans sent to Ireland no less comprehensively than it could deal with those on home soil.

## Scandinavia

Only in the fifteenth century, and for a few years on either side of it, were the five countries that form modern Scandinavia – Denmark, Finland, Iceland, Norway, and Sweden – ever united under one political head. They retain some consciousness of common origins, a good deal farther back in time. From about AD 800 to about 1100 the Vikings provided the main driving force in the world west of China, and extended their influence from Vinland to Baku: there were Norse kings of England; Norse dukes of Normandy, who conquered England later; Norse monarchs in Sicily; Norsemen on the Rhine, the Loire, the Rhone, the Volga. Norse predominance faded away, since there was no firm home base to sustain it;[1] yet even after a thousand years, Scandinavians can recall their ancestors' long ships and sharp swords with pride.

The Finns, set apart from the rest by language as well as tradition, as separate a people as the Magyars or the Basques, do not share the long ship memories, but they share the climate – the brilliant northern sun, the long hard winters – the stubborn soil, and the nearness to the Baltic. Iceland, set apart from the Baltic by distance, is in the main stream of Viking tradition, and plays a leading part also in Scandinavian culture, with its literary wealth.

In the war of 1914, only the Finns had taken part, because when it broke out they had been for a century part of the Russian empire; the collapse of which in 1917 gave them their chance to break away into independence. Neutrality and Scandinavia were all but synonyms; no Scandinavian (outside the tiny communist and fascist parties) wanted it otherwise. The next world war disappointed most of their hopes.

Greenland and Iceland, both overseas possessions of Denmark in 1940, are hardly germane to our themes. Greenland, that vast and frozen desolation, provided chances for a few Danes and Americans who had mastered the problems

[1] Cp. A. J. Toynbee, *A Study of History*, ii. 351 (1934).

of Arctic long-distance travel to tangle with the staffs of some German weather stations: there are no doubt personal sagas yet to be written about this, but German weather reporting from Greenland was never quite closed down.[1]

Iceland, occupied successively by the British and the Americans for air staging and convoy protection purposes, declared itself independent of Denmark – by unanimous vote of its parliament, the Althing – in February 1944, and had completed all the formalities of becoming a new state by that June. Its sparse population suffered culturally and economically, but not militarily, from the war; which inflicted a raging inflation. Is this a usual consequence of being occupied by Americans? – but we must return to our narrative. Before we take up the significant work in resistance of Denmark, Norway, and Sweden, Finland needs a few lines.

The Finns are trapped, like the Poles, between larger and stronger neighbours. Sweden's grip relaxed early in the nineteenth century; in the mid-twentieth, the Finns felt themselves grist between the millstones of German and Russian power. On 30 November 1939 they suddenly found themselves attacked by the USSR. To the general astonishment, they held out for over three months: though hopelessly outnumbered and under-armed. Such were the combined impact on the supposedly invincible Red Army of Baltic winter weather and of Stalin's great purge.

Chamberlain, the British prime minister, even conceived the quixotic idea of sending armed help to the Finns. An Anglo-French expeditionary force was prepared; a battalion of British officer volunteers had six weeks' skiing training in the Alps; an RAF Blenheim night fighter squadron was instructed to 'volunteer' to serve in Finland, much as the Condor Legion had 'volunteered' to fight in Spain.[2]

Had this scheme succeeded, it must have driven Germany and the USSR into still closer cooperation; with consequences perhaps fatal to the survival of open societies. Tanner, the Finnish socialist prime minister, a personal enemy of Stalin's, had a stronger grasp of reality than Chamberlain; made three secret trips to Stockholm to negotiate with Mme Kollontay, herself a Finn by origin, an old bolshevik and the soviet envoy there; and secured peace by surrender on 12 March 1940. He accepted his own retirement as part of the price to pacify Stalin.

Marshal Mannerheim, who succeeded him, continued to follow the line of least resistance. He allowed German troops to assemble in Finland before 'Barbarossa'; during that operation, he led Finnish troops in a series of moderate counter-offensives against the USSR; when it was clear that the USSR was going to win, he caused Finland to change sides again. In August 1944 he

---

[1] Cp. p. 27 above.
[2] For a few hours that RAF squadron's aircraft could be seen, from the main London–Oxford road, bearing Finnish national markings: unfortunately enough, a white roundel with a large blue swastika. (*Vidi.*)

became president of the Finnish republic; repudiated his predecessor's undertaking not to make a separate peace; signed terms with Russia, and let Hitler know that any German troops left on Finnish soil after mid-September would be interned. Hitler retaliated by orders to his troops in northern Finland to do as much damage as possible as they withdrew into north Norway; which they did.

## Denmark

The Danes had fought the Prussians, with great gallantry but equal lack of success, in 1864; once in modern times was, they thought, enough. By 1940 their hearts were set on peace, and their forces were hardly more than nominal. On 9 April 1940, after minimal token opposition, they surrendered to an overwhelming German attack.

The Germans took over a going concern: King Christian X remained on his throne; his government – successively under Stauning, Buhl, and Scavenius – remained in office; Danish factories continued to produce, Danish farmers to farm, Danish teachers to teach. Denmark was occupied by Germany, but not at war with her. She was not at war with anybody: the Danes did their best to continue neutral.

This raised a real formal difficulty. In an age when ceremony and protocol counted for more than they do in the mid-1970s, outside the one communist state of the USSR people hesitated to call for resistance activity from anybody, unless the call could be channelled through some proper authority; and all the proper authorities inside Denmark appeared calmly to have accepted the fact of occupation.

Appearance, as so often, belied reality. The king acted as the focal point for his people's beliefs, and it soon became clear that he was no nazi; he remained perfectly correct, and perfectly unfriendly towards the occupier. Riding daily through Copenhagen on horseback, he ignored every German salute; while punctiliously returning his own subjects' greetings.

His ambassador in Washington, Henrik Kauffmann, provided from the start a way round the formal difficulty. On 9 April 1940, on hearing of his government's surrender, he announced that free Denmark continued to exist, and that he regarded himself as its representative. With his encouragement, 90 per cent of the Danish ships outside Danish ports – over a million tons of shipping – took the Allied side. (Two months later, 5 per cent of the French ships outside French ports rose to de Gaulle's appeal to do likewise.) 5,000 Danish sailors were the nucleus of a free Danish combatant movement: never a large one, but including a number of remarkably brave men, such as Anders Lassen, who won a posthumous Victoria Cross with SAS in Italy near the end of the war.[1]

The Danes who stayed in Denmark were offered all sorts of preferential treatment by the nazis. By racial myth, they were (a few Jews apart) impeccably aryan; and the nazis expected them to flock to the swastika, especially when the

[1] Suzanne Lassen, *Anders Lassen VC* (1965), tr. Inge Hack, a life of him by his mother.

war against Russia began. One battalion of Danes was the sole response. The government of the USSR was very slow to forgive either the raising of this battalion, or the captive Danish government's signature of the anti-comintern pact in November 1941; most Danes were in fact firmly anti-nazi, and by long tradition pro-British, though this did not necessarily mean that they were pro-soviet. The ambassador in London, Count Reventlow, hitherto formally neutral, chose this moment to join the free Denmark movement.

On the intelligence side, a group of staff officers in Copenhagen rapidly got in touch through Stockholm with the British, and produced a mass of intelligence, particularly valuable to NID; some of it passed to Sweden by the absurdly simple method of telephone calls. Absurdly simple methods are often best against the unimaginative; the imaginative Germans seem not to have been in Denmark, something of a backwater in the stream of war.

This group, known as the 'Princes', worked for three years, and covered most points of military and police interest – Hans Lunding, a senior police officer, was one of its leading lights. Among its outstanding achievements was the production, in mid-August 1943, of several photographs of the wreck of a VI, which had gone off course during a trial and crash landed, without exploding, on the island of Bornholm, north-east of Peenemünde. To make sure that something so vital got out, the 'Princes' dispatched as many as eight different copies of it: thus multiplying their risks eight times. One of the eight couriers was caught. The Germans knew that only one VI had crashed on Danish soil, knew which Danes had seen the wreck, and arrested them all; none talked. Some of the other couriers got through, providing vital data for British intelligence.

By September 1943 the Danes had worked out for themselves a thoroughly efficient intelligence-collecting system, and an adequate set of safe channels via Stockholm to London. For convenience' sake, SIS left the bulk of the collection and transmission of this material to SOE.[1]

One other intelligence contact is worth reporting, and will lead us from that subject to escape. Niels Bohr, one of the world's leading physicists, was still working unmolested at the Institute of Theoretical Physics in Copenhagen. Sounded out by one of the 'Princes' about whether he would leave, he asked for something in writing. Much to-do with microfilm hidden in a bunch of keys brought him a letter from his friend James Chadwick, of Liverpool University; to whom he sent some important news about German intentions in the nuclear field. When that autumn German measures against Jews in Denmark were intensified, Bohr was persuaded to cross to Sweden in a fishing-boat; his wife and sons followed next day. He was brought over to Scotland, and went on to play an essential part in atomic research in the USA.[2]

[1] J. Haestrup in *ERM* i. 157. His *Kontakt med England 1940–1943* and *Hemmelig Alliance 1943–1945* (2 v; both 1959) will be useful to Danish speakers; they are based on a mass of SOE's papers, accessible in Copenhagen but not in London.
[2] J. O. Thomas, *The Giant-Killers* (1975), 32–7.

The drive against the Jews was a failure. Of 7,000, only 50 were killed; indeed only 800 were arrested. All the rest were either hidden, in the Dutch fashion, or smuggled across to Sweden: not an impossibly difficult journey. 11,000 other Danes made it as well. In a cold midwinter, when the Baltic was frozen, if one had the strength and the courage one could walk: the Sound is in places under four miles across.

Subversion progressed more slowly than intelligence. The British foreign office was worried by the formal problem that Great Britain and Denmark were not at war, and did what it could to inhibit SOE from any sort of precipitate action. Charles Hambro, then head of SOE's Scandinavian department, went to Stockholm in November 1940, and met Ebbe Munck the journalist,[1] whose cover was that he was Stockholm correspondent of *Berlingske Tidende* but whose real task was to forward information from the 'Princes' to the British. Munck besought Hambro to get some sabotage going; Hambro hedged. He sent Ronald Turnbull to Stockholm in February 1941, to act as SOE's link man there; but for another eighteen months there was little activity. Not till the autumn of 1941 was there even a single clandestine newspaper. The 'Princes' pressed for the forming of a secret army that could burst into activity when a main Allied force came near – clearly not for a long time yet; and for no sabotage meanwhile. R. C. Hollingworth, the naval commander who headed SOE's Danish section, was compelled for the time being to accept this policy.

Not till late December 1941 did he send his first pair of agents; of whom the leader, Dr Bruhn, was killed by a faulty parachute. Bruhn's transmitter was destroyed with him, and his companion Mogens Hammer knew little about their mission's aims; he became eventually the link man between the 'Princes' and Ebbe Munck, an instance of how readily people could change roles in the under-ground war – and of how readily penetrable the Danish circuits were.

In spite of its democratic traditions, Denmark had its share of *V-Männer*, just as Holland did. They were not many, but there were enough of them to make the work of active resisters dangerous.[2] The great majority of the Danes were adept at the techniques of the good soldier Šveik: incompetent appearances of amia-bility. How great the majority was appeared in March 1943, when a general election was held. This was a unique event in occupied Europe, an indication by the nazis of how much they trusted the Danes to behave as their model cooper-ative subject people; and of how inaccurate nazi political intelligence was. There was a turn-out of 88·5 per cent, the highest recorded in Danish history. Over 97 per cent of the votes cast were for non-nazi candidates; the nazis' parliamen-tary strength remained at three.[3]

---

[1] Not Kaj Munk, the pastor and poet, whom the Germans shot in 1944.
[2] Examples scattered through David Lampe, *The Savage Canary* (1957), Richard Petrow, *The Bitter Years* (1975), and J. O. Thomas, *The Giant-Killers*.
[3] Cp. p. 258 above.

In such soil, SOE really could not fail to strike roots. (OSS played junior partner; it did not even form a Danish section till January 1944.[1]) The NKVD held back, because of the formal difficulty that Denmark signed the anti-comintern pact – though with a clause inserted in it, that it was to cover internal affairs only.[2] A Danish communist party said to be some 40,000 strong – almost as large as the CPGB of the time, from a much smaller and less industrialized population – was declared illegal at midsummer 1941, and its leading men spent the rest of the war in Danish prisons: also a brake on activity. Its influence was perceptible in a considerable run of strikes in the summer of 1943, which brought on a government crisis.

The Germans suddenly demanded a whole series of repressive measures, which the Danish politicians refused to enact. The cabinet resigned, the king appointed no successors, the whole Danish governmental machine came to a standstill, and on 19 August the Germans took over direct control: whereupon the Danish navy, such as it was, scuttled its ships.

The 'Princes' found it necessary at this point to close down; most of them escaped to Sweden. Most of the remaining intelligence work was organized by one of SOE's most striking acquaintances, the wireless engineer L. R. D. Hansen ('Napkin'). Hansen, having seen and disapproved both an SIS paraset and an SOE B2, invented a transceiver about the size of a Danish telephone directory;[3] and in 1944 improved his invention – because the volume of traffic was more than the available operators could handle – by inventing the precursor of the modern clandestine high-speed transmitter, which increased the speed of sending sevenfold.[4] For some weeks the Gestapo ignored these rapid transmissions, taking for granted that they were too sophisticated for the Danish resistance to have discovered; after all, they had not yet discovered them themselves. They had not met, and therefore seriously underestimated, either Hansen or the vanished 'Princes'.

From now on, SOE could step up its dropping programme, and the business of active Danish resistance burst into flame, conformably with the general course of the war. Some fifty agents, all told, were sent to Denmark, arms for about 25,000 men, and plenty of plastic explosive: a hundredweight of it was once used in a single operation, a main bridge attack in central Copenhagen (the bridge survived, but there was a hearteningly loud bang).[5] In September 1943 the Danes in resistance formed a seven-man, non-party, Freedom Council; one member of which was Flemming Muus, the senior SOE agent in Denmark.[6] Under the Freedom Council's guidance, methodical rail and factory sabotage went ahead, while the supply of information to London continued to flow unchecked, and the remaining Jews were smuggled out of the country.

[1] Petrow, 275.

[2] Haestrup in *ERM* ii. 286.

[3] Photograph in Lampe, *The Savage Canary*, at 141.

[4] Thomas, *The Giant-Killers*, 53–69.

[5] Ibid. 187–91.

[6] See his *The Spark and the Flame* (1956).

On Neptune D-day, 6 June 1944, the Freedom Council called a general strike, to make sure that no reinforcements for the Germans in France could easily leave Denmark. The strike lasted several days, and on the railways was extended for several weeks; earning in the end a special letter of thanks from Eisenhower to Gubbins.[1]

Factory sabotage and intimidation groups were busy as well, by 1944. One of the biggest sabotage groups, of communist inspiration, used SOE's explosives – none were to be got from the NKVD. So many middle-class young men joined the original founders, who had fought in the international brigades in Spain, that one of these hard-bitten older types nicknamed the group, derisively, *Borgerlige Partisaner*, the bourgeois partisans; the name, abbreviated to BOPA, stuck. Another, still larger, group named itself *Holger Danske*, Holger the Dane, after the legendary giant whose statue looms over the dungeon floor of Hamlet's castle at Elsinore: *Holger Danske* did a lot of sabotage, but was only 400 strong. A brigade of nearly 5,000 young men was raised and trained in Sweden in the last winter of the war, with some help from SOE; the Swedes taking care to look the other way. And it was to Swedish ports, by a brilliant improvisation, that the Freedom Council directed all Danish tugs to go and have themselves interned in the spring of 1945; thus bringing the movements of large ships in Danish ports to a stop.

Cooperation between Danish resistance and the main Allied forces were necessarily informal; but none the less effective. The navy, as well as the RAF, helped in the supply of warlike stores.[2] And on two occasions the RAF attacked a Gestapo target pinpointed from inside Denmark: once with brilliant and once with mixed results.

On 31 October 1944 three squadrons of Mosquito bombers made a low-level attack on a line of terrace houses, forming part of the university of Aarhus: they picked out individual houses in the row,[3] burnt up all the Gestapo's files, and had the luck to catch and kill over 150 officers in conference.[4] They had done this sort of thing before: they had raided Amiens prison to try to rescue some resistance leaders in February, and destroyed the Dutch central population registry in April. On 21 March 1945 a smaller force of eighteen Mosquitoes attacked a more difficult target: the Shell offices in central Copenhagen, a six-floor block with prisoners on the topmost floor and Gestapo files and offices in the rest. Twenty-seven prisoners escaped, including two members of the Freedom Council; six were killed. Over a hundred Germans and collaborators were killed; but all the senior staff were away at a colleague's funeral. Worse, an aircraft in the first wave came in so low that it hit a tall pylon, swerved, and crashed into a school: its

[1] Part quoted by Gubbins at the end of his article in *ERM* iii.
[2] John Oram Thomas was a participant.
[3] Photographs, taken during the attack, in Jeremy Bennett, *British Broadcasting and the Danish Resistance Movement* (Cambridge 1966), 33.
[4] Robin Reilly, *The Sixth Floor* (1969), 87–9.

bombs went off: several following aircraft bombed the school by mistake: seventeen adults and eighty-six children were killed. Resisters on the whole were pleased; they looted some arms from the wreck of the Shellus, as well as welcoming back their comrades, and they captured a filing cabinet containing particulars of all the *V-Männer* in Denmark: main base for a series of trials after the war.[1]

At the moment of liberation, there was exuberance, but no trouble: the Danish brigade came over from Sweden, and the king's government picked up the reins as calmly as they had laid them down in 1943: co-opting the Freedom Council into the cabinet (except for Muus, who got into difficulties about some missing funds).

It is a dangerous business generalizing about national character;[2] but in political matters the Danes do seem as a rule, during the war at least, to have preserved the most exemplary and sensible calm. In 1942, SOE invited an eminent conservative, Christmas Møller, and an eminent social democrat to come to London and broadcast. The social democrat refused; Møller accepted. Bennett's book gives a revealing account of his wrestlings with PWE to be allowed to say anything worth saying at all; and of the combined impact of PWE (once converted), SOE, and the BBC on Denmark, culminating in a resistance movement fit to stand comparison, for bravery and effect, with any other.

## Norway

With a population of hardly more than three million people, Norway was not likely in 1940 to add enormously to the combatant strength of either side; but its size and position gave its area great strategic importance, which counteracted the sparseness of its population, and made its territory a prize that both sides coveted: rugged, mountainous, and with poor communications though it was.

The British, intent on stopping the traffic in Swedish iron from Gällivare via Narvik to Germany, mined the Leads, the inshore channel near the Norwegian coast, on 8 April 1940; next day the Germans overtrumped them, and landed – both by parachute and from the sea – at several points. A decent veil is best drawn over the Anglo-French attempts to counter this invasion, attempts so ineffectual that they led to Chamberlain's resignation in May; the Norwegians fought for two months and a day, with no short-term prospect of success, because they could not bear to see their homeland trampled over.

Two aspects of the Norwegian campaign were not wholly disastrous from the Allied point of view. The naval one is well known. And Gubbins was let loose in the mountains with five independent companies, the germ of the future commandos. They included some of the skiers who had been trained for operations in Finland, and other products of MIR's prewar training courses, and managed

---

[1] Robin Reilly, *The Sixth Floor* (1969), 160–201.
[2] See *The Times Literary Supplement*, 27 July 1973, 877.

with local help to snarl up some German communications. No one would claim this was much, but it was something.[1]

The king of Norway, Haakon VII, escaped German air attacks directed at him personally, evaded capture, and was brought out to London by sea with his government. All preferred staying with him to entering captivity, and the troubles about legitimizing resistance in Denmark never arose with her northern neighbour. Denmark never went to war with Germany, Norway never surrendered: the government remained at war with the German government till after Hitler was dead.

Terboven, a pilot in the previous war and a hard-bitten street fighter in the 1920s and early 1930s, was plucked from being *Gauleiter* of Essen to become *Reichskommissar* in Norway. He arrived to find that Vidkun Quisling had proclaimed himself prime minister, in the vacuum left by the king's withdrawal. Quisling he elbowed out of the way, only to bring him back on 1 February 1942 with the title of minister-president and the semblance of power: for the use of which, that unfortunate romantic was executed by his compatriots when the war was over.[2]

The exiled government had two important resources: one physical, Norway's huge merchant fleet, which provided money and to spare for all their needs; and one moral, a vast degree of popular support at home. How was all this goodwill to be organized?

Virtually nothing is known about MI6's arrangements, except that on the naval side the results were excellent, once the fumblings of the late spring of 1940 had been got over. There was a useful coast-watching operation in the Kattegat, and much of NID's best information on German naval movements came from Norwegian sources.[3] Even in April 1940, the department was alert: the night duty officer asked,

> Had the Germans got to Trondheim? It seemed so petty to say I don't know so I picked up the telephone, asked for Continental Trunks and got through in a few minutes to the Vice-Consul there in Trondheim, a naval officer.
>
> 'Any sign of the Germans?' I said breezily. 'Yes,' was the reply. 'I can see the Huns coming up the hill and I've just burned my books.'[4]

6's scientific adviser had got one very useful report from Norway before ever the occupation began: it came from a German defector, during the winter of the

---

[1] One officer in one of these parties, R. B. Redhead – who, like Gubbins, received an immediate gallantry award for his work in Norway – found himself at the tail end of the war at work under Allen Dulles, collecting very senior Germans' signatures to the surrender in Italy (pp. 219–20 above: conversation with him, 1975).

[2] Paul M. Hayes, *Quisling* (1971), 317, the latest moderate study, concludes that he was 'muddled rather than thoroughly corrupted'.

[3] McLachlan, *Room 39*, 52, and passim.

[4] Ibid. 385 quoting (Sir) Ian Campbell.

'phoney war'. He called on the British naval attaché in Oslo, and gave (as it turned out) a highly accurate account of the directions in which he understood German major weapon research to be moving: including mention of large rockets (V2s), rocket-driven glider bombs (V1s), and Peenemünde the projected testing ground for them both. As Jones the adviser said, 'In the few dull moments of the War I used to look up the Oslo report to see what should be coming along next.'[1] This is a good example of how high-level scientific intelligence worked in those days; Norway's connexion with it was the accidental one of providing the spot at which the defector thought it safe to pass the material on.

What happened to him? Perhaps he moved on into Sweden. Escapes into Sweden were far from impossible, except in the depth of winter (the southern-most tip of Norway is north of Aberdeen). One epic escape, Jan Baalsrud's, must surely challenge Cherry-Garrard's epic title of *The Worst Journey in the World*; surviving seven days lying in the open, within the Arctic circle, and without food or drink, must constitute some sort of record.[2] Fifty thousand of his compatriots crossed the same frontier, in less daunting conditions.[3]

Some hundreds escaped by sea; some in their own boats, some by what was affectionately known as the 'Shetland bus': that is, by SOE's private navy, operating from two successive spots in Shetland, Lunna and the village of Scalloway.[4] According to the contribution to the Oxford conference on resistance history, by C. S. Hampton, who had been liaison officer between SOE and Scottish Command in 1944–5, SOE's sea traffic was this:

**Table 3**  SOE'S SEA TRAFFIC WITH NORWAY[5]

| Season | Trips | | Into Norway | | Out of Norway | |
|---|---|---|---|---|---|---|
| | sailed | successfully | agents | stores (tons) | agents | refugees |
| (a) *fishing boats** | | | | | | |
| 1940–1 | 14 | 10 | 15 | — | 18 | 39 |
| 1940–2 | 43 | 30 | 49 | 117·5 | 6 | 56 |
| 1942–3 | 37 | 19 | 20 | 32 | 2 | 14 |
| (b) *submarine-chasers†* | | | | | | |
| 1943–4 | 34 | 22 | 41 | 21 | 13 | 8 |
| 1944–5 | 75 | 72 | 94 | 137·5 | 33 | 235 |

* Eight boats and 50 men lost in the three seasons combined.
† No casualties. Cp. p. 117 above.

[1] Professor R. V. Jones in *RUSIJ*, xcii. 353.
[2] David Howarth, *We Die Alone*; A. Cherry-Garrard, as in text, 2 v (1922).
[3] Michel, *SW*, 110.
[4] David Howarth, *The Shetland Bus* (1951), admirably clear and at the same time discreet.
[5] Based on Hampton's paper in *ERM* iii. 13.

These figures tell a little of their own story: the law of diminishing returns applied to the fishing craft, which were too frail, too slow, too vulnerable both to the enemy and to the weather. The American-built submarine-chasers were far more effective. All were crewed by Norwegians, who worked with base support from SOE and the Royal Navy, and occasionally with RAF air cover.

But in the summer months Norway lay outside effective Halifax range – Lysanders could never get there, and return, at any time of year; this limited air supply effort. The USAAF was prepared to attempt day supply drops to Norway in 1944–5, and lost five aircraft doing so; in such lonely and mountainous country they were less dangerously conspicuous than in somewhere like Belgium. The RAF lost twenty-three aircraft in special duties missions to Norway. The total tonnage delivered by air is uncertain – about 1,000; nearly all of it after 1943. In the spring of 1945, small arms for over 25,000 men were dropped, including 2,250 bren light machine guns, and so were 50,000 lbs of explosives; because by this time resistance was well alight.[1]

There had nevertheless been some starting embarrassments and difficulties. The Norwegians had not foreseen occupation, and had no underground movement prepared; but a large number of officers and men who had served in the army, and survived the two-month campaign – a force quickly numbering some 20,000, reaching 32,000 later – got themselves ready secretly to seize control of their country from the Germans whenever another Allied expeditionary force came near. They called themselves the *Militær Organisasjonen*, Milorg for short; were headed by several senior officers on the general staff; and, through their contacts with the exiled government, had an important difference of opinion with SOE.

Milorg was anxious to do the least that it could, compatible with getting its people together at all; in order to minimize reprisals. Two commando raids on the Lofotens, in March and December 1941, were followed by frightful reprisals against the local fishermen; these strengthened Milorg's opposition to any active measures. The second raid was the less popular among Norwegians everywhere because Martin Linge was killed in a subsidiary operation which he was leading. Before the war he had been an actor; in it he showed such splendid qualities that the group of volunteers from which SOE's agents in Norway was drawn was named after him.

Milorg stuck to its secret, long-term, preparations; calling for an infinite degree of skill and caution, in a largely rural country in which everybody knew everybody else, and it was hard to keep any secret for very long. SOE pressed nevertheless for some degree of activity; and thanks partly to the élan of the volunteers in the Linge company, partly to the strength of personality and common-sensical efficiency of J. S. Wilson, head of its Norwegian section from 1 January 1942, secured it.[2] Rheam indeed, SOE's chief sabotage instructor,

[1] Figures ibid.
[2] Photograph in J. D. Drummond, *But for These Men*, at 48.

looking back in retrospect on all those he had taught, reckoned that for bravery, skill, and quickness to seize a point the Norwegians had been the best of all.[1]

One party of nine men carried out, on 27/28 February 1943, what can reasonably be claimed as the most important act of sabotage on record. Succeeding where a larger party of airborne commandos (whose gliders crashed far off target) had failed, they attacked the Norsk Hydro heavy water plant in a gorge at Vemork, near Rjukan, some 80 miles west of Oslo. With a few well-placed plastic bombs, they destroyed several months' production of heavy water, and incapacitated the plant; a further large stock of heavy water was destroyed, by a separate operation, on its way to Germany.[2]

This operation put paid to the nazis' attempt to secure an atomic bomb. Simultaneous Allied work suggested that the route via heavy water towards a nuclear weapon might in any case be a blind alley. All the same, this raid, so a German expert told R. V. Jones, 'prevented them from doing the vital experiment which might have convinced them that the atomic bomb was possible. As it was, they decided that the bomb was not practicable and so finally did little about it.'[3] Seldom if ever has so modest a *coup* had such far-reaching results.

One other notable aspect of Norwegian resistance deserves record: the triumph of the schoolmasters. An early move by the Quisling régime insisted on a revision of the school history syllabus, to bring it into line with national-socialist thought. Every history school teacher in Norway refused to conform. They were all arrested. Quisling followed this up by an attempt to get all teachers to join a political union; 12,000 out of 14,000 resigned. The schools were closed. About fifty of the prisoners were too old and too frail to stand the treatment accorded them (eg. 500 crammed into a ship with 250 berths, and two water closets), and gave in; the rest did not. After six months, Quisling relented, and the schools re-opened.[4] It is as striking an example, in its quiet way, of what resistance can do as is the Vemork raid.

The combined effect of so resolute a stand by so many of the population against occupation; of a continual run of small coastal raids by commando parties; of SOE-inspired acts of sabotage, also continual; of the looming threat of Milorg; and of the threatened Allied attack from Scotland, one of the major successes of the 'Fortitude' deception plan; was to keep as many as seventeen German divisions in Norway in the summer of 1944, when most of them could have been far more usefully deployed elsewhere. Railway sabotage ensured that they could only be moved away slowly and with difficulty. There were a few Norwegian volunteers for the German armed forces: about 3,000.

[1] Conversation with him, 1968.
[2] Knut Haukelid, *Skis Against the Atom* (1954), a participant's account, with a foreword by Gubbins.
[3] *RUSIJ* xcii. 364.
[4] See Magne Skodvin in Adam Roberts ed, *The Strategy of Civilian Defence* (1967), 136 ff.

And in the spring of 1945, as the Reich collapsed, Milorg's parties were able to play a useful role in protecting power stations, harbour cranes, major bridges from any last-minute German devastation; except in the far north, where the troops who had sacked north Finland were too strong and too experienced. A few score SAS helped Milorg take over the running of the country in May 1945, till the king returned.

### Sweden

The last three sections have already shown what good neighbours the Swedes were, to their fellow Scandinavians: ample aid (short of warlike aid) to the Finns, ample facilities for escapers from Denmark and Norway to arrive without trouble, a blind eye turned to the Danish brigade in training. Sweden, like Switzerland, was another beacon of sanity and civilization, shining steadily on the edge of a world half crazed with war. The Swedes, like the Swiss, assembled their armed forces on a citizen base, in a fashion formidable enough for no one to want to risk attacking them; their territories remained intact.

Though they were prepared to help their friends and neighbours, the Swedes stuck to the rules of neutrality. Politically, they had moved far already towards a social-democratic welfare state. Socially, they retained a large aristocracy from the sixteenth and seventeenth centuries, when Sweden had been a leading naval and military power. Economically, they had added iron and engineering to timber and shipbuilding among their industries; the German market for Swedish iron ore, which has been noticed already,[1] was vital alike to the Swedish and to the German economy, and provided a degree of unavoidable pro-German bias to counteract the pro-Allied bias to which most Swedes instinctively inclined. Not all: the wartime commander-in-chief, for example, General Thörnell, was frankly pro-German.[2] Swedish ball bearings were indispensable to the British armaments industry, and SOE had a hand in bringing out a convoy of freighters laden with them in the second winter of the war.[3]

The iron ore traffic, by sea across the Baltic in summer, by rail through Narvik and thence by sea when the Baltic was frozen in winter, provided a sabotage target of prime importance. SOE got onto this quite promptly, and bought a Swedish gangster who was supposed to do the work; but he was detected, tried, and convicted. He made no secret of who his employers had been; thus producing acute embarrassment for the British embassy.[4] Having once burned their fingers, SOE presumably thereafter held back. Foreign office pressure to do so would certainly have been strong.

And Sweden provided other advantages than targets, for both wings of the Allied cause. It had long been convenient to the comintern, as a base from which agents in Germany and farther west could be run. Exactly what was done from it during the war is not yet known; though it was in Stockholm, as was noticed just

[1] p. 278 above.
[2] McLachlan, *Room 39*, 212.
[3] Sweet-Escott, 59–60.
[4] Harris Smith, 200.

now, that the luckless Finns negotiated the end of their winter war with the USSR.[1] The negotiator on the soviet side was the formidable Aleksandra Kollontay, one of the last surviving old bolsheviks. (Old bolsheviks were anathema to Stalin in his spells of grandeur, for they could not help remembering how comparatively lowly his own position had been at the moment of the seizure of power: joint editor of *Pravda* with Molotov. On the other hand, Mme Kollontay had an important propaganda role in the soviet myth, as the first woman head of a diplomatic mission – so she escaped the great purge.[2]) As head of mission, she would work of course quite independently from the GRU 'resident', and would have disavowed him as promptly as the British minister disavowed SOE's unlucky gangster, had so unfortunate an occasion arisen.

The GRU was not the only secret service to work through Sweden. OSS had some of its usual quarrels with the state department; mitigated in this case by the fact that its Stockholm office was in charge of an editor of *Vogue*, whose cover was that she was promoting American clothing designs.[3] Hansen, working for OSS as readily as for SOE and SIS, fixed up telephone, telegraph and ultra-short-wave wireless communications between Elsinore and an American consulate set up for the purpose at Helsingfors, just across the Sound at its narrowest point, where the Americans could claim diplomatic immunity. These lines were used for the daily press bulletins issued by the Danish resistance news agency; sensibly, not for anything more secret.

SIS no doubt had effective communications with Sweden; and the country provides a nice example of the power of the SIS myth to outweigh the facts. It has been claimed for several Scandinavian intelligence circuits that it was they who gave the first news of *Bismarck*'s fatal sortie into the north Atlantic in May 1941, that encompassed *Hood*'s destruction and ended in her own.[4] The Germans themselves were convinced that this all-powerful service was at the root of their downfall. The more prosaic truth, reported by Donald McLachlan from the inner citadel of NID where he worked at the time, was this: *Bismarck* was accompanied through the Kattegat for a couple of hours on 20 May by a Swedish cruiser, which reported the fact. The chief of staff of the Swedish (not the British) secret service mentioned the report, as a *fait divers*, to his friend the Norwegian naval attaché; who had a drink that evening, as he did regularly twice a week, with Captain Denham, the British naval attaché. The *fait divers* was mentioned at the second meeting, and instantly passed on by Denham to the Admiralty; which had already been alerted by extra German reconnaissance activity to the fact that something was in the wind.[5]

Of SOE's work, organized on the spot by Turnbull, something has been said already. By 1944 the Swedes whom Michel could describe as almost satellites

---

[1] p. 272 above.  [2] Obituary in *Times*, 12 March 1952.  [3] Harris Smith, 24.
[4] Cp. opening of C. S. Forester, *Hunting the Bismarck* (1959), or of Per Hansson, *The Greatest Gamble* (1967).
[5] D. H. McLachlan, *Room 39*, 143–7.

of the Germans, early in the war,[1] were shaking free of their economic shackles to German industry, and were prepared not only to let the Danish brigade train on Swedish soil, but also to let it have access to Swedish weapons and ammunition; a fair quanity of which promptly found its way across the Sound.

Getting into Denmark or Norway or Finland was fairly easy: how did one get to or from Great Britain? The sea route was virtually closed; the RAF opened a new one, by air. The Mosquito light bomber, in its photographic reconnaissance version, carried no arms at all; and was therefore capable of being represented to the Swedes as a civil aircraft. It could out-fly anything the Germans could put against it (such faster aircraft as the Me 163 or 262 had not the range to reach the route it flew);[2] and several score staff officers and escapers travelled by Mosquito between Sweden and Scotland. The journey had to be made in the bomb bay, and was bitterly uncomfortable; Bohr, for one, slept most of the time and made no complaint.

One other set of negotiations, on the edge of resistance, needs to be mentioned: Himmler's dealings with various personalities in Stockholm, notably his doctor Felix Kersten, and the diplomat Count Folke Bernadotte. Himmler suffered now and then from agonizing stomach cramps, which only Kersten's healing hands seemed to be able to relieve; and Kersten, like Harry Rée,[3] devised an admirable form of blackmail. He would pause in his treatment, and bargain with his patient for captives' lives: usually Jews. If Himmler relented, the massage went on and the captives were released. If Himmler refused – but the pain was usually too severe for him to refuse for long.[4]

Bernadotte's dealings with him were more straightforward, and less successful. They had a number of meetings in the spring of 1945, at one of which Himmler agreed to let Red Cross teams into concentration camps – this saved some 20,000 lives. Himmler's main object, revealed on 24 April 1945, was to get Bernadotte to propose to the British and Americans a separate peace with Germany, after which all three could unite against the Russians: a proposal instantly rejected by those to whom it was addressed. News of it reached Hitler; who dismissed Himmler from office and party, too late to save the millions of prisoners that between them they had had killed.

### Eastern Europe

Before the two intricate and difficult cases of Poland and Russia, a word or two on points of political geography that are no longer perfectly familiar.

In the third week of September 1939 Poland underwent its fourth partition: Germany annexed the whole of the Polish corridor, Danzig (for twenty years a free city) included; the province of Poznan; a large slice of Upper Silesia; and

---

[1] Michel, *SW*, 22.
[2] Cp. Pierre Clostermann, *Flames in the Sky* (1957), 138–9.
[3] Cp. p. 91 above.  [4] See Kersten's *Memoirs* (1956).

a district round Suwalki, at the eastern edge of East Prussia. Lithuania annexed (for a few months, as it turned out) a long strip of territory centring on Vilna (Viln'yus). The USSR annexed all Poland east of a line Lomza–Brest–Przemysl. The remaining stub of formerly Polish territory was dubbed the General-Government, declared a German satellite, and administered by Germans from Cracow to suit the whims of Berlin.

After the winter war with Finland, the USSR took by the treaty of Moscow[1] a strip of Karelia, including Viborg; this moved the frontier away from Leningrad, to Coventry's distance from London instead of Windsor's: the main perceptible object of the war.

In June 1940, as France collapsed, the USSR extended its own *cordon sanitaire*; taking, as well as Bessarabia and the northern Bukovina from Romania,[2] the whole of all three Baltic states. Lithuania, Latvia, and Estonia vanished respectively from the world map on 17, 20, and 21 June; between Pétain's announcement that he would seek an armistice, and its signature. 'Fall of the fascist dictatorship and creation of a people's government' is the official euphemism for the process.[3] It was followed in every case by the deporting of the entire educated class – all officers, all pastors, all graduates – to Siberia. No revolting student, living outside the USSR, who advocates the incorporation of his own country within it should retain any illusions about his personal fate if his wish comes true.

When on 22 June 1941 the Germans' invasion of the USSR began, it took them some weeks to cross this belt of new soviet territory; they were not, for instance, in sight of Leningrad or Moscow till early September. Yet they were not exactly crawling; their northern army group advanced 470 miles in three weeks.[4] They divided the territory they overran from soviet control simply into three blocks: a front zone, and two Reichskommissariats, Ostland and Ukraine, with as frontier between them – running eastward from just south of Brest-Litovsk – the border between the federated soviet republics of White Russia and the Ukraine. Ostland, run from Riga, consisted of the three Baltic states plus White Russia. Ukraine, run from Rovno, equalled the soviet Ukraine, less the province of Lvov; which was added to the General-Government of Warsaw. The two Reichskommissars were subordinated to Alfred Rosenberg, the nazi race-philosopher; who envisaged their territories as fields for experiment and colonization. There was in short every prospect of trouble for any of the previous inhabitants who survived.

### The Soviet Union

The USSR is one of the world's few states to include no territorial element in its title: right from its foundation, its leaders have envisaged the gradual incor-

---

[1] *BFSP* cxliv. 383.     [2] p. 169 above.
[3] H. Kühnrich, *Partisanenkrieg*, 645, tr.
[4] Calvocoressi and Wint, *Total War*, 179.

poration into it of every other state.[1] In the years with which this book deals, it was the only great power – almost the only power – to have adopted socialism as its state policy; and state power had rested for many years solely in a single party's control.

The territorial base of the USSR has remained more or less that of the Romanov empire of Russia; and territory does exercise some influence on state policy. Many ambitions of old Russia are still pursued by the newer USSR. Russian history is a history of agglomeration: of joining segment after adjacent segment to an existing core. Stalin saw himself as a follower of Marx; he was aware also that, in a different sense, he followed Ivan the Terrible and Peter the Great. As Marx put it, in a remark better known west of the iron curtain than east of it, 'the policy of Russia is changeless, according to the admission of its official historian, the Muscovite Karamsin. Its methods, its tactics, its manoeuvres may change, but the polar star of its policy – world domination – is a fixed star.'[2]

Some ten years earlier, he had remarked that 'Muscovy was raised and educated in the vicious and miserable school of Mongolian slavery. It won its strength only by becoming a virtuoso in the arts of slavery. Even after having liberated itself, Muscovy as conqueror played its traditionally slave-like role.'[3]

The tsarist empire collapsed, borne down by the weight of its own incompetence, in March 1917; the well-intentioned but ineffectual liberal régime that replaced it was elbowed out of the way in the following November by the Bolshevik revolution, that Lenin guided, Trotsky executed, and Dzerzhinsky protected with the Cheka. By 1927 Lenin and Dzerzhinsky were dead, and Trotsky was out of the running for the succession; which had been quietly assumed by Stalin, the Georgian revolutionary who had come to control the machine of the CPSU(B). For years Stalin and his colleagues wrestled with the problems of getting industry back on its feet under bureaucratic guidance, and dispossessing the peasants of their land; saw through the shattering economic revolution of 1931; and then all got entangled in the great purge.

This formerly inadmissible event is now accepted, even by devout communist historians, as a fact in history; so far, the political and agonizing personal sides of it have attracted far more attention than the military. It did have military weight as well; for it rendered the soviet union pretty well impotent, for some years, on the international stage. The USSR played no part in the Munich drama of 1938, not only because it was not invited, but because it was unable to leave the wings: its high command that autumn was about in its state of maximum disarray. The Red Army's pitiable display against Finland fourteen months later bears this out.

---

[1] Cp. Wolfgang Leonhard, *Child of the Revolution* (1957), 403.
[2] Speech in London, probably 22 January 1867; re-tr. by P. W. Blackstock and A. F. Hoselitz in K. Marx and F. Engels, *The Russian Menace to Europe* (Allen & Unwin 1953), 106.
[3] Ibid. 254.

And, given that his country was in no state to fight, Stalin's conduct in consenting to the pact with Hitler's Germany in August 1939 becomes more easy to explain; if not to excuse. He had got himself by then into a fix from which he was unable to see any other way of salvation.

Weak his armed forces may have been; his unarmed ones were still strong. The secret services were shaken by the purge, but the spy *apparats* of the comintern at the ordinary working level were most of them intact. How shaken their secret high command was we can only guess; no shadow of an indication has appeared from the official side, and the memoirs of those who had defected to the west, while often interesting, are necessarily prejudiced. One defector is worth mentioning, all the same: Krivitsky. He had been a senior secret police agent in western Europe, saw the purge coming, and skipped to the USA; where, not long after, he was found dead in a hotel bedroom. It was he who had let out his colleagues' proverb: 'Any fool can commit a murder; it takes an artist to commit a natural death.'[1] What artist disposed of him, is not known.

The comintern, as a world organization, had considerable though not unlimited power; as it could command the services of intellects as steely as Palme Dutt's and spies as competent as Radó or Sorge, it was not a body to despise. How many other nets, as competent as – or more competent than – Radó's or Sorge's the GRU and the NKVD ran, no one outside a closed inner circle yet knows, or is ever likely to know. Anything non-soviet services find out about this, they do their best to keep to themselves; secret service officers have a *déformation professionelle* that inhibits them from revealing anything unless they have to.

Stalin could not fail to know this; having had an early career as a bank robber, after he had given up being trained to be a priest, and having had some training in the elements of clandestinity, early in the century, from Lenin himself.[2] The purge, also, had enhanced much more recently his tendencies to be suspicious of everybody and everything. It is therefore not altogether surprising that he neglected the many warnings that reached him of Hitler's impending attack. Sorge from Tokyo, Trepper from Paris, were (though not Russian nationals) his own people;[3] but as the message also came to him from royal Yugoslavia, from exiled Czechoslovakia, from Great Britain with the personal blessing of Churchill, from the USA on the direction of Roosevelt, he preferred not to believe it; to feel that his own people had had it planted on them. It would be so excessively inconvenient if it were true.

So, up to a few minutes before the opening salvoes of 'Barbarossa' were fired, trainloads of militarily useful goods were still passing across prostrate Poland from Soviet into nazi territory; and the *Luftwaffe*'s attacks at first light found most of the Red air force's aircraft lined up neatly at the edges of their airfields,

[1] W. Krivitsky, *I was Stalin's Agent* (1938).

[2] H. Montgomery Hyde, *Stalin* (1971), 75, 85, suggests, but does not conclusively prove, that Stalin's relations with the tsarist secret police were a good deal closer than his colleagues realized.

[3] Sorge was born in Baku, but of German parents.

awaiting destruction. That the USSR survived the first few weeks' campaign is one of the most extraordinary, as well as the most creditable, facts in its history.

Readers will have noticed already that this writer is unable to join in the polite conventions of literature behind the iron curtain; or to assume that whatever the government of the USSR did, was necessarily right; or even to agree with a number of the philosophical assumptions on which marxist–leninists try to act. It is all the more necessary to emphasize that the stand the soviet people made against the nazis' barbaric attack was altogether admirable, and must command the gratitude of everyone with a brain to think and a heart to feel. My quarrel is not with the indomitable Russian, and other soviet, fighting people; but with the leadership – individual and collective – that landed them in the morass of death and suffering through which they floundered so gloriously into the grey dawn of 'peaceful reconstruction'.

Some of the tremendous intellectual resources of the USSR were devoted to the business of intelligence; with, so far as can be perceived, considerable effect. Certainly the Germans attempted to bamboozle the Russians, as they attempted to bamboozle all their enemies, through wireless games. As many as 160 attempts are on published record; was there ever a single success? Certainly, none is known fit to be mentioned in the same breath as the *Englandspiel* that the SD played against SOE; let alone 'Fortitude', MI5's crushing return victory over the German security and strategic services.

On the cryptological front, not much is known about the Russians' successes; a number of defectors have made it clear that they did have thoroughly efficient deciphering teams. Kahn clearly has high respect for their efficiency; most of the examples he quotes refer to the period after the hot war, when the cold called for extra cipher effort,[1] but there is no suggestion that their wartime ciphers were any weaker than any other great power's. That is to say, about a quarter of their traffic was probably readable immediately, and another quarter may not have been read even yet: this seems to be, at a rough guess, the average state of play for great power ciphers of the period.

Several efficient Russian-run intelligence circuits have been noticed already, and it would be reasonable to assume there were a great many more. The tone of such exchanges as have been published between the GRU and the field[2] suggests that the Russians did not read 'Enigma', and were therefore forced to rely even more than the British did on occupied Europe as a source for tactical intelligence and order-of-battle minutiae. On their own doorstep, indeed painfully far within it, deep in their own territory, they had a first-class source of tactical intelligence in the partisans.

When the war with Germany began, its outbreak proved the accuracy of secret reports from abroad, and in any less suspicious-minded organization than the USSR would have proved the good faith towards it of the friendly foreign countries who had given warning that war was imminent. It must have been a

[1] D. Kahn, *The Codebreakers*, 639–61.    [2] Eg. Radó, '*Dora*', passim.

salutary lesson to Stalin, encouraging him to believe the intelligence that reached him instead of doubting it.

It certainly precipitated a sharp turn in the soviet propaganda machine; long drilled in making sharp, even right-about, turns, while preaching the infallible continuity and directness of the communist party line. No attempt was made to mobilize popular feeling in defence of communism. An older and surer appeal was made instead, to patriotic feeling; only after the war did the party explain that the party had won it. While the war raged, Suvorov and Kutusov were re-called, while Marx and Lenin were laid by; not forgotten, but not stressed. The common people were summoned to defend the good old cause, in what is still referred to in the USSR as the Great Patriotic War. Inessentials of revolu-tionary propaganda were put aside, to preserve the main political results of the revolution: power for a single party, and control over that party by a single head.

A call for partisan effort behind the occupier's lines followed automatically from the patriotic call at home. With Rosenberg and Himmler directing the work of the *Einsatzgruppen* on occupied territory, it was not hard to find recruits for the partisans: anything, *anything* was better than the treatment an *Einsatzgruppe* enjoyed dealing out. Where the local inhabitants were less than welcoming to partisan emissaries, a little judicious terror could soon prod them into line.

The Germans might have secured themselves a welcome as liberators from the captive subject populations of the USSR; had they in turn not been under single-party control, and had that party not been obsessed with so much gib-berish about race. In some villages, bread and salt were brought out to welcome them: the traditional gesture of peasant hospitality.[1] One of the grand ironies of modern history, though an exceptionally prickly one for any historian to handle, is this tale of the mutual disillusion of the Germans and the Russians' subject peoples; one in which the partisans played a considerable part, that has not yet had the full treatment it deserves. Such books as the present writer has seen or heard of are either inadmissibly one-sided, or inadequate in their research base, or really concentrate on some different subject: such as the general course of the war;[2] or General Vlasov, whose existence is hardly admissible in the east.[3]

That hundreds of thousands of Red Army soldiers deserted is not an admis-sion that the government of the USSR can be expected to make, even after thirty years; it is none the less true. That millions of inhabitants of the USSR would have preferred another régime than the one they had before the war is true also; but the alternative Hitler offered them was still less acceptable. Hence the hold of the partisans.

Red Army doctrine had favoured, from the earliest days, cooperation with the peasantry in enemy territory. One of the advantages of marxist thinking about

[1] Deakin, reaching Montenegro by parachute in the middle of a battle, was offered bread, salt, and slivovits at the first cottage he entered (*The Embattled Mountain*, 19); that cottager supported the partisans, and knew how to treat a stranger.

[2] John Erickson, *Stalin's War against Hitler* (1975).

[3] Kühnrich does not mention him.

war is that it does take a sharp turn away from a lot of old-fashioned conventionalities, such as the idea that 'front', 'flanks', 'rear' need have any continuing meaning on a modern battlefield.[1] Marxist myth lays down that a populace which has once tasted the benefits of government by a communist party will remain ardent in that party's support: occasionally, that myth and reality could be made to coincide. Taylor has justly drawn attention to the reluctance of Eisenhower's staff who conducted 'Overlord' to trust the forces of resistance, whose help the 'Overlord' planners persisted in regarding as a bonus, something that might turn out useful on the day but was not to be relied on: 'a political blunder of the first magnitude'.[2]

SOE did drop into France arms for about half a million men, the figure Taylor gives in the same passage for the overall strength of the partisans on the eastern front; no doubt a good many of SOE's arms went astray, and certainly their use was not a tenth as carefully coordinated with the Allied armies' advances as was the work of the partisans. Kühnrich's book, a party apologia and therefore needing to be handled with some circumspection, does give numerous examples of direct tactical cooperation between partisan bands and Red Army formations.[3] He instances a group of 15,000 partisans, operating west of Vitebsk, who cut the lines of supply of the German Third Panzer Army for some months in the winter of 1943-4. This sort of work was invaluable to the soviet high command, both because it sapped the enemy's fighting efficiency and because it damaged his morale: all over the eastern front, from 1943 at any rate onwards, the Germans felt insecure in their hold over their own rear areas, could safely leave no dump unguarded, could only travel in sizeable bodies between towns; just like Spain in 1811 or France in 1944.

Kühnrich provides plenty of figures; though he says very little on some essential points of historical interest. He mentions that there were numerous operations by light aircraft, with no details; says little about armament, nothing about training, little about explosives, nothing about cipher. One name he lets drop carries interesting implications: also in White Russia, near Orsha.[4] A partisan brigade – any body over 100 strong called itself a brigade – took the name of 'Chekist'. Even the Waffen-SS did not run to a unit that called itself after the Gestapo.

The name brings out the salient feature of partisan warfare in the soviet union: it was under extremely strict party control. The Red Army could ask partisan units to undertake particular tasks, such as seizing the far bank of a river the army wished to cross, or blocking a particular line of railway at a particular time; every operation needed the assent both of the political commissar at the initiating end, and of the political commissar in the field. Every partisan unit

---

[1] 'Ludwig Renn', *Warfare* (1939), an early but still useful summary.
[2] A. J. P. Taylor, *The Second World War* (1975), 203.
[3] *Partisanenkrieg*, 366–78.
[4] Ibid. 375.

with which the Red Army worked had its political commissar; he who was not for them, was against them.

To this day, one of the two ways of joining that self-perpetuating oligarchy, the Red Army officer corps, is to be the son or grandson of a partisan. The other is to be the son of an officer. Four-fifths of the Red Army's original officer corps had held the tsar's commission.

Party hold over the partisans was most important in the disaffected areas: Georgia, the Ukraine, the Baltic States, Poland. It is time we grasped the Polish nettle.

*Poland*

The war in Poland was not simply two-sided: there were three sides to it at least, and the corners of this triangular war were – and remain – sharp.

Polish history ensured that there would be resistance; Polish geography, and the world politics of the mid century, both militated against its success. Every Pole had known from childhood about occupation and the need to fight it, and had drunk the spirit of resistance with his (or her) mother's milk. Fate's dice were loaded differently this time. It only took three days for the *Blitzkrieg* to break the back of the Polish armed forces; few of the aircraft survived the first three hours. Within three weeks, the prearranged fourth partition wiped Poland off the map – on paper.

The legitimate government of the Polish republic nevertheless remained in being. Its members withdrew to Romania; thence the core of them removed to Paris, where they wintered. On the fall of France, they moved on to London, to carry on the affairs of state at a distance and to supervise the remaking of Poland. 17,000 Polish fighting men moved with them; all very angry.

The war had not caught them, as it caught the Danes or the Norwegians, wholly unaware. Their régime had been dictatorial and military in tone; its military flavour enabled it to have a skilled and lively intelligence department. Probably the most important service the Poles ever rendered to the anti-nazi cause was something they did before the war had even begun. On 25 July 1939, in Warsaw, they handed over to the astounded Bertrand, chief of the French section D (*déchiffrement* – decipher), and to the still more astounded 'Dilly' Knox and Denniston, MI6's decipher experts, two copies of the modified 'Enigma' machine on which the Germans conducted all their most secret cipher traffic.[1] Enormous consequences flowed from this, as the next chapter will discuss.[2]

If the Germans' secret services had been more efficiently organized, for intelligence rather than party purposes; and if the Poles had been less efficient and less secure; the Germans would have picked up some traces of this in Warsaw seven or eight weeks later. But they never suspected a leak, on this most vital point; and they despised the Poles. The whole Polish 'Enigma' deciphering team

[1] Bertrand, *Enigma*, 59–60.　　　　　　　　[2] pp. 308–10 below.

got away, with all their apparatus and papers; by mid-October they were in France, helping Bertrand to run 'source Z'.[1]

Under the inspiration of Colin Gubbins, then Jo Holland's number two at MIR, who visited Poland in the spring of 1939, the Poles had devoted a little thought to the possibility that they might be overrun, and had made a few tentative arrangements. Gubbins was present with Carton de Wiart's mission at the start of the September avalanche, and reminded them; they hardly needed reminders. No sooner were the surviving troops disbanded than their officers and men got busy, at once, with changing identities, caching arms, making plans, preparing escapes. The whole Polish-speaking population seemed ready to help.[2]

Escapes, with so much local aid available, were many; a few have been noticed above.[3] It was even possible, with a Polish population surrounding it, for Poles to get away from a concentration camp; normally, an almost unthinkably difficult task. From the group of extermination camps at Auschwitz–Birkenau, west of Cracow, as many as 667 prisoners escaped; by two and threes to start with, but 310 of them in 1944 and 209 in 1945. At least 270 of these 667 were recaptured, sooner or later, and publicly executed with every circumstance of humiliation; yet over half of them got away altogether. This would have been inconceivable without help from the surrounding villages, which were full of Polish miners and their families; who would help, at the drop of a rag, anyone escaping from the nazis they detested, even if the escaper was a soviet citizen – as about one in seven of these 667 were. They guided the escapers on to the various partisan bands in the neighbourhood, in spite of the risks of reprisal.[4]

The cardinal escape problem in Poland was what to do about the Jews, who formed so tragically large a proportion of the overrun inhabitants. The Poles have left on the rest of Europe an impression of having been almost as anti-semitic as the Germans, in inclination: they were far from being so in practice, another instance of the inaccuracy and unfairness of stereotyped ideas about national character. Under the challenge of nazi occupation, all but the extremest near-fascist elements on the far Polish right responded stoutly in a pro-Jewish direction. The trouble was that the Germans were present in overwhelming force, and quite literally were out for blood. Poland seemed to Hitler, Rosenberg, Himmler, and their henchmen a good testing-ground for the *Endlösung*, the final solution of the Jewish problem: of which Hitler was already talking before the war. 'We are going to destroy the Jews', he said to the Czech foreign minister on 21 January 1939; and he meant it.[5]

Special commandos, renamed special groups – fifteen of them, all highly trained SS – worked over Poland in the winter of 1939–40, and thereafter over

[1] Bertrand, *Enigma*, 69; and see p. 243 above.
[2] Eg. K. S. Rudnicki, *The Last of the War Horses* (1974), 67–114.
[3] pp. 33 (Gustav Herling), 114–15, 199 ('Christine Granville' and others).
[4] J. Garliński, *Fighting Auschwitz* (1975), 238n, 101–3, 163–5, etc.
[5] H. Krausnick *et al.*, *Anatomy of the SS State*, 44; and ibid. 43–124 for the consequences.

such occupied territories as were available in the east. Their original task was to herd all the Jews they could find into the General-Government, pending a decision whether to send them all to Madagascar or to polish them off on the spot. Mass executions in fact began in July 1941. Former Polish territory sprouted extermination camps: Chelmo, Belzec, Sobibór, Treblinka, Majdanek, Birkenau. In the Auschwitz–Birkenau complex, which covered some fifteen square miles, over three million people were put to death within five years: an act of unexampled infamy. Himmler asked,

> All of us have asked ourselves, What about the women and children? I have decided that this too requires a clear answer. I did not consider that I should be justified in getting rid of the men – in having them put to death, in other words – only to allow their children to grow up to avenge themselves on our sons and grandsons. We have to make up our minds, hard though it may be, that this race must be wiped off the face of the earth.[1]

Women and children had no special treatment in the Warsaw ghetto, when it rose in the spring of 1943: they were shot just as dead as the rest. Those twenty-eight days of absolutely hopeless, absolutely heroic revolt provide a passionate denial of that other popular stereotype, of Jews who shambled off unprotesting to the slaughterhouse.

That was what Jews had often (not always) done before, over twenty centuries of persecution: this time they fought back. Calvocoressi prints a map of eastern Europe showing areas of Jewish resistance in 1940–4: including, besides Warsaw, sixteen other ghettoes in which armed risings took place against the nazi oppressor. Let their names at least be cited: Bendzin, Bialystok, Brody, Cracow, Czestochowa, Lvov, Lutsk, Minsk, Mir, Riga, Sielce, Sosnowica, Stryzow, Tarnopol, Tarnow, and Vilna. In nine areas – one of them, between Vilna and the Pripet marshes, measuring about fifty miles by thirty – Jewish partisan bands controlled the district for months, sometimes for years on end. Such areas, when known to the nazis, provoked frightful reprisal attacks; diverting men and weapons from the main front, at however fearful a cost. And in one of the concentration camps into which surviving Jewish prisoners were crammed, to be worked to death or more summarily wiped out – in the camp at Sobibór, not far from Lublin – the prisoners did revolt. Led by the eighty survivors from a group of 1,750 Russian Jews – some of them Red Army soldiers – who had arrived in September 1943, a party of them armed with carpenters' axes, stolen pistols and makeshift clubs rushed the main guard. About 400 got clean out of the compound; most to die straightway on the minefields near by, some to be killed by anti-semitic Polish partisans farther away, many to be tracked down by the avenging hounds of the SS; but enough escaped altogether for the tale to become known. It was too much for Himmler; he had the camp obliterated.[2]

[1] At a Gauleiters' conference in Posen on 6 October 1943: ibid. 123, tr. R. H. Barry.
[2] Calvocoressi and Wint, *Total War*, 234–5; and R. Ajnsztein, *Jewish Resistance* (1975), 742–69.

On the intelligence front the Poles did as well as they did on the escape front; or even better. The 'Enigma' team worked away in exile all through the war. Both the GRU and the London Poles got excellent intelligence reports from Poland; as both were secretive bodies, not much beyond that bare fact is known. But the London Poles did pass on their major finds, such as knowledge of the impending attack on Russia, and some vital data from Peenemünde; which gave rise to one operation in every sense too big to hide.

One effect of the big RAF raid there in August 1943 was to force on the Germans a move of their main rocket experimental station to somewhere that was out of bomber command's range. They chose the province of Cracow; guessing, correctly, that the Russians would not allow bomber command to operate from bases on soviet soil.[1] But they had reckoned without Polish intelligence. Though the Germans had the military upper hand, and petrol-driven vehicles, they were not quite a match for an enemy who was at best horse-drawn, but who could rely without question for help – as the Germans could rely without question for hindrance – on every single civilian in the country.[2]

Practice shots with V1s and V2s were constant; the two sides raced for the fragments of the wrecks. One day, on 20 May 1944, a V2 landed in a swamp near the river Bug, about 80 miles east of Warsaw, and failed to explode. Polish resisters got there first, dug it out, *hid it*, took it to pieces later, and reported the results. On 25/26 July a Dakota from Brindisi reached Poland and collected the essential parts, which were in London seven weeks before the first V2 fell there.[3] This removed, at least, the secrecy from the secret weapon; its hitting power was unaffected.

The subversive side of resistance was even more active in Poland than the other two; and was even less easily distinguished from plain politics than in other parts of Europe. Personal jealousies and animosities played a considerable part in it; so did romance. Attitudinizers, the sort of people who are prominent in the early days of a big revolution, before the professional politicians and the soldiers move in to take control, were plentiful in wartime Poland, but they took risks as well as striking attitudes: café-conversationalist resisters who pullulated in Bucarest or Paris had no place in Warsaw, where everybody took the problems of resistance seriously.

The basic political difficulty, for a Pole, was that there were two enemies, not one. Frightful measures of repression were undertaken by the Germans, both within the Reich's new frontiers and in the General Government; the Russians did not then pursue *vendette* of race at all, but were equally fierce in their pursuit of the prewar Polish ruling class. Dzerzhinsky had been a renegade Polish nobleman, and seems to have left behind in the soviet secret police a lasting

---

[1] Has anyone noticed that V1s and V2s were never used in action on the eastern front at all?

[2] J. Garliński, *Poland, SOE and the Allies* (1969), 52.          [3] Ibid. 149–64.

tradition of hatred for the class from which he sprang. As in the Baltic states, the Russians removed from their zone of Poland – or in their terms, from reoccupied western White Russia and western Ukraine – the whole educated class: about 1·5 million people.[1] This group included over 12,000 officers of the Polish armed forces; too many of whom have never been seen alive again. Polish national consciousness remained vivid; the first of the underground newspapers, appearing weekly from 10 October 1939, was called *Polska Zyje*, Poland lives.[2]

From about the same date, there was continual contact between elements of the Polish underground and the republic's government-in-exile; partly by messenger, which was slow,[3] partly by wireless, which was prompt and effective. According to Willetts, Polish clandestine wireless was judged at the time to be 'outstandingly good', in advance of any comparable service in the world, and at times as many as 100 sets were working at once out of Poland to bases in England or Italy[4] (of the move to liberated Italy, more in a moment).

Security was also good, thanks to the Poles' age-long experiences of occupation. There was no case of an agent being arrested on or near a dropping zone; there were no wireless games, attempts to play captured sets back, that even began to succeed. The Poles not only designed and made their own wireless sets, they devised all their own ciphers: of which GCCS thought highly. When in the spring of 1944 an absolute ban on all cipher traffic out of Britain, except in British ciphers, was imposed as part of the security planning for 'Overlord', three exceptions were secretly made: for the USA and the USSR, a necessary courtesy to greater powers; and for the London Poles. And as Raczynski has pointed out, 'Poland had no Quisling and no Pétain.'[5]

The London government-in-exile believed it was preparing the restoration of a democratic Poland – more democratic than the prewar colonels' régime, with which Sikorski was well known to be no sympathizer.[6] The cross-currents of insurrectionary, romantic and cautionary traditions in Poland, the general course of the war, and the superior police abilities of the NKVD defeated it.

By Christmas 1939 it had organized an Association for Armed Struggle (*Zwiazek Walki Zbrojnej*), which was renamed in February 1942 simply the Home Army (*Armia Krajowa*, henceforward AK). This body touched a nominal strength of 400,000 in 1944, but was only weakly armed; it got about two-thirds of its supplies from local caches, and a third from RAF operations, which at a cost of 73 aircraft brought in 600 tons of stores.[7] Poland was right at the limit of the RAF's range; eastern Poland was always outside it. Early flights, there and back, might last as long as fourteen hours.

---

[1] Count Edward Raczynski, 'Poland and Britain', *ERM* iii. 6.
[2] Garliński, *Poland, SOE and the Allies*, 31.
[3] Four weeks from Paris to Warsaw, 4 December 1939 to 1 January 1940: J. M. Ciechanowski, *The Warsaw Rising of 1944* (Cambridge 1974), 84.
[4] H. T. Willetts, 'Britain and Poland', in *ERM* iii. 3.
[5] *ERM* iii. 10.          [6] Ciechanowski, 2.
[7] Details in Garliński, *Poland, SOE and the Allies*, 235–8.

The air supply problem could have been made infinitely less severe if the Russians had allowed aircraft to refuel on their territory; which they hardly ever did. They said, correctly, that they were busy with their own war, and that they had no high-octane fuel to spare; they did not need to add that it was no interest of theirs to supply a movement the aims of which they disapproved, and the existence of which conflicted with aims of their own.

On 30 July 1941, the USSR established diplomatic relations with the London government-in-exile, thus enabling a number of Poles deported to the USSR to get away to fight in the Polish army in the near east.[1] Nothing was said in this pact about the one real point of impending difficulty in Russo-Polish relations, the question of the eastern boundary of Poland; this silence made trouble later.

The AK's commander, General Grot-Rowecki, was ordered by Sikorski in February 1942 not to oppose the Russians, nor even to hide from them, but rather to use his men as their guides when they entered Polish territory; at that moment, an event unlikely to happen soon. In the previous month, a Polish Workers' Party (*Polska Partia Robotnica*) had been created in Warsaw, with Moscow's approval; it formed its own private army, the People's Guards (*Gwardia Ludowa*), merged in 1944 into a People's Army (*Armia Ludowa*, AL), which – like the FTP in France – was in fact controlled by communists. On the far right, on the other hand, was a body calling itself the National Armed Forces (*Narodowe Sile Zbrojne*), which was strongly anti-semitic and almost fascist in its outlook.[2]

There was no Polish Jean Moulin to knit these ravelled strands together; on the contrary, the divisions grew deeper, and the broadest-minded leaders disappeared. In January 1943 the PPR began negotiations to join the AK; while these were going on, the bodies of over 4,000 Polish officers were found in Katyn forest, piled neatly in mass graves, each with a bullet in the back of the neck and none bearing any document later than 1940. The London Poles, unhinged by this mishap, appealed to the International Red Cross; and on 26 April 1943 the USSR broke off relations with them. This was bad enough; troubles came later in battalia.

Grot-Rowecki was arrested in Warsaw on 30 June 1943, and soon identified (Himmler had him shot fourteen months later, during the Warsaw rising). Within a week, Sikorski too was dead.[3] Their successors were lesser men. Mikolajcyk, the new prime minister, could not hold the soldiers; Sosnkowski, the new London commander-in-chief, was a man whose past inspired suspicion, for he had been an associate of the dictator-liberator Pilsudski. Bor-Komorowski,

---

[1] One of these is worth a word in passing: Colonel (later General) K. S. Rudnicki, who had been arrested on the Russo-German demarcation line while on important business for ZWZ; had concealed his real identity; was living, under a false name, in Kirov, a town of 700,000 people; and scoured the whole town without success for two sheets of paper on which to write a letter. (His *The Last of the War Horses*, 175.) Herling was another.

[2] Ciechanowski, 4, 84–9.

[3] Cp. p. 229 above.

the new commander-in-chief in the field, personally a quiet and charming noble-man, had been an excellent commander of a cavalry regiment; his new post, forced on him by fate, was not one for which he was well fitted.

He did not insist on a break between the AK and the near-fascist NSZ, the 'National Armed Forces'. No one on the Polish side, after Katyn, wanted any truck with Moscow; unless they were taken in by Moscow's propaganda story, that the Katyn murders had been committed by the German and not by the Russian secret police. Had the London Poles been able to bring themselves to come to some sort of terms with Moscow, had they listened to Churchill's and Eden's repeated advice that they really must cede some territory on their eastern border, much suffering might have been avoided; had Moscow, in turn, been ready to arrive at a fair deal.

The communists among the million and a half Poles in exile in Russia – the survivors of the educated class, extracted from eastern Poland in 1939[1] – started up in Moscow in March 1943, just before the Katyn troubles broke out, a Union of Polish Patriots (*Zwiazek Patriotow Polskich*) in the USSR, a front organiza-tion intended to incorporate all their fellow-exiles. This ZPP included a lot of people who wanted to fight, who were formed into a small army under General Berling. Its leaders saw themselves as an alternative to the Polish Workers' Party (the PPR), and were reluctant to share power with it.[2]

The AK meanwhile pursued, under its new leaders, the line of policy worked out by Sikorski and Grot-Rowecki: first 'Fly' (*Musha*), a series of pinprick sabotage raids, then 'Tempest' (*Burza*), local revolts, and lastly 'Rising' (*Pow-stanie*), which was to be a national insurrection. 'Fly' got on well enough, with a series of small maddening attacks that exasperated the Germans without mor-tally affecting their plans.[3] The main obstacle to more of these was a shortage of arms and explosives.

Hardly fifty successful drops had taken place by April 1943, when the short summer nights closed the operational season for the RAF. During that summer, the Germans erected a huge anti-aircraft artillery and fighter barrier west of Berlin, from north Denmark to Bavaria; impossible for supply Halifaxes bound from England to Poland to penetrate. Italy's surrender came just in time to pro-long the Poles' agony.

In October 1943, 301 (Polish) Flight RAF, which included three Liberators provided by the Americans, was based at Brindisi. Beside it was an SOE base commander, H. M. Threlfall, who looked after administration as well as liaison with the RAF; and Polish signals and operating staffs. The arrangement was complex, but at least the air range into Poland was shorter: many more air operations were now possible.

Soon thereafter, the great inter-Allied conference at Teheran settled the fate of Poland: it was thenceforward bound to be liberated from the Germans, if by

[1] p. 286 above.  [2] Ciechanowski, 104–5.
[3] Numerous examples in Garliński, *Poland, SOE and the Allies*, 101–65.

anybody, then by the Red Army: unless, many Poles were proud enough to think, it could liberate itself first. The political *Delegatura*, working in Poland for the exiled government, was widely felt to represent all the non-communist Poles. But at the end of 1943 a National Council was formed in Warsaw – by the PPR, the workers' party, not by anyone working with London. London's Poles responded by ordering 'Tempest' where the Red Army approached Polish soil. 'Tempest' duly began, in Volhynia, early in 1944. The AK's forces got on well with the fighting troops of the Red Army whom they met; cooperated with them tactically, and advised them on minor local problems of ground and supply, just as Sikorski had foreseen. As the battle moved forward, NKVD troops arrived. They arrested the AK's officers, and offered the other ranks a simple choice: enlist in Berling's army, or go to Siberia.

Much the same happened later in the spring round Lvov and round Vilna. By the end of July 1944, the Red Army was approaching Warsaw; and Bor-Komorowski, the AK commander, had to decide what to do. The role of urban guerilla leader, at a moment fraught with political as well as military consequences of the gravest sort for his country and his class, was one he was ill fitted to uphold. He was not the man, and August 1944 in Warsaw was neither the time nor the place, to sustain that role successfully. As Marvell said of Charles I on the scaffold, 'He nothing common did or mean'; but he could not win.

He had heard of the attack on Hitler on 20 July, which seemed to indicate that the Third Reich was crumbling; he heard on 31 July of the American capture of Avranches, which heralded open warfare in the west. Between those two events came a political turn: under soviet supervision, a Polish Council of National Liberation (*Polski Komitet Wyzwolenia Narodowego*, PKWN) was set up at Lublin, midway between Warsaw and Lvov. Bor could see the PKWN as an alternative focus of loyalty for those Poles who were reluctant to accept the lead of the government-in-exile he represented.

Ciechanowski has explained how Bor acted, on inadequate information, and without proper touch with the advancing Red Army. By the last week in July, that army's advance guards were in Praga, which adjoins Warsaw on the eastern side; and Moscow radio was calling on the capital's population to rise. On the 30th, Mikolajcyk arrived in Moscow for consultations with Stalin;[1] and Sosnkowski was away for a ten days' visit to Polish troops in Italy. Bor thought the Russians were about to enter Warsaw, and was eager to strike first; he ordered 'Tempest' to start at five in the evening of 1 August.

In hard fact the Russians in Praga had run into a check; a German counterattack held them; and they were probably unable, as well as visibly unwilling, to resume their advance for some five weeks. The Red Army had a good deal else on its plate as well; including, in the second half of August, the rising in Slovakia.[2] Even with Warsaw ablaze with street fighting, the Russians would not

[1] He did not actually get into Stalin's presence till 3 August: too late.
[2] pp. 208–9 above.

relax their rule forbidding special duties aircraft to land on their soil; save once, as late as 18 September, when an armada of B-17s from east Anglia dropped 1,284 containers – from some 15,000 feet; so only 228 reached what was left of the Home Army's lines.[1]

200,000 Poles were killed in the two months' fighting; the remaining 800,000 inhabitants were then evicted by the Germans. No capital city had suffered so severely since the Huns sacked Rome.

Slessor, as air commander in the Mediterranean, had followed these operations night by night, and had eventually to forbid the Poles at Brindisi to fly any more on a venture that had become too desperate. Looking back, he commented: 'How, after the fall of Warsaw, any responsible statesman could trust any Russian Communist further than he could kick him, passes the comprehension of ordinary men.'[2] Ciechanowski shows there may have been a shadow at least of a military excuse for the Red Army's inaction. Politically, it was certainly convenient for the communists to sit still and watch their enemies destroy each other. As Auden put it of a different battle in the same wide war,

History to the defeated

May say Alas but cannot help nor pardon.[3]

The moral impact of the failure in Warsaw on the AK was shattering. Bor survived; he was honourably treated as a prisoner-of-war, was sent to Colditz, and did not die till the middle 1960s.[4] His sublime effort had torn the heart out of his movement.

The Home Army was disbanded in January 1945. A colder fate awaited its so far uncaptured high command. Like all the other principal non-communist leaders, they were tricked into a meeting with the NKVD whence none returned: they died in prison.[5]


## Germany

The story of German resistance to Hitler is made up partly of splendid legends, partly of truths. It was launched internationally on an unsuspecting party of professional historians and ex-resisters at the first conference on European resistance, at Liège in 1958.[6] Professor Krausnick, who supervised the launch, has earned every historian's gratitude for his other work;[7] this came as something of a surprise.

---

[1] Garliński, *Poland, SOE and the Allies*, 198–203.
[2] Sir John Slessor, *These Remain* (1969), 151.
[3] W. H. Auden, *Spain* (Faber 1937), end.
[4] *Times* obituary, 26 August 1966, 12 f.
[5] Garliński, *Poland, SOE and the Allies*, 225–33.
[6] A survivor of the Warsaw ghetto, and a survivor of the main SD operation in Brittany, were so shocked that they walked out; practically unnoticed (*sed vidi*).
[7] Particularly for *The Anatomy of the SS*, several times cited above.

Here time, always important for the historian, is vital: the Germans' readiness to resist varied even more with time than did that of most of the nations whose lands they occupied. In the early days of the nazi régime, the question hardly arose. Early police operations by Göring and Himmler put the communist and social-democratic leaders behind barbed wire; the headless chickens of their leaderless parties collapsed. Some years' close cooperation with the nazis against the social democrats[1] had revealed practically the whole of the communist machine to the nazis; everybody of any importance and capacity was cleaned up, or had to run away. The party's rank and file either went over to the nazis – a cruel witticism said 1933 was the hottest summer in German history, everyone who was red turned brown – or lay low. The arrested leaders put up a magnificent display of courage in the camps – sometimes: fellow prisoners outside their party found at some other times that they had great gifts for tyrannous organization, and ran the camps for the SS with painful efficiency.[2]

The social democrats, long marked down also by the NSDAP's intelligence service, suffered severely and in much the same ways; save that they did less well for themselves and their party in the camps.

The lower bourgeoisie most of them supported the nazis anyhow; notoriously, some of the upper bourgeoisie, frightened of an impending red revolution, had financed them.[3] The armed forces were so delighted to get weapons, consideration, promotion, the prospects of military power, that they accepted the régime with enthusiasm on professional grounds. And by the late summer of 1934, when the sharper-sighted of the high command might have begun to have doubts about nazi methods and aims, every officer had taken at a ceremonial parade the following oath: 'I swear before God to give my unconditional obedience to Adolf Hitler, *Führer* of the Reich and of the German People, Supreme Commander of the *Wehrmacht*, and I pledge my word as a brave soldier to observe this oath always, even at peril of my life.'[4] This *Fahneneid*, an oath taken on the regimental colours, had inordinate weight for a body conscious of descent from the Teutonic knights, who had been men of their word from the late twelfth century onward.[5] The oath was a serious brake on resistance activity by officers.

The intelligentsia said to themselves, and to each other, The nazis are oaves; they simply have not got the intellectual power, or the administrative capacity, to

---

[1] McLachlan, when a newspaper correspondent in Leipzig in 1932, saw an election riot at the evening rush-hour. The trams along a kilometre of main street were overturned and set on fire: the odd-numbered trams by nazis, the even-numbered by communists. (Talk with him, 1936.)

[2] Contrast Allen Merson, 'Problems of the German Anti-Fascist Resistance' (CPGB, *Our History*, no. 41, 1966), 9–12, with Eugen Kogon, *Der SS-Staat* (1947), 55–68. Kogon was a founder-prisoner in Buchenwald, one of seven out of 200 who survived.

[3] F. Thyssen, *I paid Hitler* (New York 1941), the *locus classicus*.

[4] Tr. (Sir) John Wheeler-Bennett, *The Nemesis of Power* (Macmillan 1953), 339; q.v., with R. J. O'Neill, *The German Army and the Nazi Party, 1923–39* (1966), for general discussion.

[5] Compare and contrast M. R. D. Foot, *Men in Uniform* (1961), 56, 69.

manage a great modern industrial state like ours. It is not easy to treat characters like Alfred Rosenberg as people of serious intellectual standing. But on their main point, the incapacity of the NSDAP to govern, the intelligentsia were proved wrong: quite fast.[1]

By the time people might have pulled themselves together, Himmler had a firm hold; concentration camps were open and working; the *Blockwart* system had buttoned up the urban proletariat, and the lesser bourgeoisie; delation had become a routine instrument of school and university policy, instead of a crime at which everybody shuddered.[2] And besides the régime was in many ways popular.

Such movements as *Kraft durch Freude*, strength through joy, gave a great deal of innocent pleasure. Unemployment, the fearful curse of the Weimar republic during the world slump, vanished; it is not in fact hard to cure, if you put clever men to make arms, and less clever men to make motorways, and have a Schacht to keep the accounts. The civil service went on with its routine tasks of running the country, with the degree of competence for which it had long been proverbial.

The absolute frightfulness of nazism in practice did not leap to the eye. In retrospect it can only too clearly be seen: at the time, on the spot, it was less easy. A few people, exceptionally well placed to realize what was going on, took alarm: among them Carl Goerdeler, the mayor of Leipzig, who was so disgusted by the anti-semitism of his city councillors that he resigned in 1936, to try – without much success – to carry warnings abroad. 'It took a Hitler to make such a man a revolutionary', as Dulles says.[3] Vast popular enthusiasm for the régime, its banners, its uniforms, its slogans, kept most people's eyes shut to reality; the mesmeric oratorical powers of the Führer did the rest. Ravenscroft believes that Hitler *was* Antichrist; Dietrich Eckart certainly claimed to have summoned up Antichrist from hell into Hitler's body, as his own legacy to Germany.[4] Millions of Germans hardly cared whether Hitler was Antichrist or Antimacassar: he seemed to be on the winning side, and they wanted to be there with him.[5]

Dull would he be of soul who could pass by one ineffectual, but wholly honourable resistance movement, the 'White Rose' group, led in Munich university by Hans and Sophie Scholl, sibling students who were better Christians than they were nazis. They too saw Hitler as Antichrist, but on Christian grounds, not grounds of black magic. They circulated anti-nazi letters round a group of friends. After Stalingrad, on 16 February 1943, the *Gauleiter* of Bavaria who had seen some of these letters – for the hand of the secret police reached everywhere – addressed the student body with his habitual coarseness; and was shouted down.

---

[1] Cp. Allen Dulles, *Germany's Underground*, 17–19.
[2] Cp. p. 187 above.
[3] *Germany's Underground*, 30.
[4] T. Ravenscroft, *The Spear of Destiny*, 91–3, 101–5.   [5] Cp. p. 75 above.

The Scholls had a leaflet printed, denouncing him and his master, and distributed it between lectures three mornings later. They and over a hundred of their friends were all dead within ten days, most of them after torture; at least they had spoken up for what they believed in.[1]

Their record is certainly no less honourable than that of the Kreisau circle, the group of young Christian aristocrats who gathered round Helmuth von Moltke; whose father-figure was Ulrich von Hassell, the German ambassador in Rome.[2] They expressed strong, deep, and sincere feelings; but privately. Privacy did not save many of them, in the end, from the gallows. They and others made various approaches to the British and Americans: Dietrich Bonhoeffer, for example, met G. K. A. Bell, the anglican bishop of Chichester, in Stockholm in May 1942. He was not to know that Bell was an unsuitable emissary to Churchill, because the bishop disapproved area bombing. Nothing came, nothing could come of this approach; later moves ran into the obstacle of the doctrine of 'unconditional surrender', laid down by Roosevelt at Casablanca in January and reaffirmed by Stalin at Teheran in December 1943.

Stalin's own agents in Germany were not at a level to affect policy; unless Roessler's mysterious informants are counted among them.[3] Trepper's group, the *Rote Kapelle*,[4] did include some junior officers in the Reich air ministry, but as Höhne has pointed out, they did not carry much real weight, and their circuit's importance has been a good deal exaggerated.[5] Hildegard Knef's memoirs show how difficult, how virtually impossible it was for the ordinary working man or woman to do anything at all.[6]

One body that had some access to the levers of real power in Germany, the army general staff, did give birth to a conspiracy. A group of senior officers, headed by Colonel-General Beck, first thought of moving in 1938; Hitler's success at Munich dissuaded them. Six years later, after several false starts, they brought themselves at last to the moment of decision. Oster, Canaris's deputy in the *Abwehr*, provided some SOE plastic. Colonel Count Claus von Stauffenberg, who had lost an arm and an eye in Tunisia and therefore looked unlike an assassin, at the fourth attempt did manage to make a bomb go off in Hitler's presence: at Rastenburg in east Prussia on 20 July 1944. As Namier remarked, had he handled his bomb himself, he would have died twelve hours sooner, but would have taken Hitler with him.[7]

For luck ran against the conspirators. Stauffenberg slipped out of the conference room 'to make a telephone call'; the man at whose knee he had left the

---

[1] K. Drobisch ed, *Wir schweigen nicht!* (Berlin 1968) has useful documents.
[2] See *The von Hassell Diaries 1938–1944* (1948); and Christopher Sykes, *Troubled Loyalty* (1968), a life of Adam von Trott zu Solz, ch. xv.
[3] See pp. 214–15 above.      [4] pp. 255–6 above.
[5] Höhne, *Codeword: Direktor*, 234–47.
[6] *The Gift Horse* (1971), 7, 22–8, 64–5.
[7] *The Listener*, l. 854–5, 19 November 1953. Christian Mueller, *Oberst i.G. Stauffenberg* (Düsseldorf 1972) is excellent, not least for the light it throws on general staff attitudes to Hitler.

bomb, hidden in a briefcase, pushed the briefcase further under the table and out of his own way; thus putting a stout wooden barrier between it and Hitler. Stauffenberg bluffed his way out of the Führer's headquarters and onto an aircraft for Berlin; but his colleague Fellgiebel failed to send an agreed message to Berlin to say that the bomb had gone off, and worse still failed to cut off the HQ communications network, of which he was in charge, from the outside world. Hitler, wounded, debagged, and shaken by the bomb, was nevertheless very much alive; and impressed his personality by telephone on Berlin, and by wireless on the German nation. Thousands of arrests, hundreds of executions followed. Hitler had all the executions of the senior conspirators filmed, and enjoyed watching their last struggles as they dangled from butchers' hooks on nooses made of piano wire. A tyrant of the dark ages might have attended in person; can we count it an advance in 'civilization' that a modern despot watches the fruits of despotism through the intermediary of a film camera?

When it was all over, when nazi terror had crumbled into ruin and suicide, and Germany had momentarily vanished from the world map, some of the saner surviving Germans crept out of the wreckage and started to create local democratic systems that would start to clear up the mess: provide at any rate water and sewage and bread, with gas and electricity and meat to follow later. Ulbricht's propaganda secretary, who entered east Berlin with him, has given a graphic account of how they were disillusioned: if they did not figure on Ulbricht's lists of the reliable, they were unpersons and would get out of the way.

As for innumerable complaints of rape by the Red Army, no such thing could be regarded as having taken place.[1]

---

[1] W. Leonhardt, *Child of the Revolution*, 300–12.

# 7 RESULTS

This book has looked at resistance, as people had to do at the time, from a couple of dozen separate national points of view. Is it possible to look at it as a whole?

Kühnrich, and hundreds of pamphlets written in the same sense, maintain that of course it can be seen as a whole: as part of the secular struggle of the world proletariat against fascist imperialism. Anyone who cares to adopt Kühnrich's standards for accepting, rejecting, and suppressing historical evidence, and to remain blind to the brute facts of communist imperialism,[1] is welcome to share Kühnrich's view. Only an exceptionally obscurantist bourgeois historian, of a Kühnrichian degree of one-sidedness, is going to try to deny a distinguished communist record in resistance: after 22 June 1941. Is there any wider, less party-bound, more comprehensive angle from which resistance and resisters can be viewed?

Let us first consider what resistance was able to effect in each of its main aspects – intelligence, deception, escape, sabotage, attacks, and politics – and then attempt to sum up.

## Intelligence

Readers may recall that a spy's task was double: to get hold of something worth sending, and then to send it safely.[2] Equally the task of the IO who received the report was double: to assess its worth, and then if it was worth anything to get action taken on it. How much notice did commanders take of their intelligence staffs?

This varied widely, according to their own training and capacity and to the quality of their staffs. Wavell, for example, a highly intelligent man who had been a Winchester scholar and passed senior into the staff college, took a keen and informed interest in the whole business of intelligence – besides being one of the

[1] Looking more brutish than ever in Angola, while this is in the press.
[2] p. 22 above.

main props of the deception system – and was always ready to modify or even scrap his plans in the light of fresh information. Portal, also a Wykehamist though not in college, shared Wavell's respect for brain. Others – Pound, Harris, Georges, Giraud, Budyenny might serve as examples – were more inclined to think that they were unlikely to learn from their own staffs, and that battles were won by force of character and strong moral fibre rather than bright ideas.

It does deserve remark that hardly anybody who made his service career in intelligence work rose to high rank, in Hitler's war or any other. We ought perhaps to make exceptions for Canaris and Peresypkin. In the British army, for example, battalions and brigades had a lieutenant at their HQ as intelligence officer (independent brigades had a captain). Because the IO usually came from within the unit, and lived and worked at the elbow of the adjutant or brigade major, he often came to be used as his senior's deputy, to the detriment of his own proper work. Exceptionally good commanders, with exceptionally good IO's, trusted them and used them and their intelligence sections to get useful data in battle. Yet most of these data came from observation, raiding, and brisk forward interrogation of prisoners, rather than from resistance.[1] Only two officers of the Intelligence Corps have ever attained any sort of public prominence: Strong and Buckmaster, the one a major-general, the other a colonel; it is not one of the regiments to which the army habitually looks for its high commanders.

And the British are not alone in this. According to Bertrand, he and his Polish friends had already done so well with 'Enigma' that the French high command was provided, throughout the battle of France (10 May–17 June 1940), with the enemy's order of battle, situation reports, and operation orders: intelligence as perfect as any commander could desire.[2] With or without its help, Georges endured the heaviest defeat ever inflicted on a French army in the field: worse even than Sedan or Waterloo, incomparably worse than Dien Bien Phu. Moral: even perfect intelligence does not guarantee victory, if the high command has lost the will and the means to win. Stalin, again, received ample warning – more directly from resistance sources – of the imminence of 'Barbarossa'; he preferred not to know, and his country underwent a very expensive defeat.[3]

Sometimes at the highest level of strategic planning intelligence did come into its own. Whether Roosevelt made wise use of 'Magic' is not a question this book has to answer;[4] it is just worth remark that there was no European equivalent to one of 'Magic's' triumphs, the death of Yamamoto.[5] Churchill often had to weigh vital intelligence material against equally vital economic and military data, to decide how to deploy to the best advantage the empire's limited resources for the tasks of war; he certainly, having worked with Hall at the admiralty many years before, and with Lindemann (Lord Cherwell) since the 1920s,

---

[1] Cp. Stuart Hood, *Pebbles from My Skull* (Hutchinson 1963), 13: 'I knew some tricks. That of two prisoners, the second will probably speak if the other is led away behind a truck and there is a burst of fire. That in such cases no blood need be shed.'

[2] See Bertrand, *Enigma*, 80–101, 273–92.  [3] Cp. p. 288 above.

[4] See Roberta Wohlstetter, *Pearl Harbour* (1963).  [5] Kahn, *Codebreakers*, 595–601.

was not inclined to despise intelligence, though he did have a tendency to distrust intelligence services.

In this rarefied air, of course, individual reports from individual agents hardly ever appeared unprocessed on the great men's working tables. Even a Sorge's or a 'Prince's' or a Roessler's report would arrive dressed, for security's sake, in some sort of garb and accompanied by some index of how sound people thought it was; and it would be considered in the light of all the other data that came with it, or were present already in the ideas and prejudices of the planners and statesmen who worked on it.

There did seem to be something sly, wry, waspish in the manner of a lot of SIS's staff; as of the staffs of some other intelligence services. This is perhaps another case of *déformation professionelle*; or it may only have been part of the cover, like SOE's fondness for looking shoddy.[1]

One day the highly intelligent dons who worked in SIS during the war may feel able to explain what they did, or at least what they remember of how and why they did it. Meanwhile they can say, with equal grace and truth, to the casual inquirer that it is none of his business, and that in any case they are bound by the official secrets act to lasting silence. They might at least write memoirs, to be left under seal in their college bursaries or even in the public record office, so that one day posterity can know what deeds they did, or kept others from doing.

If they leave their memoirs with their old chiefs, or with a current government department, they will be subject to that historian's bane, the archive clerk – knowing nothing of the subject – who is told to reduce by $n$ per cent the amount stored in a given area, so that there is room to store some more.[2]

We are getting rather remote from resistance; let us turn back to it through the work of one more don, John Austin the Magdalen philosopher, who was chief of the I a – news about the enemy – branch (the Americans called it G-2) at Eisenhower's supreme headquarters in 1943–5. When at last the Germans did surrender in May 1945, their armed forces were in such total confusion that they did not even know accurately where they were. The German negotiators in the team of staff officers arranging the details of how the *Wehrmacht*'s arms should be laid down said that they would be glad if they might give themselves up according to Colonel Austin's order of battle, as it was so much more complete and detailed than their own.[3]

Nothing could show more vividly the excellence of the information the Allies had by this closing stage of the war acquired; where had it come from?

A great deal of it certainly had come from resistance sources; part of it built up laboriously over many years' painstaking effort, by information circuits and

[1] Cp. p. 141 above.
[2] Photograph of 'weeders' at work, *Times*, 12 July 1975, 12a; and see Professor Watt's justified protest, ibid. 23 July 1975, 15g.
[3] Conversation with a common friend who had been in SIS, 1969.

the staffs who pored over their results; part of it from much more recent, casual, transitory connexions between forward fighting troops and resisters on the spot, who had told them through improvised channels about what the enemy was up to, and who he was, in some particular locality. This was a main task for partisans on Russian territory, and SOE, SAS, SIS (through 'Sussex') and thousands of resisters participated in it in the west and south as well.

Till recently, it was generally thought that resistance provided a large, probably a very large proportion of the tactical and order-of-battle intelligence that fighting troops needed, and that without its help the war would have had to go on even longer than it did. On the eastern front, this was probably the case; though there is a good deal here that has to be guessed at, rather than known for certain, about exactly how partisans and the Red Army exchanged news.

In the south and the west, we now have a quite new set of ideas to accommodate: dating from General Bertrand's *Enigma* (1972) and from its British equivalent, Group-Captain F. W. Winterbotham's *The Ultra Secret* (1974). Winterbotham dots some i's and crosses some t's in Bertrand's account (to which, oddly enough, he does not refer); the two together give a fair idea of what the 'Ultra' system was. Peter Calvocoressi's articles[1] are even more informative than Winterbotham's book about the mechanics of work on it at Bletchley.

A summary is due to those who have not read any of these three striking works. The Germans used an 'Enigma' machine cipher, which they credulously supposed unbreakable; the Poles, the French, and the British broke it (with each others' help) in turn; as a result, masses of order-of-battle and operational data became available, to a very restricted circle of the Allied high command. Bertrand, as head of the French section D, was in charge of decipher, with Polish help.[2] Winterbotham was in charge of distributing the material round the British and American high commands: a delicate task, carried out through an unspecified number of Special Liaison Units, under the code name of 'Ultra'. Many of the staffs of these SLU's are no doubt still alive; all still bound by the official secrets act to silence; and, as like as not, no more aware of the real import of the material they handled than a cabinet office typist could necessarily recall what she had spent the day on copying.

Some 'Ultra' material was of almost unbelievably high quality: operation instructions, from Hitler personally to his supreme commanders, which now and again were read by his enemies even before they had been got into the hands of their momentarily absent addressees. A great deal of it was intensely dull: posting orders for other ranks, for example, sent by 'Enigma' because the machine was there and fast and easy to use. It all originated with the prewar Polish secret service; but by the time it had been encapsulated into MI6's GCCS structure at Bletchley it looked more like a commercial operation and less like an act of resistance.

[1] *Sunday Times*, 24 November 1974, 33–4; *Listener*, 20 and 27 January, 3 February 1977, xcvii. 70, 112, 135.  [2] Cp. pp. 243, 292 above.

By now the materials that might once have been used, to assess what weight resistance sources supplied direct to the total of intelligence available to Allied commanders, and what weight came from 'Ultra', have probably perished. Those materials that survive under secret cover are presumably supposed so secret, in the methods that publication would reveal, that their secrecy will be maintained indefinitely. Whether the supposition is right or not – Calvocoressi, in his article, makes it clear he thinks it is not, and he might know, as he became head of the main body of 'Enigma' IOs at Bletchley – secret authorities still seem to believe it. So for once the recent historian is in the same fix as his mediaeval and ancient colleagues: instead of having an avalanche of material through which to tunnel his way, he has only a few broken shards of fact, and must make as assured a guess as he can.

Were resistance sources only a sort of insurance policy, kept fully paid up in case the Germans one day scrapped 'Enigma' and turned to one-time-pad? Must the survivors of 'Rémy's', of 'Marie-Madeleine's', of a dozen other famous intelligence circuits now ask themselves whether what they did was a genuine help to the war effort, or only a staff superfluity?

In the present state of published knowledge, it is quite impossible to dogmatize. A few points are worth making. There is no evidence that Russian-dominated circuits were in any sense in competition with 'Enigma', as the Russians do not seem to have read its traffic. The 'Enigma' code wheels were frequently changed – at some stages in the war, a major change every twenty-four hours and minor changes every eight hours in between; so the 'Ultra' teams could by no means rely on knowing everything, or on knowing it at once. On one essential point, what proportion of the intercepted data they read, nothing has been let out at all; nor is it quite clear that they intercepted all the data, because 'Enigma's' signal was not particularly strong, nor easy to read from Allied soil. And sometimes the Germans had the common sense to maintain total wireless silence on a particular front, thus foxing 'Ultra' and the Y service alike, completely (and what, by the by, were the relations between 'Ultra' and Y?). At such moments resistance circuits were not merely useful, they were indispensable. The Ardennes offensive in December 1944 is a good example: Rundstedt insisted on total wireless silence, so neither 'Ultra' nor Y could give a single word of warning; good IOs on the Allied side were nevertheless aware that something was in the wind.

All the textbooks on the history of this war need of course to be rewritten in the light of our knowledge, such as it is, of 'Ultra'; except for Calvocoressi's own.[1] He could not help writing from a position of inside knowledge; and it is this point of view that helps to make his book so readable. Alexander put it that the data provided by 'Ultra' added an extra dimension to the business of war.[2] In fact 'Ultra' did not do more than a really first-class spy would have done,

---

[1] Calvocoressi and Wint, *Total War*.
[2] Winterbotham, op. cit., 187.

operating in the headquarters from which 'Enigma' transmitted; but as the Germans had several hundred 'Enigma' machines (again, we are not told how many), 'Ultra' could produce in a quantity that no single spy could dream of rivalling, and its material ranged all over the Axis-occupied world. Alexander and other commanders trusted it the more, because it reached them from their own side and from their own superiors in the military establishment, from above; it therefore fitted in with the prejudices on which they had been brought up – once they had been told what it was. In May 1941, the Allied high command in Crete was told in great detail what General Student was going to do to it, but with no revelation of the source; the reports were therefore brushed aside, as 'more of this intelligence nonsense'; with disastrous results. Thereafter, a very few very senior people were told exactly what was going on; all the survivors kept silent till Bertrand went into print.

The problem of the relative value of spies and 'Ultra' reports remains one of great technical interest and import, and it is much to be hoped that a serious study of it has been made in secret; or will be made, before all the material for it goes down the maw of the secret shredding machines. Meanwhile, unless the contrary is later proved against them, survivors of intelligence circuits can continue to believe that they played a cardinal role in the conduct of the war.

## Deception

Deception was a key problem in the intelligence war, but a comparatively marginal one for almost all resisters.

A lot of the Germans' time and energy was taken up by *Funkspiele*, wireless games: attempts to play back captured agents' sets to Allied secret service headquarters. The results can be summarized in a few lines.

In the Netherlands, the Germans did very well for eighteen months against SOE, and thus made their task of holding down an exceptionally gifted and hostile population a good deal more easy: this was an undoubted German gain. Against SOE elsewhere they seem to have done poorly except in France; even there, they did not do very well.[1] Against OSS they had one or two slight successes; against SIS they scored at Venlo and in Amsterdam, but thereafter seem to have done poorly. Against MI5 they suffered a very heavy defeat; and against Moscow they appear to have struggled largely or even wholly in vain. The XX committee's preparations for 'Fortitude' secured practically 100 per cent success, of a shattering kind.

Resistance's main claim here is that it provided the context in which these games could be played; there is neither need nor occasion to claim more. Strategists are always more ready to sacrifice irregular than regular troops for deception's sake. The only serious occasion when this happened in this war was

[1] pp. 264–7, 249–50 above.

in Greece in the summer of 1943, as part of the cover for 'Husky'. Greek losses were not severe; and the fall of Mussolini, a direct result, was worth it.[1]

## Escape

A lot of effort, an incalculable amount of courage, and several million pounds sterling went into escape lines: were they in any way justified?

Their cost in money is inestimable; but scholarship hardly has more to do with money than has bravery, and we need not do much arithmetic. One simple figure can be given: by the summer of 1944, the chance of a safe return to this country for unwounded English-based aircrew shot down over Europe west of Germany, who parachuted clear of immediate arrest, was about evens – one was quite as likely to come back unscathed as to be taken prisoner. This figure by itself justifies a great deal of escape line effort, even in financial terms. At that time, it cost up to £15,000 to train a single fighter pilot, and £23,000 to train the seven-man crew of a Lancaster bomber.[2] When we remember that by 1969 it cost £250,000 to train a single operational pilot for the RAF,[3] we can see why some degree of caution has been exercised over the years by the British government in releasing stories about escape and its techniques. In times of grave international tension, people have to contemplate the prospect of one day going through the whole exercise again; hence, some care about security may still be worth while.

How many people did get away? One grand total is available: 33,517 people in all, in the forces of the British crown or of the United States, returned from enemy-held to Allied territory during the war. Among these 23,208, of whom 1,534 were officers, escaped, and 10,309, of whom 3,694 were officers, evaded. Most of the evaders were aircrew; hence the high proportion of officers among them. Indeed, of the 2,692 members of the USAAF who evaded capture, officers accounted for 1,380, over half.[4] These figures fit in well with Neave's claim that MI9's lines brought over 4,000 aircrew back.[5] The escapers' figure is inflated, to an extent not yet ascertainable, by a large number of men, anything up to 10,000, who got out of camps in Italy in September 1943, when the Italians changed sides in the war; in any case the grand total, larger than two full-sized divisions, was no negligible contribution to military manpower.

Of escapes eastward, as has been said already, little is known. If there was a soviet Humphreys, his identity is still a secret. The disasters that overtook prisoners from the forces of the USSR were too formidable for more than an anguished mention here. All the patriotic rejoicings of the British about those who made the home run from Germany – and there were only fifty of them,

---

[1] A. Cave Brown, *Bodyguard of Lies* (1976), attacks this view with vigour, but with surprisingly little substantial new evidence. The reader who still rates the credibility of *Bodyguard of Lies* high after reading Hugh Trevor-Roper, *New York Review of Books,* 19 February, and Michael Howard, *Times Literary Supplement,* 28 May 1976, is welcome to differ. [2] Neave, 24; and Haslam to Foot, 4 December 1972. [3] Ibid. [4] Ibid. [5] Neave, 22.

including Neave and Millar – pale into a shocked hush when we look to the east. Among a total of 5,700,000 Red Army prisoners conditions were so deplorable that hardly a million were left alive at the end of the war; a consequence both of the nazis' racial doctrines, which led them to treat Slavs as a sort of superior cattle, and of the fact that the USSR had not signed the international convention on prisoners of war, so that their captives were outside even such protection as the Red Cross could give.[1]

Again, to lift our minds beyond the parish boundaries of officer aircrew escape sagas, we ought to glance at least at another aspect of nazism, what happened to European Jewry; and how much of it was saved by resistance. The 2,600 children rescued through Wilfred Israel's efforts and sent to kibbutzim in Palestine in 1944–5[2] do not look many beside the total done away with in extermination camps: somewhere between 4,000,000 and 6,000,000. Even when we add over 6,000 saved by the Danes, about 25,000 hidden by the Dutch, and so on, to the 280,000 odd who got away before the fighting, we are still not up to half a million; against 4,000,000 to 6,000,000 dead. Tremendous efforts were made to save Jews, many of them by Jews, many of them by resisters; but their rescue is not the brightest page in resistance history.

Not all the balance in this sort of historical accounting even lies in credits on the Allied side. As Giskes put it in a pregnant aside, 'the principle that intelligence is more valuable than elimination carries weight with security services'.[3] Some penetration of escape lines may have been effected, unostentatiously, by the Germans, who no doubt used such opportunities as they could get for watching how the lines worked and for interrogating those who were passing down them. Valuable order-of-battle data could be squeezed out of a man who thought he owed it to his escape line comrades, into whose hands he trusted his life, to be straight with them, whatever the squadron security officer had told him before he took off on his last previous flight. The Germans thought the data they thus gained well worth the price of a few escaped pilots: they may not have appreciated correctly how sensitive a point pilot training was in the Allied manpower imbroglio, for lack of high-level sources of their own.

And the individual who escaped successfully, as well as the individual who helped him do so, never had a moment's doubt that they were doing something worth while. Let us step just outside Europe's confines for a few examples that bear record. Twenty Gurkhas walked back together from surrendered Tobruk to El Alamein in the summer of 1942, sooner than give in; so did a South African private bearing the proudest name in African military history, Chaka. Seven South African signallers, hitherto base details with a cushy job, on the same occasion commandeered their divisional commander's car, defied his order to surrender, and drove it away to freedom.[4] Anyone who has performed such an

[1] H-A. Jacobsen in Krausnick et al., The Anatomy of the SS State, 523–31.
[2] Ian Colvin, Flight 777, 201.     [3] London Calling North Pole, 110, tr.
[4] PRO AIR 20/2330.

escape, or aided in it, knows he or she has taken part in an enterprise that was enormously worth while; whatever the accountants say.

## Sabotage

In sheer physical factory sabotage, resistance made a sizeable but far from decisive dent in the nazi economy. How large the dent was, and how much notice the nazis took of it, remain open questions.

Alan Milward argued at Salford, in an austere passage, that the dent was all but imperceptible, and instances the evidence of Speer; who, if anyone, ought to have known, for he was nazi production minister in 1943–5. Speer's first reply (at once retracted; but still, he made it), when asked what impact French resistance had had on arms production, was to inquire 'What French resistance?'[1] A great many resistance historians take for granted, without pausing to look for evidence, that the impact of sabotage must have been large; Professor Milward suggests that it was probably small, and perhaps very small.

A lot of work remains to be done here by economic quite as much as by military historians; there is a need for some people who command the capabilities of both sub-disciplines. We need also, within the sub-discipline of military history, some move to resolve a difference among ourselves. Some historians, particularly those with air interests or connexions, are convinced that air bombardment was a highly efficient weapon of economic warfare, and that sabotage was virtually useless, a political toy to keep the more restive of the occupied populace happy. Others, particularly those with resistance interests or connexions, hold a contrary view: that a good saboteur was infinitely preferable to the best of bombers, as well as far less expensive. For he could go straight to the one vital machine in a whole production line, and make sure he put it permanently out of action; while the most accurate of bombing raids might only cover the vital machine in unimportant debris, from which a few hours' work could dig it out and put it back to makeshift if not to full production.

Clearly the truth lies somewhere between these two extreme views; to establish just where, is one of the tasks facing historians of the war. An earlier attempt to start discussion on these lines in this country has (so far as I know) come to nothing.[2] A few points are still worth repeating.

Operations such as Harry Rée's at Montbeliard, which have been called blackmail sabotage, are in every respect preferable to air attacks: cheaper in lives, cheaper in property, much more certain in their impact. They are unconventional; what on earth is the point of acting conventionally in war?

The trouble in 1940–5 was that convention had a firm hold on all the belligerent powers; and force of habit, the immense flywheel-effect of a smooth administration at work, reinforced it. The British and American war machines were geared

---

[1] Milward's tr.; quoted in Hawes and White, *Resistance in Europe*, 197.
[2] Foot, 287–8, 352–5, 435–9.

to the production of huge fleets of bomber aircraft; superbly brave men manned them; superbly ingenious scientists worked out devices to enable them to know where they were, and where the weapons they carried might fall. Yet as instruments of firepower, though they surpassed artillery in range and in load of explosive, they lagged far, far behind it in precision.[1] They were aluminium tubes, filled with men and gadgets, still largely at the mercy of fright, weather, and chance. Agents were also at the mercy of fright, weather, and chance; might be even more expensive to train well; provided much less employment and much less immediately usable matter for propaganda; but militarily at a few points at least were much the better bet.

Alan Milward picks on the Rjukan heavy water raid[2] and a series of small raids on French wolfram mines as the only examples he knows of really worthwhile sabotage.[3] The agents of F and RF sections in France made or instigated some 150 attacks on French factories, mines, and power installations which were investigated in some detail after the liberation.[4] In few cases did they bring production to a total stop, but they certainly exercised some impact, even if only the impact of a sharp pin-prick, on the German war machine; and all this with a total of about 3,000 lbs of explosive, less than the bomb load of a single light bomber of 1944. In Denmark in 1943–4, particularly, there was more of the same. And the Rjukan raid alone may well have turned the course of the war: nine men can seldom have deserved better of their fellows. Transport sabotage, a separate and more special case, will be looked at in a moment.

Treatment of sabotage necessarily leads over also into treatment of politics; as the Russians learned better than most. Sabotage in 1940–5 was almost always political in its motivation: not quite. There was some degree of plain bloody-mindedness among forced labourers everywhere, particularly inside Germany, that stemmed as much from the miseries of being in exile and under compulsion, and having too little to eat, as from anxiety to make sure the Germans lost the war.

The Germans expected no miracle from their slave labour, and did not get it. Rates of absenteeism in coal mines in northern France in the early 1940s were much the same as those in Lanarkshire in the early 1970s.

One slave labourer is worth recall among millions; one of those who even when in captivity could not forget that he was a resister, and must go on fighting the war. Michel Hollard, the former head of 'Agir', found himself, in a concentration camp working party, manufacturing weapons for the Germans, under rigid supervision. He rose to the challenge to his ingenuity and resistance skills, and never let a day pass without abstracting at least one piece of equipment – always the same piece – that would render at least one weapon useless. He may

---

[1] Such squadrons as 617, which hit the Ruhr dams, or the Mosquito squadrons that went for Gestapo headquarters, deserve a word of special exception.

[2] p. 282 above.  [3] Milward in Hawes and White, op cit., 193–6.

[4] See Foot, 505–17.

have done the Germans out of 300 machine guns; he certainly exposed himself to frightful extra risks. It was not a quite useless spell in their hands.[1]

## Attacks on troops

There is an urgent task for military historians who can tear themselves away from reciting citations and recording details of changes in uniforms: someone, more probably some team, needs to work out the impact of resistance on the German army in retreat in 1943–5. While units' war diaries, and a decent proportion of subaltern officers, survive, there is quite a lot worth investigating.

So far the air forces have taken all the credit, particularly on the western front. They are of course much more photogenic than peasants or workmen lying in ambush; and they had superior public relations teams in action with them at the time. The story is for example familiar of how a carefully coordinated run of bombing attacks in May and early June 1944 cut all but one of the bridges across the Seine below Paris, and all but one of those across the Loire below Gien; in order to isolate the 'Neptune' battlefield from reinforcement. Somebody might have reflected that after their Russian experiences the Germans would have plenty of field bridging equipment with them. Hardly anybody outside France has noticed how little use they could make of it, because of resistance attacks on bridging parks; or how many – nearly a thousand – were the resisters' rail cuts effected on the night 'Neptune' went ashore.

The case of the panzer division that got from the eastern front to Strasbourg in a week, and took three weeks more to cover the much shorter distance to Caen, is well known; surely it was not an isolated one? That some delay was imposed on German columns by resisters' ambushes is certain;[2] will or can no one work out how much it was, and how far it affected the Germans' fighting quality?

Their hold on their own rear areas was certainly often shaky in the east, and became shaky in France in July–August 1944 (at latest) and in Italy in April 1945. The extreme bleakness of the eastern front, particularly in winter, is something that the west European imagination cannot easily conjure up. It is worth a few moments' reflexion. Through that desolation of scorched earth, corduroy roads, illimitable marshland, supply columns had to struggle for hundreds of miles; knowing that if they went without guards, they would be stripped by partisans; and that even if they went with them, any awk turn might be seized on by the ubiquitous partisan for an ambush or at least a mortar strafe. War is not a comfortable business; partisans, who lived as a rule in the utmost discomfort, lousy, starving, frozen and grilled season and season about, did a lot to impose the utmost discomfort on their enemies. Partisan types in the concentration camp of Auschwitz even made plans to infect the least lovable of their

---

[1] G. Martelli, *Agent Extraordinary*, ad fin.

[2] Elaborate example in Foot, 395–6, of eleven men interrupting the march of a thousand.

SS guards with typhus-laden lice: can a tougher resister than that be conceived?[1] Probably on the eastern front partisans did much more than air attack to make the life of German soldiers behind an often fluid 'front' into hell on earth; it would be interesting to know how much of the same effect was exercised in the west by maquisards, in the south by *andartes* and partisans.

## Political

Nothing on the political front could ever be quite the same again: no conservative, however reactionary, can in fact turn time backward.

The revolution of which so many resisters had dreamed remained a dream; unless some fragments of it were achieved in Yugoslavia, in the teeth of geological poverty and suspicious friends and neighbours. The war ended everywhere with a victory parade; bodies of men in uniform, marching conformably in step – the generals everywhere insisted on it. Ordinary people might remember more vividly the happy chaos of de Gaulle's apotheosis down the Champs Élysées,[2] or the crowds dancing in St James's on VE night by the light of the torches that had been lit for Trafalgar and for Waterloo, or more lurid scenes of happy ex-slave-girls giving themselves to all comers on piles of mattresses in the street, by the light of burning bourgeois houses in the smartest suburb of Marburg.[3]

Conformity has enormous social and political value, in quiet times; it helps to make and to keep the times quiet. Conformists, though, were the one class to which resisters did not belong. Liddell Hart, the unorthodox, probing critic of the deadwood high command of the war of 1914, when he looked at resistance was nevertheless orthodox enough to draw attention to the social dangers inherent in it, for the future of a settled society.[4] But who wants his society settled?

War and resistance between them produced a general shaking-up and shaking-out of societies, and got rid of a new generation of dead wood; some of the dullards and *embusqués* have crept back again, whether in the baggage of capitalist or of communist bureaucrats. In much of eastern Europe there has been a nominal revolution, brought in by the Red Army, which raises an awkward problem for resisters: now that communism is displaying some of the revolting features of the nazism they resisted, what do they think of it? The dourest maquisard of the FTP, the toughest Pripet partisan might begin to have doubts. Those who are crazed with the spell of far Muscovia remain captivated; and from inside, the system does carry all sorts of overtones of being 'forced to be free', delightfully, by the compulsions of Hegelian logic. 'For us,' said the young

[1] J. Garliński, *Fighting Auschwitz*, 142.
[2] See A. Dansette, *Libération de Paris*, 410–12.
[3] See René Cutforth, *Order to View* (1969), 115. I owe this reference to Dr J. K. Hyde.
[4] (Sir) Basil Liddell Hart, *Defence of the West* (1961), ch. vii; copying Clausewitz, *On War*, IV. xxvi.

Leonhard, 'freedom meant insight into historical necessity.'[1] People unable to accept this form of bondage to freedom continue to feel uneasy, at best, about the state of the soviet union and its satellites.

Old resisters cannot safely be ignored, by any authoritarian régime. The strongest of the survivors still glow with a special kind of courage: more cold-blooded than a boy's adventurousness, more hot-blooded than a chess-player's calculation of chances. They had a divine rashness; and can only be shrugged off as unimportant by people even more rash than they.

Yet even at the time, mixed in with the titans in resistance there were sly and supple men, with a good eye for odds, who thought anti-nazism was the sounder horse to back; some of them doubled their bet with pro-communism; many have made themselves satisfactory political careers. Their presence in the anti-nazi alliance did not make it any more fragrant; hence the profound pessimism about the nature of the war, and even of resistance, in such a devout ex-crusader as Evelyn Waugh, whom SOE for some inexplicable reason sent as a liaison officer, with Randolph Churchill, to the Yugoslav partisans.[2]

Over against these doubts and indecisions, one political point can nevertheless be scored up in resistance's favour, besides the obvious one that a great many leading European statesman of the two decades after the war owed their prominence to their resistance careers. Though there was no such thing as a 'European resistance movement' – there were only politically all-too-separate movements, within the geographic confines of Europe – resistance did re-create a sense of common European feeling and interest. Young men and women encamped in the wilds, far too excited to sleep, debated interminably the proper principles of national and international organization. (The fact that the communists among them most often rose to positions of political power demonstrates communist hold on political technique, not on political truth.) There were barbarians loose, in the SS, particularly in those special groups who hunted out the nazis' enemies in the east, and in the *Totenkopf* (death's head) division that guarded the camps, whose barbarity everyone of goodwill could recognize and reject. Many of the good impulses born of war have been frittered away by politicians during the uneasy peace. But when Mr Gladstone said, in a Balkan context, over a century ago, that 'the bare breasts of free men' were the best barrier against tyranny,[3] was he not right? Or has he too been overtaken by technology?

[1] Leonhard, *Child of the Revolution*, 385.
[2] See David Pryce-Jones ed, *Evelyn Waugh and His World* (1973), 3, 134–5, 148–9.
[3] Cp. E. J. Feuchtwanger, *Gladstone* (1975), 183.

# 8   REAL IMPACT

To work out what the real impact of resistance was, between 1940 and 1945, we need to consider in outline what were the results of the war.

The error of 1919–20 was not repeated: there has never been a formal peace settlement, on the supposed errors of which revisionist nations could hang their claims. More than thirty years have now passed since the European war's end, and a few main trends are perceptible.

Russia ended the war in a vastly stronger position than she had occupied in 1939; in spite of appalling devastation, much of it self-inflicted, and a rate of casualty that a weaker national grouping and a weaker political system could never have supported. As soon as the fighting was over, the state propaganda machine carried out another U-turn, and has explained ever since that the soviet victory was due to the wise guidance of Comrade Stalin and of the CPSU, of which latter body a good deal less had been heard during the war.[1]

The USA was in a very much stronger position still: undoubtedly the world's leading nation, fully mobilized, territorially undamaged, comparatively lightly affected by casualties, and in sole possession of the secrets of nuclear power. A simple, perhaps an over-simple way of looking at world history from 1945 to 1975 is to regard it as the period in which the USSR reduced this enormous lead over itself by the USA to the wafer-thin margin of today. The lack of use the Americans made of their power in the mid 1940s provides a short proof that they are not really imperialist tigers.

The British, the imperialist tigers of the previous century, reached 1945 apparently strong but really weak; having won the war, but having ruined ourselves in doing so, by over-extending ourselves militarily and economically after 1941. We had one remaining enormous asset, of goodwill towards us on the continent; built up over the war years by visiting agents of the secret services, and by the special duties crews of the RAF; founded indeed in the summer of 1940 when, thanks to our anti-tank ditch of the Channel and to the pilots and

---

[1] See p. 289 above.

radar operators of fighter command, we managed to hold out against the nazis' attack that had so far overwhelmed all its enemies. Most of this stock of goodwill was squandered; a little remains to welcome us as we tiptoe at last from the shallow end into the pool of the common market, from which de Gaulle barred us out, because – among weightier reasons – he could not bear to remember how he had depended on us and our American cousins during the war.

De Gaulle had come to power more by the will of resisters, than on American bayonets; the France to which he returned – going straight to his 1940 office in the rue Saint-Dominique, where even the blotting-paper on his desk remained unchanged – had been broken in battle in 1940, but had recovered resilience and self-reliance in the underground war. Of Italy, of Norway, indeed of every occupied country, much the same can be said: in southern, western, and northern Europe at least. In eastern Europe where new régimes had been, or were being, imported by the Red Army, things were not exactly on a par with the west: the promise of a new heaven and a new earth, delivered in a Russian accent, could ring hollow. Kühnrich picked out for praise a French resistance manifesto of March 1944 that pressed for freedom of thought, knowledge, and speech; inviolability of domicile; a free press; untrammelled private correspondence: did he simply forget Hungary in 1956?[1]

China, all southern Asia, were in turmoil; strange new things were preparing there. In Europe they had begun already, with the revolutionary wars resisters had fought in Yugoslavia and Albania, that had captured state power.

Above all, Hitler and Himmler were dead; the two worst men even this century has so far seen. Most people who survived them felt that the struggle to have done with them was worth it; even at the frightful price in death and devastation that had to be paid. The survivors could try to learn not to allow psychopaths to run great states into great disasters; and wonder how to handle the terrors of nuclear power, that have ushered in a new age.[2]

André Gillois has recorded that 'General de Gaulle said to me one day, "Between you and me, Resistance was a bluff that came off." '[3] There is an element of truth in this: resistance's real strength in battlefield terms, in an age of armour and air warfare, was puny. But it had titanic, as it turned out invincible, strength in moral terms. It gave back to people in the occupied countries the self-respect that they lost in the moment of occupation. People who had been in it, or near it, or simply with it in spirit, were able to face themselves calmly in a looking-glass, and to know that they had not in the end been cowards; they had belonged to a band of radical companions, mostly unknown to each other, who had put their utmost into fighting evil.

The ancient Greeks were obsessed with the worth of creating a κτῆμα εἰς ἀεί,

---

[1] H. Kühnrich, *Partisanenkrieg*, 322.

[2] Cp. G. Barraclough, *Introduction to Contemporary History* (1964).

[3] A. Gillois, *Histoire secrète des Français à Londres de 1940 à 1944* (Hachette 1973), 164, tr.

something that men who came later would always remember and respect. What resisters did often had something in it that was in this sense memorable.

This is not a trendy or a 'contemporary' way of looking at the world; it is out of fashion and out of favour; it does not suit what seems to be coming to us. Outgribing futurologues offer us a prospect of unyielding despair: muddle, starvation, suffering that will make Stalingrad or Lahore, let alone Coventry or Guernica, seem like a children's picnic; either that, or submission, a quiet knuckling under to the will of a bureaucratic universal state. If this is how we must go down, 'Not with a bang but a whimper', let us as we sink remember those who resisted Hitler, especially their dead: people for whom human dignity was not a hollow phrase.

Organization of some sort there must be; the intricacies of mechanized life demand it. But organization need not forget humanity. We are none of us so long down from the trees that we can afford to neglect what Hobbes taught us in a famous passage, over three centuries ago, about life in 'a time of war, where every man is enemy to every man', and people will not agree to live with some degree of discipline: 'no arts, no letters; no society; and which is worst of all, continual fear, and danger of violent death; and the life of man, solitary, poor, nasty, brutish, and short.'[1] But we need not let it dominate our every moment.

If you who read this can say, I am not under fire; I am not under torture; I am not on the run; if I hear a noise at six in the morning, I know it is a neighbour or a milkman, not the secret police; no one in my country is arrested and held without prompt charge and trial; I can read newspapers, see and hear broadcasts, of several different views; within the laws of libel, I can say what I like about anybody; then you owe it, in a larger degree than most historians have so far allowed, to the resistance that occupied Europe put up to Hitler.

There is a Dutch saying worth recall: only dead fishes float down the stream, live ones swim against it.

[1] *Leviathan* (1651), part I, ch. xiii.

# NOTE ON BOOKS

Here, as above, books in English are published in London, and books in French in Paris, unless another origin is given.

## General

For the historical background from which the war developed, see John Roberts, *Europe 1880–1945* (Longmans 1967) or James Joll, *Europe since 1870* (Weidenfeld and Nicolson 1973).

Among many histories of the war, five stand out: Gordon Wright, *The Ordeal of Total War* (Harper, New York 1968) for justice combined with brevity; Peter Calvocoressi and Guy Wint, *Total War* (Allen Lane 1972), the best single-volume treatment at length; Henri Michel, *La Seconde Guerre Mondiale* (Presses Universitaires de France, 2 v, 1968-9) for breadth of view; and H-A. Jacobsen and Hans Dollinger, *Der zweite Weltkrieg in Bildern und Documenten* (Kurt Desch, 3 v, Munich 1962) for pictorial as well as historical cover. A. J. P. Taylor, *The Second World War* (Hamish Hamilton 1975), like Jacobsen's book, consists of pictorial history; liberally sprinkled with taylorisms, and not inclined to over-stress resistance.

Casterman: *Encyclopedie de la Guerre 1939–1945* (Casterman, Brussels 1977), prepared under the editorial direction of Marcel Baudot, Henri Bernard, Hendrik Brugmans, M. R. D. Foot, and H-A. Jacobsen, is a convenient source on points of fact.

*BFSP: British and Foreign State Papers*, a collection in English, French, and German of the principal diplomatic documents of international importance (now HMSO; almost yearly volumes since 1841).

## Bibliographies

Henri Michel, *Bibliographie critique de la Résistance* (Sevpen 1964) is admirable, but deals mainly with France, and is over ten years old. Max Gunzenhäuser,

*Geschichte des geheimen Nachrichtendienstes* (Bernard & Graefe, Frankfurt am Main, 1968) has a wider range than its title suggests, but is some long way from being perfect. Here is a large gap, hard to fill.

## Resistance

On the single subject of the concentration camp at Auschwitz (Oświęcim) there is already a bibliography of over 7,000 items. The particular case is exceptional; but may serve as an instance of the profusion of cover provided for many resistance subjects. Books used for specific points have been detailed in footnotes above. A very few of those most often cited are worth repeating here:

*ERM: European Resistance Movements 1939–1945*: i (Pergamon Press 1960) covers the international conference of 1958 at Liège, ii (Pergamon Press 1964) that of 1961 at Milan, and iii (typescript, not yet published) that of 1962 at Oxford. References to *ERM* iii give the page number in each item; there is no general pagination.

Foot: M. R. D. Foot, *SOE in France* (HMSO 1966, second impression 1968), includes an idiosyncratic bibliography (pp. 453–64).

Harris Smith: R. Harris Smith, *OSS* (University of California Press 1972).

Lorain: Pierre Lorain, *Armement Clandestin* (l'Emancipatrice 1972).

Michel, *SW*: Henri Michel, tr. R. H. Barry, *The Shadow War* (Deutsch 1972).

Neave: Airey Neave, *Saturday at MI9* (Hodder & Stoughton 1969).

Sweet-Escott: Bickham Sweet-Escott, *Baker Street Irregular* (Methuen 1965), by a former senior staff officer in SOE.

Lastly,

*RHDGM*: Henri Michel ed, *Revue d'histoire de la deuxième guerre mondiale* (Presses Universitaires de France, quarterly since 1950), far and away the leading learned journal on its subject; francocentric in view; includes useful book reviews.

A note may be added on **film**.

In spite of the intensely dramatic nature of much of resistance – interspersed, like any other form of war, with long dull stretches – there is hardly any authentic film: for an obvious reason. Taking film simply provided a run of extra risks, in a context where every risk was weighed, and sensible people took on no more risks than they must. Using cameras on tripods was unthinkably conspicuous. Hand-held film cameras were then still rich men's toys, far too easily traceable; and film once taken *could not* be disguised as anything else. It is remarkable that any was taken at all.

A little simulated film, made soon after the event, is of some use to historians as a picture of resisters' manners and customs: eg. René Clement's *Bataille du Rail* (1944) or a film made by some amateurs in SOE and the RAF, called *Now it can be told* (also 1944), starring Harry Rée and Jacqueline Nearne. As a corrective, one should also see *Nacht und Nebel* (1955); if one is a sound sleeper.

# INDEX

Diacritical marks ignored, in fixing alphabetical order; except for German ö and Danish ø, both treated as oe. Hyphens also ignored: S-phone between 'Sphère' and Sporre. Titles in brackets (thus) conferred after the war. Entries in brackets: relevant name not given on page concerned. Main passages in bold type. R = resistance.

Katyn, 146, 295, 298
Kauffmann, H., 273
Kautsky, K., 62
Kavka, F., cited, 209
Keble, C. M., 159
Kell, Sir V., 134
Keller, R., see K
Kelly, Sir D., 213, 216–17
Kemp, P., 118, 198, 232
Kennan, G., 233
Kennedy, J. F., 51 and n, 62–3
Kennet, Lord, see Young, W.
Kenya, 163
Kersten, F., 285
Kessel, J., 21, 103, 171
Kesselring, A., (220), 227–8
KGB, 144–6
Kharkov, 50, 188
Khrushchov, N. S., 62–3
Killearn, Lord, 158 and n
Kilmartin, T., (125n), (250)
'Kim', 100, 134, and see Philby
'King Kong', see Lindemans, C.
Kipling, R., 15, (17), 79, 100, 134
Kislenko, 220, 373
KKE, xvi, 176, **179–82**
Klaras, A., 180
(Klop, D.), 259
(Klopper, D.), 312
Klugman, J., 159, 198
Knatchbull-Hugessen, Sir H., 164–6, (201), 222n
Knatchbull-Hugessen, Lady, 166
Knef, Hildegarde, 303
Knight, C., 256
*Knokploegen*, group, 261, 267
Knox ('Dilly'), 243, 292
Koch-Kent, H., cited, 258
Koenig, P-J., 248
Koestler, A., 144, 233
Kogon, E., 301n
Kolbe, F., 218–19
Kollontay, Aleksandra, 272, 284
*Kommandobefehl*, 32–3
Korneev, 197
Koryzis, A. 177, 178
Kosice, 209
Kosovo, 183
Kossuth, L., 200 and n
KPD, xvi, 214, 218, 300–2, 304
Kragt, D., 269
Kragujevac, 226
Krausnick, H., 34n, 149, 211n, 293n, 300, 312n
Kreipe, K. 181–2
Kreisau circle, 302–3
Křen, J., cited, 104n, 206n
Krivitsky, W., 288–9
Kruuse, J., cited, 55n
Kubiš, J., 205–7
Kühnrich, H., 207n, 208n, 286, 290n, 291, 305, 319
Kun, B., 198–9, 201
Kuomintang, 156

Kupi, A., 184–5
Kutusov, M. L., 290
'Kuznetsov, F. I.', 145

Labour, 54, 81–2, 96, 114, 162, 174, 227, 233, 314, 316; *and see* Strikes; Women
Lactantius, cited, 50
Lalatović, M., 194
Lamia, 180–2
Lampe, D., cited, 139n, 275n
Lampson, Sir M., see Killearn, Lord
Langer, W. L., 142
Langley, J. M., 31n, 97n, 137, 244, 245–6, 256, 257n, 268n
Lapierre, D., cited, 253n
Lassen, A., VC, and S., 164 and n
Latin America, 33, 142–3, 153–4
Latin Europe, 77; *and see* Belgium; France; Iberia; Italy; Romania
Latvia, 12, 285–6
Laurens, Anne, cited, 97n
Lausanne, 215–16
Lauwers, H. M. G., 264–7
Laval, P., 237
Lawrence, T. E., 20n, 47, (118), 129, 138, 158
LCS, xvi, 133; *and see* Deception
'Le Carré, J.', 136
Le Chêne, E., cited, 211n
Leadership, 17–18, 54–5, 58n, 62–3, 73, 85, 134–9, 142, 192, 203–4, 223, 229, 236, 238–40, 244, 249, 252
League of Nations, 162–3, 214
Leahy, W. D., 161 and n, 236
Lebanon, 163–4
'Leclerc', *see* Hautecloque
Lee, A. G., cited, 169–72nn
Leeper, Sir R., 138
Legitimacy of R, 6 and n, 235–7, 273, 279; *and see* Exile, governments in
Leigh-Fermor, P., 181–2
Leipzig, 301n, 302
Lenin, V. I., xii, 11, 50, 61, 75, 85, 90, 129, 144, 145, 149, 198–9, 213, 270, 287–90
Leningrad, 3, 33, 263, 286
Leonhard, W., 286, 303–4, 316–17
Leopold III, king of the Belgians, 255
Lepage, F., 256
Leproux, M., cited, 48–9, 131n
Leroux, R., cited, 55n
Levant fishing patrol, 118
Leverkuehn, P., cited, 148n, 166n
Levi, P., 11
Lewis, Flora, cited, 218n
Leyden, 263
Ležáky, 52, 206
Liberalism, 72, **81–2**, 173, 226–7
Liberation, national organizations for, 9
  Belgium, *see* Secret Army
  Bulgaria, *see* Fatherland Front
  Czechoslovakia, *see* Obrana Naroda
  Denmark, *see* Freedom Council

# Europe under German domination early December 1942

Limit of axis control

Boundaries of Germany in 1937

RK Reichskommissariat

Shetlands

Orkney

1940 RK OF NORWAY

Oslo

Rjukan

Belfast

Edinburgh

IRELAND

UNITED

Dublin

KINGDOM

DENMARK

Copenhagen

Tempsford

1940 RK OF NETHERLANDS

Peenemünde

Amsterdam

London

The Hague

Beaulieu

Tangmere

Rotterdam

Venlo

Ber

Channel Islands

Dieppe

Brussels

BELGIUM

Lille

Luxembourg

G E R

Rhine

Elbe

SWED

PROT.
M

Vien

Normandy

Paris

Brittany

Seine

St Nazaire

Nantes

Loire

F R A N C E

Berne

SWITZER-
LAND

Bordeaux

DEMARCATION LINE

Vichy

Geneva

Lyons

Rhône

Venice

Milan

Toulouse

Perpignan

Marseilles

Ravenna

Andorra

PORTUGAL

Lisbon

Madrid

S P A I N

Vatican City

Rome

I T A

Naples

Tangier

Gibraltar

SPANISH
MOROCCO

Algiers

Sicily

Casablanca

MOROCCO

A L G E R I A

Tunis

TUNISIA